Unsettling Spirit

Unsettling Spirit

A Journey into Decolonization

DENISE M. NADEAU

Foreword by Deanna Reder

McGill-Queen's University Press
Montreal & Kingston • London • Chicago

ISBN 978-0-2280-0157-7 (cloth)
ISBN 978-0-2280-0290-1 (ePDF)
ISBN 978-0-2280-0291-8 (ePUB)

Legal deposit second quarter 2020
Bibliothèque nationale du Québec

Printed in Canada on acid-free paper that is 100% ancient forest free (100% post-consumer recycled), processed chlorine free

This book has been published with the help of a grant from the Canadian Federation for the Humanities and Social Sciences, through the Awards to Scholarly Publications Program, using funds provided by the Social Sciences and Humanities Research Council of Canada.

Funded by the Government of Canada   Financé par le gouvernement du Canada   Canada

Canada Council for the Arts   Conseil des arts du Canada

We acknowledge the support of the Canada Council for the Arts.

Nous remercions le Conseil des arts du Canada de son soutien.

Library and Archives Canada Cataloguing in Publication

Title: Unsettling spirit : a journey into decolonization / Denise M. Nadeau ; foreword by Deanna Reder.

Names: Nadeau, Denise Marie, author.

Description: Includes bibliographical references and index.

Identifiers: Canadiana (print) 20190234482 | Canadiana (ebook) 20190234938 | ISBN 9780228001577 (cloth) | ISBN 9780228002901 (ePDF) | ISBN 9780228002918 (ePUB)

Subjects: LCSH: Nadeau, Denise Marie. | LCSH: Indigenous peoples–Canada–Social conditions. | LCSH: Decolonization–Canada. | LCSH: Decolonization–Religious aspects. | LCSH: Decolonization–Psychological aspects. | LCSH: Reconciliation–Social aspects–Canada.

Classification: LCC E78.C2 N33 2020 | DDC 305.897/071–dc23

This book was designed and typeset by Peggy & Co. Design in 11/14 Minion 3.

Contents

Figures   vii

A Note on Copyright and Intellectual Property   ix

Foreword   xi

Acknowledgments   xv

Introduction   3

PART ONE
Mission Impossible

1   Missionary Musings   17
2   The Denendeh Seminar   29
3   Shifting Missions   40

PART TWO
The Great White Helper

4   From Taking Space to Making Space   57
5   Healing and the Politics of Trauma   69
6   Decolonizing the Great White Helper and Reconciliation   86

PART THREE
Going Home: Gespe'gewa'gi

7   Blood   101
8   Unmapping   120
9   Decolonizing Rivers   141

PART FOUR
Making Relations

10   Moccasins   153
11   Walking with Our Sisters   164
12   A Water Journey: Indigenous Water Laws   173
13   Ceremony   187
14   Reciprocity   206
15   Living Treaty   218

PART FIVE
Unsettling Spirit

16   Lejac Residential School and Rose Prince   231
17   Can You Hear the Drum? Indigenous Christianities   241
18   Returning to the Heart   251

Afterword   263

Notes   271

Bibliography   295

Index   323

Figures

1.1   Me in my cowgirl outfit (Denise Nadeau photo)   7

8.1   Nm'tginen map of statement of Title to Gespe'gewa'gi (Mi'gmawei Mawiomi Secretariat)   121

8.2   Picture of Indian at the Musée Maison Legrand (Denise Nadeau photo)   125

8.3   1765 map of Port Daniel (Bibliothèque et Archives Nationale du Quebec)   128

8.4   1787 map of Port Daniel (Bibliothèque et Archives Nationale du Quebec)   128

8.5   1888 map of Port Daniel (Bibliothèque et Archives Nationale du Quebec)   129

9.1   Logs under railway bridge, Port Daniel West River, 1912 (Stedman Bros, Madeleine Quesnel Postcard Collection)   146

9.2   Mi'gmaq place names along the Gesgapegiag River Watershed (Mi'gmawei Mawiomi Secretariat)   148

A Note on Copyright and Intellectual Property

The author respectfully acknowledges the inherent cultural Rights and ownership of all oral histories and cultural information shared with her by Knowledge Keepers from Mi'gmaq, Coast Salish, Anishnabe, Métis, and Cree Nations. Those seeking to quote Elders and Knowledge Keepers cited here must honour these First Nations' inherent authority in regard to their cultural information in their specific knowledge system and must seek permission from the author or her duly appointed representative.

Foreword

Deanna Reder

Despite a long tradition of Canadian history textbooks that have celebrated settlement and the development of a colony into a nation, there can be no accurate understanding of the past without a central focus on the experiences of Indigenous peoples prior to colonization; an evaluation of the mechanisms, including theft, that transferred the land from the use by First Peoples to settlers; and the ongoing policies that have affected and damaged Indigenous nations. This is difficult work that flies in the face of the assumption that Canada is innocent, decent, well-intentioned, and fair-minded. While there has been scholarship that has helped Canadians reconsider this history,[1] this book, *Unsettling Spirit: A Journey into Decolonization* by activist-scholar Denise Nadeau, demonstrates how to unsettle one's understandings of a variety of key issues – from belonging and identity, blood quantum, the politics of trauma, and the relationship with water to treaty responsibilities – by seeing them from Indigenous points of view. She models a method based on autobiography, research, and critical reflections on colonization.

Despite continuing assertions to the contrary,[2] as an Indigenous scholar in literary studies, I continue to emphasize that autobiography is a foundational Indigenous intellectual tradition.[3] Identifying who you are and explaining your relationship to your family, as well as the land and people whose territory you are living upon, is a key attribute of Indigenous rhetoric, evident in a diversity of discourses from oral storytelling[4] and community addresses[5] to the genre of Indigenous autobiography[6] and, more recently, to Indigenous scholarship.[7] In this book Nadeau models her work on this tradition as she interweaves research with her own story. This inclusion of the personal fundamentally changes our reading, causing us to respond intellectually, emotionally, and viscerally in complex reactions that can differ from reader to reader, depending on one's position.[8]

While everyone in Canada in the post–Truth and Reconciliation Commission era can recognize the context from which the author writes, for me there is a sustained sense of recognition as I've lived in a lot of the places she mentions, and I know and admire the many well-respected Indigenous community leaders with whom she has worked. And despite the hardships that I struggled with as a youth, I recognize the anxieties she expresses about being raised in privilege. Even though I can attest to disadvantages and the casual racism I experienced as a Métis girl growing up, from racial epithets to the low expectations of my abilities, regardless, as an adult I have lived comfortably with loved ones, with access to university study, counselling, opportunity, and home ownership in a city where homelessness is a well-known crisis. The very mechanisms of agency and status that I have gained are generally still not available to many Indigenous people.

I also recognize the struggles of faith discussed in this book, as someone who as a girl became very religious from about the age of eleven until my father's death about a decade later. As a teenager I believed that my family needed salvation and the grace of God. Looking back, even as I no longer call myself religious, and wince at the narrowness of some of my beliefs, I don't think I was wrong to hope for divine intervention.

So when Nadeau writes about her summer spent in Fort Simpson, in "Native ministry," in the footsteps of a French Catholic religious order that has been in Canada since 1841, I understand her disquiet, but I also feel my own. As she shares honestly and self-critically, I have to examine my desire to distance myself from this history that wrought so much damage to Indigenous nations, even though I remember my evangelical zeal as a teenager. There is this moment when the reader might want to cast blame on others, but Nadeau models for us how to reflect, to analyze, and to listen to our bodies so that we can allow multiple reactions to sit together. This isn't a strategy to stifle outrage or complaint but, rather, a way to have it sit alongside other emotions, if they exist, in order to understand possible connections. This practice is consistent with Indigenous protocols that encourage us to embrace contradiction rather than dispose of relationships, so that we can look at these histories with clarity while understanding the complexities, in order to know how to move on.

As I think about the prayers of my youth for the alleviation of a variety of distresses, I realize how my mother's stories created a similar space to that which Nadeau crafts – a space of reflection and analysis, along with humour and belonging. We were fortunate to be able to listen to mom's constant storytelling, which conveyed a sense of closeness to our relatives, despite their living far away. Each story steeped us in the values of *wâhkotowin*, the Cree term for the interrelated bonds of kinship. It was through her stories that she taught us who we are by teaching us about our relatives.

I remember, in the summer of 1993, that my mother's mother, my Kohkum, passed away at the age of ninety. My husband and our two-year-old son got into our Pontiac Acadian and drove from our new home in the Fraser Valley, about an hour outside of Vancouver, to La Ronge, Saskatchewan, about six hours north of Saskatoon – a trip that took two days to complete. Given that my mother came from a large family, and almost every one of her siblings had several children, a throng of us arrived at the village, reuniting for the funeral at the local Catholic church.

It was clear from the start of the service that the priest did not know Kohkum. He did not know her as a matriarch, the mother of ten, a midwife, or a healer, or even as Mrs Patterson. Throughout the service he referred to her as Victoria, a legal name that no one ever called her. He bumbled through a service that had little connection to her life and then at the graveside admitted that he had forgotten the Holy Water to sprinkle on her coffin. The family expected so little of the clergyman that no one expressed surprise. The fact that some of my cousins are status Cree and have stories from residential school added to this low opinion.

I felt my frustration growing, to think that someone who had been so influential in all our lives was given such an inadequate memorial. But just as we reassembled for a final family reception, with no clergy in sight and completely unscripted, my cousin Patsy began to address us all and talk about Kohkum, who had raised her when her mom was unable to do so. Patsy talked about Kohkum's strength, about her power, about her knowledge, about her flashes of anger. It set off a stream of stories from many members of our family, each of whom knew Kohkum in different ways. These impromptu words were testimony to her amazing, difficult, joy-filled, sorrowful life, a tribute that several of us needed to articulate and all of us needed to hear.

I know that Nadeau has also listened to many stories told by the many Indigenous women with whom she has worked. She is a seeker who honours the values of Indigenous ethics, which direct us not to judge others but, instead, encourage us to share our stories and to value the autonomy of our personal perspectives so that we can be responsible for our own ideas and actions. It is through her example that we can try to understand how colonization works and has worked in all of us, Indigenous and non-Indigenous readers alike.

Acknowledgments

This book has taken several years to write and has been influenced by many people and lands as I moved from occupied K'ómoks Territory on Vancouver Island to unceded Tiohtià:ke (Montreal) in Kanien'kéha Territory, and recently to the unceded Coast and Straits Salish Territories of the Lekwungen peoples, the Songhees and Esquimalt, and the W̱SÁNEĆ Nation (Victoria, British Columbia). I have also spent time during the summers in Gespe'gewa'gi, unceded Mi'gmaq territory in Quebec. I acknowledge that I have been an uninvited visitor in each of these territories and am grateful for the lessons I have learned and that have challenged me to take responsibility for being a settler in these lands.

In many ways this book is not the product of one person but, rather, of many conversations, challenges, mistakes, sharings, and the generosity of many who have helped me on my journey. I have learned from Indigenous citation practices how important it is to acknowledge the collective and all the people who have contributed to one's knowledge and experience.

There are many friends and colleagues to whom I owe much in the writing and thinking about the themes in this book. Over the years I worked at different times with Alannah Young Leon and Marjorie Beaucage; each of you pushed me, often resisting, into new worlds and ways of seeing. Bernadette Spence and Madeleine MacIvor have shared much wisdom and given me support when I was questioning what I was doing. To Mi'gmaq Elder Pnnal Jerome, wela'lin, for the laughter and stories you shared with me during my too brief summer visits to Gesgapegiag. To Manon Jeannotte, who provided me with some of the Mi'gmaq history of Port Daniel, thank you for opening up a world that had been hidden from me. To Musqueam Elder Larry Grant, huy ch q'u for the many times you agreed to speak at workshops led by Alannah and me and for sharing so much about the hən̓q̓əmin̓əm̓ language and Coast Salish Protocols. I am forever grateful to Madeleine Quesnel, who gave substance and historical context for my work in her sharing of her research on the history of Port Daniel.

My writing group members in Courtenay – Jessie Schut, Mae Padgin, Valerie Raoul, and the late Anna Miriam Leigh – all worked hard to make my writing less academic and more accessible. I hope I haven't failed you. I thank my prayer group in Courtenay – Karen Roe, Mary Catherine Ruel, Willa Cannon, and Joyce Relyea – for the prayers and support when I flagged and got discouraged. Many people read parts of this book and gave invaluable feedback – James Loney, Alannah Young Leon, Marjorie Beaucage, Lyana Patrick, Bernadette Spence, and Madeleine MacIvor. I thank Marie Zarowny and Joyce Harris, two Sisters of Saint Anne, who supported me as a person of faith through many years of being a "fringe Catholic." Wayde Compton and Barbara Pulling were my editors for an earlier version and validated my efforts to combine story with more academic reflection. I want to thank Tim Pearson, who helped with some of the editing and, in particular, with bibliographic details. Many thanks to Chelsea Horton, who is both a friend and editor extraordinaire and who edited both an earlier and later version that I submitted to McGill-Queen's University Press. Chelsea is a companion in spirit and supported me when I felt the loneliness of doing this type of writing.

There are many others who contributed to what this book and journey have been, if not directly, then indirectly though their friendship, sharing, and inspiration. Joy Illington, Lindsay Borrows, Maxine Maltilpi, Dara Culhane, Carole Brazeau, Rita Wong, Dorothy Christian, and Bonnie Hanuse are just a few of the women who have inspired me in their commitment to justice for Indigenous women and for the land and waters.

A special thanks to my anonymous peer reviewers who gave excellent suggestions for revision and helped clarify my thinking. McGill-Queen's University Press editor Mark Abley took encouraging interest in this work and was both patient and supportive in many ways. I am grateful to Mark for "hanging in" through the many evolutions of this book. Thanks to the editing team at MQUP, especially Joanne Richardson, all of whom have been a pleasure to work with.

Wela'lin to Bernadine Martin from Gesgapegiag who beaded the beautiful Saint Anne brooch that graces the cover of this book. Self-taught, Bernadine has been beading for twenty-four years and made her first Saint Anne brooch for her mother.

I am grateful for my son Kael and my grandson James Jiwoo for providing moments of delight and laughter when I was feeling over-whelmed. I owe a special thanks to Elisa Lay, without whose support this project would not have been possible. She kept me from being discouraged and grounded me in everyday reality, while taking on my share of domestic labour so that I would have the time to complete this work.

Unsettling Spirit

Introduction

Should I buy it or not? I look at a beaded car ornament that lies among other beadwork under the glass counter at the Micmac Coop in Gesgapegiag, a Mi'gmaq community near the town of Maria on the Gaspé Coast. The beading consists of a circle of pale blue beads with darker ones around the edge. At the centre is a medallion-shaped image of a white Saint Anne holding her daughter Mary. Dangling from the circle are several long strands of dark blue beads. A piece of white deer-skin is sewn on the back of the medallion, tiny stitches visible around the brass circle enclosing the image. I think it is beautiful, but doubts crowd my mind.

I internally weigh the pros and cons of getting it. Putting it on my dashboard would be a statement. I usually avoid public professions of my Christianity in any situation in which it might represent an uneven power dynamic. For many Jews, Muslims, and Indigenous peoples, Christianity is freighted with a colonial and racist past and present.[1] I travel in some secular circles in which all religions, including Christianity, are considered anathema. The beadwork would imply I am Indigenous, which is not the reality. I worry that I may be considered a fraud on both sides. Yet it has been those who bead – Indigenous women and their teachings – who have transformed how I now understand and see Christianity.

Saint Anne is Jesus's grandmother. I am attached to her for many reasons. Over the years when I have felt alienated from the Catholic Church, it was the faithfulness and welcoming openness of the Sisters of Saint Anne that kept me Catholic and Christian. I have visited Lac Saint Anne and Saint Anne de Beaupré, which are just two of the pilgrimage sites frequented by Indigenous people in this country named Canada. Saint Anne is revered by many Indigenous Catholics because she is an Elder, a grandmother, and a mother, roles that are sacred and powerful in Indigenous traditions. During times of difficulties as a mother, I prayed to Saint Anne in a grotto in the woods at the former retreat centre of the Sisters of Saint Anne in Victoria, British Columbia. The Saint Anne figures I have often seen usually depict her with her head draped in a veil or bearing a crown, her pious daughter Mary in her lap with hands clasped, either gazing at her mother or joining her in reading a book. This grotto image in Victoria was different, a contemporary and plain grey plaster sculpture with multiple edges showing Anne simply holding her daughter. Somehow that faux stone figure gave me solace. I was not yet a grandmother and was worried I never would be, so I prayed to Saint Anne to help me on that front.

In the end, I decide to buy the beaded Saint Anne. My doubts are unresolved, yet somehow it feels right. I am a person caught between two traditions. One has transformed my experience of the other. I need to figure out how to live with integrity when the old stories I was raised on no longer have meaning and, in fact, are part of a culture that contributed and still contributes to the genocide of Indigenous people in Canada. I put the dangly Saint Anne in an envelope in my suitcase and wonder when, if ever, I will actually put it in my car.

※

That was in 2008. My conflict over whether to buy the beaded Saint Anne represented the multiple layers of questioning of my identity that have been central in my adult life. First there was the question of ancestry. My father had said there was Mi'gmaq blood in the family, though far enough back that it was not something that any family member took seriously. This statement led me on the path of wondering if that made me "part Indian" or not. The second question was that of my identity as a settler. By 2008, my life history and the political developments in this land that is called Canada left me in no doubt that I was the daughter of many generations of settlers who had been colonizers, occupying and exploiting the land's resources. How could I as a settler live with integrity and responsibility in relationship with the Indigenous peoples of these lands? The third area in which I was troubled involved a religious question. What was a faith I could live with as someone raised as a Christian when Christianity has been and continues to be a major player in the colonial project?

The Truth and Reconciliation Commission (TRC) of Canada took place between 2008 and 2015. In its final report of 2015, in which it made ninety-four Calls to Action, the TRC commissioners stated that "'reconciliation' is about establishing and maintaining a mutually respectful relationship between Aboriginal and non-Aboriginal people in this country."[2] Because the meaning of the word "reconciliation" seems to vary and is interpreted by Indigenous and non-Indigenous people in a multitude of ways, I have chosen to focus here more on settler decolonization than on reconciliation. While I don't have a clear definition of decolonization to offer, I see it as a process of unlearning a worldview and values and ways of acting and being in the world that have prohibited and continue to prohibit any meaningful and mutually respectful relationship between Indigenous and non-Indigenous people. This book is in fact an exploration of what the term "decolonization" may mean for non-Indigenous people living in Canada. I believe we will not uncover its full meaning in this lifetime or even in a few more generations.

My journey into decolonization has led me to ask what it means to be a settler in a country in which the land we live on was taken – stolen – from the original peoples who lived here. How does that change how I understand myself, my family, my history, my community, my religion, and my relationship to this land? This journey has been more than intellectual, it has been deeply personal, spiritual, and embodied. It has involved a change of heart, of my relationship to land and water, of how I understand religion, and of how I live in my body. It has changed how I live my life. I have had to figure out what being a settler is really about and my implication in what Michi Saagiig Nishnaabeg Leanne Betasamosake Simpson calls the *processes* of settler colonialism, the state-controlled structures that maintain the ongoing dispossession of Indigenous peoples from their territories.[3]

The process of decolonization is different for all of us. For me it is an invitation to see how white settlers like myself, whose family has been here for generations, are complicit in the structures of settler colonialism. Like settler scholars Emma Battell Lowman and Adam Barker, my definition of settler refers to those who "live on lands that have a pre-existing and undisputable claim on them."[4] At the same time I recognize that non-black people of colour who have settled here have come from countries colonized by Europeans and that many now experience racism and oppression here in Canada, dependent on their class, gender, migration status, and the nation from which they came.[5] These newcomers still experience settler privilege in that they, too, benefit from the occupation and exploitation of Indigenous land. Black people whose ancestors came here under conditions of slavery, refugees fleeing homelands they do not want to leave, temporary foreign workers, and black people who choose to come to Canada from historically colonized countries complicate how we can understand the term "settler." However, the one thing common to all is that they have a relationship to and a presence on Indigenous lands that have been occupied for more than five hundred years.[6] I use the term "settler" to include all those who benefit from settler privilege. In this work I focus on the structures that accompany settler colonialism, structures through which those who arrived from Europe imposed their culture and laws on the Indigenous peoples already living here.

I grew up in Montreal, Quebec, in the 1950s and 1960s. My father was from a twelfth-generation entrepreneurial Catholic family from a small village on the Gaspé Coast. His roots were French, with some Scottish, and possibly some long ago intermarriage with the Mi'gmaq. The Mi'gmaq were the original inhabitants of Gespégawági, which is the seventh district of the Mi'gmaq Nation, called Mi'gma'gi.[7] My mother was from a prosperous third-generation Irish Catholic family in Brockville, Ontario, in Haudenosaunee and Michi Saagiig territory. I had little awareness of any of these territorial connections while I was growing up. Each of my family lineages contributed to the assumptions I had regarding relationship to land, to others of a different race and class, and to our very purpose in this life, which was, in essence, "to get ahead."

As a child I knew little about Indians except, of course, playing "Cowboys and Indians." Though I loved the story of the Lone Ranger and his faithful sidekick, Tonto, I wanted to be Annie Oakley, the sharpshooter and star of the 1950s American TV series. There is a picture of me in one of my mom's albums when I was about seven or eight. I am smiling, wearing a fringed cowgirl dress with two plastic guns in their holsters, my hands on my guns and one foot placed jauntily in front of the other, my shoulders held high. In a world of mean cowboys, it was clearly better to be a woman with a gun than an Indian.

Figure I.1   Me in my cowgirl outfit

My family was Catholic within the very Catholic culture of Quebec of the 1950s and 1960s. This meant that it was quite common to see roadside shrines to Mary on trips out of town, to observe annual pilgrimages to holy sites like Saint Joseph's Oratory or Saint Anne de Beaupré, and for girls like me to attend convent schools. In Quebec, most of the streets and towns were, and still are, named after saints. I can pass the street of Saint Zotique in Montreal or drive through a town like Saint Apollinaire and assume the name is normal. In the 1950s and 1960s, dietary rules about fish on Friday and no sweets for Lent were considered the cultural norm. There was frequent praying of rosary beads at school, at church, and in the homes of many of my friends, all as part of daily life. We didn't pray the rosary at home as my mother was not that devout; she was influenced by her own mother, who was a Protestant and who lived with us for many years. However, I had a home altar in my bedroom from about the age of nine; on it I collected holy cards, flowers, medals, a statue of Mary, and a votive candle in a glass jar.

As a teenager I attended Sacred Heart Convent School in Montreal, a somewhat upper-class school that had annual fees of five hundred dollars. There I joined the Children of Mary Sodality, an order for those who were devout and pious, plus had good marks. Your reward was that you got to wear a medal of Mary on a blue ribbon around your neck, an outward symbol of your religious achievement. However, this did not stop me from sneaking a cigarette with some of the "bad girls" when off school grounds. Still, my faith meant something to me. Religion was a solace. My childhood was difficult. Some children are more susceptible to religion than others, and I was clearly one of them. As a child I felt I was engaged with the spiritual realm every day. It was a world in which there was a set of values and behaviours I aspired to practise (and failed at miserably) and that brought me a sense of calm and of a connection to something larger than myself. And, somehow, I internalized a deep sense of social justice under the influence of a Sacred Heart nun, Mother Power, who took me under her wing.[8] Her commitment to social justice was transmitted and stayed with me long after I had left the church. My university years were marked by a fervent engagement with Marxism and feminism, the former more about theory, the latter more about practice – marches, rallies, support groups, and personal relationships. I became a social justice warrior, an avocation rooted in my Catholic past and carrying the energy of my childhood cowgirl bluster.

Throughout my life I have moved between two callings. One has been as an educator and facilitator, which included teaching in the fields of social work and ministry. In recent years this has morphed into a part-time practice as an expressive arts therapist and somatic educator, always with a focus on embodiment. My other calling has been in the field of religion, first in training in Christian ministry, later in inter-faith work, and still later as a university sessional lecturer in religious education and, more recently, in religious studies. I have always been somewhat of an intellectual, drawn to theory but at the same time more engaged in practice, and the tension between the two has been with me all my life. This tension has allowed me to develop a lens that, to some extent, is holistic in that, when I look at personal and social change, I consider the body, spirit, mind, and emotions as well as the historical, political, ecological, and social context. I have been able to connect my two worlds, the theoretical and the practical, in the area of decolonizing the body. I have found that the body is both a site and a marker of colonialism, and its study provides insights into the politics of trauma, healing, and reconciliation.

In the last three decades I became aware of how the Christianity in which I grew up transmitted a worldview that was not only antithetical to the knowledge systems of Indigenous peoples but was also premised on eradicating their traditions. I have struggled to remain a Christian as well as to understand how any Indigenous person can be Christian. Then in 2011 I heard the late Lakota evangelical Christian Richard Twiss speak at a conference on theological education in Winnipeg. He asked: "Why do we talk about 'what do I do about being an Indian now that I am a Christian,' but not 'what do I do about my whiteness now that I am a Christian?'" He added, "How do we rescue theology from the cowboys?"[9] Twiss's comments shook me. I am a practice person, more defined as a religious educator than as a theologian, but I have been a cowgirl, and the well-meaning helper. I take seriously his challenge to disentangle Christianity – European Christianity – from whiteness and colonialism. It is this challenge that informs the first two parts of this book: "Mission Impossible" and "The Great White Helper."

In the late 1980s and the early 1990s I had a brief foray into the field called "Native Mission." In critically examining my experience in this period, I identify the figure of the White Helper and how that role, shaped by whiteness and gender, would continue to inform not only my behaviour as a social justice advocate but also how it has been an integral part of the helping and healing professions in social work, therapy, and Christian ministry and practice. I include the political and social ramifications of White Helper behaviour and the larger geo-political context of helping by addressing the politics of trauma, which play a significant role in how Indigenous lives are problematized by governments and churches. Drawing from liberation therapy, somatic psychotherapy, systems theory, and Indigenous approaches to wellness, I explore directions for decolonizing the White Helper in both individual behaviour and institutional structures.

In Part 3 of this book, "Going Home," I go back in time and place to explore my ancestry. I face what for me has been a personally troubling matter, the issue of blood and how identity arguments based on blood are inherently racist. Drawing on the work of Pam Palmater, I realize that it is connections, relationships, and long-term history with an Indigenous nation that matter and that I really have no claim to Mi'gmaq ancestry.[10] Accordingly, from a settler perspective, I examine my ancestors' role in the dispossession of Mi'qmaq peoples from their territory and how colonialism functions in terms of constructing land and waterways as property and resources to be exploited.

As someone who is interested in religion and religions, I have been privileged over the years to be exposed to several different Indigenous Knowledge Traditions.[11] This was sometimes through work, other times through personal relationships. For many years I partnered with an Anishnabe Cree traditionalist and ceremonialist in healing and cross-cultural education work. In the last decade I have taught part-time and done research in the area of Indigenous-settler relations, colonialism, and gender in the Department of Religion and Cultures at Concordia University. In this later context I learned how the academic study of religion, which emerged in the late nineteenth century in Europe, imposed the Christian imperial gaze and its essentially Christian framework onto non-Western wisdom traditions, such as Hinduism and Buddhism. Indigenous Knowledge Systems, based on orality, were considered "pagan" and not religions. The Europeans applied a definition of religion that was based on Christian categories – the importance of doctrine, sacred texts, and true and false beliefs.[12] Though the framing of Indigenous traditions as religions is now recognized in some academic circles, at the level of daily and community life this is often contested by some Indigenous people.[13] So I understood when a young Mohawk man whom I had met at a gathering in Montreal told me that he would never take a course in a department of religion because his traditions were not a religion but a way of life.

My contact with Indigenous lifeways and knowledge systems, which I describe in Part 4, "Making Relations," has broadened my understanding of religion and the spirit world, and challenged any separation of body and spirit, humans and non-humans, that I inherited from Christianity. While I believe most religions can claim to be a way of life, I certainly have had trouble experiencing the Christianity I learned in this way. I internalized the colonial framework of European Christianity and culture. Accordingly, decolonization for me has meant way more than critiquing European Christianity, settler colonialism, and whiteness: it has meant being confronted and challenged in my daily practice and values in the encounter with Indigenous traditions. I use the plural – traditions – because each language grouping, each nation based in a specific territory, has a knowledge system that differs from that of its neighbours.

Embodied relationship is at the core of Indigenous traditions, and building relationships involves a value system and way of relating not only to fellow humans but also to land, water, sky, and other non-human beings. My exposure to Indigenous lifeways has brought me into contact with a way of being in the world that is premised on these relationships and all the responsibilities that the gift of relationship entails. I have had the privilege of developing relationships with women and men who practise specific lifeways – Anishnabe, Mi'gmaq, Coast Salish, Cree, Métis, and Kanien'kehá:ka – a range that I confess reflects my deterritorialized settler self. I have learned lessons from Indigenous women from each of these homelands. I draw on these relations to explore the question: "What does it mean to be a good relative?" This includes examining my relationship with Indigenous women's practices of making moccasins and beading, my relationship to the murdered and missing Indigenous women, and my relationship to water and Indigenous water protection. I reflect on how my experiences of Indigenous ceremony and the Indigenous principle and value of lived reciprocity not only challenged my way of being but also informed my critique of colonial Christianity. I examine, in turn, what the process of making relations can involve in any decolonization practice. I include, in this exploration, my own journey to unlearn habits of mind and body, what it means to live as an uninvited visitor in Indigenous homelands, and what responsibilities one has to treaties and the Indigenous legal orders of a territory.

Finally, in Part 5, "Unsettling Spirit," I return to my initial question: How can I respectfully hold together Indigenous traditions and Christianity? I reflect on how the process of decolonization involves unsettling the relationship of settler colonialism with the spirit world. I consider different examples of where Indigenous people have integrated Christianity into their cosmologies. I suggest that it is our relationship with an embodied spirit world that will point the way forward in Indigenous-settler relations. It is the deep principles of Indigenous traditions, embedded in Indigenous languages and relationship with the land and waters, that can offer a direction for a decolonized Christianity and for interfaith relations. I conclude with reflections on the importance of listening to Indigenous women, the need to transcend the dualistic thinking and binaries that underlie European Christianity and Western culture, and the imperative of transcending a frontier mentality, all of which are necessary if there is to be any possibility of co-existence between Indigenous and non-Indigenous peoples. In the afterword I situate my work within specific academic disciplines and include scholarly resources for those interested in teaching and learning more in the area of decolonization.

I am writing this book at a time when many white settlers feel threatened by economic uncertainty and fear recent immigrants and the "Other" – a fear that is fuelled by demagogues and nativist ideologies. In the fall of 2018 I attended a panel titled "An Indigenous Law Response to the Boushie/Fontaine Verdicts."[14] In the discussion of the case of the young Cree man Colten Boushie – a case in which the white farmer Gerald Stanley, accused of killing Boushie, was acquitted – Métis lawyer Robin Gervais shared some of the racist comments that appeared on the internet. One was "Yeah Cowboy!" Another was "Go cowboy go!" It made me realize that we have not moved far from the era of cowboys and Indians and that racism against Indigenous people is alive and well in Canada.

This book is about a journey, both painful and joyful, during which I learned to feel comfortable in my own skin and on this land, while still accepting that racism and colonialism continue to be part of me and the culture in which I live. Throughout, I hold up those traditions and practices that have caused me to see myself differently, that have challenged the worldview I inherited, and that have transformed both my faith and my commitment to live "in a good way" on this earth. I am not someone who has been to a few sweats and is now going to describe Indigenous ceremony or ways of healing, nor any topic on which Indigenous people are now writing prolifically. I am not attempting cultural translation, nor is this an apology for Christianity. My purpose here is not to presume to write about Indigenous lifeways; rather, it is to write about decolonization as a process, a calling, and a positive way of being.

My experience of decolonization has not been linear. It is more like a spiral that has returned me to a place I have been and that has enabled me to gain more insight. I have chosen to reflect on stories, on incidents in my life in which I had to face how my ideas and values were challenged by a situation in which Indigenous values and world views were present. I refer to books that may be useful for both an academic and a general audience concerned about building respectful relationships between Indigenous and non-Indigenous peoples. I do this in order to invite my readers to explore the rich world of Indigenous literature and scholarship that exists in this country. I have chosen to present a series of chapters/essays that can be read sequentially or dipped into, according to the reader's interests.

Many, always settlers, have asked me why I would write this book. It is not a comfortable topic with which to engage. But to be able to feel comfortable all the time is a white settler privilege. It is time to see discomfort as positive. My hope is that the reader will learn, as I have, that decolonization is not about "me" and that the journey forward is collective. In a time when the predictions of climate devastation are being realized, there is still a constructive alternative to be found in learning to recognize Indigenous laws and to live within a value framework that prioritizes balanced relationships with all beings. Decolonization is necessarily a spiritual journey and an urgent one. It is time to move beyond the cowboy and cowgirl mentality.

PART ONE

Mission Impossible

1

Missionary Musings

Denendeh, summer 1986. Every day, for several days, I have sat in the mission kitchen for a few hours, waiting and waiting for something to happen. It is a warm and hazy afternoon, the July sun strong enough to keep the mosquitoes at bay. I am just waiting, hoping someone will drop into the Sacred Heart Mission Parish. Nobody has so far. Catholic parish life is not very active in Fort Simpson. I ask myself, "What am I doing here?"

✳

How I ended up that summer at a Catholic mission in Fort Simpson in the Northwest Territories seems both miraculous and logical as I look back on the twists and turns in my life. I had been deeply religious as a child but when I entered university religion suddenly became irrelevant. I discovered Marxism and feminism and concluded that religion was the opiate of the people and, quite rightly, that Catholicism was anti-woman. By the end of the 1970s the call of goddess religions was strong for me. These re-emergent traditions treated women with dignity and recognized them for their spiritual power. I went to women's festivals where naked women chanted to the goddess and danced in circles. I had figurines and pictures of goddess figures from all over the world. Black ones, brown ones, red ones, Santeria figures, pre-Greco-Roman. Appropriation was not an issue then. Tapping into the energy of the goddess seemed to fill the spiritual hole in me. At the same time I was becoming involved in social justice issues, the fight against apartheid in South Africa, and the struggle of non-status Indigenous women to gain status.

Then, in 1983, personal tragedy struck for me. I was struggling to keep my son through an ugly court custody battle, where I was named an unfit mother because I was a lesbian. Ironically, I reverted to my Catholic faith, which, although officially homophobic, enabled me to find solace through Emmaus, a small Catholic social justice community in the Comox Valley where I was then living. Christianity had resources like the Psalms to deal with suffering and I found comfort in the rituals of the Mass. In the end, my son's father and I chose mediation, which provided us with a less conflictual solution than did the courts. That same year, 1983, I attended the World Council of Churches (WCC) gathering in Vancouver, solely with the purpose of promoting and selling the women's self-help handbook that I had been involved in developing. At the WCC I discovered liberation theology and its role in the liberation struggles in El Salvador and South Africa. I was hooked! The combination of religion and radical politics was something I was looking for. That very fall, I applied and was accepted into the 1984 class at Vancouver School of Theology (VST) as a master of divinity student. Here I would transform my interest in the goddess into a theological reading of the feminine face of God.

As a Catholic woman, not to mention a lesbian, I could not get ordained in the Roman Catholic Church. However, I resisted the invitation to convert to Protestantism in order to become a minister. I felt little emotional or spiritual resonance with the rational restraint and solemnity of churches that lacked icons, incense, or saints. I was uncomfortable with the overlay of Anglo culture that one finds in varying degrees in the Presbyterian, Anglican, and United Churches of Canada. I was and am still interested in what is called "popular religion" – the devotion to saints, Marion figures like Our Lady of Guadalupe in Mexico, Our Lady of Las Reglas in both Cuba and the Philippines, or Saint Anne here in Canada. I love home altars and keeping sacred objects, and I believe there are spirits around us. Not exactly Protestant fare.

So it was not surprising that two years later I was in Fort Simpson as part of my ministry field placement at VST. It had been difficult for this Protestant seminary to find a place for me as a Catholic woman, not to mention as a semi-out lesbian. As someone clearly on the margins of the church and with social justice leanings, I was drawn to ministry with marginalized peoples. I had some experience in "Indian Country," including a five-year intimate relationship with an Anishinaabe-Métis girlfriend and involvement with Project North, a Christian group advocating for Indigenous self-determination. One of the faculty members at VST, Terry Anderson, had picked up on my history and had suggested that I go north to work with René Fumoleau. Fumoleau was an Oblate priest who had just started running the Denendeh Seminar, an "exposure tour" for Christians from the South. I learned that he was a historian, a filmmaker, and an outspoken advocate for Dene Land Rights, and he needed a facilitator for the seminar. René agreed that I was a good fit, and as the seminar would only involve three weeks of my time, he arranged that I spend the early part of the summer placement in Fort Simpson at Sacred Heart Mission with Camille Piché, another Oblate who had been supporting Dene Title to their lands.

So here I am in Fort Simpson, exploring the field known as "Native ministry." The Oblates of Mary Immaculate are a Catholic religious order, originally from France, that arrived in Canada in 1841. They established missions in Native communities throughout the Northwest, competing with the Anglicans, who were also determined to save the souls of the Dene.[1] The Slavey name for Fort Simpson is "Liidli Koe," and Camille had given me a booklet titled *Liidli Koe: Two Rivers of Faith,* so I could learn more. He and a Métis community member, Lanny Cooke, had prepared the booklet for visitors for what was ultimately an aborted visit of Pope John Paul II to Fort Simpson in 1984.[2] In it I discovered that the Catholic Church established itself formally in Fort Simpson in 1913 when the federal government granted the mission eighty acres of land. The mission ran a farm, a school, and a hospital, all of which were long gone before I arrived.[3] The church and rectory, built in 1923, are white wooden buildings set back from the main dirt road in the centre of town, on the edge of the Mackenzie River. Fort Simpson is now the base for the Sacred Heart Mission, where a single priest covers a large area extending from Fort Providence to Fort Liard. I am here as Camille Piché's temporary "parish assistant," and it is my fourth week in this village of about twelve hundred people.

Camille has gone to pay a pastoral visit to a Métis family that has recently lost their elderly mother. There isn't much for me to do at Sacred Heart Mission. The parish membership, a blend of Métis, Dene, and white settlers, has dropped considerably over the past few years. Evangelical churches have recently moved into the region and are drawing in converts. As well, the issue of sexual abuse at Catholic residential schools is beginning to emerge publicly, and there is a growing interest in the return of traditional Dene spiritual practices. Camille tells

me there have also been some Dene leaders who have travelled to the
South and returned with intertribal ceremonies like sweats. My image
of myself spending the summer counselling battered women and doing
popular education in the community has been quickly shattered. The
church does not seem to have much of a place in the lives of most of
the Dene and Métis in Fort Simpson, and a newcomer like me is even
more irrelevant.

In the last few weeks I have had to learn to be comfortable with doing
nothing, with just hanging out, hardly my forte as a highly energetic
activist, educator, seminary student, and part-time mom who is now
without her son, books, and a cause she can mobilize around! At first
I felt a high level of anxiety as my body was used to being in high gear.
Then I started to feel ennui and boredom, and then guilt that I wasn't
"doing anything" that I could call constructive and meaningful. So,
today, with nobody dropping by after three hours, I decide to go out
and wander slowly down to the Mackenzie River. I make my way on a
path that passes between the rectory and the nuns' trailer, past the tall
grey-green grasses and the willow bushes, and I sit down on the bank
to watch the mighty Mackenzie.

A slight river breeze keeps the mosquitoes and horseflies away. Here,
the Liard River flows into the Mackenzie, hence the traditional name
for Fort Simpson: Liidli Kue, "the place where rivers come together."
The Slavey name for the Mackenzie is the Deh cho, meaning "big river."
There are no rapids or large jutting rocks here, just the steady flow of
the meeting of two powerful rivers, a confluence that seems to be almost
one and a half kilometres wide. I have never spent any time just sitting
by a river, especially one that feels bigger than the Saint Lawrence,
the river I know from growing up in Montreal and travelling to the
Gaspé. I am mesmerized by the physical power of this river and am
just becoming aware of its centrality to the lives of people here in the
North. In this land of few roads, the Mackenzie has been and is the main
trading and communication route for the Dene, for the fur traders, and
for the settlers.

How tiny I feel beside it. Humans seem so small in the North, the
distances between communities so great. Today, there are no boats or
barges visible on the river, just this great expanse of steadily moving
blue-grey water, reflecting the hazy sky. For the first time, I feel some
peace here. I have never had time to slow down and just be. Maybe this

is why I have come up North, to learn from the river, to learn to be still, to stop being busy and to feel in my body that the land is sacred.

A breeze chills the air and I return to the mission kitchen, restless again. No one has dropped by, and Camille has left a note saying he is out visiting a family whose son has just committed suicide. I am sure no one will come this late in the afternoon, so I decide to go up into the attic of the rectory to explore what is there. Camille had been a key figure in organizing the pope's planned visit in 1984, and he has suggested I might want to see the paraphernalia – T-shirts, posters, buttons, flags – associated with the visit. Two years ago, more than four thousand Indigenous people from all over Canada had gathered in Fort Simpson to greet Pope John Paul II. However, his plane had been unable to land due to a thick fog bank. The plane flew on to Yellowknife, where the pope delivered a speech from the airport, leaving the crowd at Simpson disappointed and angry. With his tight schedule, there was no more time for the Native people.[4]

I climb the creaky wooden stairs from the second floor to the attic, open the door with its rusty hinges, and pull the cord for the overhead light bulb. I first go to the left, ducking my head under the dusty beams, and discover a worn wooden desk in the far corner. On it are some of the old catechisms that were used for First Communion preparation, which have now been replaced by the "new catechism," prepared under Pope John Paul II. Beside it is a pile of newspaper clippings and some shiny pope posters, papal flags, and pens. I find another poster rolled up behind the desk – it is a black-and-white photo of thousands of penguins with a caption in red reading, "Millions Await Pope in Arctic." I laugh.

Against the opposite wall there are a few cardboard boxes and another poster rolled up behind them, this one somewhat yellowed with age and on a duller paper than that of the slick pope posters. Curious to see a poster that may be from a different era, I cross over, pick it up, and unroll it. It is very long and narrow, printed in colour though faded, with many small images and few words. I immediately sense I have found something both old and interesting. I examine it carefully.

On the poster are two paths or roads going from top to bottom. One of these seems to lead to an image of heaven, with Jesus and Mary floating on clouds and embracing a young woman. The other road leads to a ball of flames – hell. At the base there is a triangle representing the Trinity (a Catholic representation of God that includes Jesus and the Holy Spirit) as well as a scene of the creation of the world in six days and then a scene of Adam and Eve. Evicted from the garden, Adam and Eve move towards a fork in the road. On the left road, coloured pale yellow, are small images of Abraham and Moses walking, then a bit further along, after some more good guys, the birth, life, and death of Jesus and, eventually, the Roman Catholic Church. Between both roads, the discovery of North America is represented with a tall ship and faithful missionaries. On the left road a few white angels accompany the journeyers. From the bottom of the other path, coloured black, where the road diverts to the right, there are key turning points in biblical history – Cain and Abel, the flood, Noah and the Tower of Babel, Martin Luther, and a few black-horned devils leering on the side of the road, plus enactments of the "seven deadly sins." Purgatory, the in-between place where those dead who are repentant sinners must wait before being admitted to heaven, is a smaller fire off near the top left. The left road leads, via purgatory, to heaven. The right road, leading to hell, is clearly the one that pagan people and Protestants, who live in error, travel.[5]

I have a feeling close to nausea in my gut. This is clearly an old tool for conversion, created to teach "salvation history" to the "Indians." Not only does this represent a Christianity of judgment and harshness, but the message is clear: the only way to God is through Christianity and the Catholic Church. You were a pagan destined for hell if you did not follow this path.

I go downstairs with a heavy heart. What if this poster is still used? Or even if it is from the past, what scars has it left? And am I complicit in reinforcing that message by being here? Later that evening, at dinner, I ask Camille about it. He nonchalantly explains that it was an old catechetical tool used by the missionaries in the nineteenth and early twentieth centuries but that it is not in use now. "Of course, it is dated and reflects an old theology," he adds. I decide not to discuss it further as I don't know exactly what to say to him.

I knew this poster was dangerous, but I did not yet understand the degree to which it was harmful. I wondered how these modern missionaries were different from the old ones. Camille, like many Oblates, spoke the local Indigenous language, which was South Slavey. Historian Raymond Huel has argued that the Catholic missionaries' early commitment to learn Indigenous languages was rooted in the desire "to preserve

Indigenous languages as a bulwark against Protestantization and sub-
sequent Anglicanization."[6] Camille's motivation was rooted more in
the era of liberation theology, in which preaching God's option for the
poor often involved learning the language of the poor. In the 1970s,
he had taken a leadership role in some co-op projects with the Dene
and supported the chiefs in their opposition to the Mackenzie Valley
Pipeline.[7] In Fort Simpson, a decade later, his role seemed to be reduced
to that of a sacramental functionary. The Dene were leading their own
organizations. Most of the Dene and Métis in Fort Simpson and the
adjacent community of Fort Providence didn't attend church. However,
they still had their children baptized, got married in the church, and
often had a Catholic funeral. This approach to the church is what my
Métis friend Marjorie Beaucage has described as a "just-in-case" theology, covering all the bases.

In Fort Simpson that year, I had no context for the poster and was
quite disturbed by it. But I was a Catholic woman with limited options
for ministry in the Catholic Church. I had the belief that there must
be some reason that I ended up here. I observed Camille, who had
channelled so much of his energy into organizing the Pope's failed visit
and who, that very summer, was facilitating a visit to Fort Simpson from
Jean Vanier, the founder of L'Arche, in the hope of starting a L'Arche
community in the North.[8] So I kept my criticism to myself and put the
poster out of my mind.

A few weeks later, Camille invited me to go to Fort Rae (now
Behchoko) with him to attend the ordination of Denis Croteau, another
Oblate, as bishop of the Mackenzie-Fort Smith Diocese. The Dogrib,
or Tłı̨chǫ, community of Fort Rae was (and still is) very Catholic, and
I was told this would be part of my learning about the "Church of the
North." Possibly because it was an ordination of a bishop and possibly
because the Dogrib were engaged with the church, a significant crowd
had gathered in Fort Rae, about two hundred people, mostly Dene, but
also some Inuit who had flown down from the Artic, along with a scat-
tering of white people from Yellowknife. With my Polaroid I managed to
take a picture of two Inuit women wearing amautiit (parkas with large
pouches on their backs) into which their babies almost disappeared.
I was acting like a tourist, later taking pictures of the rows of Dogrib
women, most wearing headscarves and loose blue or maroon windbreakers, who sat separately from the men in the large outdoor space.

I quickly noticed just how male the event was. The ordination took place over three days, with at least twenty priests and a few bishops in attendance. A half-teepee-like structure, a white pointed canvas that covered an open space on a raised dais, had been built on the front of the church. I wasn't sure that they had teepees in the North, certainly not like that one. Several Dogrib drummers had drummed on the stage before the big event began. After this, a procession of white men, dressed in cream-and-gold-threaded robes and wearing red stoles, moved through the seated crowd, which was again separated by gender. The highest ranking of these priests, the bishops and monsignors, went up the dais to sit, facing us, the lowly laity. What followed was an endlessly long Mass.

With all this male pomp and circumstance, I was more than thrilled that I had been invited to stay with the Grey Nuns in their residence in Fort Rae. The day before the ceremony I had escaped to have tea with them, wondering, as I looked into the lined faces of the two older nuns who lived in Fort Rae, what their experiences in the North must have been like. But there was little talk of the past, and I was soon lured away by my new companion from Fort Simpson, Jeannine Coulombe. Jeannine invited me to the afternoon praying of the rosary in the church. At first I was reluctant as I considered the rosary one of the greatest pacifiers of women. I stopped saying the rosary when I was fifteen. I was sure this would be one more example of how the Native people of the North have been stripped of their culture by the church. Yet I was curious as I looked out the window of the nuns' residence and saw several older Dogrib women shuffle by on their way to the church. Most were wearing their blue nylon windbreakers, head scarves, shapeless skirts, and thick beige stockings with ankle socks; on their feet, they wore moccasins protected by rubber galoshes. I was curious, so I put on my jacket to ward off the June chill and joined the last stragglers.

When I arrived there were about forty women in the old wooden church and the rosary had started. However, it seemed to be more singing than repeating the words of the Hail Mary. A high melodic chant filled the air in a language I did not understand. The melody was haunting and I was soon swept up in the rhythms and sounds of the singing. Suddenly, the language of the rosary had become something else, not the repetitive mumbling of my childhood prayers. I felt a sense of awe and of being somehow privileged to be there in that holy space created by the women. As the last decade of the rosary ended, the sole man in the room, the Dogrib deacon, who was standing at the front, spoke a prayer in Dogrib. The women replied "amen" and then there was silence. Slowly, they began to shuffle out. I whispered to Jeannine beside me, "In what language have the women been singing the rosary?" She answered, "Cree."[9] And she pointed to the hymnals in the pew. "They are also in Cree. There has been as yet no translation to Dogrib."[10]

I met Jeannine Coulombe the second day I was in Fort Simpson. She was a Sister of Charity. The Sisters of Charity are a Catholic religious order, also known as the Grey Nuns, founded in Quebec by Marguerite d'Youville in 1737. The Grey Nuns had worked in partnership with the Oblates in the North for many decades, first in the missions and later in the residential schools.[11] In Fort Simpson, the Grey Nuns lived in a trailer beside the priest's house. In the old days, the nuns had cooked and cleaned for the priest, and washed and ironed his clothes and church linens. In 1986, a few of the older Grey Nuns were still doing the job of maintaining the priests in Fort Rae and Yellowknife, in addition to their numerous other jobs – teaching at schools, providing catechism lessons and sacramental preparation for the young, and visiting the sick. Jeannine, however, was a modern-day nun. She would have none of that "serving-the-priest" business, and she lived by herself in the trailer beside the church in Fort Simpson. She had short brown hair sprinkled with grey, an engaging smile, and dressed simply without a habit.

Jeannine was the sole alcohol and drug counsellor at the Deh Cho Society Friendship Centre across the street from the church, where she'd worked for two years. The Friendship Centre served the mixed population of Dene and Métis of not only Fort Simpson but also the smaller outlying Dene communities like Trout Lake and Jean-Marie River. Jeannine often seemed weary at the end of a long day. Sometimes she saw a few clients who were in critical condition from severe drinking; most days, she had none.

One afternoon, we were sitting together on a bench on the side of the dusty main drag, a dirt road that was part of the Yellowknife Highway. As usual, there was not much traffic, just a few pedestrians. We watched two older Dene men slowly walk by, followed by a couple: the woman had a black eye and trailed behind the man. Not much later, some young Dene guys sauntered by, ball caps on their heads. No one looked at us. I thought to myself: "Why should they look at us? We are two white women associated with the church and they know we are passing through and will leave soon." I felt so out of place here, sitting on the bench like an awkward tourist. I turned to Jeannine and asked her if the alcohol counselling she has been doing has had any impact. She replied, "I doubt it," and turned and looked me straight in the eye and said, "The fact is, we shouldn't even be here."

Jeannine's words left me confused. I was there trying to find my place in the Catholic Church, yet aware that what I was doing, or not doing, did not feel right. What did her words mean for all of us well-meaning non-Native people from the South who had come to help out in the North? I was still sure I could offer something useful.

Luckily, Camille had arranged for me to do a week-long popular education workshop in Fort Providence on preventing violence against women. This was something I had done in the South so I was hopeful that, at least here, I could make a difference. Fort Providence was part of Camille's pastoral responsibilities; he travelled there weekly and hence he had the contacts to arrange this workshop. Fort Providence is named Zhahti Kue, which means "mission house," referring to the Catholic mission and the residential school that was there for many years. Fort Providence had been the first centre of the Sacred Heart Mission, and, in 1867, the Fort Providence Boarding Home had been the first such home created in the North. The Grey Nuns arrived in Fort Providence that year and, in the next few decades, set up the boarding school, an orphanage, and a small hospital. The school was rebuilt a few times and the last and largest one closed in 1953.[12] For almost one hundred years, children along the Deh Cho River were sent to the Fort Providence Residential School.[13]

Camille drove me to Fort Providence and set me up in the empty nuns' trailer at the edge of town by the river. It felt strange to be staying in this unoccupied trailer, still neat and tidy, with lace doilies on the side tables, beige curtains over the windows that faced the river, and the requisite crucifix on the kitchen wall. This plainly furnished abode was occasionally used by the few church workers, mostly lay, who now passed through Fort Providence. By 1986, no buildings from the residential school era remained. I had no knowledge of this history or of its significance. Not far away was the priests' residence, also empty, and around the corner was a beautiful old wooden church, its white paint starting to peel. The church was still used on the Sundays when Camille came to town.

That summer of 1986 I was unaware of the connection between residential schools and family violence. Family violence, and especially violence against women, was endemic in these Northern communities, and any approach or help was welcome. I had worked on Vancouver Island for several years using popular education to help prevent spousal assault. Popular education, as it was called in Central and Latin America, had its roots in the teachings of the Brazilian educator Paulo Freire. It challenged the role of the "expert," drawing on people's own knowledge of their situation to enable them to develop a critical analysis, which, in turn, would enable them to take action.[14] I had trained as a popular educator in Nicaragua and Costa Rica, where this approach was used mostly with rural and peasant populations, so I was pretty confident that it would be of use with rural Native women.

However, as I was soon to discover, not much is predictable in "Indian Country." Before he left, Camille brought me over to meet Harriet Geddes, the family violence counsellor for the band. She lived in a small green wood frame house in the middle of the community. Harriet, a sturdy woman with crinkly eyes and short curly dark hair, welcomed me warmly. She immediately offered to help me make copies in the band office of a graphic poster I had designed to advertise my workshop. We posted at the recreation centre, the town store, and at the community hall. I was excited and that night could barely sleep in the narrow bed in the trailer, anticipating the workshop.

However, it turned out that the topic and image of violence against women that I had chosen, even if in cartoon format, was not a big draw in a small Native community where everyone knows everyone else. The first day only two women, Harriet's friends, showed up. Discouraged, but not giving up, that evening Harriet and I worked on a different graphic and title, promising theatre games and fun activities to explore women's strengths. Harriet did more outreach and five more women arrived the second day. By the end of the week, the group had laughed, a few had cried, and I had managed to share a few safety strategies. I would leave Fort Providence with the illusion I had made a difference and glad that I had at last been able to "do" something rather than just sit around as I had been doing in Fort Simpson.

Little did I realize that I was learning more than I was teaching, not only from the group but also from Harriet. Harriet was the first woman to introduce me to Dene traditional knowledge, though I did not know then that there was a name for it. She invited me over to her house one night for a dinner of moose stew. I discovered that she herself had shot the moose and, with her husband long gone, was a resilient survivor on many levels. Harriet was a hunter, able to skin and work with moose hide; a fisher; someone who was knowledgeable about plant medicines; a former court worker; and now a family violence worker.

Another evening, after a workshop session, she invited me to come berry picking. The berry area was on the edge of town on the road by the river. The sun was still visible in the Northern evening sky, and Harriet offered me a green hat with a fine netting that covered my face to fend off the mosquitoes. I discovered we were to pick the tiny red wild strawberries that grew beside the road, close to the ground – berries I had ignored at home because they were so small. Harriet began picking in earnest and seemed to have infinite patience as we were swarmed by buzzing mosquitoes. She chatted away about the teachings of the strawberries and of the other plants on the side of the road as I miserably picked a bowl a third the size of hers, barely listening. Only many years later would I appreciate the gift of picking the first strawberries of the season and understand the spiritual and ceremonial significance of these berries in many Indigenous cultures.[15]

I would only pass through Fort Providence one more time. It was 1990 and I was driving the Yellowknife Highway with my son and stepson on a journey from Vancouver to Yellowknife to co-facilitate the Denendeh Seminar that was to be held in Dettah that year. We dropped in on Harriet, whom I had written in advance, and she was as welcoming and gracious as I remembered her. When I left I promised to write, but I never did, caught up as I was in my life in the South.

The Denendeh Seminar

Of the two placements I had in the Northwest Territories in 1986, the Sacred Heart Mission with Camille Piché and the Denendeh Seminar with René Fumoleau, the latter had the most impact on shaping my life direction. I had had a few telephone conversations before I arrived in the Northwest Territories with René, the Oblate priest who had begun the Denendeh Seminar. But I only met him for the first time at the bishop's ordination ceremony in Fort Rae. A short man, slightly built, with thinning grey hair around a square face and glasses, he greeted me warmly with a delightful French accent, which he had not lost despite being away from France for more than forty years. I noted right away that he was not wearing a priest's collar at this formal event; rather, he wore just an old plaid work shirt. He seemed to know many of the Dene who were at the ceremony, and I watched him chatting away with many of the locals during those three days in Fort Rae. We arranged to meet at his home in Yellowknife the next week to prepare for the seminar, which, that year, was to take place in Rádeli Kóé, then known as Fort Good Hope, now known as the Charter Community of K'asho Got'ine.

This meeting was to be the first of many rendezvous between René and me at his home base. René lived on Latham Island in a small, very basic two-room cabin in the Old Town part of Yellowknife. He referred to the cabin, constructed of green painted plywood and a wood frame, as his shack. Like many who lived in the Old Town, where the homes were built on rocks, his sanitary facilities consisted of what was called a honey pot – a bucket in a small washroom. I was impressed, as all the priests I had known elsewhere in Canada lived in rather comfortable rectories.

Over the five years we worked together, I discovered a lot about René, about the church in the North, and about Dene politics. René had been a priest in the Northwest Territories since 1953. He had moved from

France to Fort Good Hope to be the parish priest there. Like many of the Oblates, he learned the local language, which was North Slavey, the language of the Sahtu people, and he had travelled with the people during their seasonal moves out on the land, hunting, trapping, and fishing. In 1970, he moved to Yellowknife to work as a researcher for the emerging Indian Brotherhood of the Northwest Territories, the organization that became the Dene Nation in 1978. The result of René's research was the book *As Long as This Land Shall Last*, which is still considered a definitive history of Treaties 8 and 11.[1] René was also a filmmaker and a photographer and, at the time I met him, was functioning more or less as a free agent in the diocese, not allocated to any parish.

René had created the Denendeh Seminar as a type of "exposure tour" for Southern church people. The term "Denendeh" means "The Land of the People." The idea was to educate Christians about the Indigenous people of the North, specifically the Dene and their land Rights, and to mobilize Southern support for the Dene fight for sovereignty. René was trusted by many Dene, and, though he was very critical of the church and how it operated in the North, he was tolerated by the bishops because of his strong connections with the locals. He was knowledgeable about the complex politics in the North, and, as more and more Dene became educated and could do the research and documentation he had formerly done, René figured out that his ministry was now to educate white people. He no longer believed in the role of the parish priest in Dene communities. His was a form of liberation theology, but it was more nuanced than most in that he had few illusions about reaching a "revolutionary goal" in his lifetime. René had been with the Dene so long that he saw God in relationships and always in process. Whenever the Denendeh Seminar group wanted a definitive answer to a question, René would respond with, "life is constantly moving and changing and we can find God in the process, we find God in relationship."[2] René offered me a model of ministry that was radically different from anything else I had seen. He had been Indigenized to the extent that he saw the world through both Euro-Western and Indigenous lenses. It was because of this that I decided to continue to work with René and the seminar.

The Denendeh Seminar had begun in 1985 and ended in 1991. I was fortunate that the first facilitator, who had worked with René in 1985, was unable to return the next year, which gave me the opportunity to work as René's co-facilitator from 1986 until the final seminar in Hay River in 1991. Over the five summers that René and I worked together, we visited four different communities: Rádeli Kóé/Fort Good Hope, Lutsel k'e/Snowdrift, Dettah (near Yellowknife), and Hay River, where the 1991 seminar was sponsored by the Dene Cultural Institute.

Little did I know just how political René's agenda was. Since 1975, a document known as the Dene Declaration had articulated the Dene vision for sovereignty.[3] The Declaration was the result of the combined work of the Indian Brotherhood of the Northwest Territories and the Metis and Non-Status Association of the Northwest Territories. It proposed an autonomous nation within Canada, a nation based on Dene values, traditions, languages, and ways of living. This nation and its land would incorporate economic self-sufficiency and use consensus decision making, all within Dene-defined political institutions. Not surprisingly, the Canadian state was not interested in this vision, which undermined the ongoing capitalist exploitation of the resources in the North. So the federal government had begun a long process of land claims negotiations with the Dene and Metis under its Comprehensive Land Claims Policy, its framework for modern-day treaties. René was hoping to educate seminar participants about Dene values and relationship to the land, and the sham of land claims process, so that they would go back home and lobby for the Dene framework. He had sent me the Dene Declaration and material on the federal comprehensive land claims policy to read before the seminars. I could hardly grasp the complexity of it all, so I decided to leave that part of the seminar to René. I was basically like the rest of the participants – new to the North and discovering as we went along, guided by René and the few Dene and Metis who occasionally joined us.

René was very critical of the federal claims policy. He explained to me that the very term "land claims" reflects the federal agenda. It implies that Indigenous people must apply to have possession of their land rather than addressing the fact that they already have an inherent Right to the land, inherent Title, which means a collective Right to the use of and jurisdiction over the ancestral territories of their specific nation. After more than a decade of negotiations, by the late 1980s, the federal government had succeeded in removing recognition of Indigenous political Rights from the negotiations. In the words of contemporary Yellowknives Dene scholar Glen Coulthard, the federal government agenda was "to 'extinguish' the broad and undefined rights and title claims of First Nations in exchange for a limited set of rights and benefits."[4] During the period that the Denendeh Seminar took place, from 1986 to 1990, the federal government managed to pressure the Dene and Metis to remove Indigenous political Rights from the negotiations. In 1988 the Agreement-in-Principle was signed, which, as Coulthard explains, "required the Dene/Metis to agree to 'cede, release, and surrender' any residual Aboriginal Rights and Title to the remaining lands of the Northwest Territories."[5]

For me, the Denendeh Seminar was a trial-by-fire experience, learning about what I was facilitating from day to day. As for the participants, it was both a challenging and a troubling experience. Most of the people who attended it over those five years were white. Two Native women once came from Winnipeg, not realizing it would be a mostly white crowd. On average, there were twelve to seventeen people each year. These included a few priests, most of whom were going on to placements in Native communities either in the North or elsewhere in Canada; several nuns; a few Protestant ministers; and many laypeople who were involved in Project North, an ecumenical Christian church organization that did Native solidarity work.[6] There were also a few interested individuals who just wanted a more "in-depth" tourism experience of the Northwest Territories – that is, they wanted to meet Native people.

What struck me during those five years was how the seminar groups were viewed and were both accepted and not accepted in the Dene communities. My basis of comparison was my experiences in Nicaragua and Costa Rica, where I had trained in popular education and had been involved in making solidarity links with educators in Central America who were fighting the US-backed Contras who were attempting to depose the Sandinista government. Different organizations arranged solidarity tours in which participants stayed in the homes of locals. However, during the Denendeh Seminar, we did not stay in people's houses, much to the disappointment and frustration of some of the participants, who wanted this type of experience. In the communities we either stayed in an empty priest's residence or a school gym. As well, we were regarded with some distrust by many in the communities. We were rarely invited into peoples' homes, and the level of daily interaction that participants wanted with the locals often did not happen. We were invited to the occasional community event, but there were fewer interactions with individuals and families. On the visit to Rádeli Kóé I had brought my seven-year-old son Kael with me, which opened up a few doors with some of the women. When the local kids threw stones at him one night when he went to play with them, I could only remind him what it must be like to be the only Native kid in a white school.

In the seminar we facilitated daily sessions that focused on social analysis of the North, reflection on our own group process, the politics of solidarity, and deconstructing the language of comprehensive land claims. It was politics without taking a close look at ourselves. Each day, if we were lucky, a local Elder, Dene or Metis leader, male or female, would come to share whatever she or he wanted to speak about. In the late afternoons and evenings we could wander about the small villages and would occasionally get the chance to attend a local event. A few times we were invited to a "tea dance," which is a Dene drum dance ceremony. Once, in Dettah, we were invited to a community feast. Each seminar included a one-day "fast on the land," a brief but not insignificant invitation to get to know the land. This involved spending twenty-four hours on the land without food and water, which we did in order to get a tiny glimpse of what "Aboriginal spirituality" might be.

What has stayed with me over the years, and I think with many others who participated in the seminar, is my experience of the vastness of the land in Denendeh. The visit to Rádeli Kóé involved a plane ride to Norman Wells and then a boat ride up the Mackenzie River to reach our destination. Our fast that year was on the Ramparts, a sacred place of towering cliffs on the banks of the Mackenzie that is accessible only by boat. As at Rádeli Kóé, all fasts involved a boat trip to a more remote area. One year, to get to Snowdrift/Lutsel k'e, seminar attendees had two options: a flight on a small float plane or a day-long boat ride across Great Slave Lake in a "kicker" (usually a small 3.5- to 4.9-metre aluminum boat with an outboard motor). Each of these trips brought up fears – fear of flying in tiny float planes, fear of being in little boats in rough waters, and, on the land, fear of unknown animals and of going without water for a day. For many of us the seminar was about facing our fears.

The boat ride that I took from Yellowknife to Snowdrift/Lutsel k'e is still etched in my mind and body memory. It is one thing to watch the land of Denendeh from a plane, observing the hundreds of little lakes and the seemingly endless scrub forest of low pines and black spruce. It is quite another to sense the immensity of the land and water when you are on it. I was quite scared to embark on the boat trip to Lutsel k'e; the boat seemed so tiny, an open Lund aluminum craft, about four metres long, with an outboard engine and two gas tanks in the back. There was just enough room for four of us: J.C. Catholique, our Chipewyan helmsman who owned the boat; a youngish priest from Toronto who had just been transferred to the Mi'kmaq community of Eskasoni in Cape Breton; a retired social worker, Henry; and me.[7] We had given our packs to those who were travelling by float plane, and we settled in for what looked like a smooth boat ride.

Great Slave Lake is the second largest lake in the Northwest Territories (after Great Bear Lake), the deepest in North America, and the tenth largest in the world. Snowdrift is on the east arm of the lake. I did not know any of this then. As our boat rounded the point and slowly left Yellowknife Harbour in Old Town, in the distance I saw nothing ahead but a vast blue expanse of water. It was a clear morning with a few clouds on the distant horizon. After a few hours in silence, we stopped at a small island to have our lunch and tea, heated on a small fire that J.C. quickly built. Just as we were about to head out again, the sky darkened and a wind came up from the east, churning the grey water into whitecaps. J.C. and I moved over to the side and discussed whether we should go forward, turn back, or stay where we were. I was torn, not wanting to look like a frightened woman and concerned we would miss the activities that evening and the next morning, which I was supposed to facilitate. J.C. did not seem that worried about going ahead, so we decided to do it.

With trepidation, I took my seat on the small wooden bench behind J.C. Soon, some of the waves were as high as the boat, with spray occasionally covering us, splashing our faces and glasses. J.C. handed us pieces of dried caribou to chew, which relieved the tension. I watched my panic rise. At one point, it seemed we were lost in the middle of the lake, with no land in sight and the wind howling. Here I was, a nervous woman with three men, none of whom seemed as afraid as I was, least of all J.C., who did not seem at all perturbed. So I bit my lip and prayed. Gradually, J.C. steered the boat closer to the distant shoreline. It would take several more hours, hugging the shore, until we reached Snowdrift in the late evening, with the rest of the seminar group anxiously waiting for us on the shore.

This trip humbled me to the power of the water. I got a small sense of how the Dene negotiated daily with the land and waters, how the rhythm of their lives was linked to respect for the power of the lake, and how human schedules were secondary to this relationship. I saw another aspect of this relationship with water when, a few days later, I was invited by J.C. to go to one of the nearby sites that was sacred to the Chipewyan people. I went in the boat with him and his young daughter, Kai. It was a time of few words. After walking up the Snowdrift River a short distance, the two of them stopped and looked over the river bank into a deep pool where several fish were lazily swimming. I watched with them, in silence, without moving, for what seemed like an eternity. Gradually, I became mesmerized and lost a sense of separation between myself, the fish, the water, and my companions. Then, slowly, we continued on our way in silence.

My land experiences in Denendeh stayed etched in my mind. I was learning to see the land differently from what I had learned as an urban Canadian. I discovered in a visceral way that we are really not in control, certainly not of "nature." And if we are not in control then what is our relationship with the land and water and the non-human beings that are part of them? While I could not yet articulate or understand that relationship I had become aware that the land was vibrant and alive and that I was a small figure in relation to it.

As I watched people in the small villages observing us warily, I became aware that our agenda was not theirs. I had not yet grasped the extent of the colonial power relations within which we were enmeshed. In a way, the Denendeh Seminar was not that different from the experience of the white missionary or helper parachuting into a community for a few weeks or even months. We did not spend time looking at our role in the colonial structure that had left these Northern villages poor, marked by a history of residential schools, with the challenges of alcoholism and abuse. While René made sure we became aware of how the Dene were asserting their rights and working to overcome the impacts of colonial history, we did not spend time looking at our whiteness, which was invisible to us but not to those we visited. We did not question the fact that we had the funds and mobility to travel up North, while many in these communities would travel no farther

than Yellowknife, if they were lucky. Despite the fact we were not officially associated with any particular church, there was no denying that
we were a Christian group, composed mostly of well-meaning white
Christians wanting to make a difference. And many Dene and Metis in
the North regarded Christianity, with its various factions competing
for souls, not to mention all its sexual abuse scandals that were being
revealed, with clear suspicion.

As for the difference René and I hoped its participants could make,
the Denendeh Seminar focused largely on the political arena. René
had chosen Dettah for the 1990 seminar so we could be there for the
Dene National Assembly, where a motion was passed to have Aboriginal
and Treaty Rights affirmed, not extinguished, within a comprehensive
claims agreement.[8] This meant that the Dene/Metis Final Agreement
was rejected. Though this decision was later overridden, as two of the
regions and nations within the larger Dene Nation, the Gwich'in and
the Sahtu, withdrew and settled separately with Canada, our hope was
that the seminar participants would return to the South and support
Indigenous Nations' assertion of sovereignty.[9] However, even this was
ambitious, as every year the participants were new, and it was not easy
to quickly grasp the complex political dynamics of the North. Most
participants were just pleased to be at Dettah to observe a consensus
decision-making process that was new to them, to observe how the
Dene National Assembly handled speakers who spoke in the many languages of the Dene Nation, and to be included in the daily community
feasts. That was enough to take in within two weeks. Yet, over the years,
I would occasionally run into former participants who were active in
making their churches or communities more responsive to Indigenous
Rights and issues, and I realized the seminar continued to have a considerable impact on many.

After Dettah, there was one more seminar, in 1991, this time in Hay
River, located on the south shore of Great Slave Lake at the mouth of the
Hay River. We stayed on the Hay River Reserve, the Slavey community
now known as K'atlodeeche. The seminar was sponsored by the Dene
Cultural Institute (DCI). The purpose of the DCI was to research and
promote Indigenous Knowledge. As in every other community in which
the Denendeh Seminar was held, we learned about the history and
culture of the Native peoples in that region, but we also learned about
the work of the DCI. The focus on the collection and formulation of

traditional Indigenous Knowledge reflected an expansion of the political focus of the DCI's Metis founder, Joanne Barnaby. René had worked with Joanne over the years and she had been an invited speaker at a few of the seminars when she worked in Yellowknife. The DCI was collecting traditional plant knowledge, as well as information about traditional hunting, trapping, and fishing practices along with traditional governance and justice systems. It would take me several more years to understand the significance of this, that the foundations of Indigenous world views and laws were rooted in relationships with the land and that the conservation of that relationship and knowledge is critical for maintaining a distinctly Indigenous way of life and form of governance.

In Hay River, most of the participants stayed in the gym of the recreation centre on the reserve, while I, pleading that I needed time to do my prep and rest before facilitating every day, stayed with a Metis couple who were practitioners of the Baha'i faith. What I noted in Hay River was the extent of religious diversity and religious conflict in that community, which was like so many other Northern communities. Besides the churches of at least three mainstream Christian denominations (Anglican, Catholic, and Baptist) there was an Assembly of God tent, run by a Chipewyan woman from Snowdrift; some travelling evangelicals from Texas, whom we met at the local restaurant; the Baha'i group; and, finally, several members of the Hay River reserve who were returning to traditional Dene spiritual practices while also running a sweat lodge. Clearly, the fight for "Indian souls" had not diminished but, rather, had quite possibly intensified since those first years of colonialism when the Oblates and Anglicans had competed for religious control of the North.

The visit to Hay River marked the end of the Denendeh Seminar. Joanne did not offer to host it again. The priority of the Dene Cultural Institute to recover and promote Indigenous Knowledge was clearly more important than hosting a group of well-meaning Christians. Yes, there had been critical weaknesses in the Denendeh Seminar, yet there had been some important lessons as well. René served as a model to show those of us who participated in the seminar that our role was to be there as witnesses, not to pretend that we could do anything to help the Dene. The Dene had been mobilizing since the early 1970s to protect their Indigenous Rights and needed no help from us. Many of the participants were disappointed that so often all we did was sit and watch what was going on, be it an assembly, a community meeting, or a feast. Yet the Denendeh Seminar did achieve some of its goals: white Christians from the South got a tiny taste of the reality of Native people in the North, and, afterwards, many got involved in church-based Indigenous solidarity organizations, either within their own churches or within the ecumenical Aboriginal Rights Coalition, which replaced Project North.

The five summers that I spent in the North were critical in shaping my relationship to Christianity. What had become clear to me was that the churches, which had played a not insignificant advocacy role in the defeat of the Mackenzie Valley Pipeline proposal through the vehicle of Project North in the 1970s, had become politically irrelevant in the North. I was tempted to drop any identification with Christianity because I could see that the churches had been complicit in so much evil. Around me, both in the South and in the North, some white people were attending Indigenous ceremonies and adopting Indigenous forms of dress. Many had rejected Christianity completely, a pattern that would intensify as the sexual abuse scandals and later the horrors of residential schools were revealed. Yet that summer, my second to last in the North, I made a decision that was to be one of the most significant in my life.

I remember one moment so clearly. I was sitting on a large rock outside Joanne Barnaby's house in Yellowknife. Joanne had hosted a barbecue for the last night of our Denendeh Seminar at Dettah that year. She had invited some locals as well. A young white man with long hair who lived in Yellowknife was chatting to me about how much he loved the tea dances and "Indian spirituality," and he said that he was going to look for a sweat lodge to attend. He had had it with Christianity. Somehow his enthrallment with Indigenous spirituality made me uncomfortable and propelled me in a different direction. As I sat there, after facilitating the seminar that had witnessed the Dene National Assembly, I realized that, for me, opting out of Christianity would not only be cowardly but would also make the problem worse. Staying a Christian suddenly felt like a responsibility, an admission that I was born into white privilege in a country that had a terrible colonial past and that I needed to account for my faith and its role in the violence. I am not clear what triggered this realization, but that decision and that moment has stayed with me throughout many decades, despite my ambivalence towards, and often anger at, all the Christian churches.

The desire of well-meaning white Christians "to make a difference" was one of the central problems of the Denendeh Seminar. We, including me, didn't really know what that meant and didn't realize that it might be problematic. But one thing I learned from René was commitment. He was a stubborn little man: his astrological sign was Leo, like mine, and we sometimes clashed. But I had the privilege of working with someone who was in it for the long haul, deeply committed to supporting and being a witness to Indigenous people in the North. In his late seventies and early eighties, he organized and deposited with the Northwest Territories Archives the more than fifteen thousand photos and multiple film reels that he had taken of the Dene and the North.[10] In this period, he also wrote and published a few books of poems and stories as he morphed into a storyteller, constantly faced with the challenge of not appropriating Dene stories.[11] In the late 1990s, René moved to Lutsel'ke, where he stayed in the seniors' residence for several years. When the Oblate order wanted him to move into its home for aging priests in Edmonton, he refused, eventually leaving the order. When he was almost ninety, René returned to Yellowknife, where he had a room in a church residence used by people travelling into Yellowknife from area communities. I still see his book, *As Long as This Land Shall Last*, on Treaties 8 and 11, referenced in present-day struggles for sovereignty. I know that René made a difference in my life, modelling to me to not be afraid to question the church, to commit to long-term relationships, and to not be in a hurry – the hardest lesson for me.

Shifting Missions

Between 1986 and 1991, besides my experiences with the Denendeh Seminar and my fieldwork in Fort Simpson and Fort Providence, I had other opportunities to observe the many contradictions and problems of "Native mission." I had felt vaguely uncomfortable with the word "mission" when I was in theology school, but I couldn't quite identify why. I was immersed in an environment in which the word was taken for granted, so it was fairly easy for me to ignore my discomfort in the busyness of study, field placements, graduation, and figuring out what role I could play in the church. The etymology of the word "mission" may be traced to the Latin verb *mittere*, meaning to send. The term emerged in the sixteenth century to describe the sending of the Holy Spirit into the world.[1] Christian mission was the undergirding of European colonial conquest throughout the globe. During my time in theology school I could see that, within liberation theology, there were attempts to make mission palatable, but I had little life experience to challenge its usage. This would soon change.

During roughly this same time period, from 1988 to 1991, while facilitating the Denendeh Seminar in the summers, I was working in Vancouver on a three-year contract at the Native Education Centre as an evaluator of the Native Family Violence Workers Counselling and Community Services Training Program (hereafter referred to as the Native Family Violence Program). The goal of this program was to equip students to deal with spousal and sexual violence in their communities. It combined some Euro-Western counselling techniques with healing approaches based on Indigenous traditions and culture. In the program, I observed the extent of the damage caused by sexual abuse in the residential schools, and, among the participants, I saw both anger at, and little sympathy for, the churches. At the same time, I was supporting the work of Project North, which was an ecumenical organization of

Christians whose purpose was to support Indigenous communities fighting resource extraction and pursuing sovereignty. As well, I had been hired to teach popular education methods to Canadian and American Jesuits who were working in Native Ministry. The late 1980s was a period during which white Christian solidarity with Indigenous people was being redefined, a period of shifting alliances and strong Indigenous mobilizations, and the role of the mainstream Christian churches was no longer clear.

In 1988, I worked with Marjorie Beaucage, a Métis woman, to facilitate the annual general meeting of Project North in Winnipeg. The organization had been involved in an advocacy and support role in the fight against the Mackenzie Valley Pipeline as well as in the legal and environmental struggles of the Haida, Lubicon Cree, Nisga'a, Innu, and Gitskan and Wet'suwet'en. It was also advocating for Aboriginal Rights to be included in the Canadian Constitution. At that point in time, Project North was in the process of morphing into the Aboriginal Rights Coalition, an ecumenical alliance with members from different mainstream churches and religious organizations. Project North's work had usually taken the form of campaigns involving letter writing, fundraising, and putting pressure on government and industry. When Marjorie and I facilitated this meeting, we were aware that there was criticism that some of these campaigns were initiated by the organization with little input from the Native people on the ground.

The three-day meeting was held at Villa Maria, an Oblate House in St Norbert, outside Winnipeg. Participants were primarily the leadership and the most committed members of Project North, the majority of whom were men representing different churches, with some determined older women as well as a few Aboriginal leaders who had come to get some concrete support from Project North on specific issues. Marjorie, a gifted educator, was friends with the invited Elder, Art Solomon. Art was an Anishinabe traditionalist and writer known, among other things, for getting Indigenous spiritual practices into the prison system. Within a few hours of the start of the meeting, we became aware that there was a considerable gap between what the Indigenous and white participants expected as outcomes of the meeting. The majority of the Project North contingent disliked our participatory style. Wanting to avoid conflict, I was getting nervous about how we were going to manage these challenges. At a break, Marjorie and I went outside with Art and he said he would support whatever we decided to do. At lunch, we went outside again and Marjorie brought me over to a white birch tree, its leaves dancing in the breeze. She put her arms around the trunk and leaned against it. Then she invited me to hug the tree and to ask it for support and guidance as we planned what to do. This seemed a bit strange to me, but I trusted Marjorie and I did it. I immediately felt more centred. At that point we decided to call the issues that were lying dormant in the room rather than to prolong the undercurrents of discontent.

When we returned to the group, Art took the floor and gently challenged the assembled members. He said it was time they listened to the leadership of women and recognized the gifts we brought to the table. Then we asked participants to locate themselves in any one of four stations in the room, based on the question: "What do you want to spend your time doing to support effective mobilization for Aboriginal Rights?" The four choices were: write letters, join a demonstration, sign a petition, or civil disobedience. The only ones who went to the civil disobedience station were Don Ryan, head negotiator for the Gitxsan, who had just established a blockade to stop logging in the Sam Greene Creek area of their territory, and his Wet'suwet'en colleague, Herb George. The Project North people were scattered between the remaining stations. Ryan and George spoke from their station about their situation and what they needed from the churches. After the afternoon coffee break, he and his companion left, flying back to British Columbia.

This moment crystallized for me one of the main problems of church social justice coalitions. The Aboriginal Rights Coalition would be hampered by its unwieldy structure, which demanded that member churches had to approve actions and direction taken by the staff and frontline people. The leadership of the churches – Catholic, Anglican, United, Lutheran, Presbyterian, and others – were often not willing to rock the boat. Their vested interests were in maintaining the status quo.

During this same period, I was recruited by the Jesuits to lead several workshops in their "Native Apostolate." The Jesuits I worked with were less focused on the politics of Indigenous Rights and more on how to increase Aboriginal participation in the church. I had first made the acquaintance of the Jesuit Mike Murray at a popular education workshop in Montreal in 1985. Mike was a committed adult educator, and he wanted to explore popular education as a method that might work to increase the involvement of the Anishinabe men and women the Jesuits were training for the Catholic Diaconate in Northern Ontario. He invited me to lead a one-week popular education training workshop at the Anishinabe Spiritual Centre at Anderson Lake near Espinola, Ontario. The Jesuits had constructed this beautiful centre as a base for a Native ministry training program. Few Native men had opted for a priestly vocation, which involves celibacy, largely because in Indigenous traditions having a family is considered a sacred calling and responsibility. The focus of the program was therefore on training deacons. Realizing that gender balance was integral to Anishinabe culture, the Jesuits decided it was strategic to train the wives of deacons into what was then called the Diocesan Order of Women. So I arrived in 1989 to facilitate a group of what turned out to be deeply Christian and deeply Anishinabe women and men.

I quickly discovered that the members of this group had more to teach me than I them. I was using a methodology for reading the Bible developed by Brazilian biblical scholar Carlos Meister. Meister had worked with Basic Christian Communities in Brazil and articulated the process by which people in these communities read the Bible.[2] He identified how three elements led to a liberatory reading of a text, a reading that motivated a group to challenge both the established church and social structures. These elements were the *pre-text*, which was the larger economic, political, and social situation within which the group lived; the *context*, or specific community; and the meaning the people discovered in the biblical *text*. In reflecting on a biblical text, participants needed to acknowledge and name both the pre-text and the context. I had used the method with some success a few times with Christian social justice groups and with the Denendeh Seminar groups. However, in this group of solely Indigenous people, I marvelled at how they required no effort to move into a lived analysis and application of the scriptures. They had interpretations of the biblical texts that not only had I never heard before but that were also deeply radical, in the sense of getting to the roots of the colonial reality in which they were still living.

One example was the story of the Good Samaritan, which Jesus told in response to the lawyer's question, "Who is my neighbour?" I had always been taught that this text was primarily about the good role model provided for us by the Samaritan, who bound the wounds of, and fed and provided shelter to, the man hurt by robbers, as opposed to the passing priest and Levite, who ignored him. To my amazement, this group focused on the robbers in the story, easily naming the forces, including the Indian Act, that were keeping their communities in poverty, as well as the companies that were exploiting the resources on their land in Northern Ontario. So for some, the Samaritan they envisaged was doing way more than providing Band-Aids to ease the suffering of the wounded man: he was bringing the wounded man to a community member who, together with others in the community, would go about solving the problem at its roots.

At the end of my week with this group, one of the women rose to her feet and moved to the centre of the circle. The circular room was large, with imposing fir beams and high windows. The sun was out that day, and through the many large windows we could see the lake sparkling behind her. She carried an eagle feather and she slowly ran her fingers down each side of it. Then she explained to all of us that her faith was like the feather, on one side was her Indigenous traditions, on the other was the Christian tradition, and they came together as one in the feather, without contradiction. This was the first time I wondered if there was a possibility of a Christianity that was genuinely Anishinabe, not European like my own.

Mike seemed satisfied with my work and flew me next to Bozeman, Montana, where I conducted a workshop on popular education methods with about thirty Jesuits involved in Native ministry in the United States and Canada. The numbers surprised me, and I got a sense of just how geographically extensive the Native Apostolate was. However, none of these men were Indigenous; all were white, with the exception of a Chicano Jesuit. Yet many of these men had been living in Indigenous communities for years, were language speakers, and were struggling with how to "inculturate" Catholicism.

I was uncomfortable with inculturation, yet not sure why. I first heard the term used by the Oblates. One of them, Achiel Peelman, had published a book on inculturation in Aboriginal communities in Canada.[3] Inculturation, from what I could see in the late 1980s, seemed to involve adopting some aspects of a local culture – kind of like window dressing. Somehow, whether a priest wore a deerskin stole, or deacons were allowed to use sweetgrass in the church instead of incense, or a service began with drumming, or even if the Mass were offered in the language of the people, none of this seemed substantially different to me. As I was just out of theology school, I was still keen to find out more and did a little research. The definition of inculturation that was getting the most play came from Pedro Arrupe, the superior general of the Society of Jesus, who wrote in a 1977 letter to his fellow Jesuits worldwide:

> Inculturation is the incarnation of christian [sic] life and of the christian [sic] message in a particular cultural context, in such a way that this experience not only finds expression through elements proper to the culture in question ... but becomes a principle that animates, directs and unifies the culture, transforming and remaking it so as to bring about "a new creation."[4]

I guessed that this was the new meaning of mission for the Catholic Church – transforming and remaking a culture using its own cultural elements. I confess I got easily lost in theological thinking (and still do), but somehow what I was observing did seem like the old Christianity with new window dressing. This was not what had been happening with the Bible reading experience I had had with the Anishinabe Christians at Anderson Lake, but it seemed to be what the new mission was all about.

My next glimpse into this arena occurred when Mike asked me to facilitate a preparatory session at Lac Saint Anne for the annual Tekakwitha Conference, proposed to be held in Alberta in 1989. Kateri Tekakwitha was a Mohawk Algonquin woman born in 1656 who became a convert to Christianity. Over the centuries, she became something of a Catholic cult figure. I remembered holy cards of Kateri, called "Lily of the Mohawks," given to us in the convent, where the nuns promoted both her asceticism and her virginity. Years later, I would discover from historian Allan Greer how the early Jesuits had constructed Kateri's image, appropriating and exoticizing her story to serve Catholic doctrinal ends.[5] Greer illustrates how, for European and European American Catholics, Kateri was "made to stand for the antithesis of modernity."[6]

However, for Native Catholics she had come to represent the possibility of being fully Indian and still fully Catholic. Many Indigenous people regarded her as a saint long before she was officially canonized by the Catholic Church in 2012. The Tekakwitha Conference had begun in 1946 as a support group for priests in Native ministry. In 1977, it was "opened" to Native Catholics. As Greer describes it, in the context of the American Indian Movement, Native people were no longer willing to let the priests lead. The Tekakwitha Conference then expanded into an international network with numerous local chapters and "Kateri Circles," small groups of mostly women who already regarded Kateri as a saint.[7]

I agreed to go to Lac Saint Anne, my main motives being curiosity and my still unsatisfied desire to find a place for myself in the Catholic universe. This was 1988, and Lac Saint Anne had been suggested as the venue because it was already a pilgrimage site for Native Catholics. Lac Saint Anne is a Métis community in Northern Alberta and the location of a lake named by the missionaries after Saint Anne, Mary's mother. The lake was a Cree sacred site before contact. Every year Indigenous Catholics from Northern Canada and from the Northwest United States come to honour Saint Anne and to bathe in the healing waters of the lake. I knew of this place because, during the summer I was in Fort Simpson, Camille had left the mission for a week to take several Elders to this very place.[8] My task was to facilitate the planning session for the annual conference. This was not easy. The attendees consisted of some priests and several Native nuns and Native representatives from different Tekakwitha chapters. I definitely felt like an outsider with little to offer. And I questioned why I was there when there were clearly Native people at the meeting who could facilitate it better than I could. The tension and lack of clear direction that I observed was the result of a rapidly changing church, in which authority roles between priests and Native people were beginning to shift. I left that meeting frustrated with my inability to move the process forward and aware that there was no role I could possibly play in this dynamic. In the end, the conference was not held in Lac Saint Anne but in Fargo, North Dakota.[9]

Once more I worked with Mike Murray. I give him credit as he continued to search for ways that would give Indigenous people more say in the church, something few clergy believed in. In 1989, he included me in a four-member team visit to the Diocese of Chiapas in Mexico, where Bishop Samuel Ruiz had fostered what was as close to an Indigenous church as possible.

Close to 80 percent of the diocese of Chiapas was Indigenous. As well, Ruiz supported the more than forty-five thousand Indigenous

Guatemalan refugees who had fled to Chiapas during the Guatemalan Civil War, which had begun in the early 1960s. There are nine distinct Indigenous groups in the state, and Ruiz had learned not one but several of the Indigenous languages in his diocese. He was committed to both social justice and to Indigenous leadership in the church. The Indigenous peoples and their lands had been exploited for centuries by wealthy landowners, and Ruiz emphasized a gospel of justice for the impoverished. He critiqued a church that had been in Latin America for five hundred years and had still done nothing to change the impoverishment, oppression, and marginalization of Indigenous peoples. Ruiz was not afraid to speak the truth, and he held the missionary work of the churches responsible for destroying the cultures of the Indigenous peoples.[10] Both the local landowners and the Vatican hierarchy were unhappy with Ruiz; he was criticized as a communist and endured many threats and efforts to replace him. But the several Indigenous nations within his diocese respected him, and he was able to eventually develop what has been called an "autochthonous church," in which, to some extent, Indigenous people could participate on their own terms.[11]

I knew little of this history when I arrived. My Spanish was functional but our visit was still limited by language and the contrast between the different worlds in which we were operating. The trip included a visit to the Bartolome de Las Casas Human Rights Center in San Cristobal, which Ruiz had helped establish. Advocacy for Indigenous Rights and liberation was a visible and structural commitment in his diocese. We made several forays into some of the outlying communities to meet the local church leaders. We visited one small town on the edge of the Lacandon jungle where our parish guide translated for the Lacandon team, a man and a woman who were the pastoral educators. My job was to figure out how much popular education informed the pastoral education work of the diocese. Alas, I could see it in the cartoon-animated catechetical booklets, but I also deduced there was much more going on than that. Education methodology was just a small part of a church committed to justice for Indigenous peoples. This was a church grounded in the needs of communities, not in those of the hierarchy, and, as I later discovered, Ruiz, involved in dialogue with the Indigenous communities in his diocese, had developed a theology that I would call more interreligious than inculturated. As well, a "teologia india" was emerging – an Indigenous theology articulated by Indigenous people themselves.[12]

One evening the bishop provided us with a local guide to observe a service at a Tzeltal community not far from San Cristobal. Our team, all non-Native, a fact of which I was becoming painfully aware, squeezed into his small pickup and proceeded to be bounced around as the truck climbed on very rough dirt roads into the mountains. We eventually arrived at a small chapel on the top of a hill. It was so crowded that we could not enter, so we just stood outside and listened to the singing and observed through the open windows and door a ceremony that seemed to be mostly Tzeltal ritual. The colours, the bright blue shawls of the women and the reds of their intricately embroidered blouses, the coolness of the dusk air, and the haunting sound of their singing in their language left an indelible impression on me. There were no priests leading, only two Tzeltal deacons. The only thing overtly Christian about the service was the cross on the top of the small adobe building.

I later learned that Dom Samuel Ruiz, or Dom Sam as he was called by the people, had started from the position that the work of God already existed in the Indigenous communities and that "God's Spirit is present in all cultures – the Spirit was at work in the world before Christ."[13] For him, this meant respecting the language, traditions, and ceremonies of the different nations in the diocese, and supporting a liberation struggle that was based in the peoples' identities, not in an abstract vision of liberation. He recognized the capacity for self-governance among the different populations, developed strong local leadership chosen by the communities, and made sure that all participated in decisions to be taken within the church. As we left Chiapas, I was excited and hopeful that we could transfer some of this back in Canada.

However, the follow-up in Canada was only disappointing. In order to share lessons we had learned, Mike arranged for me to facilitate a day-long dialogue in Ottawa between himself and three bishops in whose diocese there were significant Indigenous populations. As I sat there watching these men, I quickly realized that these guys were like CEOs. They were smart, diplomatic, with a sense of confidence and smooth authority. There was a lot of talk at the meeting but not much action afterwards. Bishops have power, which is why there had been significant changes in the church in Chiapas. But most don't want to rock the boat. The institutional machine of the Roman Catholic Church is very hard to turn around. The scandal of residential schools had not yet publicly come to light, and there was no reason to do anything differently. The Catholic Church was far from allowing or supporting an Indigenous church in Canada, or even understanding what that meant. A few years later, one of the bishops at that meeting, Hubert O'Connor of the Prince George Diocese, was charged with the sexual abuse of several girls in residential school and with impregnating one of them. I was not surprised.

In 1991, the Catholic organization Development and Peace brought Dom Samuel to Canada. The "tour" served to educate Catholics about two things: (1) a different model of church and (2) the work of Development and Peace, which, at that point in time, was providing funding for projects in the Chiapas Diocese. After his talk at a local church a few of us went back to the home of one of the Development and Peace organizers for an informal visit with him. Ruiz was standing by the sink in the kitchen of this older East End Vancouver house. He was a humble, short man who did not take up much space, and he was dressed in a modest grey suit that gave no hint that he was a bishop. He shared with us, through a translator, how he saw signs of hope and liberation for all peoples in the values and struggles of Indigenous nations. He believed that interfaith dialogue was the way to work with Indigenous peoples and had committed his life to that work and to standing with the poor. Ruiz was an inspiration to me. An interfaith approach to relationships with Indigenous peoples was more appealing and realistic to me than was a "mission." It was a framework that I would explore and that would guide me in the next decades.

In 1994, certainly not to my surprise, the Zapatistas emerged out of the Lacandon jungle in Chiapas to protest both the North American Free Trade Agreement and the marginalization of Indigenous peoples. Many of the deacons and catechetical instructors of the diocese were in their ranks. Committed to non-violence, Dom Samuel Ruiz became the mediator between the Zapatistas and the Mexican government. I was more interested, as an educator in Canada, in promoting the Zapatista vision of autonomy and local control of natural resources on the part of Indigenous peoples than in propping up a church that offered communities little help to deal with the real material conditions of poverty that they were facing. The disconnect between the churches and increasingly militant Indigenous populations in North America, many of which were returning to their traditional practices, would continue to increase throughout the 1990s.

By the end of 1992, I had finished with doing any work for the Catholic Church. My last contract, under the progressive bishop Remi de Roo, had been to promote the Catholic teachings on labour rights through leading a series of Bible studies up and down Vancouver Island. This ended with a male priest and a male lay leader complaining about me, largely because of my sexuality and gender. I was content to leave the world of mission and the institutional church behind me, and became involved in doing anti-racist popular education work in unions and teaching popular education at the UBC School of Social Work and Vancouver School of Theology. The colonial structures of the Catholic Church were too fixed, and, as in many other areas where non-Natives had been too prominent, Native people could do the work I had done, and in their own culturally appropriate way. I had become even more critical of the term "mission," remembering that awful poster in the upstairs attic of the rectory in Fort Simpson. The entire European imperial project had been as much a Christian mission venture as it was a way of getting the raw resources that Europe needed. I felt that, unless mission addressed colonialism, the power imbalances inherent in the church structures, and the damage the church has done, nothing would change.

In the next two decades, the scandal of sexual abuse in residential schools, as well as in the rest of the church, continued to erode Indigenous peoples' participation in the church. Fewer and fewer young people were attending church, and the massive social and economic problems resulting from residential schools, displacement, and colonialism, processes in which the church was implicated in ways it could not yet see, were crying for attention. In the North, a shortage of priests, combined with little commitment to Indigenizing training for local leaders, contributed to the church's irrelevance as a social force.

In the Jesuit realm, fewer Native people would come to the Anishinabe Spiritual Centre and its diaconate training program. Some were drawn to the Three Fires Midewiwin Society, sometimes called the Anishinabe "Grand Medicine Society," which had been suppressed during the years when Indigenous ceremonies were forbidden by the Indian Act. Throughout "Indian Country" there was a revival of many other traditional practices, including intertribal ceremonies like sweat lodges and Sundances. It's possible that the white missionary hierarchy that still pervaded institutions like the Anishinabe Centre was a critical factor in many Indigenous people distancing themselves from the Catholic Church. While some Anishnabe remained Catholic, at the same time there were and still are many who were not interested in combining traditional ways with Catholicism. The forms of "inculturation" that the Catholic Church has adopted – sweetgrass on the altar, integrating Anishinabe symbolism into Christian images, or bringing the drum into church – were rejected by "traditionalists" who, in the words of settler scholar Theresa Smith, feel that "traditional Native ways are being stolen or perverted in the name of inculturation."[14] In 2003, when I drove across Canada in a move from Vancouver to Montreal, I visited the Anishinabe Centre. It was eerily quiet, almost empty, and was in the process of being transformed into a retreat centre offering yoga, meditation, and Jesuit Ignation spirituality programs.

When Indigenous people choose to remain or become Christian, it is now increasingly on their terms and within their cultural frameworks. Many Indigenous people "converted" during the early colonization period because it was strategic. Some had hoped that the Christians had medicines that might have helped with the diseases that were wiping out communities; others saw that Europeans had political power and thought that conversion could be useful.[15] For many, conversion was forced upon them in residential schools. The Dene and Sahtu Elder George Blondin once commented:

When the Church came they were professionals in converting people. I guess they were trained for that. The Indians were not hard to convert. The priests talked the same language almost right away ... Once a whole bunch of them got converted it was easy, since they were poor people, depending on somebody all the time. The Church was something they really went for. Indians are very religious people.[16]

Choctaw religious studies scholar Michelene Pesantubbe cautions that it would be inaccurate to paint Native people solely as victims of manipulating missionaries "without recognizing their agency expressed in subversive and imaginative ways."[17] It will be a long time before

Christian mission in North America can be free of its colonizing history and accept the lessons of "reverse mission" – that is, to respect and honour the values and worldviews of the cultures who were and are already here. Indigenous Christians are reclaiming and redefining the word "mission" for themselves, as seen in a recent Indigenous theology of mission in the Canadian context articulated by Carmen Landsdowne, a Heiltsuk woman who is an ordained minister in the United Church of Canada.[18]

In the year 2000, I enrolled in the International Feminist Doctor of Ministry (DMin) Program, which was based in the San Francisco Theological Seminary. This program was geared to providing advanced theological education for women from the Global South. As part of the program, a few women from the North were admitted, and our fees helped to pay for the women in the South. My fellow students were from South Africa, Ghana, Costa Rica, Kenya, Japan, Samoa, Chile, Bolivia, and Scotland. I was exposed to a postcolonial feminist alternative to Christian mission and to a politic of interreligious dialogue rooted in social movements for justice and peace.

In the DMin program I learned how biblical narratives had been used to justify the conquest of Indigenous peoples and their lands. I had discovered earlier an article by Osage scholar Robert Warrior, which offered a Native American critique of liberation theology and how the proponents of the latter used the exodus story in the bible as a liberation motif. Warrior argued that Indigenous people could identify more with the Canaanites, those whom the Israelites had dispossessed, and he talked about how the early Puritan preachers used the story, referring to Native Americans as Canaanites.[19] I then unearthed the work of Osage theologian George Tinker, who articulated a Native American critique of mission as well as an Indigenous theology of sovereignty.[20]

As well, my DMin program exposed me to African, Asian, and Latin American feminists and, in particular, to biblical scholars like the Botswanan Musa Dube, who adds a gender perspective to stories of imperial conquest. Dube illustrates how the Bible was used by the colonizers to justify travel to foreign lands by representing foreigners as people in need and as inferior. She shows how both biblical and imperial travel stories were used not only to depict the Native woman as savage and sexual but also as a metaphor for the land, which is something to be occupied and possessed.[21] Dube defines mission as "the exportation of biblical religions to non-biblical cultures," with the goal of possessing land and legitimating empire.[22] Dube is engaged in dialogue with African Indigenous Religions and the African Independent Church, while at the same time incorporating some of the values of these traditions into her ongoing biblical work. Her agenda is to support decolonizing readings of the Bible. This means, for her, "refusing to privilege any cultural or racial supremacy" and offering readings that seek "healing by seeing the interdependence of cultures rather than emphasizing exclusive oppositions."[23] Dube, like many feminist scholars from the Global South, critiques white feminist blindness to the imperial settings of biblical texts. Through the DMin program I learned how to engage with different religious traditions, including Indigenous ones, from an interfaith perspective, which includes criticizing frameworks that still support imperial domination and the colonial patterns that have shaped North American Christianity.

So it was with new eyes that, in 2006, looking through the stacks at the library of the Sisters of Saint Anne in Victoria, I came upon a book titled *History of the Catholic Ladder*.[24] I discovered that the poster I had found many years ago in the attic in Fort Simpson was a version of the "Catholic Ladder" created by the Oblate priest Albert Lacombe. The first Catholic ladder had been a visual aid constructed on a stick by the missionary Father Blanchet for the "Indian Chief" Tslallkum at Fort Vancouver at the mouth of the Columbia River in 1838. In 1839, Blanchet created what the Coast Salish called the Sahale stick, meaning the "wood from above" in the Chinook language, a preaching aid that had the main points of salvation history marked on it. The Sahale stick was seen as an effective teaching tool for dealing with orality-based cultures that functioned through storytelling. It was later converted to a paper chart and further developed as the Catholic Ladder. Its main purpose was to convert non-literate populations of Indians to Catholicism. Lacombe created his ladder in 1872 to use with the Indigenous populations of the Northwest Coast. At least ten thousand copies were printed by the Oblates in the 1870s, with the Sisters of Notre Dame creating a colour version. In 1895–96, Pope Pius IX ordered several thousand copies of a variation of Lacombe's ladder, which were printed for missions around the world. Different versions, including Protestant ladders, were used worldwide until the mid-twentieth century.[25]

Now I see how the Catholic Ladder worked. By defining spiritual life in terms of strict dualisms – right and wrong, good and evil, the white road leading to heaven and the black road leading to hell – Christian missionaries introduced something completely foreign to Indigenous value systems, which were and are based on a principle of balance between differing forces (all of which are in relationship) and on the interconnectedness and interrelatedness of people and non-human beings. The Catholic Ladder divorced the world of spirits from the everyday world of living on the land, imposing a belief system that had little relationship to the culture, land, and place in which people lived. With its condemnation of paganism, which was relegated to the black road, this poster insidiously promoted fear, along with shame of Indigenous ways of being and, hence, of being Indigenous.

When I look at the Catholic Ladder I am left perplexed by the complex relationship that some Indigenous people still have with Christianity, and this is something with which I have struggled over the years. Meanwhile, I salute those non-Indigenous people who have redefined mission from a postcolonial perspective. Mennonite Kate Friesen offers a different vision of mission as well as a critique of Christian missionary conquest. She focuses on the rootlessness of missionaries who had no sense of connection to land and watershed. She asks how people with no sense of home can stand with other people's struggles to protect their homelands. Friesen challenges "the spiritual pathology of placelessness," and she advocates "reconciliation with our home place" as a foundation for Christians who proclaim the Gospel.[26] This means either returning home or staying in place in order to get to know and love the watershed in which one lives. She poses "watershed discipleship" as a restorative justice alternative to "watershed conquest."

While this vision of mission is rooted in a rereading of Christian biblical teachings, it does not imply conversion but, rather, respect for what is already there, an ecosystem that includes animals, plants, and waters and whose value is equal to that of humans. This includes respect for Indigenous traditions and all faith traditions. Indigenous traditions, whose worldview is that of interconnectedness, are not conversion religions: each tradition is tied to specific lands, territories, languages, and cultural practices that are not transferable. Any interfaith relationship with these traditions requires respecting this fact and letting go of any claims to the universal validity of one's own tradition.

PART TWO

The Great White Helper

From Taking Space to Making Space

When I finished Vancouver School of Theology with a master of divinity in 1988 I was uncertain about what to do next. I had chosen to remain a Catholic, even when many of my fellow students had suggested that I convert to Anglicanism or become a member of the United Church in order to be ordained. I did not remain a Catholic because I was enthralled with the Roman Catholic Church – far from it. The Catholic Church's sexism and homophobia excluded women like me from any leadership role in the Church. Its official position on reproductive rights – against birth control and choice – denied women any agency. But I instinctively felt parish ministry was not for me. Yet how was I going "to use" my degree? I had started the ongoing summer job of working with the Denendeh Seminar and had some popular education contracts with the Jesuits, but that was not enough to keep body and soul alive, not to mention support my son, whom I was raising under a joint custody agreement.

Then, unexpectedly, in the summer of 1988, I received a phone call from Connie Chapmen, who had just been hired as coordinator of a new pilot program, the Native Family Violence Program, at the Native Education Centre in Vancouver. I knew Connie through the feminist anti-violence movement in Vancouver. She invited me to apply for the job of evaluator of the program. I hesitated as to whether, as a non-Native, I should apply, but with few job options I decided to submit my resume, having been assured by Connie, who was not Native herself, that it was only white people who were considering the job. Possibly because I said I would use a participatory evaluation model in the interview, possibly because I had facilitated the Denendeh Seminar for a few years, I was offered the job. I accepted the post, nervous but curious that something like this had arrived in my lap, so to speak. Even if this didn't look like "ministry," I wondered if there was some divine intervention going on.

The Native Family Violence Program was a three-year federal demonstration project. Its purpose was to develop a training program for workers who would return to their communities to provide counselling and advocacy in the area of family violence. My role involved teaching and facilitating an evaluation process for the trainees and the community members they served and, in so doing, to assess the quality of the training. This meant I consulted with the trainees and some community members about how to design research questions, interpret data, and draw conclusions. This participatory evaluation model included the course content, the group process, the effectiveness of the training model, and the impact of the students on their communities. The job involved my not only attending many of the students' training sessions in Vancouver but also, over the three-year period, travelling to the communities in which the students were doing their fieldwork. These communities included Whitehorse and Carcross in Yukon, and Kispiox, Fountain, Pavilion, Mission, Chawathil, and Lytton in British Columbia. In each of these I met with band members who had had contact with the students as well as with the students' local supervisors.

At the Native Education Centre where the training was delivered, I often had the opportunity to sit with the students and to observe the different teachers and Elders who were invited in. Each day began with a circle, smudging, and a check-in. I hadn't been at the centre more than six months when I realized that I was learning more about spirituality here than I ever had at the Vancouver School of Theology. I felt fine about my dual role as a participant observer and an "outside" evaluator: I could share some experiences with the group and then enter their communities as the impartial external eyes and ears of the project.

Just as the Eurocentric scientific concept of impartiality is an illusion, so too was my concept of myself as the helpful observer. It had been difficult to sit in the circle while the group members shared and grieved over the loss of children, partners, and relatives through suicide, murder, and accidental death. Some of the women shared stories of childhood sexual abuse, violent relationships with husbands and boyfriends, and rapes by white men. I had listened to the one man in the group share how he had been sexually abused in residential school, how he had become an abuser, and how he had made several botched suicide attempts. I had watched all this as an observer, feeling slightly ashamed and guilty for the orderliness of my childhood and my "decent" upbringing in an upper-middle-class suburb of Montreal.

One day, in the third year of the project, the definition I had of myself shattered. We were checking in during the usual morning circle when one of the women in the group, who had just returned from a court appearance, decided to share her story. She broke down in the middle of its telling and, in a voice shaking with sobs, shared her fear that no one in the group would really love her now that they knew she had witnessed a murder twenty years ago when she had been on the streets of Vancouver. When she had finished, she was surrounded by the acceptance, love, and affirmation of the group. As this was happening, something in me suddenly snapped. A huge black hole I had kept carefully hidden opened up. Deep down, I believed the same thing: no one would love me if they found out what I was really like, who I really was, with all my gaps and failures. I began to sob uncontrollably, and as I sobbed and sobbed, I heard the gentle voice of one of the members of the circle saying, "Denise, we wondered when you would finally join us."

It had never occurred to me that I hadn't really joined them. My inability to face my own pain was the result of many factors. It certainly wasn't that I hadn't had difficult things happen in my life. I had lost my stepson in a lesbian custody case, had only partial custody of my biological son, had been in an abusive relationship with my Anishinaabe partner (whose behaviour I now understand was reflective of severe intergenerational trauma), had a mother who only wanted me to reflect her (I later discovered the psychological term "narcissistic" to describe her behaviour), and had been sexually molested as a child by a family "friend." Yet I had bracketed all this, constructing an image of myself as a helper and social justice warrior, while at the same time disassociating myself from my feelings. Steeped in my psyche was an "us" and "them" mentality: "they" were the victims and "I" was the helper. In that circle, for the first time in my life, I began to feel my own pain and losses. I had finally taken a mask off, one that I didn't even know I was wearing. In coming from the heart, I was no longer the "helper" but just one more member of this circle of equals, able to be *with* the group rather than above it.

Throughout this period at the Native Education Centre I was still not aware that I had internalized a deficit model of healing, not to mention my inflated sense of myself as a helper. The notion that others are or have problems that "we" can help them to solve, that we can fix, and that we know best how to approach had been deeply ingrained in me since childhood. From an early age I had internalized the idea that it was my "duty" to help others, a concept that is linked to a subtle sense of unconscious white superiority. I grew up in a sea of white Catholic benevolence. While my convent schooling in Montreal included a smattering of Lebanese and Latino girls from well-off families in the mix, the majority were privileged girls from European Canadian backgrounds. These girls were mostly Irish, English, and French, as were all of the nuns. My family lived in a prosperous and mostly Anglo and Jewish neighbourhood, segregated from the impoverished French Canadians in the East End and "the immigrants," at that time mostly from Italy, Portugal, or Hungary. At school we prayed daily for the poor and were each given a holy card with a picture of a child in Africa or India for whom we were to donate our allowances. We had events like the "potato novena," a nine-day period during which we brought in a potato from home to help feed the local poor.

One year my Catholic family went dutifully to help serve food at Benedict Labre house, a house of hospitality for the poor in the Little Burgundy area of Montreal. This one-day experience was both uncomfortable and positive. It gave me a sense of purpose, but it felt scary to be with all those "grubby" men whose stories we imagined in our heads. We presumed ourselves innocent and virtuous, in contrast to the poor, who somehow had not managed their lives well, not to mention the lazy or drunken Indians across the river at Kahnawa:ke. If blaming the victim came naturally, this was compounded by the fact that we were taught no history that even touched on Natives, blacks, or poor French Canadians, who were only visible when my family ventured out of its comfortable suburb. That there might be a relationship between our prosperity and their poverty and marginalization never crossed our minds.[1]

The teachings about helping and service I had learned as a Catholic adolescent were reinforced at the Vancouver School of Theology, which I attended from 1984 to 1988. There I discovered liberation theology. Liberation theology talked of being *with* the people rather than *for* them, and it critiqued charity as a form of paternalism. Liberation theology motivated my activism in the 1980s and 1990s, and it was what first drew me to popular education, the form of adult education developed through the work of the Brazilian Paulo Freire. Freire recognized that students were not empty vessels to be filled up but, rather, people who were capable of thinking critically and solving their problems with knowledge rooted in their own experience. It was this philosophy that informed the methodology of participatory research that I brought to the Native Education Centre. However, it is one thing to think critically about reality and another to have internalized, in one's body and heart, the attitudes and ways of being of the well-meaning helper. I had the politics of liberation but not the self-awareness to keep myself from being "for" others.

That moment at the Native Education Centre was the beginning of my awareness of how whiteness constructs a false self by defining that self in comparison to others. This self is often quite hollow as it is not built on one's innate goodness or compassion but, rather, on what one sees as lacking in others – be it education, class, race, ethnicity, abilities, sexuality, or gender – and on comparisons with the conditions of others. At the Native Education Centre, I was forced to face my own emptiness.

If addressing my own pain was a first critical step in disrobing what I would eventually call my Great White Helper, there were many more steps for me to take. In fact it would take many years and I am still catching myself. During the 1990s I gradually learned that many white behaviours are encoded in the body. In 1995, I co-facilitated with Carmen Miranda Barrios, a Guatemalan popular educator who had immigrated to Canada, a workshop for women focused on working with differences in organizing. The participants were mixed – white women, women of colour, and a few Indigenous women. We were using small groups to discuss issues so that participants could observe how different contexts and social locations informed how they understood and analyzed a situation. We were grouping the participants in different places around the room, starting with something relatively innocuous like age, when Fay Blaney, a Coast Salish Xwemalhkwu woman and an indefatigable organizer against violence against Indigenous women, challenged the group to notice how the white women took up bodily space. The white women, even taking into account class differences, moved quickly and unconsciously "bigly," and usually first, to the allocated spaces. This was to be the beginning of my understanding of how taking bodily space was part of the invisible behaviour of whiteness and how this was connected to a sense of entitlement to space and place.[2]

Another time, in the same workshop, Fay challenged me because I had grouped Indigenous women and women of colour together; she pointed out that their struggles were significantly different despite the common experience of racism. Indigenous women were dealing with colonialism and dispossession, which were reinforced by racism. I was not used to being challenged by a participant and I left that day feeling considerable shame. In fact, I felt bad about myself for weeks, taking up way more psychic time than was necessary rather than accepting such constructive criticism as part of the work. Someone needed to point out to me the fact that I had not picked up on two different aspects of excluding behaviour: I could have been grateful instead of turning in on myself. But what this had tapped into was a self-hatred that I could barely articulate. I was carrying emotional baggage that was preventing me from benefitting fully from that encounter. It would be a few more years before I would start to do the personal work that would free me of my feeling of shame for having messed up. And while much of my internal pain had to do with my personal history, a lot had to do with my inability to see my whiteness.

It is not easy to grasp what whiteness means when it is an invisible quality within which you are immersed. I had participated in numerous "unlearning racism" and anti-racism workshops in the 1990s, but aside from the ubiquitous "Unpacking the Knapsack of White Privilege," the focus was on racist stereotypes and structures "out there," not on what was "in here."[3] I had read many books on racism and on whiteness, but it was only when I was challenged by some of my co-facilitators that I discovered aspects of my own behaviour that embodied privilege.

In the early 1990s, I co-taught a course called "Education for Liberation" with the Chinese Canadian religious educator Wenh-In Ng at the Vancouver School of Theology. Later, in 2003, we co-taught a course called "Anti-Racist Ministry" at Emmanuel College at the Toronto School of Theology. Wenh-In was originally from Hong Kong, and she offered me perspectives on the history of racism and colonialism in Asian Canadian communities that I had never even considered. With her, I became conscious of how I could so easily take over either our planning or our facilitating. Wenh-In was older than me, so, unlike a younger generation of anti-racist activists who would call me out to my face, she indirectly challenged some of my more dominant behaviours. There was often tension in the room, and what I know now is that I was probably enacting a big bodily space, taking space even in the way we negotiated the course design and how to teach. Because I had many years of popular education under my belt, I somehow felt I was the expert. By 2003, I was a bit more conscious of what I was doing and worked at holding myself back to allow more space for Wenh-In's brilliant insights.

From 2000 to 2003, I co-facilitated a course with Alannah Young, an Anishinabe Cree educator, at the Downtown Eastside Women's Centre in Vancouver. Alannah was younger than me, and she would get visibly irritated when I either tried to take over the planning or missed an important point. She would immediately point out when I didn't "get it." She made sure that I understood what taking space meant not only with regard to our planning but also with regard to the importance of making space for the voices of women of colour and Indigenous women everywhere.

It was these struggles and challenges that I faced when co-facilitating with Wenh-In and Alannah that helped me "get" some of the theory around whiteness. Between 2003 and 2005 I co-developed with Amal Rana, a South Asian Muslim poet and educator, an anti-racism education kit for the Canadian Union of Public Employees. I had observed many anti-racism workshops and was frustrated at how, once the person "understood" racism, the focus on racism seemed to facilitate the "I'm-no-longer-a-racist" perspective. So I wanted to incorporate into the kit more on how whiteness functioned.

I conducted research into the area of whiteness studies, an academic field that had developed in the 1990s and early 2000s. I'll never forget a line from David Roediger, a scholar of whiteness, who said that whiteness is the "empty and terrifying attempt to build an identity based on what one isn't and on whom one can hold back."[4] Through Roediger I discovered two African American writers, James Baldwin and W.E.B. Dubois, who had analyzed how dominance functioned through whiteness. Baldwin clearly articulated how "thinking oneself as white" was premised on a "moral erosion" that justified the slavery of black people and the killing of Native Americans and the taking of their land.[5] A white mentality is necessary in order to maintain one's moral superiority, which, in turn, justifies the exploitation of "others." W.E.B. Dubois, the African American civil rights activist and scholar, first articulated the concept of whiteness "as a sort of public and psychological wage" that low-paid non-black Southern workers received and that compensated for the fact that they were still being exploited.[6] Roediger articulated that this "wage of whiteness," this assumption or belief in one's whiteness, functioned in a way that enabled white workers to separate themselves from blacks "as non-slaves and as refusers of 'nigger work.'"[7]

I developed a history of whiteness timeline for the Canadian Union of Public Employees kit. This illustrated how the concept of whiteness developed and was used to maintain a hierarchy of workers. Whiteness was and is always fluid. When the Irish and Jewish people first came to the United States, they were not considered to be white, yet gradually they assumed the values that came with whiteness and began to consider themselves white and, therefore, neither black nor Indian.[8] In Quebec, I can remember speaking French in the schoolyard and being told by some classmates to "speak white!" It would take many years for me to get what that meant at a deeper level. Whiteness came with speaking English and working at non-menial jobs and getting out of poverty. Now I understand the anger of Pierre Vallières, one of the leaders of the Front de libération du Quebec, who, in 1968, wrote *Les Nègres blancs d'Amérique*. Translated as *White Niggers of America*, this pivotal work addresses how, in Quebec, the French-speaking working class was exploited by the English capitalist class. Even now I look at how the hierarchy of whiteness functions with regard to labour in Canada, where white people don't want to do "menial" jobs like farm labour or house cleaning, leaving such work for non-white people, recent immigrants, and temporary foreign workers.

During the mid- to late 1990s I taught courses on popular education at the University of British Columbia School of Social Work. Here I discovered many commonalities between social work and Christian social justice work and pastoral counselling. Both the white woman as professional helper and the white social justice worker are rooted in the late nineteenth- and early twentieth-century creations of the white middle class woman as missionary and Christian social reform worker. The task of both was to help the less unfortunate to fit into the normative standards of white English- or French-speaking society.[9] Now, through what Kersten Roger calls "the privatization of health and well-being," the civilizing mission of settler Christianity has been transformed into the vocation of the professional helper, counsellor, and therapist who offers professional empathy and advocacy.[10]

The belief that one is somehow of more worth than, and above the struggles of, those who have been "dealt a poorer lot in life" comes with race and class privilege. It often translates into speaking "for" rather than "with." The proverbial role of being "a voice for the voiceless" that I heard so often in theology school is extremely problematic. As an Indigenous colleague of mine once said, "We have a voice, it is just that you never listened."

So what is an alternative way, a way of making space rather than taking it? I have had to learn new ways, one step at a time. Whenever Alannah and I organized an event that involved Indigenous Elders and Knowledge Keepers we "made space" for them in very significant ways. This meant doing more than adopting the Protocol of territorial or treaty acknowledgment. Elders are not just window dressing, people we ask to open and close an event that is usually dominated by non-Indigenous people. Significant time must be allotted so that they can share their wisdom with us, both during an event and in its planning. I learned to consult with an Elder well in advance of any workshop we did and to get her or his input into its design. However, as usual, I learned the hard way.

In one case, in 2010, Alannah and I had been invited by a United Church minister, Sally McShane, to develop a two-day workshop on reconciliation with two United Church parishes in the western part of Vancouver near UBC. These churches were located in xʷməθkʷəy̓əm Musqueam territory, so first we needed to ask a xʷməθkʷəy̓əm Musqueam Elder to join us. At that time, Larry Grant was the Elder-in-Residence at the First Nations Longhouse at UBC, so Alannah told me we would first meet with him to see if he was interested in the workshop and, if so, find out what he thought we should do in it. On our way to meet him at his office she asked me if I had brought tobacco for him. Apparently we couldn't ask him for anything until we had first offered him tobacco. Oops, I hadn't even thought of it! Luckily, Alannah had lots, and she sent me back to her office to find a small bag for me to put it in.

But there was to be way more to that meeting with Larry than an initial offering of tobacco. We sat talking for about an hour, and it seemed to me we discussed everything but the workshop. My tendency to get down to business immediately was interrupted by Alannah, who asked about his family and other people she knew in the territory. When Larry eventually asked me how we thought we would proceed following his opening welcome, I suggested an introduction exercise that involved grouping people by social location – race, class, sexual orientation, and so on. Larry looked at me and chuckled and said, "You mean, where is your granny from?" I was dumbfounded and then had to laugh. Not only was his way simpler, but it told a lot more about a person, and in a much more relational way, than did my classificatory categories, which had little to do with family, community, or land.

We would meet with Larry two more times before the workshop. I learned that it is important to spend time with Elders and to give them information about what you are planning. There were many ways in which Larry shaped our program design. He offered to tell the history of the Musqueam people and the land in which these church people were guests. He would share his own story and views on reconciliation. He suggested we invite an Elder from another local nation to offer a different perspective on the region and reconciliation. So we did this. Alannah had already worked with Gerry Oleman, from Tsal'alh (Shalalth) of the St'at'imc Nation. So she and I drove across town to meet with him at a coffee shop. Once again, she asked me to produce tobacco. Once again, I had forgotten to bring some. Fortunately, I had with me a Mi'gmaq leather pouch containing tobacco, which I gave him, trying to make it look like I had planned all along to do this.

So making space, rather than taking space, requires a lot of time and relationship building. Every workshop that Alannah and I have done that incorporated Traditional Knowledge Holders has involved numerous meetings before the event. Even the offering of tobacco is not straightforward. In 2009, when we were meeting with the University of Victoria Elders group about planning a staff and faculty Aboriginal cultural awareness training, Alannah and I had prepared small bags of cedar rather than tobacco, as we were advised by Deb George (Quw'utsun', Scottish and English), the University of Victoria cultural Protocols liaison worker.[11] I handed the bag to Skip Dick, a Lekwungen Elder, and he put it on the table between us and said to me: "You cannot presume I will take it. If you place your offering between us I can then decide if I want to work with you or not." He said it sternly, but with a twinkle in this eye. Wow! I was embarrassed and felt stupid for still not managing to do it the right way. But it was a lesson I have never forgotten.

Making space for Indigenous people means non-Indigenous people setting aside their own agendas. When Indigenous people are not treated as tokens, they may be comfortable staying at an event, but the agenda needs to include their concerns. Making space works at multiple levels. For me, it is about stepping back from the pattern of colonial dominance to let others take the lead because for so long it has been white people who have done so.

I share an example from my more recent history. In 2017, in the Comox Valley, I was part of a women's drum circle that was started by a group of mostly Anishinaabe and Cree women and included some local Kwakwaka'wakw and Metis women. The group was open to all nations, and the invitation was to sing traditional First Nations hand drum songs. When I joined the group it had been functioning for several months and there were many non-Native women who showed up at the circle. Over a period of time, I observed the dynamics. A few of the non-Native women began to "take space," talking longer during the introductory circle and strongly stating their needs in decision-making circles, be it their preference for weekly potlucks or for talking circles. Tension began to rise between different players in the group, including some of the Indigenous women, and I was torn as to what to do. I wanted to support the leadership of Indigenous women, but I was not sure how or if to intervene or even what my motives were. Luckily, I ran into one of the white women at the market. She was very upset about how she was now being excluded and was in considerable pain as there had been minimal communication with her. I was able to offer her a few thoughts she had not considered and to place the dynamic within the larger context of a history of years, generations, of white people taking space and taking over groups.

In that situation, I was conflicted about my role as a group member, about whether I should say something. I was also aware of the ethic of non-intervention, found in most Indigenous cultures, according to which to interfere in an interaction between others is seen as a form of dominance. The exchange reminded me of how important it is for those of us who are non-Indigenous and who are engaging with Indigenous people to do our own personal work. This is true for everyone in the circle, so that we don't bring to our interactions our own histories of pain, suffering, and exclusion – histories that we have not yet dealt with.

Taking space has socio-political, economic, cultural, epistemological, and even religious dimensions. It affects how events are organized, what issues are deemed important to consider, and whose perception of reality is considered "right." When white people wonder why Indigenous people or people of colour don't stay in their planning meetings or organizations, they might want to look at the space dynamics to understand what is happening. Making space includes supporting the expression of different worldviews, different ways of knowing and organizing, cultures and practices. In my interactions it has meant learning about and being open to Indigenous Knowledge Systems, methodologies, and Protocols. It involves way more than having a certain number of bodies in the room.

The Great White Helper still occasionally pops up in my psyche, but now I can often catch her. Recently, on a visit to Gespe'gewa'gi, a cousin of mine suggested I meet an Elder from Gesgapegiag whom he knew. I was already meeting with another Elder, Pnnal Jerome, whom I had been working with for some time. A few years ago, I would have leapt at my cousin's invitation. Great, a chance to be inspired by a cool Elder and learn more! But this time I knew it was not right for me. I would be taking up the Elder's time, which was needed more by her community than by me, and I could not enter into a reciprocal relationship with her. Our exchange would have been one-sided and, hence, not ethical. I would have been taking up space. I am now much more aware of the importance of checking my motives for engagement, and if it is about me, then there is a problem.

Healing and the Politics of Trauma

If, as is shown in the previous chapter, "taking space" is a very material and bodied process, the process of unlearning that particular colonial way of being in the world requires inner and embodied work. A few years after what I named as my breakdown at the Native Education Centre, I attended a week-long retreat for women at Glenairlie, a rural property of the Sisters of Saint Anne on Vancouver Island near Sooke. The retreat was led by Alexandra Kovats, a creative retreat animator and a Sister of Saint Joseph of Peace from Seattle. A few American nuns were among the twelve of us who took part in the retreat. We were near the end of our time together, and for the closing ritual Alexandra had put a bowl with a dozen polished stones in the centre of our circle. We had each chosen a name at random and now were to pick a stone to give to that person in the circle; with the stone we were to name a gift or gifts that we wanted that person to take away from the retreat. I cannot remember to whom I gave my stone, perhaps because I was more concerned about who had a stone for me. After everyone else had their turn, Sister Dorothy, a Holy Cross nun from Spokane, who had a halo of white hair and was in her late seventies, spoke. I had noticed her before on this mostly silent retreat. She had once said she preferred to stay in her room rather than to sit on the grass looking at the water, as the beauty was a distraction. I had found this rather disturbing. Now she stood up and came over and placed a polished pink stone in my hand and said, "Denise, I give you three gifts – joy, peace, and sorrow."

I was a bit stunned. Sorrow! Why would anyone wish sorrow for a person? I thought maybe she had made a mistake. I decided I would just focus on the joy and peace message. I soon forgot about the stone, though I kept it on my home altar. Sometimes it would get lost with other stones; but somehow it would always reappear. And then gradually, over the years, with the help of other encounters and a significant loss in my life, I began to understand how feeling my own pain and sorrow could be a gift.

It would take me time to face my own pain, and in 1997 I decided to explore therapy. I chose dance therapy, a field that often appeals to people who have been dancers. I have danced all my life: I took ballet as a child, graduated to modern dance, and by the 1980s was doing "liturgical dance" in churches as well as occasional performances at social justice events. I met Sunita Romeder, a dance therapist in Vancouver, did a few sessions with her and was impressed with how working through the body provided a way for me to express locked up feelings. So I decided to apply for a two-year training program she was offering in dance therapy and expressive arts for people who were already trained as counsellors or body workers. I claimed I was a pastoral counsellor, a considerable exaggeration as I had only taken one course in pastoral counselling at the Vancouver School of Theology. As a popular educator working mostly with women in groups, I knew I needed more skills. Fortunately, I was accepted into the program.

That course was the beginning of two decades in which I learned how closely the body, mind, and spirit are aligned and how working through the body was key not only to resolving personal issues but also to transforming "relational" skills so that a collective or system could function in less oppressive ways. It was through my first dance movement and expressive arts training with Sunita Romeder that I met Alannah Young. Alannah, who is Anishinabe and Cree, was not interested in using our training to do individual therapy with middle-class and mostly white people, the majority of therapy clientele. Nor was I. We both liked working with groups, and we both wanted to incorporate a spiritual and political dimension into our work. Alannah wanted to work with Indigenous communities and I wanted to share what we were learning with women who didn't have access to therapy and the expressive arts, and so we teamed up to practise and develop what we were learning. This was the beginning of almost two decades of working together and, for me, a monumental shift in how I understood healing, trauma, and therapy itself.

On a cold day in December 2000, Alannah and I met at the First Nations House of Learning (FNHL), located in the First Nations Longhouse, a large, magnificent cedar structure on the UBC campus whose purpose is to support Indigenous students. Alannah was the cultural counsellor and leadership coordinator there. Her tiny office was crowded with ceremonial gear, drums, medicines, and rattles. We had been invited to develop an eight-week afternoon program for the Downtown Eastside Women's Centre (DEWC) – specifically, a program for Indigenous women who have experienced multiple forms of violence. The two board members who had asked us had observed that a one-on-one counselling approach did not seem to work with the women, and so they were looking for a group approach that included cultural teachings. Alannah and I decided we would approach this as an interfaith team. Some of the women who attended the DEWC were Christian and had learned from the church that their cultural teachings and ceremonies were pagan and superstitious. My role was to counter this by translating how ceremony or ritual in one tradition can have a similar function in another tradition, and to gently challenge the exclusive forms of Christianity.

We were at the beginning of our planning, and I suggested: "Why don't we first have the women name all the symptoms of trauma and violence they have experienced and the impact on them, so that they can link it all together and see it as systemic?" I had been thinking of the Native Family Violence Program at the Vancouver Native Education Centre (now the Native Education College) that I had evaluated almost ten years earlier. Much of its focus had been on sexual abuse and trauma and on different therapeutic approaches that were then being used to deal with trauma. Alannah looked at me, sighed, and said: "Native women have been told all their life that there is something wrong with them. They know what racism and sexism is and the negatives in their own lives. We need to work with their strengths and enhance their confidence about their leadership capacities."

Jolt! I realized that I was all too familiar with the approach that held that there was something wrong with people that "we" needed "to fix." I had thought it would be useful to throw in some trauma theory and have the women share what happened to them. But Alannah was having none of that. She went even further, suggesting we call this an education program rather than a healing program. I agreed because I am primarily an educator, so I felt comfortable with the terminology, but I also felt challenged. Was I still seeing these women just as victims with huge problems? I had been thinking about the women as survivors of sexual and spousal abuse, racist and sexist attacks, with possible addiction and suicide attempts in either their own lives or those of their family members. So yes, I had bought into the Native-people-have-all-these-problems mentality. This had, in turn, left me feeling somewhat overwhelmed as to how we were going to "tackle" all that. I felt both nervous and inadequate, and now here was Alannah proposing a completely different approach.

Alannah and I went on to spend almost two and half years working with a core group at the DEWC. The course that we developed was called "Still Movement." We integrated the spiritual and listening dimension implied by stillness with the movement therapy and dance practices we both loved. The course integrated ceremony, expressive arts, and dance with Indigenous and, to some extent, Christian teachings.[1] We presented the course as a leadership training program rather than as a healing program, and this may have been the reason we had a consistent group who took it more than once. The term "leadership" gave the course a positive frame and removed the stigma of illness that is implicit in the language of healing. We emphasized participants' strengths and avoided any terminology that would imply a deficit of some sort. This allowed us to shift our work into a more Indigenous framework, within which everyone is seen as a teacher and learner and everyone has gifts and responsibilities to contribute to society. We sang a lot, drummed a lot, and engaged in ceremony, all of which helped to transform the pain and struggles of individuals into a collective process of renewal.

There was considerable power in the activities we developed that were body-centred. There was one that involved us having participants slowly walk backwards in a circle to discover and name and call upon ancestral women relatives who were role models for them. Another involved dancing as a group like a flock of birds, moving together as one. We created rituals that engaged voice and incorporated movement. Equally rich was our focus on women's roles and responsibilities within their particular cultures. We stressed the values inherent in kinship, extending to non-human relations, both through activities in the class-room and by taking the group on a one-day retreat outside the city onto the land. We incorporated ceremony when hard issues came up, so that even when someone was releasing anger we were able to hold it within a container, directing it towards the earth.

During some of these activities I often found myself stuck in my Euro-Western worldview, only to be shocked out of it by something that happened in the group. Once this occurred when we were doing an activity called "Animal Relatives," which involved a short guided meditation on one's favourite imagined or real place on the land, and then an invitation for an animal relative to visit. After spending time with this animal, bird, insect, or whatever had appeared, each participant was to draw and then dance her animal relative. Finally, they were to write down on the back of their drawings any message they may have received from that relative.

After the session Alannah asked me, "Did you notice anything about Paula's drawing?"

"Yes," I said. "It was an image of a large brown bear on the side of a forest."

Alannah replied, "Is that all? Did you notice that she referred to it as coming from her dream? That was a powerful dream and we could have asked her to speak more about the dream."

"Yes," I replied with a shrug and a feeling of shame.

I had completely missed that! I paid little attention to my own dreams. Yet here I was confronted with something I had read about, but obviously not absorbed – a central belief of Indigenous teachings, which is that dreams are a significant source of knowledge.

During another moment in the course, a Nisga'a woman named Doris stated that a constant pain in her arm was the result of someone from her home community in the North having inflicted bad medicine on her. I did not know what to think, but I was aware that it was hard for me not to immediately label her as "superstitious." However, Alannah was unfazed and drew on a ceremonial way of working with the woman's arm that cleared out any remnants of pain and bad medicine. Rather than dismissing the woman's claim she worked with it, and the woman's pain disappeared. I decided then and there not to be so judgmental regarding how people understood their pain.

I later learned that my first reactions during these incidents were a form of what is called "epistemological racism" – the belief that your knowledge and way of knowing is superior to that of others, that it is only certain types of knowledge that are valid. According to this perspective, Euro-Western knowledge and science is "better" or superior to other knowledge systems. In terms of how colonialism functions, the belief that Indigenous knowledge systems are inferior reinforces the claims of settler dominance and the right of settlers to control and extract resources from Indigenous lands.

Over the years I have learned that Euro-Western medicine does not consider as valid many resources that are part of Indigenous medicine. Dreams, spirit helpers, stories, ceremonial cleansings, songs, dances, plant medicines, and more are integral to Indigenous worldviews and to supporting individual and collective journeys to wellness.[2] In Indigenous traditions we do not find the fragmentation that exists in the dominant culture, where health is separated from the political, economic, social, and religious lives of the people. Many Indigenous approaches to wellness are rooted in Indigenous values and cultural knowledge, and many look beyond the individual to include the family, community, and nation, including Indigenous laws of governance, viable economic systems, and respectful relations with the non-human world as necessary factors for sustainable and healthy lifeways. In other words, to "heal" the individual, the entire society needs to be repaired. This expansive view of health addresses the root causes of Indigenous ill-health and effectively challenges the narrow emphasis on trauma that is so dominant in the White Helper World.

Our approach during our work at the Downtown Eastside Women's Centre was to help the women see that their responses and/or symptoms didn't need to have a label and that they reflected the survival skills they had developed to deal with unbearable conditions. We supported their strengths with cultural resources and affirmed their resilience in the face of significant obstacles in their lives. We stressed that, in Indigenous cultures, each person has a unique role and responsibilities that contribute to the family, clan, community, and nation. Even if these women were living in the inner city, often cut off from their families or traditions, they each had a role and gifts to offer to their family members and their urban community.[3]

However, as useful as was our work with the DEWC, the reality was that as each woman left the program she re-emerged into an environment within which she was consistently devalued. It is hard to stay in one's body and remember one's goodness when faced by constant crises in one's family, the racism and sexism of day-to-day interactions, a housing shortage, no job, and the ongoing vulnerability and exposure to violence that is part of an Indigenous woman's life in the Downtown

Eastside. When Alannah and I later wrote about our work, we stated that programs like ours would remain limited as long as they were not part of a comprehensive decolonization strategy that includes community economic and social development that places at its centre the material, spiritual, and social needs of Indigenous women and children.[4] What sovereignty and self-determination means for Indigenous women living off reserve and in urban centres, most of whom do not have access to band resources or a traditional land base, is a question that has been and will continue to be determined by them.[5]

As for me, I continued to explore the question of what was useful in the field of healing and what was harmful. It has become clearer to me that healing work is embedded in systems. In the last decade I have engaged and struggled with what I call the politics of trauma and how trauma discourse is used for different political ends. Probably one of the most overused words of the last two decades, trauma has both personal and political resonance for me. But let's start with the personal. I remember my friend Shayna Hornstein asked me what I was doing about trauma when I was taking my training in dance movement therapy and expressive arts. I was struck by it in several ways: first, there had been little explicit focus on trauma during that training; second, I wasn't confident I had the skills to deal with it; and third, how did it fit into this strength-based model of regeneration that Alannah and I were exploring at the Downtown Eastside Women's Centre? I didn't even think about it in terms of applying it to myself. I didn't know the answer to Shayna's question and decided I had better do something about it. In my training practicum I was working with sexual abuse survivors, and in my work with Alannah I was dealing with individuals who had suffered from many circumstances that could only be described as traumatic.

I use the term "trauma" to refer to a group of symptoms that a person experiences in her/his body and that keeps her/him from being in the present moment. These symptoms can range from what is called hyperarousal (one's nervous system is extremely agitated, and the psychological component is anger, the need to fight, or high anxiety) to hypoarousal (one feels numb and experiences a sense of low or no energy in the muscles, and the psychological component is giving up).[6] There are other bodily symptoms that vary with different people, but all reflect how individuals have been unable to process their emotional

reactions to a situation in their past. This inability to process may have
been the result of the fact that it was unsafe to express these reactions,
something that occurs in "relational trauma," where there has been
abuse of power. Examples are sexual abuse, beatings in residential
school, workplace harassment, or abuse or neglect by a parent. The
other type of situation in which there has been an inability to process
emotions occurs when there was no time to do so, as in the case of life-
and-death trauma experiences such as a car accident, a fire, or fleeing
war. Any situation that presents even a tiny similarity to a specific past
situation may trigger traumatic symptoms in a person.

In my practicum work with sexual abuse survivors in the late 1990s
I had learned to recognize that some group member behaviours could
easily be triggered by something fairly benign that occurred either
during the group meeting or in daily life. These behaviours included
disassociation (moving away from being in the present both in thought
and in body awareness, often accompanied by a glazed or distant look
in the eyes), being overwhelmed by flashbacks (images and body sensations associated with a disturbing event in the past, which may or
may not be remembered), hypervigilance, and high levels of anxiety.
The reactions associated with the trigger, which could be as minor as
a tone of voice or a back turned, did not match the situation and, as I
would later learn, are in fact stored in the body from a past traumatic
experience that has not been processed. I had been around enough
women who have experienced some sort of abuse and violence in their
lives – be it sexual, racist, physical, and/or emotional – to know that
it was very hard for many of these women to believe in their strengths
and to move beyond repeating self-destructive behaviours.

For many years, I did not include myself because I felt that what
had happened to me, a white middle-class woman, was nothing compared to what had happened to the women with whom I was working,
especially Indigenous women who had experienced multiple forms of
violence and intergenerational trauma. I overlooked how my own history had marked my body and behaviours and how I had bracketed my
experiences of violence and abuse. I had grown up in a context of white
privilege and settler dominance and had no clue that this affected my
behaviour. Eventually this past, which I had not resolved or processed
emotionally or physically, showed up in my own erratic behaviour both
in groups and in interpersonal relationships. For example, whenever

a situation got too difficult for me, especially in interpersonal relationships, my automatic impulse was to become cold, almost frozen inside,
and to leave rather than to try to work things out. Another reaction was
to lash out in a rage at some minor thing someone had done. It would
take several years for me, first, to notice what I was doing, and, second,
using skills I had learned, to remain in the situation without getting
cold as ice and projecting onto it a story that was connected more to
my past than to my present.

Because I wanted to be more effective in the groups I was leading
and because I realized that I needed to help myself, I began to see on an
ongoing basis a therapist who was trained in body-centred modalities.
As well, I registered in Body-Mind Psychotherapy training, developed
by Armenian American Susan Apoyshan, in the fall of 2002.[7] Alannah
took this training with me and we both took the annual "refresher"
for more than a decade afterwards. In 2008, I began to take courses
with Merete Brantbjerg, a Danish somatic physiotherapist who visited
Vancouver annually and who was developing a method she eventually
called "relational trauma therapy."[8] I took her training workshops from
2012 to 2017.

The work that Alannah and I did together, especially with Indigenous
women, raised for me serious questions about how trauma and healing
had become one of the main foci in many Indigenous communities
and, more important, whenever Indigenous people were discussed by
non-Indigenous people, be it through media, churches, government,
or the helping professions. I remember a conversation I once had
with Dara Culhane, who is an anthropologist who teaches at Simon
Fraser University. Many years earlier, Dara, who is of Irish and Jewish
heritage, had married into to a Kwakwaka'wakw family from Alert Bay.
The marriage ended, but she remains connected through kinship and
relationship ties. Dara is deeply committed to challenging the structures
that have impoverished and dispossessed so many Indigenous peoples,
especially women. I was sharing my frustrations with the challenges of
doing healing work in the Downtown Eastside when she made a tren-
chant comment that stood out for me like a neon light: "When I listen to
students these days, I find myself worrying that the emphasis on trauma
and addiction in media, the arts, and education may be reproducing
old pathologizing stereotypes of Indigenous people as 'damaged' in a
new language of the healed and the unhealed."

Dara was instrumental in my developing a critique of the healing industry. During my work for my doctor of ministry dissertation, which was about the methodology that Alannah and I were developing, I conducted research in the field of trauma, aided by some references from Dara. The word "trauma" is often used in conjunction with the term "post-traumatic stress disorder" (PTSD). PTSD is often used in mainstream medicine to describe the symptoms of people suffering from a wide range of situations that extend from being bitten by a dog or surviving a car accident to spousal abuse, the experience of war, racism, and various forms of deprivation. Arthur Kleinman and Robert Desjarlais, two pioneers in medical anthropology, note that the diagnosis of high rates of PTSD is usually applied to "special populations" who have experienced certain conditions associated with war or state terrorism or who have been subjected to unjust political, economic, and social structures. They use the term "social suffering," and name the conditions that produce it as political violence, and observe how the language of trauma removes these people from a religious, ethical, and social framework.[9] Social suffering refers to the collective pain and distress that results from violence and to the "interpersonal and community-wide effects of violence" that are obscured in the medicalization of violence.[10] The individualizing language of PTSD overlooks how social suffering undermines relationships – the core value of Indigenous communities. It ignores the fact that humans are relational beings, not autonomous selves (as we are led to believe by the dominant culture). The PTSD label reduces suffering to a condition of medical pathology, to just a complex of body symptoms, rather than addressing it as an ethical or moral problem.

When labels like PTSD or even trauma were applied to the women with whom we worked, this only served to individualize each woman's condition and to deny the extensive race, class, and colonial violence that they had experienced. These structural factors were lost in the diagnostic terminology of PTSD. Accordingly, Alannah and I never used that term or the word "trauma" in the group. Equally unhelpful was the term "syndrome," which equates symptoms with a supposed cause – for instance, "residential school syndrome" or "battered wife syndrome." Terms like these serve to pathologize people and their suffering and to obscure the context within which the abuse has occurred. Indeed, they can reduce a person's entire life to symptoms.

Another person who influenced my thinking about trauma was the Salvadorean Jesuit Ignacio Martin-Baro. Martin-Baro was one of the six Jesuits killed by a Salvadorean death squad in 1989. He had developed a "liberation psychology" after observing the effects of war in El Salvador. He used the term "psychosocial trauma," a term that gives primacy to the social network within which the human is embedded.[11] Psychosocial trauma is trauma that is foreseeable and predictable; it affects an entire network of social relations. As long as dehumanizing social relations continue, the symptoms of trauma remain both in individuals and in communities. Accordingly, as I later applied this theory to Indigenous-settler relations, it became clear that it is only in changing the social relations between colonizer and colonized that psychosocial trauma can be alleviated.

In the case of Indigenous communities, another level of relationship has been damaged, not just the human-to-human level. Indigenous worldviews are grounded in principles of kinship according to which all beings are kin, relatives with whom we have relationships and to whom we have responsibilities. This means that plants, animals, minerals, and humans are all kin; we share time and space, and we can't exist without each other. Multiple forms of colonial violence to Indigenous peoples over generations have resulted in a spiritual disjuncture, a loss of connection with these relations and with the spirit world. This historical spiritual disconnect operates at an additional level when applied to Indigenous women, who experience personal, structural, and racial violence. As Cree-Métis scholar Kim Anderson explains, while previously "our cultures promoted womanhood as a sacred identity, an identity that existed within a complex system of relations of societies that were based on balance," now, through the process of a sexist and racist colonialism, Native women have lost their collective status as sacred.[12]

If individualizing trauma is problematic for the person who is suffering, there are significant political ramifications, as I learned from the work of Dian Million. Million, an Athabaskan social worker and scholar, has provided a powerful critique of what she calls "therapeutic nations."[13] She has examined, within the context of international human rights discourse, the past few decades of healing that have been occurring in Indigenous communities. Her concern is that the focus on individual healing benefits neoliberal development. She shows how this plays out in the way that the historical legacy of colonialism is being addressed largely by a trauma economy, and in the way that the solution to endemic poverty, poor health, and suicide risk in Indigenous communities is being reduced to the healing of trauma. "The colonized subject," Million writes, "became a trauma victim."[14]

Million notes that the Royal Commission on Aboriginal Peoples produced a five-volume report in 1996 that included 440 recommendations designed to improve the relationship between Aboriginal and non-Aboriginal people and governments in Canada.[15] However, the only recommendation the federal government took up was that of addressing the healing of the children affected by residential schools. In 1998, this resulted in the establishment of the Aboriginal Healing Foundation to address "historical trauma" and, a few years later, federal support of the establishment of the Truth and Reconciliation Commission (TRC), which, according to Million, "reaffirms the people's systemic inequality and endemic social suffering as a pathology, a wound that is solely an outcome of past colonial policies."[16] Million addresses the inadequacies of healing programs that fail to address the normative racial and gendered violence inherent in the ongoing structure of the Canadian state and the Indian Act. She argues that only the return to Indigenous forms of governance under Indigenous laws will provide a genuine alternative to capitalist "development" and end the endemic social suffering in Indigenous communities.[17]

Million is not alone in identifying how the concept of trauma has been used for different political ends. In their book *The Empire of Trauma*, French social anthropologists and physicians Didier Fassin and Richard Rechtman analyze how the concept of trauma has been used politically both in Europe and in the United States. They underline how the condition of victimhood has been reinforced by the extensive use of trauma discourse and treatment, with the result that "survivors of disasters, persecution and oppression adopt the only persona that allows them to be heard."[18] They also illustrate how trauma discourse has become part of the politics of reparation, testimony, and proof, whereby victims claim their rights as traumatized individuals rather than as survivors of injustice.[19] What I like most in their analysis is that they point out how trauma language erases the context and complexity of human experience, reducing it to symptoms and avoiding moral judgment of the causes. Most important, trauma language overlooks the heritage of resistance and survival that has enabled Indigenous people not to disappear.

These critiques of trauma and therapy focus on how, throughout society, the healing industry has served to maintain ongoing structural injustices. Million sees therapy as a way of helping people to adapt to the realities of capitalism, with the goal of producing "a certain type of individual, one that works to continuously manage one's own emotional and mental hygiene."[20] Oops, that could be me! And many people I know who have the option of spending considerable amounts of money not just on therapy but also on various forms of bodywork, yoga, and stress management practices so that they can continue to function in work that is extremely oppressive and unhealthy. In other words, we can all be dupes of an uninformed and apolitical healing machine that helps us to cope with the injustices and stresses of daily life under capitalism rather than to challenge and change injustice.

The dominant media, the federal government, and the churches framed the Truth and Reconciliation Commission as victim-centred, and, as a result, it focused on healing and cultural recovery. While useful for survivors, this has played into the Great White Helper mentality that is so integral to colonialism. The emphasis on healing from "historical trauma" continues to appeal to churches and NGOs that provide funding for it. Settlers are comfortable with this focus on healing Indigenous people because it means that they don't have to look at themselves. The Canadian government reinforces the individualization of social suffering by negotiating financial settlements with individual Survivors who experienced sexual and physical abuse in residential schools. But neither this money nor the focus on healing addresses the causes, the harsh realities, of ongoing colonial structures: dispossession and occupation of Indigenous land, tutelage under the Indian Act, impoverishment, broken treaties, lack of housing, the exploitation of territories and waterways for resource extraction, loss of language, and, last but not least, racism. All these are integral to the structure of the Canadian state as we know it. These are the issues that make most Canadians uncomfortable.

Even if trauma is politicized there remains the reality of suffering in the everyday life of all who live under a colonial regime. People do experience trauma and there is much suffering that comes with this.

There is a need to work with trauma but not in a way that uses trauma language to pathologize a person's behaviour. In the past few years more attention has been paid to developing what is called a "trauma-informed practice," whereby, although understood within the framework of trauma, a person's or groups' behaviour is situated within a history and social context.[21] At the same time, such practice must be careful not to transmit the idea that a person's body is "marked" by, or inherently carries, intergenerational trauma. Treatment may incorporate culturally specific approaches to healing, but a broader understanding of trauma moves people away from seeing themselves as victims. If training is provided through "culturally safe" and trauma-informed practice, then service providers – be they paramedics, police officers, nurses, therapists, teachers, or ministers – can learn, at minimum, about colonialism and about how traumatic events and history affect the body. They may also learn how a person with a history of intergenerational or situational trauma might react in situations of stress. So informed, the service provider is less inclined to make judgments and more inclined to be present and just listen.

Today many Indigenous people in the health and wellness field do not buy into the Western individualizing of trauma, preferring to work out of an anti-colonial worldview. There are rich developments in the Indigenous psychology, religion, and social work fields that point to practices and understandings from which all can benefit. One example is the work of Anishinaabe religion scholar Larry Gross. He has developed a concept known as "post-apocalypse stress syndrome."[22] "Apocalypse" is a term used in religious studies, and it refers to the end times. Gross uses it to refer to the end of a world as it was known by its inhabitants, and he identifies the experience of colonization as apocalyptic. He includes in his analysis not only how this apocalypse has had psychosocial impacts on individuals but also how it has involved the collapse of educational, governance, health, and family structures as well as the loss of the cultural traditions of his ancestral Anishinaabe communities. Some Indigenous people did survive this apocalypse, and, for Gross, the revitalization of the sacred stories and ceremonies of the many Indigenous traditions that the colonizers attempted to eliminate is critical. He sees the necessity of restoring the values and ethical frameworks inherent in these traditions, which, in turn, can inform Indigenous structures of education, governance, and health, which can provide an alternative to the structures of capitalist societies based on individualism.[23]

Mohawk psychologist Rod McCormick has shown that we needed to transform Western attachment theory to fit with the realities of Indigenous life and values. Attachment theory is a term from developmental psychology, and it posits that a child needs to have a strong emotional and physical bond to at least one primary caregiver in order to have a basis for healthy development. Without this bond there is "attachment trauma." McCormick maintains that, for Indigenous people, attachment trauma differs from what is experienced by non-Indigenous people. He argues that, for Indigenous people, healthy attachment is grounded in a relationship to a large kinship network, to the land, and to the web of relations that inform Indigenous worldviews. Accordingly, healing involves restoring those connections.[24] When the colonial project severed family bonds through residential schools, it also severed cultural practices whereby a child was embedded in this relationship with the land and "all our relations." McCormick, among many others who work in the mental health field or as cultural advisors, now advocates for practices like naming ceremonies, in which a youth at risk is given a traditional name and family members commit to watching her/him and helping her/him live up to that name.[25] This is but one of many effective cultural practices that reinforce family and kinship connections, enable a person to develop a sense of responsibility, and support an individual's relationships with the land.

I have many friends and colleagues, all women, who are working hard to ensure that the best of their Indigenous cultural traditions are used to provide for the well-being of communities. Some bring these traditions into dialogue with Western psychology; others don't. All are working to transform a system that has been oppressive. In the area of child welfare significant damage occurs when Western psychological theory is applied to Indigenous peoples. At the time of writing, there are disproportionate numbers of Indigenous children in care – ratios that are being compared to the number of children who were removed from their homes during the residential school period.[26] One factor in the apprehension of Indigenous children has been the application of, again, Western attachment theory, which focuses on the bonding of mother and child in the first year. This has resulted in many children being removed from the care of the mother with no attention being paid to the larger family and community system of which she may be a part. In opposition to this, Métis social workers Jeannine Carrière and Cathy Richardson have articulated an Indigenous attachment theory, which focuses on kinship and connectedness, connectedness not only to biological parents but also to "a spiderweb of relations" that includes extended families and the natural world.[27] They argue that it is in being part of a kinship system that a child develops a sense of belonging and connectedness.[28] Carrière and Richardson's work is informing the Indigenization of child welfare. One example is the Vancouver Aboriginal Child and Family Services Society. Bernadette Spence, Cree, who is executive director of the society, spoke at the First Roundtable on Indigenization of Child Welfare, which was held at UBC in 2013. She described how the society is committed "to represent[ing] Aboriginal worldviews, cultural expression, cultural interpretation of issues and dilemmas in child welfare and grounding our practice in customary laws pertaining to children and families as reflected in customs and Protocols."[29]

Indigenous health care practitioners across many nations are now grounding their work in cultural teachings and philosophies. Many have had training in Western models of counselling psychology or alternative healing modalities like massage or acupuncture, but they have made conscious efforts to develop a decolonizing practice, integrating stories, ceremony, and culturally based strategies into what they do. Anishinaabe scholar and social worker Renee Linklater calls this "decolonizing trauma work."[30] One example of this is Indigenous (formerly Aboriginal) Focusing-Oriented and Complex Trauma Training, which originated out of the Justice Institute of New Westminster.[31] It is important to note the cultural specificity of much of the work done in many communities as this grounds the person who has come for help in her own tradition. An example of this is some healing work being done in Nuu-chah-nulth communities on the west coast of Vancouver Island. Anita Charleson-Touchie (Nuu-chah-nulth) and Dea Parshanishi explore the relationship between Western somatic therapies, in this case Somatic Experiencing, and Nuu-chah-nulth approaches to healing.[32]

Most Indigenous approaches to healing integrate the values of specific traditions and emphasize enhancing the strengths and gifts of each individual. Often education and healing are not separate: both operate within a much larger framework than just repairing the damage caused by violence. Even the word "damage" is loaded. I have learned not to describe people who are struggling with addictions or self-sabotaging behaviours as damaged. It is a term that objectifies the human spirit and erases the larger political context of the suffering. Wellness or well-being in Indigenous traditions operates on the emotional, spiritual, physical, and mental planes, and includes restoring family relationships, clan affiliations, and connection to land and nation. What many may call "spirituality" is integral to this healing process. Perhaps more accurately, what is central is a holistic worldview that includes the spirit world, which itself is part of a cosmology that is lived in daily life. These healing approaches are informed by an analysis of historical and contemporary colonialism.

Indigenous approaches to healing trauma provide directions for how to decolonize settler society. They move from the individual to the community to the land and to the nation. Dian Million quotes Indigenous governance scholar Kiera Ladner in her final chapter of *Therapeutic Nations*, where she stresses the need for Indigenous forms of governance that can create "healing cultures."[33] Indigenous governance "is an expression of the way in which a people live best together ... as a part of the circle of life, not as superior beings who claim dominion over other species and other humans."[34] In transforming relationships of dominance into relationships that are balanced we learn that healing cannot be separated from the relational field. The foundational practice is to build relationships and to honour and respect them. We can build relationships one person, one river, one plant at a time. That is the beginning.

Decolonizing the Great White Helper and Reconciliation

As discussed in the previous chapter, uncritical helping professions and much of the discourse about trauma have significant political and structural ramifications. Not surprisingly, the historical origins of the profession of social work reflect many of the values of Christian mission.[1] Christian mission was, and to some extent still is, part of an ongoing imperial project, a project articulated by the English writer Rudyard Kipling as "the White Man's Burden."[2] It was a duty to help others, to lift the uncivilized out of their abject state and, hence, to liberate them. And, of course, the white man and woman could then feel good about themselves and ignore the fact that they had occupied the territory of another people.

My youth church experience included exposure to many Christian development and mission programs that involved praying for the brave missionaries who had gone to help those in the "underdeveloped" world. We were told that their heroism was something we could aspire to and we prayed that we might be called to the vocation of missionary, though, of course, for girls this meant being a nun, which was definitely less heroic. Through all this I received the coded message that I would be a good person if I donated money or volunteered to help those poor people struggling with poverty and disease, people who were almost always black or brown and who lived far away. We, of course, had no idea of the role of our country or of the systems that had contributed to deprivation and oppression in these contexts; nothing was done to help us think critically about the political and economic histories that had led to the conditions of these people.

It is this helper within myself, the efforts to be a "good" person, and the systems of which I have been part that I have struggled with over the years. When I chose to continue my own "healing" process, first through Body-Mind Psychotherapy and, more recently, through relational trauma training, I had no idea that I would discover that, in pursuing my helping relationships, I was transmitting an oppressive system. Basically, I wanted to be a more functional human being in my personal and work life, and I chose body-based therapies because I had few illusions that I could just talk myself out of destructive patterns. I gradually learned that some of these patterns are a product of the society in which I live, not just of dysfunctional interpersonal relationships. I have been inspired by the scope of many Indigenous models of health and well-being and by the fact that Indigenous understandings of health and trauma are more holistic than is the Western medical model. Perhaps because I have been informed by these understandings I began to see how being raised as a white settler has contributed to some of my dysfunctional behaviours and that I have enacted this culture unconsciously in many of my relationships.

So my question has been, "How does this oppressive system play out in bodies?" I am interested in how relationships of dominance and submission show up in daily encounters and, in particular, in the helper role – the role I have been raised to adopt as a woman and as a Catholic. During the body-mind psychotherapy training I took in 2003, I had one of those "ah ha!" moments. Susan Apoyshan has brought together her two-decades-long practice of Buddhism and body-mind centring with recent developments in somatic psychotherapy and neuroscience.[3] At a certain point in the training I was supporting a fellow member who was weeping, my hand on her shoulder. Susan came by and gently noted to me that my head was overreaching and asked if I could feel my body as I "helped." I couldn't feel my body at all at that moment. I was so involved in helping the other student that I had lost touch with myself. She pointed out that by touching the woman I was stopping the processing of her pain, imposing on her my discomfort with her suffering. Despite knowing in my head that I was supposed to just be *with* another in pain, my body was doing something different.

Susan taught "embodied listening." Embodiment is "a moment to moment process by which human beings allow awareness to enhance the flow of thoughts, feelings, sensations and energies through our bodily selves."[4] Animals are embodied in that they always allow the flow of life through their bodies. But humans, because of personal experiences of violence and living in a violent culture that promotes body-mind dualism, often experience a sense of disassociation or separation from the body, which is a form of disembodiment. Susan trained us in "embodiment practice," whereby one learns to be aware, moment by moment, of sensations in the body and to give these permission to move and flow throughout the body so that one stays in the present moment. This practice allows the "helper" to be aware of what is happening in her body as she listens to and engages with another, and, it is hoped, leads her to stop when she notices that she is trying "to fix" the other. Echoing Buddhist teachings, Susan would always remind us there is nothing to fix, nothing to do, but just be with the other.

With relational trauma therapy and the work of Merete Brantbjerg, which I have been engaged with from 2008 to 2017, I found a similar approach to not fixing as well as an emphasis on what she calls "mutual regulation" and "empathic resonance" grounded in body skills.[5] What has been most useful for me is the fact that Brantbjerg offers a systems method and addresses how issues of authority and power are played out not only in the body but also in systems.[6] System work is critical to trauma therapy because we are embedded in systems of racism, colonialism, white supremacy, patriarchy, ableism, and heteronormativity that affect all of us. This approach accordingly looks at how attachment, authority, dominance, and submission play out not only in the body but also in relationships within a group. Brantbjerg describes how authority, in particular, is inscribed in the "relational field" of trauma, whether the struggle is over territory, influence, or power. Where there is no access to emotional resonance, the relational dynamic is guided by dominance and submission – someone gets to define direction without listening to other voices and decides who gets what, and then the others move into reaction. Brantbjerg uses the terms "one-up" for a dominant role and "one-down" for a submissive (or victim) role in a relationship.[7] When someone moves into the one-up role then it is easy for the other or others to move into a submissive role, the "one-down" role. This "role induction" happens automatically, most often outside of conscious awareness. Resonance can only occur when there is no one-up or one-down in the dynamic, where there is genuine contact and relationship.

This has enabled me to understand aspects of my own behaviour. In one training session, Brantbjerg asked us to go into a "one-up" role with which we were familiar and that related to authority. I decided to choose my political activist self, a familiar role. It has played out for me in activist circles in which I have struggled with an almost compulsive drive to speak first and to offer my analysis of a situation as the "right" one. Even in the many groups I have led as facilitator, I can often leave tired, carrying the role of someone who "had" to help the group move on in a myriad of ways because she knew the answer, knew what was "right" to do. I can see now that I go into a one-up position; I assume the role of an authority. In the role play I chose to look at my behaviour at an initial planning meeting for a conference. I was frustrated that the group, all white, was not prioritizing Indigenous participation in an event that was based in a small working-class community in Indigenous territory. As I replayed the dynamic in the role-play, I noticed two things: the tone of my verbal language ("You don't get it" and "I know the answer") and my body language (aggressive). My voice was somewhat loud, my neck was pushing my head forward, and I couldn't feel my body. I was holding my breath and was out of touch with the group. In judging the others I had assumed a dominant role. I was the helper as problem solver, unwilling to go through the process of learning what was going on with the group, unwilling to deal with the complexity of the context or spend time building relationships. I was not dealing with my own reactions and frustrations with what had come up so far but, rather, letting these guide my response. As a result, I moved out of "empathetic resonance" with others in the group.

Later, when I asked a somatic physiotherapist colleague to help me be precise with what happens in the body in the dominant role, she suggested that dominance is held in an arched back, hips that are externally rotated, shoulders that are wide and externally rotated, a neck that is pushed forward and a jaw that is retracted, and a locked-in kind of spine/core with the associated shallow breathing. She added that she saw this in a lot in clients who were military personnel and with young guys who worked out a lot.[8] I see the helper role as a bit more subtle than the more overt military or boss role but as still part of the one-up/ one-down dynamic of unequal power relations. The one-up position of the helper can be expressed bodily in a moving out of inner awareness, a losing of contact with one's physical core or centre, and a hardening of muscles that occurs when one is constantly making judgments of the "other." The one-down position, which often goes along with feeling like a victim, is lived in the body – in the shallow breath of someone who is always under siege and has to be vigilant. There is also either considerable tension in the body, part of the need to be vigilant, or sometimes a flaccidness, a giving up in the muscles.

As I began to recognize these patterns in my own behaviour I was able to associate some of them with whiteness. By whiteness I mean not only white privilege but also the structure that maintains this privilege, what is called white supremacy. It is becoming more commonly accepted that this term refers to much more than sympathizers of the Ku Klux Klan. The Black Lives Matter movement, which has arisen in the context of ongoing police violence against black people and a resurgence of right-wing identification with whiteness, both in the United States and in Canada, has pushed non-black groups to name and challenge white supremacy as a structure that maintains racism and exclusion. White supremacy is more than the belief that white people are superior to the people of other races. It refers to a political, social, and economic system in which white people benefit over non-white groups, and it operates through a set of institutional assumptions and practices. African American anti-racist educator Tema Okun names these values and practices "white supremacy culture." She examined a range of characteristics that she and the late Kenneth Jones, in Dismantling Racism workshops in the United States, identified in white-dominated organizations. Some of these characteristics are: either/or thinking, perfectionism, a sense of urgency, defensiveness, paternalism, fear of conflict, individualism, a belief that there is only one right way, worship of the written word, and the right to comfort.[9] I can clearly see these in myself, not only in many of the institutions of which I have been part.

I see that the implicit "I know what is good for you," either for an individual or for a collective, is part of the white helper mentality. By pushing for solutions (mine), I had not even allowed the members of the group to get in touch with their feelings about the situation, a necessary first step to moving out of paralysis or guilt and to taking action. If they were resistant, it was probably because they were resistant to me, not only to what I was saying. Tema Okun sees this "only-one-right-way" attitude as being "similar to the missionary who does not see value in the culture of other communities, sees only value in their beliefs about what is good."[10] Even if some members of the group may have agreed with me, there was resistance to *me*, not to what I was saying. I see now how ingrained the impulse to do something my way, the right way, is for someone like me, raised to help others as part of my identity. Caught in a common dilemma with no Indigenous people at the table, I moved into "speaking for." The content of what I was saying was constructive but it was countermanded by my attitude of righteousness, something I had internalized from growing up in a culture that cultivated the Great White Helper.

Brantbjerg provided me with some other therapy language that is helpful when considering the internal dynamics of systems of which we are a part and that reproduce oppression. She expanded her analysis to include the dysfunctional "stuck roles" that play out in situations of conflict. I was familiar with these stuck roles from working with drama therapist Nisha Sanjani in the area of prevention of violence against women in Montreal.[11] The roles are the victim, the persecutor, the rescuer, and the bystander. Often these roles have been learned earlier in life to help one survive in a hierarchical system, be it a family, a community, or a nation-state. In relational trauma therapy, these roles are understood as behaviours adopted to solve situations of conflict, unequal power dynamics that never got regulated or addressed. They become habitual ways of dealing with a situation of conflict and are based in the past rather than in the here and now.

I mention these dysfunctional roles because I see how they can play out in the social dynamic around settler colonialism and reconciliation in Canada. Both settlers and Indigenous people can get caught in these stances. Many settlers opt for the passive bystander role, doing nothing, either out of a blame mentality ("it's their own fault," "Why don't they take responsibility for what has happened" – i.e., one-up) or out of a feeling of guilt and hopelessness ("there's nothing we can do," I feel so bad" – i.e., one-down). There can be the angry victim, which is still one-down: on the Indigenous side, "all white people are bad"; on the settler side, "we had nothing to do with the past," "we meant well". There is the helpful do-gooder rescuer ("we know what will help" – i.e., one-up) and the persecutor ("just move on and get over it," "they are all lazy, cheating us on welfare"– i.e., one-up). In conversations with individuals, I observe how many white settlers get stuck in either feeling guilty about being white, and so are paralyzed, or who assume a rescue role (e.g., I Love First Peoples, a campaign to send shoe boxes with little gifts to First Nations kids in the North).[12] I cringe every time I hear "*our* First Nations." Nobody owns or possesses First Nations people, they are sovereign self-determining humans and the "our" reeks of paternalism. All of us can probably find where we tend to go automatically in this system. The challenge is figuring out how to move out of stuck roles. For instance, the rescuer is very familiar to me: taking responsibility for someone else's problem (i.e., assuming I can act or think for them). But I, and all of us, can also, at different times, be a bystander, a persecutor, and a victim.

In recent years, the rescuer is a role in which many Western white feminists have managed to get caught up in the international arena. The impulse is expressed in the need to take responsibility for doing and thinking for "Others." The Other can be Indigenous women, women of colour, black women, or Muslim women in war-torn countries like Afghanistan, Iraq, or Somalia. The many projects initiated by well-meaning white women to help "other" women are modern-day versions of the role white women played in nineteenth-century colonialism.[13] In Quebec, I have seen the Great White Helper in the efforts of some feminists to save Muslim women who wear the "veil," be it the hijab or the niqab. This helper does not ask the woman who wears the veil what she wants; nor does she research the history, religion, culture, and context of the woman.

How the structure of the Great White Helper still functions is well illustrated in the debate that followed the *Kony 2102* video. This was a film made by the NGO Invisible Children about Joseph Kony and the Lord's Resistance Army, which operated in Uganda and the Central African Republic and that recruited child soldiers.[14] The video went viral in 2012 and later sparked criticism of how Westerners (mostly white) could point the finger at an evil African warlord and avoid looking at American economic and military intervention in Central Africa and in numerous wars. Randelle Nixon and Katie Macdonald, two settler scholars who use the *Kony 2012* video to look at the impulse of white helpers to immediately move to action, invite us to reflect "on the wildly unsuccessful (predominantly white) Western history of helping in both global and local contexts (from colonization to international aid) and to question deeply the implications of the unreflected-upon moves to action that have shaped this history."[15]

Yet Invisible Children is but one of the many NGOs, church programs, and charities that are part of a large industry that, in the end, only serves to maintain the unjust conditions that keep people poor and oppressed. Black American writer Teju Cole has called this structure the "White Savior Industrial Complex," in which the well-meaning person's involvement is not about working for justice but about having a strong emotional experience that validates and reinforces privilege.[16] It is easier for me to send money or volunteer for one of these charities than to question my own motives and take the time to analyze the structural underpinnings of the situation. If I did this, I might have to face how my own political and affective histories are implicated in my choices to help. There are other options. We can choose to track and challenge our country's role in resource extraction and in the militarization of other countries. We can learn about and support what the local people themselves are doing to change their conditions. Then we can ask them what they might want from us.

If Christianity has played a central role in the construction of the Great White Helper, at least there is now a significant effort on the part of some Christian churches in Canada to begin to address their role in settler colonialism. When I say "Christianity" I mean European Christianity, which was the vehicle through which Europeans enforced the cultural values that justified their occupation and possession of Indigenous lands. It was a Christianity shaped by imperial values, reflecting little of first-century Palestinian Christianity or many of the non-European Christianities that exist today. Some mainstream Christian churches in Canada are addressing their colonial past and present by responding to the Truth and Reconciliation Commission's Calls to Action. By "mainstream churches" I mean the Roman Catholic, United, Presbyterian, Anglican, Baptist, and Lutheran churches; the Quakers; the Salvation Army; and Unitarian Fellowships – all of whose leadership and membership is predominantly white. I do not include Indigenous Christian churches or churches with large recent immigrant populations, such as the Congolese Catholic Church in Montreal or the Korean United Church in Toronto.

The TRC Calls to Action address the major role the churches have played not only in residential schools but also in the civilizing mission that promoted Christianity and European culture as being superior to all other cultures. Call to Action 59 calls for the churches to educate their members about their church's role in colonization, about the history and legacy of residential schools, and about why church apologies are necessary.[17] Call to Action 60 calls for church leadership and theology schools, in collaboration with Indigenous spiritual leaders, to develop and teach curriculum "on the need to respect Indigenous spirituality in its own right" and " the history and legacy of religious conflict in Aboriginal families and communities, and the responsibility that churches have to mitigate such conflicts and prevent spiritual violence."[18] Calls to Action 48 and 49 have called for the repudiation of the Doctrine of Discovery and for the churches to formally adopt and comply with the principles norms and standards of the United Nations Declaration of the Rights of Indigenous Peoples.[19] To the churches that were part of the Settlement Agreement, in Call to Action 61, the TRC has called for church funding of community-controlled healing and reconciliation projects, language and cultural recovery projects, and education and relationship building projects.[20] These are powerful calls, and it will take years, if not generations, for these actions to affect the local churches. But it is important to note what has and has not been done.

The Canadian Ecumenical Anti-Racism Network, which is under the umbrella of the Canadian Council of Churches, has produced two documents on the Doctrine of Discovery: one a resource for ministers and educators, the other an overview of how churches in Canada have responded to the TRC's call to repudiate this doctrine and the concept of "terra nullius" that was used to justify European dispossession of Indigenous land.[21] The latter document summarizes select statements of repudiation by the churches, with a few making a commitment to implement the United Nations Declaration of Indigenous Peoples.[22] However, I cannot forget Tema Okun and how she included "love of the written word" in her list of the characteristics of white supremacy culture. Churches love making statements. I confess I am looking for more than statements in response to the Calls to Action.

Some church organizations have been more scrupulous in their response. The Mennonite Church of Canada, through its Indigenous-Settler Relations Program, has published three readable journal-style books, one on the United Nations Declaration of the Rights of Indigenous Peoples, one on the dispossession of Indigenous lands and the Doctrine of Discovery, and one on how the churches can respect Indigenous spiritualities.[23] The very fact that the Mennonites funded a national Indigenous-Settler Relations Program, which involves congregational education, is hopeful. In 2018, the Mennonite Church, again through that office, published *Unsettling the Word: Biblical Experiments in Decolonization*, which is accessible to the lay reader and begins to explore how the Bible was used and manipulated to justify colonization.[24] KAIROS, the national ecumenical justice organization that represents several churches, has several action programs: one advocating for the implementation of the UN Declaration of the Rights of Indigenous Peoples, another is an information hub on murdered and missing Indigenous women and girls, and a third, the Blanket Exercise, is an education program about the history of colonialism in Canada and has been offered extensively both inside and outside church circles.[25] Several of the churches now have ongoing funds for both Indigenous healing and cultural recovery, while different religious orders have provided funding for various Indigenous projects. For example, the Sisters of Saint Anne, in response to the TRC's Call to Action 50, which calls for funding and supporting Indigenous laws, donated a significant amount of money to the University of Victoria's new Indigenous Law Program and degree.[26] This particular action provides concrete support for Indigenous governance, which is a critical pillar in self-determination and sovereignty for Indigenous nations.

In terms of anti-racism materials, the United Church has been producing anti-racism materials for more than a decade, and in 2018 it began to look at anti-Black racism and Afrophobia.[27] The Anglican Church of Canada passed the Charter for Racial Justice in 2007, and in Victoria, where I now live, the Anglican Diocese is initiating a series based on the excellent Dismantling Racism Program from the United States.[28] The Canadian Ecumenical Anti-Racism Network has also produced anti-racism materials and, in particular, an education workbook on "white identity," which includes addressing white supremacy culture.[29]

If we look at the churches there is definitely, in church organizations and at the academic level in theology schools and seminaries, a minority who are resisting and challenging the colonial project in their commitment to reconciliation and anti-racism. However, this rarely filters down to the people in the pews. A United Church minister told me that it is up to her to gain access to the anti-racism resources; there are no mandated programs of any substance, only a three-hour anti-racism course for ministers in her presbytery. In some theology schools, courses that address racism, white privilege, and colonialism are electives. A colleague, who is researching why so little of what is taught in theology schools filters down to the congregational level, observed that one problem is that there is no follow-up to educational exercises like

the Blanket Exercise. People feel they have "done it." She added that
the majority of people who come to these mainstream white churches
want to be comforted, to be consoled, rather than to face discomfort.[30]

The individual resistance to addressing church contribution to
ongoing colonial structures is supported by the fact that most white
churches haven't looked at their own structures. In other words, there
is a structural whiteness that reinforces a comfortable apathy. I have
observed this when I have facilitated some "Indigenization education
programs" not only in churches but also in universities. While infusion
of anti-racism education and Indigenization programs into these institutions is a step forward, as long as white people control the delivery
of these programs, real decolonization cannot happen. What is needed
most, as stated by optipemisiw/Michif/Métis scholar Zoe Todd, writing
about academia, is not so much Indigenization but a change in who
is controlling the storyline and in the decision-making structures of
the institutions.[31] As long as the majority of the decision makers and
professors in universities – and, I would add, in church structures, seminaries, and theology schools – are white "it means that arguments for
changes to institutions have to be filtered through whiteness, through
white bodies (both human and institutional), and that white people
still, largely, operate to own, control, and command what any changes
to a campus looks like."[32] This means that for real change to occur more
racialized and Indigenous people need to be occupying these positions.
Todd calls for challenging "the ongoing inability of many institutions
to engage with the deeper legal-ethical meaning of their institutions
occupying unceded/stolen Indigenous lands."[33] While Todd is talking
about universities in Canada (with some exceptions), this also applies
to churches and religious congregations (again with some exceptions)
that occupy, have owned, and still own much land on unceded or
treaty lands.[34]

There are a few positive moves at the structural level. A Unitarian
colleague told me that the Unitarian Universalists of America have committed to dismantling white supremacy culture in their organization.
Triggered by a challenge to a leadership that was continuing to hire
mostly white men, several key figures resigned and a co-presidential
interim team of three people of colour was appointed. The team produced a report, which is now being followed, on the steps that need
to occur to change the culture.[35] One comment from their presentation stands out for me: "The risks of failing to engage these issues are

enormous for this faith. Change must come if our faith is to thrive."[36] The Unitarians have sponsored "white supremacy teach-ins" across the United States and Canada.[37] The Quakers, again in the United States and Canada, have appointed the Institutional Assessment Task Force, whose mandate includes assessing "the degree to which individuals, institutions and our Quaker culture uphold white supremacy and marginalize our subcultures. How does Quaker practice, programs, etc. benefit white society and oppress people of color?"[38] So there is much that is positive going on in terms of addressing the Great White Helper and ongoing colonialism and racism.

At the same time, I need to hear the cautions of Indigenous people. Eve Tuck (Unangax, Aleut) and Wayne Yang, in an article on decolonization that addresses how the term is used so loosely, advise us "to consider how the pursuit of critical consciousness, the pursuit of social justice through a critical enlightenment, can also be settler moves to innocence – diversions, distractions, which relieve the settler of feelings of guilt of responsibility, and conceal the need to give up land or power or privilege."[39] In other words, workshops and documents are not enough. There are some Indigenous activists and scholars who argue that reconciliation is but a form of recolonization.[40] Michi Saagiig Nishnaabeg Leanne Betasamosoke Simpson, scholar, writer, and activist, calls reconciliation just one more "depoliticized recovery-based narrative."[41] Simpson advocates "resurgence," a term that includes the "simultaneous dismantling of settler colonial meta-manifestations and its reinvigoration of Indigenous systemic alternatives."[42] I understand resurgence as a movement and theoretical framework that rejects reconciliation with the Canadian state in favour of building strong Indigenous Nations from the ground up, rooted in language, art, ceremony, and land-based practices that provide an alternative to a capitalist economy based on resource extraction. Consistent in all these critiques of reconciliation is the fact that most reconciliation efforts don't address the land, the need for economic and political sovereignty, which requires returning control of the land on which a Nation's language and culture is based. As the late Art Manuel stated, "The land issue must be addressed before reconciliation can begin. "That is, it must be addressed only after Indigenous Title and land Rights have been recognized and enough land base returned to support each Nation's economic and cultural needs.[43]

When I engage with these critiques of reconciliation things become clearer for me. It is easy for a culture that is rooted in white supremacy and the helper mentality to focus on healing and cultural recovery and then to incorporate this into the "business-as-usual" of exploiting Indigenous lands. I once heard Métis and Cree educator Verna St Denis say that "cultural pride is not a remedy for racism and poverty."[44] So I want to include the wider vision of Indigenous leaders like Manuel and Simpson. I consider decolonization to be an integral part of this vision and to be applicable to both Indigenous peoples and settlers. For settlers it provides a way to move away from complicity in structures like settler colonialism, white supremacy, capitalism, and heteropatriarchy.

Decolonization is complex and it is easy for settlers to prefer the language of reconciliation to that of decolonization. However, I am not willing to dismiss some of the important steps towards decolonization that are being taken in the name of reconciliation. I think taking a polarized view – for example, all reconciliation efforts are compromised – negates the complexity of human endeavours and buys into an either/or mentality that lets white settlers off the hook. If we truly believe everything is interconnected and that "we are all One," or Nétsamaat in the Lkwungen language of the territory in which I am now living, then every action counts.[45] In this slippery area of reconciliation each person has something she or he can do.

What relational trauma training gave me was a way to analyze how trauma occurs in the relational sphere of colonialism and how it is important for all of us to look at the patterned reactions we bring to abuses of authority. If we examine the present context of reconciliation in Canada it is clear that white authority is at stake – again over land, territory, power, and influence. This is not only a structural but also an individual issue. How do I personally address my implication in this authority, especially when it is hidden by the invisibility of whiteness? As someone with both white and settler behaviour patterned into my body, how do I carry this into my relationships with Indigenous peoples and how can I begin to address my role in collective dominance? How can I support the organizations with which I have a relationship in a way that encourages critically examining and changing them and their cultures? This means not only addressing white supremacy but also being open to and learning about differing world views and cultures, all of which offer alternative ways of organizing and functioning. This is all part of decolonization, which has to come before any true reconciliation.

PART THREE

Going Home: Gespe'gewa'gi

Blood

The woman opposite me at the fast food table gives me a chilling look. This exchange is not going as I had intended. She is of Coast Salish and European heritage, has published articles on Coast Salish legal traditions, and is a practising Christian. I had arranged this meeting over a meal in the fall of 2008 because I wanted to know how she reconciled Christianity and Indigenous knowledge systems. However, she wants to know about my lineage, who my ancestors are, and how far back I can trace them, including their names.

I had introduced myself as someone of mixed heritage – French, Irish, Scottish, English, and Mi'gmaq.[1] She looks at me with a severe frown. "If you can't actually name the person and what community they come from, then you should not claim Mi'gmaq ancestry," she says. She then throws out: "Why don't you take a blood test? Then you will know for sure, and you can either feel good or sad, depending on the results." I had a flash of a woman I had worked with who had been fostered and then adopted, and had decided to take a thousand-dollar blood test, which had indicated that she was part Indigenous Pacific Islander, among various European strains.

I am taken aback. How did I get into this quagmire? My stomach clenches at the thought of a blood test. I am disturbed by what she is saying, and it is not only because it seems I have lost credibility in her eyes. After several years of anti-racism work I know that blood quantum as a determinant of race is integral to racism itself; it is a category created by white people to justify dominance and superiority. So I am confused and somehow slip into my familiar one-down position. Rather than challenge her on the issue of blood quantum, I sink into self-doubt and say nothing. We both hastily finish our meals in silence and bid each other adieu. The tension in the air had been palpable. I leave with a feeling of shame, once again feeling unsure of who I really am and, worse, feeling that I presented myself as a person who falsely claims to be "Indian."

❋

The question as to whether I have any Mi'gmaq ancestry has been an ongoing thread in my life. As a child I knew little about Indians, except for playing Cowboys and Indians as my cowgirl heroine, Annie Oakley. In an old family photo my parents are dressed for a Halloween party. My dad is dressed as an Indian, his face painted with two black lines on his cheeks, accentuating his high cheekbones; on his forehead is a head-band of feathers and his body is wrapped in a blanket. My mom seems to be dressed as a settler, wearing a scarf on her head and a big long skirt and shawl. An odd couple indeed. My dad's choice of Halloween garb was interesting. It certainly was reflective of the still-popular Halloween trope of "playing Indian." Yet I later wondered if there was possibly something else going on.

When I was around ten, rather than taking the train as we usually did, dad drove the family down to the Gaspé coast in our new green Ford. On the way to Port Daniel, where he grew up, we passed the town of Maria and he pointed out the Micmac reserve.[2] As I did not know what either a Micmac or a reserve was, he explained that a reserve was where Indians lived, making a vague gesture towards an area by the river. I got the sense it had nothing to do with us, and in my mind's eye I saw a chain link fence around it. This was not an inaccurate image, considering that the pass system had only been repealed in 1951 and there were still remnants of it here in the Gaspé in the late 1950s. The pass system, designed for reserves on the Prairies, was an administrative policy whereby permission to leave a reserve had to be granted by an Indian agent.[3] In Maria an "Indian" could not do business outside the reserve without the approval of the Indian agent. Of course, I knew nothing of this, but my dad's tone conveyed it all.

Curiously enough, after we had passed Maria, my dad added a comment that stuck with me: "we have some Micmac blood in the family." Dad never said that to me again, though years later, when I checked with my brother Gerald to see if he remembered this, he said he had heard Dad say it more than once. My father was not of a generation that thought it was "cool" to mention Indian ancestry. In fact, it was the opposite. It was something to hide because racism towards Indians was endemic in Quebec. However, the question of ancestry and identity was not important to me when I was an adolescent, nor was it important to me as a young woman. Knowing one's roots becomes a more compelling matter as one gets older, especially in a culture that promotes rootlessness. After more than twenty years working in "Indian Country," where ancestry is central to identity, I decided at the age of fifty to investigate.

My father was born in 1911 in Port Daniel, a village on the south shore of the Baie de Chaleur. My dad's father, Charles H. Nadeau, owned and operated a large sawmill there. My great-grandfather, Pierre Nadeau, had moved to the village of Grand Cascapedia from New Brunswick in the mid-nineteenth century and had worked out of Cascapedia as a building contractor. He had married a Scottish woman from New Brunswick, and when she died, he married her sister, producing twelve children in total. The favourite family story about him was that he had built two churches for the Protestants and, as a result, had been excommunicated twice from the Catholic Church. My grandmother, Anna Mae Gagnon, came from a family that had moved from Baie des Sables near Matane to Port Daniel at the end of the nineteenth century. Her father had been the postmaster and had married the daughter of an Irish settler. Family genealogists, of which we have a few (something that is not uncommon among francophone families in Quebec), have traced the Nadeaus back to the village of Genouillac, close to Angoulême in the southwest of France. The first Nadeau arrived in Quebec in 1663, while the first Gagnon birth to be recorded here was in the town of Quebec in 1657. In the case of both families, only the male ancestral line has been traced to date, though I have recently discovered a second cousin, Diane Gagnon, who is determined to track the women.

For me, Port Daniel was a summer haven and refuge, a place where I belonged. Cascapedia was the place where my grandfather grew up and occasionally went fishing. Like many adolescents, I was focused solely on my own survival. The Gaspé was a place to escape from the confusing and stultified life I experienced growing up in the Town of Mount Royal, an upper-middle-class area of Montreal. I felt trapped by the stifling atmosphere and genteel manners of my parents, who wanted to be accepted into the upper echelons of anglophone Montreal society in the 1950s and 1960s. My mother's mother, Silena Brown Downey, who was "mentally ill" (she was later diagnosed as manic depressive), lived with us. This was a family stigma that required the pretense of "all is well." Port Daniel was another world where I could run barefoot with my cousins, wander freely, and wear whatever I wanted. If my mother looked down on the manners and morals of my dad's rambunctious family of three sisters and four surviving brothers and all their children, for me their world was heaven. I "belonged" there.

I haven't traced my mother's line as diligently as I have my father's because I have felt little connection to her ancestry. This is partly because my mother herself had become both disconnected from her Irish Catholic roots and enthralled with the "American culture" that she knew through her American Methodist mother. An only child, my mother had actually been born in Manhattan, though the little family moved to Toronto when she was five. My mom's paternal grandfather had been mayor of Brockville, and her maternal grandmother, a widow, had been a farmer in Kansas, but my mother never met or visited her. After my mother developed Alzheimer's, I was unable to trace any relatives on her side. She had had a conflicted relationship with her family. When I was a child, we only went twice for short day visits to Brockville to visit her one surviving cousin and her family. As a result, I had little sense of the place and land around there, which years later I would discover was in Michi Saagiig and Tyendinaga Mohawk territory.

It was the yearly summer visits to the Gaspé Coast, my father's strong sense of family history, his connection with some of his siblings who lived in Montreal, and a cultural identity that was both French and English that forged my identification with my dad's family and his sense of place. In 2000, I attended the first Nadeau family reunion in Port Daniel. I had not been back to the "Coast" since a family wedding in Gaspé in 1989. The sense of familiarity and comfort returned to me immediately. I loved the wide expanse of Port Daniel Bay, which would be sparkling under a sunny blue sky one day and, the next, be a grey heaving sea of whitecaps under stormy clouds. I spent hours walking the beach with its different layers of rocks, pebbles, and sand, hearing the sound of the waves pulling the rounded stones back and forth. I meandered back into the woods, thick with birch, poplar, and pine, and listened to the musical rustling of the leaves in the wind. I loved this land and it did feel like home to me, even if most of the family had moved away.

I figured Monique Nadeau, the Parisian wife of my dad's cousin Gerald and a consummate dedicated genealogist, might know whether there had been intermarriage with the Micmacs. She was presenting a slide show she had developed of the Nadeau family history at a large family gathering in the basement of the town hall. When the show was finished, I raised my hand and asked: "As-tu decouvert des ancêstres Mi'gmaq dans la genéalogie de la famille Nadeau?" (Have you discovered any Mi'gmaq ancestry in the Nadeau genealogy?) She replied authoritatively, "Non, les Nadeaux ont folâtré avec les Micmacs, mais c'est tout." (No, the Nadeaus had danced with the Micmacs, but that was all.) A titter spread throughout the room.

I was annoyed but kept it to myself. After twenty years of working in the area of violence against women, including Indigenous women, I had a different lens than did the people in that room. To publicly say that my male ancestors had fooled around with Mi'gmaq women was not laughable. Like many descendants from settler families, we think *our* ancestors were never part of any rape and pillage scenario. Or, worse, as the laughter in the room implied, that sexual adventures were of no significance. I could see I was the odd one out at this gathering. However, that moment led me to decide that I would search out whether there was indeed any Mi'gmaq blood in the family.

If we went by physical characteristics, I could see that my grandmother, a few of my aunts, and one uncle had almond-shaped eyes as well as the characteristic Mi'gmaq dark hair and high cheekbones. My dad had only the cheekbones and black hair. I discovered from my Aunt Katherine that my grandmother had been teased and called "the Eskimo" when she was young because of her eyes. When I looked back at one of the few pictures of my grandmother's mother, I was sure she "looked" Native, even if her name had been Isabelle Macpherson. I decided to spend time walking through the Catholic cemetery in Port Daniel, looking for clues about my family amidst the old gravestones.

The old cemetery was on the back slope of a hill above the church. The Nadeau family plot was at the back, with a shiny granite stone for both my grandparents and two of their sons, my uncles. Behind the stone, separated by tufts of long grass and a low rusted iron fence, were several concrete gravestones. This was a neglected plot and many of the letters on the gravestones were eroded. I was able to make out the names of my great-grandparents on my grandmother's side. Beside their stone were three smaller ones, and, as I tried to distinguish the faded dates, I realized that the graves were for three young children between the ages of one and three, all of whom had died between 1897 and 1899. I felt sadness at such a tragedy. As I gazed at the weather-beaten stones, I fantasized that maybe the bereft couple had adopted a Native child to make up for this loss. I was so focused on my story that I did not even think about the reality that many Native children as well as their parents would have died from the same disease, possibly influenza, and that their families would have had no interest in letting the children who survived go to white families.

Every family member with whom I spoke told me there had been no Micmacs in Port Daniel, even when they were young. Yet I was reluctant to believe this. I asked my Uncle Charlie Jr, the most Native-looking in the family and, at that time, the only one of my father's nine siblings still alive. He had his tall-tale version of our Micmac ancestry. He told me that my great-grandfather Peter Nadeau had had a store on the beach. One day, a group of Indians raided the beach and he fled, leaving his wife hiding under the counter. When he came back, she was pregnant. Needless to say we all regarded his stories with some scepticism. Like most white Gaspesians, he had internalized the idea that any Micmac ancestry was distasteful, and certainly not something to be discussed, taken seriously, or researched.

In the spring of 2003, I moved back to Montreal after more than thirty years on the west coast. I had decided to "go home." This phrase has layered meanings for me. I had learned from my Anishnabe Cree friend Alannah Young that "going home" was very important in Indigenous traditions. It meant returning not only to one's roots and culture but also to the responsibilities that were part of renewing one's relationships to one's ancestry. At that point in my life, I saw my return to Montreal as a journey that included reviving my connection to my French roots and language as well as indulging my nostalgic love for Quebec and, specifically, for the Gaspé. But all was not as it seemed, and my life's path was leading me gradually to discover a different story of this land, of my family, and of my responsibilities.

In the process of looking for employment in Montreal, and because of my work with Indigenous women in Vancouver's Downtown Eastside, I decided to approach the Quebec Federation of Native

Women for some work leads. Now, I look back at this as both naïve and presumptuous. In "Indian Country," everything is done through relationships and, at that time, I had none in Quebec. I even had the nerve to ask for the president, and, when the front desk staff person told me she was out, she referred me to the executive director, Manon Jeannotte, who, luckily for me, was in. I entered her office and was greeted by a blue-eyed woman with shoulder-length auburn hair. I was taken aback at first, as she didn't really "look" Native. As we were talking, I noticed on the wall a large map that showed all the Mi'kmaq communities in the Maritimes and Quebec. I realized Manon must be Mi'kmaq. To my knowledge, most Mi'kmaq were English-speaking, so I was curious about her being francophone.

I asked Manon, in French, "What nation are you from?"

"Mi'gmaq," she replied. "Gespeg, but my family is from a small community on the Gaspé coast that you have probably never heard of."

"Which one?" I inquired. "Because my father is from the Coast."

She replied, "Port Daniel."

My heart jumped. "But that is where my family is from! Where did your family live?"

"McInnis Cove," Manon replied.

McInnis Cove is a beautiful little spot off Port Daniel Bay, which I had rediscovered the summer before. No one in my large extended family had mentioned that there were Micmacs there. Letting go of my original job-seeking intention, Manon and I agreed to talk again.

Stunned by this exchange, I began a two-pronged search: to revisit my own identity and ancestry and to track down more information about Mi'gmaq presence in Port Daniel. So I began another search for a Micmac ancestor, which still proved a difficult task. I decided to go through the baptismal records of the Port Daniel Catholic Church, looking for signs of intermarriage. I spent hours going through three paperback volumes published by the Gaspé Diocese for each parish, looking for some sign of intermarriage with Manon's family, the Jeannottes. The records began in 1898, with a few going back as far as 1854. After poring through pages and pages of baptisms and marriages on both the Gagnon and Nadeau sides, I did find an obscure link with the Jeannottes through the McGuinesses, my dad's third cousins, but otherwise nothing. Well, not totally true. I did discover my dad had been born six months after my grandparents got married, which was pretty racy for Catholics controlled by the church in rural Quebec. It gave me a good laugh.

I was discouraged, but determined, so tracked down copies of the family trees on both sides. Of course, both traced only the male line. There were countless women who had married into these male lines as far back as the early seventeenth century, some from the other side of the Gaspé coast and some from New Brunswick. But how long would it take me to determine the ancestry of each of these women? I was somewhat daunted by a task that was becoming not only time consuming, but possibly fruitless. With work opportunities opening up in Montreal, I became too busy to even think about it anymore.

The next year, 2004, I attended the American Academy of Religion's (AAR) annual meeting in San Antonio, Texas. I had been going to the AAR for a few years and, as my field of study was developing into the relationship between colonialism, Christianity, and Indigenous trad-itions, I had found a home in the "Native Traditions in the Americas" section. In 2003, Alannah Young and I had delivered a paper on our work in the Downtown Eastside at the annual AAR meeting in Toronto and had been greeted warmly by Inez Talamentez, a Mescalero Apache scholar and one of the founders of the "Native Traditions" section.[4] So, in 2004, I decided to attend the pre-conference gathering of the section in which Inez was, in some way, the presiding Elder. These sessions are quite informal and we go around the circle identifying ourselves. I had learned that it is important to name your ancestry when introducing yourself, so I nervously gave my name and said that I was of French, Irish, Scottish, English, and Mi'gmaq heritage.

After the meeting, many in the group went out to dinner at a Tex Mex restaurant. We sat at a long table outside, beneath brightly col-oured paper lanterns, and I ended up sitting directly across from George Tinker, a well-known Osage scholar. He refused to acknowledge me. I felt invisible, and questioned myself. "Maybe I am an imposter, perhaps I shouldn't be here," I thought. But I was there, so I just felt miser-able. I do recall that Michael McNally, a well-respected white scholar of Anishinaabe traditions, did speak to me, which made me feel better.[5] A year later, I read a book written by my uncommunicative tablemate, Tinker, called *Spirit and Resistance*, and I discovered his position: if you are not raised culturally Native, you have no right to claim Native ancestry or even attend Native ceremonies.[6]

Over the years, I stayed with the Native Traditions group, learning much and becoming aware of the values guiding those who took leadership positions. There are a few people of European ancestry in the group, and I observed that what counted was to show up, to be committed to Indigenous sovereignty, to do the work respectfully, and to build relationships over time. If I had followed Tinker's lead, I would not have stuck it out; hard as it was, I am grateful for what I learned by staying.

But the road around blood has been bumpy for me. In the winter of 2005, I decided to approach the Department of Religion at Concordia University in Montreal to see if I could teach a course there. I was already teaching a course in community organizing and popular education at the Concordia School of Community and Public Affairs, but my passion was in the area of religion and I needed more work. I arranged a coffee date with Norma Joseph, who was then the chair of the religion department at Concordia. I knew about Norma because of her early work on feminism in Judaism. Unknown to me, she also had a degree in anthropology in the area of Native religions. Norma was and continues to be a strong advocate for having Indigenous religions taught in the religion department. So when I told her I had done my doctorate of ministry dissertation on embodied and interfaith healing work with Indigenous women, she asked me if I would be interested in teaching a course on Indigenous women. I hesitated and told her I could only teach it from my location – that is, as a descendant of colonizer families who had possibly intermarried with the Mi'gmaq. Somehow the mention of intermarriage, even though I said it had been far back, seemed to be a factor in her finding me eligible for the job.

A few weeks later, I found myself sitting at a long table in the religion department being interviewed for a sessional position to teach a course on Indigenous women and colonialism in Canada. Three senior faculty members, all white, were screening me to teach one course. They questioned me on my knowledge in the field, which was clearly more than theirs. Then one of them said, almost with a sense of relief, "Well, it is helpful that you are Micmac." I quickly qualified this, "There has been some intermarriage way back, but I am not Mi'gmag." However, I could see that distant ancestry was enough for them. Then I said, "There are Indigenous people around who can do this job." And I named one or two women who I knew were in the Montreal area. One man replied, "But they need to have a degree in religion." I responded, "Indigenous studies is a field that is cross-disciplinary, and breaking off religion into a separate department counters the reality that Indigenous traditions permeate all aspects of life." I could see they weren't convinced. Then one of them made a remark that politely conveyed their concern: "We don't want someone we don't know much about in the department."

I suddenly got it. Fear of rocking the boat. I was "Indian" enough for them, but, even better, I was white enough that I was safe. I wouldn't be one of "those" disruptive types. I sensed a fear of the possibility of a militant Indigenous academic challenging the department and university structure. As I looked at this group, mostly professors near retirement, I could see that it was convenient and easy for them to hire me. At first glance, it didn't seem to be about race, as there were South Asians and an Arab Middle Eastern scholar in the department. There was even one course, Religion and Native Traditions, co-taught by a white woman, Louise Johnston, and a Kahnawà:ke Mohawk Elder, Brian Deer. I learned that Deer couldn't teach alone as he didn't have a doctorate, a policy that was university-wide. What an irony! Not only was he a Traditional Knowledge Keeper, equivalent to a PhD in "Indian Country," but, as I discovered a few years later, he had also created the first Indigenous library reference system in Canada, called the Brian Deer Classification System.[7]

I was torn as to what to do. I knew my Mi'gmaq ancestry was tenuous, but I needed and wanted the job, and I was quite sure they would not hire anybody else. I believed strongly that the religion department had to offer more than one course in Indigenous traditions. Yet, at the same time, I heard in my head the voices of the Indigenous academics who critique non-Indigenous people who take their jobs, especially full-time ones. In the end, I agreed to teach the course, rationalizing that it was only one course, not a position. But I felt some guilt that I had neither refused the course nor used the moment to challenge the trio who had interviewed me. But I have never been quick to respond to comments with which I disagree. I was honestly flummoxed by what happened in the room. And, at that point, I was not clear myself about my identity. I did not grasp then the reality that, my qualifications notwithstanding, they were perfectly happy to hire me on the basis of "blood." This was as bad as the "one drop rule" in the United States, whereby you were considered black if you had any known black ancestry, a policy that was used against African Americans to maintain segregation. This was the one drop in reverse!

In order to compensate for what could allegedly amount to stealing an Indigenous job, I rigorously researched and developed my course so that it clearly illustrated the role and impact of colonialism and colonial Christianity on Indigenous traditions. I used Indigenous women's voices and invited women from local nations to speak to the class. I presented myself as a settler of European heritage whose French ancestors intermarried with the Mi'gmag many generations ago. I almost became like the race police myself, taking a hard line on those who claimed Indigenous ancestry without a clear connection to a community. I challenged students who said they were Metis but had no connection to the Métis Nation. I wrote an article for a University of Montreal theology journal in which I critiqued the widespread tendency of many francophone Québécois to claim Indigenous ancestry.[8]

Two events in 2010 helped further shift my perspective on my ancestry. At a round table on Indigenous literature at Simon Fraser University, I heard Scott Morgensen, an academic who works in the area of queer and gender studies, call himself a "settler scholar." I suddenly felt a burden lifted from my shoulders. Finally, there was a name I could claim that granted some integrity to how I was teaching. Later that same year, I was the master of ceremonies at a book launch for the Aboriginal Healing Foundation's *Response, Responsibility, and Renewal: Canada's Truth and Reconciliation Journey* at the First Nations House of Learning at the University of British Columbia.[9] I had to introduce Jonathan Dewar, one of the editors. When I googled Dewar, I couldn't glean from his bio where he was from, and he definitely "looked" non-Native. I caught myself as I thought this, once again equating ancestry with skin colour. Dewar, in his introduction, explained that his grandmother had been part Huron-Wendat. He then went on to say how he had been reminded by a friend that he had three other grandparents and that they had been just as important in shaping his life. That gave me pause for reflection.

For no matter how you cut it, my family, on all sides, had been settlers for many generations, and one intermarriage, if there even was one, would not change that fact. I decided to end my search for an obscure Mi'gmaq ancestor. The hours, even weeks or months it could take, seemed very problematic. And what would it prove? I had been raised within at least three generations of white privilege; I was culturally white. It was time I let go of the genealogy quest. Dewar had reminded me of the importance of balance in tracing ancestry. This would lead me in another direction, that of researching the role of my father's family in the displacement of the Mi'gmag on the Gaspé coast. As well, I decided to educate myself on the politics of blood.

Indigenous identity, as defined by blood, is one of the most charged issues for Indigenous women in Canada. The Indian Act disenfranchised women who "married out" and created the legal categories of status and non-status Indians as a way of slowly eroding the Indigenous population in Canada. Even Bill C-31, passed in 1985 after years of lobbying by Native women, only restored status to two generations of women and to two generations of grandchildren. Bill C-3, which followed, due to the tireless work of Sharon McIvor, still functioned to disenfranchise the grandchildren of women who married non-Native men. I have trouble figuring out the legalese around the bills and the terms for children and grandchildren – 6(1) and 6(2). I have heard women say, "I have a 6(2) child," which in itself shows how Indigenous life in Canada is legally framed by the Indian Act. In November of 2017, as a result of an amendment to C-3 passed by the Senate, led by Indigenous senators Lillian Dyck and Sandra Lovelace Nicholas, Bill S-3 has been passed, ending sex-based discrimination in registration under the Indian Act.[10] As of this writing there has been no mechanism to bring this bill into force.

I think that those of us who are non-Indigenous have no idea how much pain and suffering has been caused by the status distinctions made in the Indian Act as part of the plan to assimilate and eventually erase the Indigenous population. I have a Mohawk friend from Kahnawake who moved out of the community because of the blood quantum controversy there. Her children were identified by the Indian Act as 6(2)s, so they are considered non-Native by Mohawk leaders who want only pure Mohawks living on reserve, even though her mother is a Longhouse member and the culture is matrilineal.[11] I have Métis friends who are accused by status Indians of taking jobs from them, and a Cree-Métis friend who fears her grandchildren will be excluded from a particular Sundance if participation gets restricted by blood quantum. I know a Kwakwaka'wakw woman who has status but a white complexion, so she has to work extra hard to be heard and accepted for who she is. I have had Indigenous students who, because they are light-skinned, have their comments treated as less legitimate not only by the non-Indigenous students in the class but also by some of the Indigenous ones. These are but a few examples of what has resulted from a government policy meant to foster these divisions and slowly erode Indigenous populations. To make it worse, white people and many other newcomers absorb these distinctions, buying into the myth of the "real" Indian.

It is this context that has possibly contributed to a few of my Indigenous women friends complicating my relationship with my somewhat questionable Indigenous ancestry. They are cautious about quickly judging women who speak of ancestral connections. Alannah wanted me to educate myself about Mi'gmaq culture and gave me books on Algonquin-French religious encounters. When she invited me to be a support for her and a witness for her initiation into the Midewiwin society, she reminded me of how the Anishinaabe and Mi'gmaq were related peoples within the larger Algonquin linguistic family. When I told Bernadette Spence, a Cree friend, that I had given up looking for any Mi'gmaq ancestry, she reminded me about the "lost ones," those who had chosen to go underground in eastern Canada as it was easier to do that than to maintain an Indigenous identity in the face of racism. She once gave me a wristband that resembled a Métis sash to remind me to acknowledge that part of my ancestry. I was very moved by this. When I shared with Bonnie Hanuse, who is of Kwakwaka'wakw and Coastal Salish ancestry, my exchange with the woman who suggested I take a blood test, Bonnie just gave me a hug and encouraged me to not hide whatever connection I have in my ancestry to the Mi'gmaq. Recently, a Kahnawake Mohawk Elder, Niioieren Patton, told me that I should not be afraid to mention even distant Indigenous heritage as for so long people were ashamed of it. With all these women, I sensed an attitude of non-judgment and the practice of non-intervention, something like, "we will support you in whatever you figure out." So it has not been easy.

Another factor that has made it challenging to move beyond the connection between blood and identity has been my looks. Black writer Wayde Compton introduced me to the term "pheneticization." Drawn from biology, it means that a person is classified on the basis of observed physical characteristics. In Quebec, I was occasionally pheneticized as Indigenous. This was by older French Québécois, many of whom believe they too have Indigenous ancestry. But I have blue-green eyes, dark brown hair, and high cheekbones. In British Columbia, where colonization has been more recent and there has been less assimilation, I have rarely been pheneticized as Indigenous. Yet one day, when I had long hair, I had a real wake-up call. I had donned a black jacket with a Thunderbird crest on the back – a jacket that I had borrowed from Alannah during a storm. I was walking on a road near a park in Victoria when not one but two pick-up trucks carrying some rough-looking white guys slowed down beside me. The guys in the first one offered me a ride, which I refused; I fled into the woods when the second one slowed down. That was probably the most powerful teaching experience of pheneticization I ever had as it showed me how easily Native women are racialized as sexual targets because of their looks.

The question of Indigenous ancestry has always been complicated in Quebec. Early French colonial policies had encouraged intermarriage with Native women as a strategy to facilitate assimilation, a strategy that backfired as the men often "went Native." Many Québécois therefore claim they have Native ancestry, and some Québécois maintain that as much as a half to three-quarters of Quebecers have at least one Aboriginal ancestor. A group has recently emerged in Beauharnois, near Montreal, calling itself the Mikinaks, apparently Quebec's newest Aboriginal community. To become a member, one only has to have an Aboriginal ancestor somewhere in one's genealogy, even as far back as several generations, and pay eighty dollars. The members of this group want to have the same rights as status Indians, which has resulted in considerable animosity expressed by members of the nearby Mohawk community of Kahnawake.[12]

The blood controversy extends to who claims to be Metis. I agree with Métis writer Chelsea Vowels's critique of John Ralston Saul's *A Fair Country: Telling Truths about Canada*, in which he claims that Canada is a Métis nation.[13] For me, Saul's argument that Canada's culture is shaped as much by the Indigenous peoples as by the French and English represents a denial of settler responsibility for our colonial history and the fact that we are still occupying stolen land. Vowel is rightly annoyed at how Saul's book implies that anybody with any Indigenous ancestry, no matter how far back, is Métis, and she ties his work to what Eve Tuck and Wayne Yang call a settler "move to innocence."[14] What has annoyed me even more than Saul's book is the film *L'Empreinte*, directed by Carole Poliquin and Yvan Dubuc, and also discussed by Vowel. This Quebec film came out in 2015 and documents the actor Roy Dupuis looking for the roots of the Québécois identity.[15] He romanticizes the relationships of early generations of French settlers with Indigenous peoples. He claims that the reason that Quebecers have a strong sense of collective identity is that generations of them are of mixed blood and have inherited the Indigenous valuing of the collective over the individual. As someone growing up in a Quebec that was and still is deeply racist, I am of the unpopular opinion in secular Quebec that it is the heritage of the Roman Catholic Church that has shaped the mentality of many in Quebec who, through vital social movements, work for the collective good, not some distant blood connection to the First Peoples.

In the twenty-first century in Quebec, it is "cool" to identify with Indigenous people, so racism has gradually shifted from looking upon the ignorant savage with superiority and contempt to romanticizing the noble warrior and beautiful princess. In 2011, I was sharing with Jean-François Lozier, a historian of New France, the information that my background, like that of many Québécois, was unclear. He wryly answered: "everyone is looking for the Indian Princess in the family." I gulped, "Oh God, is that me?" Even if I had given up "looking," I still harboured the belief, like many Quebecers, that I did have some Indigenous ancestor. If I am critically aware of the romanticization of Native people, how is the search for a "blood" ancestor not racist?

In 2013, I discovered Pam Palmater's book, *Beyond Blood: Rethinking Aboriginal Identity and Belonging*.[16] I had started paying attention to Palmater when she was runner-up to Shawn Atleo in the 2012 elections for chief of the Assembly of First Nations. She is a lawyer and has been a strong voice for the Idle No More movement and occupies the chair of Indigenous Governance at Ryerson University. Most important for me, she is Mi'kmaq, from Eel River in New Brunswick. She was raised as non-status because her mother had lost her status. Her book documents her journey to define Indigenous identity in a way that excludes the racism of blood quantum, biological characteristics, and government legal interference. Palmater states clearly what I had slowly, and agonizingly, worked out for myself over these years. She identifies criteria that individuals need to meet in order to be citizens of an Indigenous nation and members of a specific community. One is ancestral connection, which she defines as having common histories, families, communities, territories, and treaties. She states that this leaves out someone whose parents or grandparents or great-grandparents identified as Acadians, who have always identified with French language and culture, and who then discover that somewhere in the family they have a Mi'kmaq ancestor. This could be me (except my family was not Acadian). She includes those who think they have an Indigenous ancestor because of biological characteristics perceptible in relatives in old photos. Thank goodness I had let go of that one! Palmater sees these claims as being about blood quantum, not about connections; and it is connections – that is, relationships – that matter.

Palmater's work is extremely important in a context within which debates about identity are raging, as seen in the recent social media flurry about renowned author Joseph Boyden, who has been rightfully challenged for misrepresenting his ancestry as Indigenous. She has two other points that are equally significant in terms of defining Indigenous identity: (1) what she calls civic loyalty, or commitment to the survival of the Mi'kmaq Nation, and (2) respect for Mi'kmaq language, customs, traditions, and practices.[17] In the dominant Euro-Western culture in which I grew up, my search for identity has been very much an individual process. In Indigenous cultures, as Palmater says, Indigenous identity is formed through the relations between individuals and nations.[18] The rights of the individual are balanced with the right of nations to determine their identities and who can be their citizens. And it is a relational process, with the nation, the land, and ancestral connections.

This understanding of Indigenous identity as a relational process was reinforced for me in Lawrence Hill's book *Blood*.[19] I like how he insists that it is wrong to see the mixed heritage of Métis people as negative because many of us are of mixed heritage, be it Indigenous, Black, European, or Asian, among others. The Métis distinction has been another nefarious legacy of the Indian Act. Métis people are Aboriginal people with a distinct culture and sense of nation, both of which are passed on through the generations; they are not "less than." In 2016, when the Supreme Court of Canada ruled on the *Daniels* case, which recognized Métis and non-status people as Indians under the Canadian Constitution, my Métis friend Marjorie Beaucage just laughed and said,

"I'll never be an 'Indian.' I am otipimsewak, the people who own them-selves no matter what the government says."[20]

What does all this mean for "blood memory"? This is a concept that has been of interest to me as someone who is trained in body therapies and is aware of how the body holds one's history in muscles and cells. Some of my Indigenous friends describe my attachment to Gespe'gewa'gi and Port Daniel as blood memory. I have heard the term used to explain how Indigenous people who were raised white because they were adopted during the period known as "the Sixties Scoop" were later drawn back to their ancestral communities. Palmater argues that this phrase does not refer to actual blood but, rather, to the "deep connections with our past through our ancestors, with our present thorough our families and communities, and to our future through generations yet to come."[21]

I recently had a moment when I was in Gespe'gewa'gi and drove over the Gesgapegiag (Cascapedia) River bridge on my way to the community of Gesgapegiag. I noticed my body relaxing, softening – in a sense, feeling at home. Grand Cascapedia had been the home of my grandfather, great-grandfather, and great-great-grandfather and their families, and that river had been part of their livelihood. I have always felt a connection to the land of the Coast, possibly because I spent every summer of my childhood and youth in Port Daniel from the age of one, possibly because my father was deeply connected to his roots and passed this on to me. Later, when I mentioned this visceral feeling to Gesgapegiag Elder Pnnal Jerome, he commented that our ancestors' DNA continues in us. While I agree with the critique of DNA theories of ancestry advanced by Kim Tallbear, Cheyenne and Arapaho, who argues that DNA testing is a new form of racial science that can under-mine tribal sovereignty, I am also comfortable with Pnnal's reading.[22] I was experiencing a felt connection to a river that had been part of my ancestors' lives for a few generations.

Sometimes my head swims as I try to figure out my own truth in the midst of all this. Underlying all the race dynamics of identity, there is a relational truth that has stayed with me over the years. In 2005, I was attending Midewiwin initiation ceremonies in Bad River, Wisconsin. I decided to take a break to join Dawn Marsden, an Anishinaabe col-league who was at that time finishing her PhD at UBC. I was still unclear about how to name my ancestry and was feeling a bit uncomfortable

about being there, as few white people are invited to Midewiwin ceremonies. In our conversation, possibly because I felt the need to justify
my presence there, I mentioned that I was struggling with the issue of
distant Mi'gmaq ancestry. Without hesitation or judgment, Dawn said to
me, "what is important is that we are responsible for seven generations
before us and seven generations after us." Through the years, this remark
has stayed with me, reminding me that what is important is relationship
and responsibility for our ancestry and progeny, regardless of race.

It is this vision that has informed my research into my family's history.
Whether I do or don't have a Mi'gmaq ancestor, I can be responsible for
honouring both the memory and the ongoing presence of the Mi'gmaq
in the Gaspé, and for looking at my family's role in that history. It is so
convenient, and of course useful, for colonialism to foster the individualism that encourages no sense of connection to our ancestry, never
mind a sense of historical responsibility. Though there are, of course,
both good and bad stories to uncover, it is clear that my family was
implicated in the ongoing colonization of the Gaspé and the displacement of the Mi'gmaq. No blood test could avoid the fact that I have a
responsibility here. If a large part of my ancestral past was premised
on rendering the Mi'gmaq peoples invisible, then that history needs to
come to light.

Nothing is ever "black and white." My dear friends, who chose not to
judge, but to support me in my journey, were practising what I now see
as elements of Indigenous ethics or values. To not judge another as being
right or wrong is part of the process of seeking balanced relationships.
The value of non-interference – to not interfere in someone's process –
is a common Indigenous child-raising practice. This meant leaving it
to me to figure out my ancestry myself. Another value I've observed
in practice is to support whatever strengths or gifts one brings to the
table. With all these women, I sensed respect for my work in the area of
religions and traditions, and for my own journey as a spiritual seeker.
These women are all on a spiritual path themselves, as ceremonial leaders, Elders, mothers, and grandmothers. They have all been personally
affected by the Indian Act, which has either taken away their status or
that of their grandchildren, and yet each of them in her own way has
pulled herself out of the morass of blood racism and is more interested
in finding our common humanity.

I no longer feel uncomfortable in describing my ancestry, especially when I am teaching or leading workshops and modelling the importance of identifying one's ancestry. I say I am from Quebec, with a settler background of roughly twelve generations in Quebec on my father's side and four on my mother's; that I have French, Scottish, Irish, and English ancestry; and that there may have been some intermarriage with the Mi'gmaq on the French side but that that does not make me Mi'gmaq. Especially when teaching, I like to share how tracking the blood trail was a dead end for me and that I now live out my responsibilities as a settler aware of my family colonial history and as someone who has made relationships over the years in "Indian Country." It is my relationships that define me, not my blood.

Unmapping

If I didn't have Mi'gmaq blood, did that exonerate me from having any relationship with the Mi'gmaq? Definitely not, as I would eventually discover. In 2005, the Mi'gmaq of the seventh district of Mi'gma'gi published a document titled *Nm'tginen: Me'mnaq Ejiglignmuetueg Gis Na Naqtmueg*, the Statement of Claim to Aboriginal Rights and Title of their lands.[1] On the inside cover is a map that illustrates their primary claim area based on research conducted on their traditional land use. It covers an area that includes the entire Gaspé Peninsula in Quebec and extends south to Edmunston in New Brunswick and west to the south shore of the St Lawrence River past Rimouski before reaching to the east in New Brunswick past Meteapenagiag, at the mouth of the Miramachi River. Mi'gma'gi, or Mi'kma'ki, is the name for the land of the entire Mi'kmaq Nation. This area comprises the seventh district of Mi'gma'gi, which extends from the Gaspé throughout the Maritimes and includes Prince Edward Island and Newfoundland. These boundaries were shaped by the communal land needs of the families in each territory, and each district had and has its own government.[2] This assertion of title in *Nm'tginen* is a rewriting of history and an indictment of those who carved up the land into grids and provinces so that settlers could have "private property."

I spent all my summers until I was sixteen on the Gaspé coast. Since 2000, I have returned annually with the aim of reconnecting with a landscape I have always loved and felt at home in, and to discover more about my ancestry on my father's side. In 2006, on one of these trips, I had picked up the *Nm'tginen* document from the Mi'gmawei Mawiomi Secretariat, delighted with its comprehensiveness as well as with its grounding in traditional Mi'gmaq teachings.[3] I showed it to a few family members and friends. One just smirked and was not interested in even looking at it. A colleague from my theology circles, who had retired

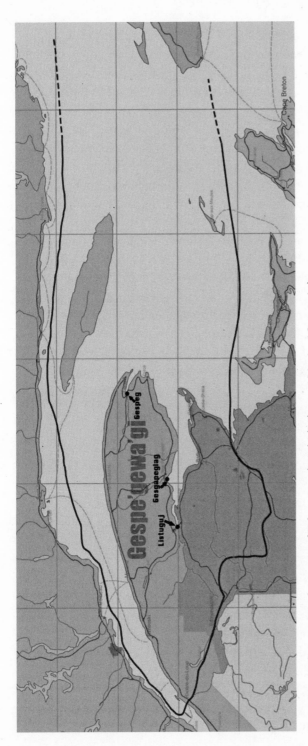

Figure 8.1   Nm'tginen map of statement of Title to Gespe'gewa'gi (Mi'gmawei Mawiomi Secretariat)

to the Gaspé coast, acknowledged the document, but put the copy I gave her on an unread pile and never mentioned the Mi'gmaq claim again. Another relative, my dad's cousin's widow then living in Port Daniel, who claimed to be interested in family history and genealogy, was also dismissive.

If ignoring the Mi'gmag claim was the attitude of some, I encountered another response that was perhaps more honest. Fred Metallic from Listuguj had asked me if I had any Catholic contacts who could help track down several sacred Mi'gmaq cultural materials that had been taken by one of the now-deceased priests who had served in their community. This priest, like many other missionaries, had over the years acquired many Mi'gmaq "artefacts" so that he could have his own exotic museum. I eagerly offered to help Fred, as I was feeling both guilty and responsible as a Catholic for how the Catholic Church had contributed to the attempts to systematically erase Indigenous culture and identity. However, I had few contacts in Quebec, having only recently returned after a long period away. But I did know an Ursuline sister in Rimouski, Monique Dumais, who was a feminist theologian and fairly progressive.[4] I decided to ask her to help me. She knew of the priest who had spent his final years at St Anne des Monts and she promised me she would do something. Thinking I would motivate her to act quickly, I showed her the *Nm'tginen* document with the claim area. She looked at it and then said forcefully, "I don't think so!" I sensed not only disbelief but perhaps some hostility, an attitude of "how dare they! This is not their land."

A year later Monique contacted me with details of where the priest's "collection" was held. It wasn't a question of how difficult it was to find, but more that she realized it was right to return the sacred objects. I admire her for shifting her perspective, which must have been hard for someone from a religious order that had been originally called to New France to educate "the daughters of the natives" in the early part of the seventeenth century.[5] The Ursulines continued to educate young girls and women into the twentieth century, including establishing a convent in Rimouski and in the town of Gaspé. Monique's identity was grounded in this history and in a love of Quebec. I suspect that it wasn't the actual Statement of Claim that unnerved her or the others to whom I had shown it. Nor was it the traditional teachings or historical photos of Mi'gmaq from earlier generations that made them uncomfortable.

It was the map on the inside cover. I could hear the unspoken voices: "there were no Micmac living here!" and "this is our land!"

This response is not uncommon among settlers. It gets even more complicated in Quebec, where nationalism is strong among French-speaking Québécois who regard both their language and their territory as a bulwark against English Canada. Just as history is written by the victors, so maps are made by the conquerors. Having lived for over thirty years in British Columbia, I know well that the question of Indigenous Title to lands is greatly contested, especially where there are no treaties. Counter-mapping, the creation of maps that represent Indigenous occupation and use of territory, has become a common strategy throughout Canada as Indigenous nations claim their Indigenous Rights to territories that were either never ceded/surrendered to the colonizers or were part of treaty relationships.[6] Like many of these nations, the Mi'gmaq have engaged in rigorous research to back up their claims, through interviewing Elders, conducting land use surveys, uncovering traditional place names, and mining oral traditions that reveal specific connections to the land. Yet most settlers are neither aware of nor interested in this work, avoiding what it may mean for their privileged lives. Most, like my family, deny the collective memory of Indigenous presence on the land upon which they live or lived. Often these settler families have lived and worked for many years in a specific community, sometimes for several generations, and have a strong sense of entitlement to ownership of their land.

The Mi'gmaq claim brought my family's history and its relationship to the land and waterways of the Gaspé Peninsula into question. What does it mean to have a different map of a place you had always understood in a certain way? How would it affect my own relationship to this land? I spent part of my summers over the next decade exploring this question. This has meant re-storying my own past and sense of place. It has led me on a fascinating quest, almost like a treasure hunt. The Mi'gmaq have their own story of this land, but I wondered how I could "retrospeculate," a term I learned from black historian and writer Wayde Compton, in order to resist and transform the settler narrative that has suppressed Mi'gmaq realities.[7] What does it mean to unlearn or unmap the map, as one metaphor for decolonization?

Up until my encounter with this new map, I had known Port Daniel as the home and birthplace of my father and the place of my grandfather's business. My grandfather had been quite an entrepreneur and had owned a large sawmill and a hardware store. The mill was the main industry in Port Daniel from about the time of the First World War and was run by my family members until the mid-1980s when it mysteriously burned down. The other town I knew as a child was Cascapedia, where my grandfather was born and where my grandfather and dad had gone fishing for salmon. There was a hospital nearby in the town of Maria, where some relatives lived. These were the facts that I knew when I started my investigation.

Equipped with new eyes, I went back to some markers in Port Daniel that I had not paid much attention to previously. The first was a large wooden cross, without a human figure and painted brown, with the date 1534 and Jacques Cartier's name carved in faded letters on the arms. It stood on a small point facing the Baie de Chaleur on the narrow road to McGuiness Cove. For many locals, the cross represents the village's assertion to being the first place where Cartier landed and claimed the land for New France.

However, this is a somewhat distorted reading of the facts. Jacques Cartier's journal is more useful, and it tells us that this is where he first encountered the Mi'gmaq. He recorded that about two hundred Mi'qmaq arrived in their canoes to greet his ship when he first arrived.[8] It was in Port Daniel Bay that Jacques Cartier first anchored and where his ship stayed for eight days. Here he had his first exchanges with the actual inhabitants of the country, was welcomed by the friendly Mi'gmaq to their territory, and traded with them for furs. Cartier noted that the Mi'gmaq wanted European products for their furs, which meant that this sheltered bay had already been used for the purposes of trade with Basque and Portuguese fishers.[9] Whether Cartier actually landed and planted a cross here is not clear from his journals. But what is significant is that, where that stark wooden cross stands, there is no mention of this Mi'gmaq welcome, nor is there mention of it in the town's official history book, which was published in 2005.

Histoires et souvenirs was written to commemorate the town's 150th anniversary as an official municipality.[10] The authors do acknowledge the Mi'gmaq traditional place name for Port Daniel – Epsegeneg, "the place where one warms up."[11] The book begins with Jacques Cartier and omits any reference to the Mi'gmaq who greeted him when he arrived on 4 July 1534. What is important for the authors is that Port Daniel

Figure 8.2   Picture of Indian at the Musée
Maison Legrand

was first named by Cartier as Conche Saint Martin in honour of Saint
Martin, who was the saint of the day in the French Catholic liturgical
tradition. Most significant, according to *Histoires et souvenirs*, is that
this was not only the first place Cartier set foot in North America but
also where the first Mass was said.[12] Accordingly, the book's first chapter
is titled "Berceau de la Nouvelle France" (Cradle of New France).[13] This
claim is hotly contested by the town of Gaspé, which maintains that
Cartier planted the cross there to claim "Canada" for France.

Somewhat frustrated with the village's official published history, I
then turned to the town museum, located in the former Hotel Legrand.
The museum is on the first floor of the town hall and tells the story
of the Legrand family, their hotel, and the travelling salesmen who
frequented it. The building, with its licorne windows and copper roof,
is a magnificent monument to nineteenth- and early twentieth-century
Quebec architecture. It looks over the bay and the beach between two
rivers, the Little Port Daniel River and the Port Daniel River, that flow

through the town out to the ocean. In its heyday, the Hotel Legrand was the stopping point for travelling peddlers, tourists on their way to Percé, and businessmen in the fishing and forestry industries. Now, there is a small library on the main floor and two large rooms devoted to exhibiting the kitchen, dining room, and bedrooms of the old hotel. There is no mention of Mi'gmaq in here.

However, outside the building are several life-size figures made out of what seems to be papier mâché painted over with a shiny lacquer. At one end are Monsieur and Madame Legrand. At the other end, a travelling salesman stands with his suitcase of wares besides his horse and carriage. In the front is Jacques Cartier and, off to the back, is an "Indian." The placement of this figure is significant. He represents the distant past. This rather bizarre character is wearing what seems to be a short deerskin tunic and is carrying a single feather in one hand and a fish in the other. Beside him is a plaque noting that the Micmac had spent the summers here, had greeted Jacques Cartier, and had called the bay "Epsegeneg."[14] There is an acknowledgment that the Gaspé Peninsula was criss-crossed by this "nomadic" people and that Epsegeneg was part of Micmac territory. This plaque is the only record of Mi'gmaq presence at this site.

How does a seasonal encampment of a thriving Mi'gmaq group of families become a settler village and later a municipality where Mi'gmaq presence is now only represented by the plaster Indian outside the museum? The official story is that there were no Micmac in Port Daniel when settler history began and none now. This is an example of "the vanishing Indian" trope in which Indians belong to the past and any living Indians are mere remnants of a long ago time. This view is reinforced by the colonizer's description of the Micmac as "nomadic" peoples and hence as not connected to specific places. "Nomadic" is a Western term that denies the complex relationship with land and waterways that is integral to hunting and gathering peoples. It is a convenient concept used to relegate a people to "pre-history," and it reflects a profound ignorance of the nature of Mi'gmaq life and connection to the land.

The reality was that "the occupation of Mi'gma'gi was organized by the Mi'gmaq according to a precise geographical use, and according to cycles dictated by Mi'gmaq rules of law."[15] In 1768, the well-known Jersey merchant Charles Robin noted that families returned to the same sites year after year.[16] Like many Indigenous peoples who lived by hunting, fishing, and gathering, for centuries the Mi'gmaq moved seasonally from one region of the Gaspé to another. They returned to specific areas depending on needs for food and shelter. Families travelled lightly, often by canoe, taking their wigwams with them when they moved. Each family constellation was allocated an area of territory. There was nothing random about their movements.

Unacknowledged and unrecognized by both the French- and the English-speaking settlers who followed them was the fact that the Mi'gmaq used the full range of the lands and resources on the Gaspé Peninsula, which they called Gespe'gewa'gi. They not only hunted and fished but also harvested plants for food and medicines, gathered roots and berries, and used the trees for baskets, furniture, and canoes. They made nets from the trees and fibrous plants and implements from stone. In the winter months, they moved into the interior to hunt and to escape the strong winds and tides of the Atlantic. Like most Indigenous peoples, they survived because they used the resources within the entire extent of their territory. This relationship to land was not only functional but also central to their spiritual and political worldview, and it was guided by the Mi'gmaq system of governance.[17] Hence the map in the *Nm'tginen* document records the entire territory on which the Mi'gmaq sustained their lives.

However, with forests hugging the shore and no visible structures or ruins to mark Mi'gmaq space, early settlers treated these lands as terra nullius (vacant land). This was a concept developed by the French and English to complement the even more pernicious Doctrine of Discovery that had been declared by Catholic popes in the fifteenth century. The Doctrine of Discovery, as first applied to the Americas by Pope Alexander VI in a papal bull, was based on fifteenth-century theological assumptions and held that Indigenous peoples, as non-Christians, could not claim ownership of their land, only rights of occupation and use.[18] The pope gave exploring nations title to all the land that they allegedly "discovered" "in order to pursue the 'holy and laudable work' of expanding the Christian world."[19] The French and English used the concept of terra nullius to further justify their title, claiming that, because these lands were neither farmed nor developed in an acceptable European manner but, rather, were only used for migratory subsistence, they were in fact empty.[20] Undergirding the concept of terra nullius was the legal

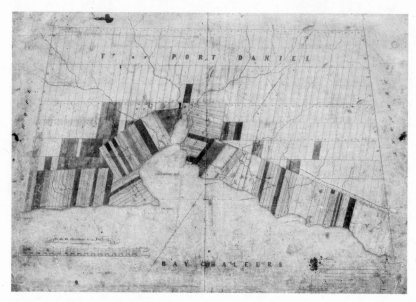

Figure 8.3   1756 map of Port Daniel

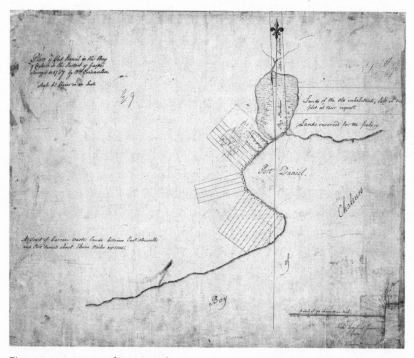

Figure 8.4   1787 map of Port Daniel

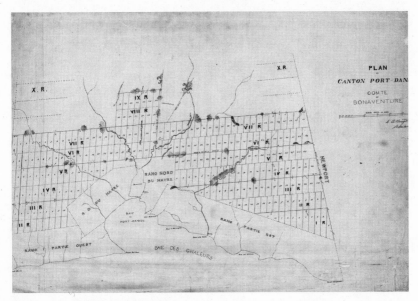

Figure 8.5   1888 map of Port Daniel

rule of "first possession," the idea that land was "open to the first taker,"
itself premised on the belief that wild and uncultivated land needs to be
conquered.[21] The Europeans saw themselves as outsiders, as conquerors of nature, and could not recognize the ways in which Indigenous
peoples related to the land.[22]

How did the title of the conquerors get enforced? Long before the
reserve system was established in Lower Canada, the Europeans had
divided up the land for settlers. Nowhere is this more visible than in
maps. Europeans loved to map land, to demarcate lines, boundaries,
and declarations of property. But maps are not innocent, particularly
when the land is contested. I learned from my friend Jo Roberts, an
English Canadian writer and scholar, how the British and Israelis used
maps to erase Palestinian memory in the context of the conflict in Israel
and Palestine. As Roberts writes, citing cartographer Denis Wood, a
"'map does not *map locations* so much as *create ownership at a location*,
it is the ownership ... [that] the map is bringing into being.'"[23] Maps
were one of the major weapons used against the Mi'gmaq of the Gaspé.

So I set out on a quest to uncover early maps of the Gaspé. I was
fortunate to have a friend in Port Daniel, Madeleine Quesnel, who

is a diligent researcher of the town's history. In her late seventies, Madeleine is a small woman with short wiry grey hair, glasses, and an aura of serious intensity. Her particular passion is the historical geography of the village, how history has shaped the land. Her father was the village doctor when I was a child, and Madeleine herself is a retired civil servant who worked for the Quebec government in Quebec City. She showed me how to gain access to the earliest topographical maps of the village from the Archives national in Quebec City. On one of my visits I spent hours with her looking at maps.

The French had not mapped in the same way as had the English. From a later surveyor's comments I discovered that the French had a system of surveying that involved allocating large plots of land to a seigneur and his heirs in perpetuity; these were usually demarcated by a river or ocean boundary and the neighbouring seigneurie. The seigneur was given the rights "to high and moderate justice, to hunting and fishing in the area and treaty with the Indians, effecting treaties with the Indians both within and without."[24] Many seigneuries were eventually subdivided, "with the view of protecting the settlers from the incursions of the savages at the time, in long and narrow lots."[25] The area around Port Daniel was allocated to the Seigneurie Deneau in 1696. It seems this land was left largely unexploited during the French Regime. Madeleine and I did not find a map of the Seigneurie Deneau, but, with the click of a mouse, there were other telling maps available.

First there was the earliest map of Port Daniel, made in 1765, six years after the battle of the Plains of Abraham at which the English defeated the French. I didn't know much about what had happened in the Gaspé during this period and was shocked when Madeleine bitterly commented that the English had burned down whole villages. She sent me an article in which I discovered that, in the fall of 1758, the British, under General Wolfe, began systematically burning French houses in the area of the town of Gaspé. This was part of the Seven Years War between the French and the English, which played out in the Maritime region between 1755 and 1758. In this war, the Mi'gmaq took the side of the French. In early 1759, Wolfe's troops moved further into the Baie de Chaleur, burning homes, boats, and fishing nets in Pabos, Grand Rivière, Ile Bonaventure, and (again) Gaspé.[26] In the summer of 1760, the French and their allies, the Mi'gmaq, were finally defeated in the Baie de Chaleur region at the Battle of Restigouche. This meant the end of French occupation of the Gaspé. In November of the same year the British made a peace treaty with the Mi'gmaq.[27]

In the records of Captain Bell, General Wolfe's aide-de-camp, there is a brief reference to Port Daniel as the chief settlement of the French.[28] Perhaps this is why the earliest township map on record, in 1765, is that of Port Daniel (figure 8.3). My guess is that Port Daniel was the first area surveyed by the English in Lower Canada, not only because of its strategic importance but also because of its bountiful fishing and its safe port access. The map identified the lots that English settlers could now occupy. On this map, we see that not only is the entire frontage on the Bay divided up into ranges with lots of fifty acres each but also that these lots extend several miles into the forest behind. Here the English practised what historical geographer Cole Harris calls "cartographic erasure," referring to "the colonial practice of 'mapping out,' through the use of blank white space, the Indigenous people, their traditional seasonal settlements, and their lives from official documents."[29]

In the next map that Madeleine and I looked at, dating from 1787, she pointed out to me how the French settlers were pushed to the east side of the Port Daniel River and allocated no specific allotments. This land is described on the map as "reserved for the old inhabitants, left in one plot per their request" (figure 8.4). On the same side of the bay are lands reserved for the fishery – that is, an area claimed as public lands. A small strip of beach near the Port Daniel Harbour is not allotted. All the land west of the river is allotted and claimed by settlers. There is no place for those whom the French called "les sauvages" here.[30] These maps served to legitimate private property on land that the Mi'gmaq viewed not as something to be "owned" but, rather, as something shared with all creatures under Mi'gmaq law. Part of the terra nullius concept of empty land was that land that was not used for agriculture or buildings (i.e., was unimproved, unused) was a blank slate and therefore eligible for appropriation and occupation.[31]

Another map that Madeleine and I investigated, written in French and dated 1888, was produced in the period when the Quebec government was promoting the Gaspé for "colonization," the word the province used to promote settlement in outlying areas. This map (figure 8.5) concentrates on farming and wood lots behind the town. However, it is clear that the entire area around Port Daniel Bay is now divided into named ranges to a point at which the mapping of the next region,

Newport, begins. The beach area has now been absorbed into several of the lots, and the beach delineated between the Little Port Daniel River and the Port Daniel River is getting smaller and smaller. By the 1880s, there is no "public" space left on the map. The only "free" space has been reduced to a shifting tidal area.

Together, these maps reveal what happened to Mi'gmaq territory due to settler incursion onto the land around the bay. The last map reveals, with the allocation of woodlots, an ever deeper penetration into the forest. When Napoleon blockaded the English, the British could not get wood from Europe for the construction of their naval boats, and so they turned to the colonies, first to Newfoundland, and then to the Gaspé coast. By the mid-nineteenth century, the mapping and leasing of woodlots had expanded up and down the coast, with sawmills in most of the towns. Forestry was to become the second major industry after fishing, supplying tons of wood to Europe and later to New England. By the early twentieth century, the English had been replaced by Americans as major owners of the forestry licences on the coast. The American market was soon more important than that of Europe, with its mills providing wood for railway ties and construction, and pulp for the growing paper industry.[32] Interestingly, Madeleine shared a saying she heard as a child, "Behind every tree is an Indian so better to cut down the tree."

To facilitate this process of transforming the Gaspé into private property and woodlots, in 1853 the Province of Canada established two Indian reserves on the south shore of the Baie de Chaleur – Maria and Restigouche. These are now known by their Mi'gmaq names, Gesgapegiag and Listuguj. These reserves were small enclaves in which Native people were confined, a further step in reducing their territorial boundaries. Cole Harris calls the reserve creation process one of "making Native space," further reinforcing the legitimacy of private property and unhindered resource extraction.[33] Soon the Mi'gmaq were considered trespassers in their own land. There eventually developed, by the mid-twentieth century, a common understanding among non-Natives that reserves were the only places where Indians lived.

Most Gaspesians were and remain ignorant of the Indian Act, 1876, and its function of dividing Indians into status (those who could live on the reserve) and non-status (those who could not). The latter included both Native women who had married "out" and Metis. The status/non-status distinction served to reinforce the idea that only those who lived on reserves were "real" Indians. As well, the federal government chose to ignore the not insignificant number of Mi'gmaq in the area around the town of Gaspé, providing no reserve for them due to the commercial value of this end of the peninsula, which was soon to become the economic hub of the region. Accordingly, many Indigenous peoples who lived throughout the Gaspé region became invisible, with many choosing to remain that way because of the rampant racism.

But had the Mi'gmaq really disappeared long ago from Port Daniel? One summer when I was visiting Madeleine, she invited over one of the older people in the village who still had a memory of earlier times. Omer Brunet was in his late eighties when we met in 2009. A once tall man, he was shrivelled with old age and had driven to Madeleine's house. He was happy to share coffee with us and talk. Omer's father had been the doctor for the village before Dr Quesnel, Madeleine's dad. His family had lived in a large house facing the beach, between the two Port Daniel rivers. He told us how, as a small boy, he had seen Indians from Maria by the side of the road in front of his house selling handcrafted tables and chairs made from trees and branches. He said the Indians had camped on the edge of the barachois, which was an intertidal area, a lagoon of sorts, created by a sandbar between the two rivers. His mother had shared stories with him about how the Mi'gmaq had appeared seasonally and lived on the beach during the summers.

On his next visit to Madeleine's, Omer brought two folded and aged pieces of paper, both documents written by his mother, Ida LeGrand. One was in a shaky script, dated 1990, when Ida was ninety-two. The other page was typewritten, transcribed by Omer, and did not have a date. I was fascinated by these documents. Ida's parents had owned and operated the Hotel LeGrand. Ida wrote about her great-grandparents arriving from Scotland via New Brunswick and Bonaventure, and then coming to Port Daniel after making the acquaintance of a Mr Carter, "who had a store for trading with the Indians, i.e. for food, and he bought baskets, etc. etc. for pay." In both documents Ida describes the Indians as "pleasant and friendly" and records how they went to the English bringing gifts and expecting presents in return, "especially white bread which they loved." In the second document, she adds how her great-aunt Hannah Lauder, who owned the first hotel in town before the LeGrands, from the mid- to late nineteenth century, had told her how the Indians "would arrive suddenly out of the woods and come visit the Lauder home, expecting gifts and bringing some." Ida then segues into a story that her aunt told her about a chief who frequented Port Daniel, who was said to have taken the name Peter Baskat. To this, Hannah asked, "Why do they always take the names of kitchen items?" She mentioned that the chief "was a great admirer of Queen Victoria" and noted that he been able to visit the Queen in England and exchange gifts "after the intervention of a county deputy." Hannah added: "I hope he didn't wear those terrible moccasins to visit the queen!"[34]

These two documents provide a wealth of information about settler perceptions of the Mi'gmaq in the late nineteenth century as well as their misinterpretation of Mi'gmaq interactions with them. It is not surprising that the Mi'gmaq were trading for bread with householders, considering that they were facing severe malnutrition and starvation as the result of disease and settler occupation of their lands. Rereading these settler stories, I was reminded that the Mi'gmag culture was based on reciprocity. In other words, giving and receiving gifts was the mechanism that ensured the proper functioning of their relationships. So, not surprisingly, they brought gifts for the settlers and expected gifts in return.

After rereading the story of the chief, I decided to ask Pnnal Jerome, a Gesgapegiag Elder, about it. I discovered that the chief's name was probably Basque, not Baskat. Pnnal told me that this family name continues to this day in both Gespeg and Listuguj. Hannah Lauder and Ida Brunet seemed surprised when the Indians were "pleasant," an image that clearly countered that of the warlike savages that the settlers were told to expect and fear. The patronizing tone used by Hannah Lauder to refer to the chief's visit to Queen Victoria reveals ignorance of the fact that the Mi'gmaq chiefs saw themselves as equal to European rulers. The Mi'gmaq chiefs were well aware that the Queen represented the Crown with whom they were in a treaty relationship. The Mi'gmaq were a proud people with a long history of autonomous negotiations with European powers, first a Concordat with the Vatican in 1610 and later the Peace and Friendship Treaties of 1749, 1752, and 1760–61 with the British.[35] This visit of the chief was an affirmation of his sense of authority and identity as a Mi'gmaq.

Beside Mi'gmaq from either the Gesgapegiag (Maria) area or the Gespeg (Gaspé) region who had come to trade in Port Daniel, possibly into the 1920s, there were Mi'gmaq who actually lived in the area. My colleague Dolores Contré-Migwans, an artist and cultural animator who is Métis, Anishinaabeh, and French, has mentioned to me that her mother grew up in Paspebiac, a town east of Port Daniel, and that her aunty, her mother's oldest sister, had married a Mi'gmaq from Port Daniel. Madeleine Quesnel told me how, when she was young, she would travel with her doctor father "up river" to visit Native families. Clearly, the Mi'gmaq were present in some settler memories well into the twentieth century.

After what I'd learned through my discussions with Madeleine, Omer, and Pnnal, I decided it was time to revisit Manon Jeannotte, whom I had met back in Montreal in 2003, and find out more about her family history and memories of the area. We met this time in Percé in 2010. It was late September and Manon was on her way to Montreal from Gespeg where she had spent the summer as director of the *Site D'Interprétation Micmac de Gespeg*. She was very willing to share details of her family's history in Port Daniel. Her great-great-grandfather, Jean Louis Jeannotte, had been born there in 1830 and had married in 1872. Her great-grandfather Olivier had lived in McGinnis Cove and had died in 1934. Both men had worked mainly as guides for non-Native hunters or forestry people. As guides, they would take these men through the thick woods on trails only they knew, sometimes even as far north as the town of Gaspé or across the peninsula. Manon added that her great-grandfather had been killed in the woods by a white man. Her grandfather Arthur had spent his youth in Port Daniel but had moved to Gaspé, where he had married a Wendat woman. It was there, in Douglastown, that Manon's father Oscar had been born. Like many Native men Oscar had to move to find work, and in 1956 he moved to Montreal for a job. When he retired he moved to the Laurentians in Kanien'keha:ka (Mohawk) territory. Manon had lived here with her parents, though she returned to Port Daniel every summer to visit family and her grandfather. One of the local lakes, Lac Caribou, is a sacred place for her family, one she revisits yearly. She recalled her grandfather teaching her to catch and boil lobster on the beach. He taught her to hunt and fish in the woods and lakes around the town. Manon told me that there were remnants of three Mi'gmaq families who had lived for several generations in Port Daniel – the Langlois, the Sinnets, and the Jeannottes. While there had been intermarriage both ways, Mi'gmaq men marrying French-speaking women over the generations or Mi'gmaq women marrying white men, those who lived there still retained a strong sense of Mi'gmaq identity and connection.

So why had my family members pretty consistently maintained that there were no Micmacs in Port Daniel? The fact I had been surprised to discover there were Mi'gmaq in the town was very much a product of my upbringing. I finally "got it" when, in the summer of 2015, I visited Denise McGinnis, a stained-glass artist who lives in McGinnis Cove with her companion, a retired construction worker by the name of Gustave Langlois. The house has bright yellow painted siding, a red metal roof, and pieces of blue, green, and orange glass covering the interior walls and stairway.

We engaged in the usual exchange that happens for me in Port Daniel. Gustave wanted to know who I was in terms of to whom I was related. By the time I had named cousins, uncles, and grandparents, Gustave had a pretty good idea of who I was. My family had owned the large sawmill that employed half the town. Gustave told me his dad had worked for my Uncle Norbert at the mill. Norbert, a large and friendly man, had been the only uncle of mine who had been liked by the workers. Despite this positive connection, Gustave still regarded me warily. In the course of the conversation, he made a remark about being in British Columbia for a short time doing construction work and not staying as there were fewer safety protections in place there than in Quebec. I commented that this was probably because the construction unions are more powerful in Quebec than they are in British Columbia, and I said this in a way that indicated I was pro-union. I then mentioned that I had worked for the Hospital Employees Union in British Columbia, after which I could see Gustave visibly warm up to me. When I told them I was writing about the erasure of Mi'gmaq presence in the town, Gustave just laughed and, with a finger pointing north, said there were more Mi'gmaq upriver.

I left that visit with a new insight. The presumed non-existence of Mi'gmaq was a story created by my family's class and race blinders. My family lived on "the other side" of the river. The poor French workers and the Mi'gmaq lived in what was known as Port Daniel East. The bilingual French and the anglophones, who were mostly of Scottish and Irish heritage, lived in the centre of town or Port Daniel West. Madeleine had once remarked that, at one time, my grandfather "owned" the town. The Nadeau family had been of the gentry class and, in the hierarchy of race and ethnicity in Quebec, therefore very white. My dad's family had become Anglicized by being bilingual, which gave them the keys to work with the American and English-speaking industry owners. For years, I had assumed my family was a benign influence in the town, a provider of jobs like any small business owner. Because of my grandfather's Chiac French, and what my mother considered bad table manners, I considered him to be far from gentry, and I considered the family to be more like the petty bourgeoisie that I had learned about in my Marxist days.[36] But power and privilege function differently in different contexts, and I was gradually uncovering that fact that some of my family members had actually played a role in dispossessing the Mi'gmaq of their territory. There was clearly more personal unmapping for me to do.

On both sides of my dad's family, the Nadeaux and the Gagnons, the first settlers had arrived in "New France" over twelve generations ago. While the Gagnons had moved to Baie de Sables on the St Lawrence River side of the Gaspé Peninsula in the mid-1700s, the Nadeaux only arrived on the Gaspé coast in the late 1800s. My great-grandfather Pierre Nadeau had moved to Grand Cascapedia from New Brunswick in 1871. He had been a building contractor and a full-time entrepreneur. He opened a sawmill, a sash and door factory, a cheese factory, a store, and a boarding house for his workers.[37] He owned several tree farm licences to feed the mill. He had numerous building contracts between New Richmond and Dalhousie in New Brunswick, including the two infamous Protestant churches that had so annoyed the local Catholic bishops that he had been excommunicated twice. From a second cousin, Bernard Nadeau, I discovered that in 1902 my great-grandfather had built the Native school on the Restigouche reserve. When I look at the few grainy black-and-white grainy photos of the mill, the factory, and the workers in Grand Cascapedia, it is difficult for me to see whether he had hired any Micmac workers. Pnnal Jerome told me that, rather than mill work, it was log driving and sorting – the most dangerous jobs in logging – that went to the Indians.

Pierre, also known as Peter Nadeau in the mostly English-speaking village of Grand Cascapedia, was also prolific in terms of his paternity. He had twelve children from his two different wives, the Scottish McIntyre sisters, whose father had been a bootlegger in New Brunswick. A few of Pierre's sons became involved in the business, and in 1911 he bought a small sawmill in Port Daniel with his son John. Visible on a 1912 Port Daniel map that Madeleine has is a lot on the east side of the barachois that bore Pierre's name, probably a site for log booms. There was a short period during which the mill was sold to an American, and then, in 1918, my grandfather, Charles Harrington, bought it back with a mortgage from the previous owner.

My grandfather seemed to have inherited the entrepreneurial gene of his father. With more research, I found out that, as the Port Daniel sawmill expanded, so did my grandfather's enterprises. He built two ships to carry his lumber to St Pierre and Miquelon, New England, and even Jamaica, where they returned with molasses and rum. He opened a hardware store in Port Daniel and eventually owned seven smaller mills further up the coast, some of which supplied the larger sawmill in Port Daniel. In the 1930s, he took a commission for subcontracting workers for La Gaspesia pulp mill in Chandler. Two of his sons and one of his sons-in-law became part of the business and eventually, as he became old and frail, one son took it over. Both the business and eventually my grandfather went bankrupt, the former because of a fall in the price of lumber and problems with managing the business, the latter because of losing his money in the stock exchange.

If three generations of the Nadeau men were involved in the forest industry, then my immediate forebears were implicated in the destruction of the land that had been the source of livelihood for the Mi'gmaq. Literally millions of trees were logged over the 250 years since the Napoleonic wars, and in the 1900s, the growing New England market, along with advancing technology and transportation, intensified the extraction of timber.[38] None of this benefited the Mi'gmaq, who were initially restricted to three hundred acres of reserve in Gesgapegiag, the closest visible Mi'gmaq community to Port Daniel.

I decided I needed to go to Cascapedia, now called Cascapedia St Jules, to see if more family members had had direct contact with the Mi'gmaq. Inquiring at the museum as to whether there were any Nadeaus left, I was fortunate to discover one second cousin of my generation. His name was Paul Nadeau and he himself had been an RCMP officer on the anti-terrorist squad involved in dealing with the Air India bombing. He told me that his father, who was my father's cousin, Charlie, from Grand Cascapedia, had been the Indian agent at Restigouche and then superintendent of Indian affairs for the region, a period that extended from the late 1940s until the mid-1970s. During this period Charlie Nadeau had much power, and this included the ability to take children away from their families and to place them either in residential schools or in white foster homes. Charlie's sister Margaret had taught in the Restigouche Native school.

It would not have been fair to track only the Nadeaus, so I made some inquiries about my grandmother's family, the Gagnons. I found another intrepid family researcher like myself, Diana Gagnon. She had traced the family, including some of the women, back to the other side of the Gaspé Peninsula. From her I discovered how many men in that family entered Catholic religious orders or became priests. The first Gagnon to arrive in Port Daniel, in 1884, was the priest Augustin Gagnon, who came from the Baie des Sables on the north shore. Augustin was an organizer priest: he built schools for the children and helped community members to construct the dock, a sawmill, a flour-mill, and a tannery. He was forced to leave after twenty years when his housekeeper became pregnant. He had brought with him his brother, François-Xavier Gagnon, who became the village postmaster and my other great-grandfather. Two of his sons, my grandmother's brothers, became monks, one a Trappist, the other a Marist. My grandmother's cousin, Eduard, became a priest, later a bishop, and then a cardinal based in Rome. This example of the extent of religious vocations in a French Canadian family was not atypical. The role of the Roman Catholic Church in the Gaspé region was considerable, controlling social mores and influencing personal and political choices. Equally problematic was how the Catholic Church inculcated in the non-Native parishioners a colonialist sense of superiority over the Indigenous peoples, who were serviced by very separate "mission" churches on the Maria and Restigouche reserves. While the religious men in my family would leave the Gaspé, they were very much products of this system.

When I look at my ancestry now, it is clear that no one in the family would have a vested interest in knowing that there were Mi'gmaq peoples in the area of Port Daniel. My uncovering of the details of my family tree had produced what settler historian Paige Raibmon calls "a figurative genealogy of colonialism."[39] My family members had reaped the benefits of government policies that narrowed "Native space" to small reserves. They had also been very much part of settler practices that reinforced the seeming erasure of Mi'gmaq from the land. Of course, no one else saw it this way. And as for my immediate family, my dad was not part of the family business and would leave Port Daniel as soon as he could for an education, eventually becoming a Rhodes Scholar and later a trust officer for Canada Permanent, a parent company of TD Canada Trust. Removed from the land, living in Montreal, we had no idea that our ancestral roots were part of the "myriad makings of [the] dispossession" of Indigenous peoples.[40]

Port Daniel had always been a place of belonging for me. The many summers during which I played on the beach with my cousins, picked up the green and sapphire blue pieces of sea glass from the pebbly shore, had sugar pie with a glass of milk in my grandmother's large warm kitchen in the big white "maison ancestral," was accepted by all my cousins just because we were blood relatives – those memories will always be with me. Yet I had internalized the idea, and taken for granted, that the forest was a resource to be exploited for our livelihood and that having private property, my grandparents' and uncles' homes, defined how one "belonged." Now there are no Nadeaux left in Port Daniel. The family home was sold to a Chilean psychiatrist who worked in Chandler, and the homes of my aunts and uncles are occupied by new families. The building in which my Aunt Katherine and Uncle Norbert lived, on top of the Nadeau hardware store, has been razed to the ground. There is no trace of the mill. We are gone. Yet the Mi'gmaq are still there.

Madeleine once remarked that I was too hard on my family. It is not a matter of saying they or I are or were bad people; it is a matter of bringing to light the structures of which we have been and are a part. As critical race scholar Sherene Razack said, "unmapping is intended to undermine the idea of white settler innocence (the notion that European settlers merely settled and developed the land) and to uncover the ideologies and practices of domination."[41] We are not innocent but, rather, deeply embedded in these structures. It would have been easy to sidestep this part of my ancestry, like many in Quebec, by going back to France and declaring my French roots. But is that really decolonization? If uncovering my colonial genealogy is one step in seeing the land differently, perhaps another is learning to understand the original maps and laws of the territory that we chose to reconstruct in our own image.

9

Decolonizing Rivers

Through the process of unmapping I had managed to uncover some of the history of how the Mi'gmaq had been displaced from the community that my father's family called home. However, I still had much more to learn about how colonialism had shaped my understanding of that land, the waters, and the other-than-human beings who lived there – in particular, the salmon beings.[1] When I was young I would go down with my father to Central Station in Montreal every spring to pick up a big salmon sent by my grandfather. We would walk to the end of the long train, the Ocean Limited, to the freight car. There, waiting for us, was a big wooden box. Sometimes my dad would let my brother and me have a peek and we could see a big silver salmon, sometimes two, still whole but cleaned, kept cold in its bed of crushed ice. We would take it home, the box dripping water in the back of the car, and for a good week we would have salmon every night as the freezer in our fridge was not big enough to store it. Salmon became a treat we took for granted every fall. I had little thought for where the salmon was from or the context in which it had been caught.

I live in salmon country now, here on Vancouver Island. I have even commercially fished salmon and been to a Coast Salish ceremony that welcomed the first salmon coming up the river. I support the fight to stop open net fish farming on the west coast. Yet I can still sometimes feel in my body that disconnection to salmon and their home waters that was my reality as a child, and I have wondered how this sense of disconnect developed. If we are going to decolonize our relationship with water bodies and the beings that live in them, it will take more than changing the name of the Strait of Georgia to the Salish Sea. I decided to go back to Gespe'gewa'gi to find out more about my first salmon and the history of some of the rivers there.

I decided to first talk with Manon Jeannotte as she was coming to speak to one of my classes at Concordia. She suggested it would be useful to chat with her father to find out more about Mi'gmaq presence in the region. So, in 2009, I was fortunate to have an interview with Oscar Jeannotte. The interview did not go as I expected – in itself a lesson in learning to listen to what Indigenous people think is important. Oscar was a traditional person of the Gespeg Nation. Gespeg is the third official Mi'gmag community on the Gaspé Peninsula, but it has no territorial base. It is located by the town of Gaspé and was only officially recognized by the federal government as a Mi'gmaq community in 1972. Accordingly, many of its members live elsewhere in Quebec, as did Oscar and his wife. I met with Manon and her parents at the Centre Socio-Culturel de Gespeg à Montréal in the winter of 2009. Manon had established the centre with other urban Mi'gmaqs from Gespeg in order to keep the Mi'gmaq culture alive in the urban context.

Her mother, who had a halo of white hair, was from Cap des Rosiers, of Jersey Island ancestry. Oscar was a somewhat burly man, with greying black hair that was thinning and combed back in a slight pompadour, weathered skin, and blue eyes. He looked to be in his early seventies. Neither spoke English so we conversed in French. Initially, Oscar spoke in monosyllables and seemed reluctant to talk, especially when I asked him direct questions. However, at a certain point in our conversation his whole demeanor shifted as he launched into a story.

He was fishing on Rivière Saint Jean, outside the town of Gaspé, when suddenly he heard a helicopter overhead. It landed on the shore of the river and two game wardens got out. Oscar was fly-fishing in the middle of the river, so he stayed there while one of game wardens on the shore asked him, "What are you doing?" He replied, "I am fishing, of course!" Then one of them said, "You cannot do that, it is out of season." Oscar replied, "It is my right to fish and to fish for food for my family. There are six of us with my children, and I need two for each person, so I will fish twelve." So Oscar stayed there and continued to fish. One of the game wardens asked, "Aren't you afraid?" And he said, "Yes, there are two of you and one of me, but it is my right."

So Oscar stayed in the water where they couldn't get him, and they just waited for him. After a few hours, he caught twelve fish and then he gathered them up and moved to shore. Expecting him to run, the game wardens approached him. However, as soon as he got to the banks, Oscar sat down and began to clean the fish. Bemused and annoyed, the game wardens watched him. He was obviously not intimidated by their show of force. Finally, the head guard backed down and said, "OK," as he could see he was taking only the twelve fish. Oscar would return every week to fish and they did not bother him again.

Later, Manon shared with me that this incident happened around 1975–76, a period when the Mi'gmag throughout the region were challenging the denial of their Aboriginal hunting and fishing rights. She said that, at that time, the Molson family from Montreal was one of the owners of the Saint-Jean River. I asked myself, how could they "own" a river? What had I missed growing up and spending all those summers on the Gaspé coast?

In Quebec, until the mid-1970s, the fishing rights on all the salmon rivers of the Gaspé coast were leased to the highest bidders. In the early nineteenth century, the Mi'gmaq faced increasing encroachment on their fisheries by Euro-Canadian fishers. In 1824, the latter succeeded in having a law passed that forbade Mi'gmaq their traditional fishing techniques, specifically salmon spearing.[2] Later, one of the first things that the new government of Canada did was to criminalize Native fishing. Not only was this a restriction of Indigenous food sovereignty, but Native people could be and often were arrested for providing food for their families. In the second half of the nineteenth century, the government of Lower Canada and then Quebec leased the salmon-fishing rivers to wealthy Americans and Canadians of status, like the governor general. Most of these patrons were English-speaking and they became known as the "guardians" of the rivers. For 118 years, neither Native people nor locals were allowed to fish in these rivers, which were patrolled by night watchmen. Poachers could be subject to fines or jail terms.[3] The Mi'gmaq continued to fish covertly, often at night, but overall the impact was devastating, limiting salmon both as a food and as an income source.

My grandfather had been born in Cascapedia and had moved to Port Daniel to run a sawmill started by his brother and father. Probably because of his later business as a sawmill owner, he had been invited to fish in the Cascapedia River by one of his wealthy American clients who had a stake in the river. I remember him talking about fishing on the Cascapedia and I accepted it as common sense that he had been a guest of someone at a fishing club. I never even questioned the existence of these fishing clubs.

But what about the Mi'gmaq? The Cascapedia was and is the most famous of the salmon rivers on the Coast because of the size of the fish and because of the prominent white people who fished there. Yet the name of the Cascapedia River is taken from the Mi'gmaq word "Gesgapegiag," which means "where the river widens." When the river was privatized and the Mi'gmaq were reduced to a small three-hundred-acre reserve at the mouth of the river, with half of these acres being swampland, their main seasonal food source was cut off. While some of the earlier generations of Mi'gmaq men worked in the fur trade and in fishing, the only work available during this period was as river guides for the sports fishers, labourers for road construction, or river drivers.[4] Log driving was the most dangerous job in the forest industry as it involved standing on and rolling logs into booms on the fast-running water. Pnnal Jerome, an Elder from Gesgapegiag, told me that in 1951 his grandfather, William (Billy) Jerome, had drowned in the river during a log drive.

The Mi'gmaq were told they were "allowed" to gather firewood and hunt and fish on this tiny reserve allotment, when previously they had hunted and fished the whole length of the mighty Cascapedia, which is between 140 and 150 kilometres in length. Even if they could fish at the mouth of the river, until 1978 the estuary front on the New Richmond side was leased to the Cascapedia Booming Company, which changed the physical integrity of the river system and denied Mi'maq access to the salmon.

The Mi'gmaq of Gesgapegiag, like Oscar Jeannotte from Gespeg, were not willing to be contained. In the early 1970s they started to take back their fishing rights as resistance took place up and down the Coast. Then, in 1976, the Parti Québécois came into power, and, looking to eradicate the privileges of the Americans and the long-hated English on the rivers, ended the practice of leasing rivers and set up Zones d'Exploitation Contrôlée, or national parklands, open to the public. The Gesgapegiag Mi'gmaq claimed the right to manage the Cascapedia River, which had been the heart of their nation since time immemorial. In 1980, they signed an agreement with the Cascapedia Salmon Club to co-manage the river. This meant the Mi'gmaq could bring forward salmon enhancement programs based on traditional Mi'gmaq ways. By the end of the first decade of the twenty-first century, there were between thirty-five and fifty Mi'gmaq working on the river at any one time, as guides, managers, and enhancement workers. As Pnnal remarked to me with a grin, "we are not just the Indian in the canoe anymore."

I learned gradually that this was about more than food and jobs for the Mi'gmaq. Their relationship with land and water was an integral part of their relationship with the spirit world. As Pnnal once told me, "our blood line depends on the river." Fred Metallic of Listuguj has described how the relationship with the salmon, with its cyclical lifespan and intimate relationship with the rivers, informs principles of Mi'gmaq governance. "In Listuguj the salmon is one guide, which reminds us of the importance of balance and good order in our relationships with and within 'Gm'tginu, our territory.'"[5] Metallic illustrates how the sharing of the first salmon catch with extended family illustrates both the governance principle of sharing, which maintains and strengthens relationships within the community, and the responsibility and obligation that comes with the right to fish.[6] These responsibilities include the obligation to respect and protect the waters in which the salmon live. According to Metallic, "in Mi'gmaq I say 'the salmon is my brother.'" He continues: "We are connected to each other. We live in and from the territory: the salmon, through the water, keeps us connected."[7]

In these reflections, I see a different relationship to the river and the salmon than that of my family and most settlers. While we ate salmon as a treat, it was definitely in the realm of sports fishing or even trophy fishing. The larger the salmon caught by my grandfather or uncles, the better. There was no interest or awareness of sustaining the fishery or even of a relationship with the river that went beyond resource extraction. My great-grandfather had run a sawmill on the Cascapedia and, like, my grandfather's mill in Port Daniel, his mill had huge log booms clogging the river. Both the booming grounds and all riparian access rights had been "given" to my father's family.

Growing up, I neither learned about the displacement of the Mi'gmaq nor saw them as part of the story of these rivers. Not surprisingly, this amnesia continues today, as can be observed in the Cascapedia River Museum. Situated on the north shore of the river in the town of Cascapedia-St Jules, it is a perfect example of "colonial nostalgia."[8] This term describes the contemporary tourists' desire for wilderness and their yearning for the experience of a sanitized colonialism. In other

Figure 9.1   Logs under railway bridge, Port Daniel West River, 1912

words, it describes their wish to experience the land without the colonial dispossession that has shaped it.[9] The museum's website invokes the history of the river, stating that if the Cascapedia could speak "it would acquaint us with the rich and the famous who escaped their busy lives to find a sense of peace and balance in the hidden forests of the Cascapedia Valley."[10] The museum's main concern is to show the size of the fish caught and the history of the royal and illustrious people who fished this river. The few times I visited, the outside wall by the parking lot was covered with wooden fish engraved with the names of some of these people, ranging from the hockey player Bobby Orr to Laurent Beaubien of Bombardier to Princess Alexandria, cousin of Queen Elizabeth. A large map of the river in one of the rooms focuses on the different fishing camps and fishing holes up the length of the river and names some of the people who fished in each camp and/or the size of the largest fish caught there.

The last time I visited the museum, in 2017, there was no mention of how the Mi'gmaq used the land and river for generations, no mention of their campsites, portages, or the geological features that are part of their sacred stories. Yes, there was a small room in the museum that illustrated some of the Mi'gmaq culture, including pictures of Mi'gmaq guides in the "early days" of sports fishing, and there was even a map with traditional Mi'gmaq place names throughout the Gaspé. Yet the social and political history of the river was sadly missing. The exclusion of the Mi'gmaq for more than a century, the privatization of rivers for the wealthy, the reserve system and the Indian Act, other legislation that denied Aboriginal hunting and fishing rights, and, last but not least, the negotiations between the government and the Mi'gmaq that had to be undergone to arrive at a co-management regime – all this was missing. Even the fact that this is now a co-management regime was not readily visible. What is celebrated is how the wealthy English could come into the "wilderness" to trophy fish and have a unique experience of the wild. Hence the museum serves to reproduce and encourage a colonial experience of the physical landscape.[11]

The salmon is sacred to the Mi'gmaq. "The salmon is medicine because it is good for you. It keeps you alive," Pnnal explained in one of our exchanges. "In our case salmon and the Cascapedia are our life line. Five generations have worked around the river and we have to take care of it because it has taken care of us." Salmon has always been used for food and for social and ceremonial purposes. There is now a middle school socials and science course created by Mi'gmaq educators that is centred on the river and the salmon. The place names of all the fishing holes where the Mi'gmaq fished over generations have been recovered, and the Mi'gmaq map of the Gesgapegiag River illustrates just how central the river was and is for Mi'gmaq title to this territory.

Integral to the middle school course and to the Mi'gmaq management of the Cascapedia River is the principle of Netukulimk. Netukulimk is defined on the website of the Unama'ki Institute of Natural Resources in Cape Breton as follows:

Netukulimk is the use of the natural bounty provided by the Creator for the self-support and well-being of the individual and the community. Netukulimk is achieving adequate standards of community nutrition and economic well-being without jeopardizing the integrity, diversity, or productivity of our environment.

As Mi'kmaq we have an inherent right to access and use our resources and we have a responsibility to use those resources in a sustainable way. The Mi'kmaq way of resource management includes a spiritual element that ties together people, plants, animals, and the environment.[12]

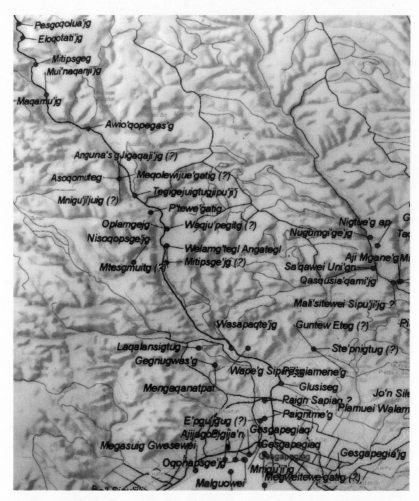

Figure 9.2   Mi'gmaq place names along the Gesgapegiag River Watershed (Mi'gmawei Mawiomi Secretariat)

This is a version of sustainability that makes sense to me. Without the rivers being healthy there can be no salmon, and no community of people whose lives, traditions, and values are connected to the salmon and the river.

Back in British Columbia, I watch the many salmon restoration projects that are in effect up and down Vancouver Island. These projects are restoring and conserving the habitat of wild Pacific salmon in watersheds, estuaries, and shorelines. There are education programs on the lifecycle of the salmon in many school districts, and every year young children are invited to release baby salmon from hatcheries into the rivers. For those who can see it, the spiritual element is there, but we still have a long way to go to integrate salmon restoration with a vision of sustainable governance that is embedded in Indigenous worldviews.

As for me, the one year when I fished salmon commercially (I was twenty-six) is a distant memory. Then, the excitement was about hauling in and clubbing a big spring salmon, and about how much money you could get for it. And, of course, there was the glamour of being one of the few women fishing on the west coast in the 1970s. I did not see the salmon as a relative, never mind giving thanks to it for giving its life. Four decades later, I am more humble in the presence of the "Salmon Nation," a term I have heard used by some of my Indigenous colleagues. Occasionally, I go out fishing with my son, who has a sports boat. He always shares his catch, giving away most of it to family and friends. I marvel at his generosity and also at his sense of interrelatedness with the human and fish beings.

The term "going home" has significant meaning in "Indian Country." It encompasses going back to one's ancestry and home territory and assuming the responsibilities that are connected to one's family, clan, and nation. I now see my going home journey as a settler as informing my relationship with the past, which I experienced as an inheritor of a colonial legacy, and my responsibilities to the present. It is a journey that invites me to transform my relationship to land and waterways from one that is disconnected to one that is embodied and emplaced. For this I give thanks.

PART FOUR

Making Relations

Moccasins

I am sitting cross-legged on the ground, watching an ant move slowly across the dry moss. Annoying pangs of hunger distract me from this moment of communion with the ant. It is midday, the sun is high in the sky, and we have been fasting (no food or water) for about eighteen hours as part of our twenty-four hours on the land. So far this is the most significant event of the Denendeh Seminar. Fourteen of us are camped on the plateau above the Ramparts, a unique geological formation on the Mackenzie River, where tall vertical limestone cliffs contain a twelve-kilometre-long canyon. This area, an open plain of subalpine tundra covered with stunted black spruce and low shrubs, is one of the sacred sites of the Sahtu Dene and is upriver from Radili Ko', named by the settlers Fort Good Hope. I see a few pup tents and a lone sleeping bag on the ground in the distance, but most members of our group are out of sight, searching for solitude.

It is 1986. I am co-facilitating the Denendeh Seminar for the first time. The fast began with the boat ride to the cliffs of the Ramparts, where we would camp for the night. A few of the Fort Good Hope men had offered to bring us and our gear in their small open motorboats; one was an older wooden flat-bottomed boat painted blue and green, the other two were aluminum Lund crafts. I loved the boat ride, the wind whipping through my hair, the rugged cliffs and banks of the wide river with no signs of human habitation. A ride on the Mackenzie was an auspicious beginning to our day on the land. I was learning that the Dene regard the land as sacred and alive, that some sites carry special significance as places of collective gathering for ceremonies or as places recounted in oral tradition where there occurred significant events involving animals or humans. The Ramparts is one of these places, though we did not learn the stories or the history associated with it. René, the Oblate priest who is in charge of this adventure, has carefully avoided the language of "vision quest" and promised no more than the experience of fasting on the land, but, for most of us, this is the most memorable part of the seminar.

Suddenly, two figures appear in the distance, at the top of the trail that leads from the river below. They walk towards me and I soon recognize René, accompanied by a Native woman. This is supposed to be a time of silence and I am a bit annoyed that René feels free to approach me, but I am the co-facilitator of the group and we are both responsible for anything unexpected that may come up. As they get closer, I see that the woman could be in her mid- to late thirties, though it is difficult to tell as her long black hair is partly covering her face. She is carrying something in her right hand. René introduces me to Mary Baptiste (not her real name) from Fort Good Hope and says she has something to sell. Mary holds out a beautiful pair of moccasins. She briefly speaks, "I finished them this morning."

Many thoughts race through my mind as I ask her, "How much?" I can't let her go to the others as it will disrupt their silent fast, and if I say no to the moccasins, she might want to do just that. I wonder why she has come all this way instead of waiting for us to return tonight. What is she going to use the money for, especially if she was willing to come all the way out here to sell them?

"Eighty dollars," she says. I take the moccasins in my hands and examine them closely. They are made of smoked moosehide, a rich bronze colour, with the hide extending to cover the ankle. The intricate beadwork on the top of the moccasin, known as the "vamp," or "upper," depicts the wild rose, a bush that is everywhere in the North, its distinctive dark pink flowers dotting the landscape. The petals of the beadwork are red, with a pale blue centre and a dark blue edge. The wild rose with its green leaves is on a backdrop of creamy white beads with a border of tiny red beads. As with many Dene moccasins, there is a red melton cuff about two inches wide, with sawtooth edging that covers the leather thongs that wrap around the ankle. In short, they are stunning.

I have wanted Indian moccasins for some time, but I always thought that they were too expensive, especially the ones that, unlike the factory ones that you see in urban "Indian craft stores," are handmade. Though pricey, this is a good deal. The thought of bartering for them flashes through my mind, but I know being on a fast is not an appropriate place to barter, so I nod, and go into my pup tent to get my wallet. I pull out four twenties and give her the cash. The exchange is quick. She nods and turns back to the pathway to the cliff. René shrugs his shoulders at me and follows her. About ten minutes later I hear the chug-chug of the kicker of the Lund boat carrying her back to Fort Good Hope. The smell of the smoked moosehide fills my nostrils as I put the moccasins in my tent. I am left somewhat disturbed, asking myself, "What if she is going to just spend the money on alcohol?" For the rest of the fast I am distracted, puzzling over the encounter.

I knew nothing about Mary Baptiste, except that she could make beautiful moccasins and that she lived in Fort Good Hope. I was making assumptions about her, based on prevalent stereotypes of Indigenous women and on my experience as a well-meaning Christian who had chosen to do my fieldwork for theology school in the North. I assumed that she and her community members were poor but could still hunt and fish on land that was still abundant, that she probably had children, that she was maybe a single parent, and that alcohol addiction was common in her community. I presumed that she had come all the way out to the Ramparts to sell the moccasins because she was desperate for money. Because I assumed that only addiction would result in that type of desperation, I wondered if that was what I was contributing to.

The exchange over the moccasins on the Ramparts disrupted my romantic fantasy of fasting on the land. I was not prepared for the messy daily reality of this Dene community and the woman who was part of it. We had focused on land claims and politics, not on the realities for Dene women in the North. At the time, I was unaware that this encounter was playing out a colonial dynamic: the Indigenous woman who needs to survive and so must sell her art at whatever price she can get, and the white outsider/settler/visitor woman camping on her sacred territory. I was taking up space on her land, and the exchange was mediated by a Catholic priest. Nothing more clearly illustrates the asymmetrical power relations that are hidden in "exposure tours" like the Denendeh Seminar than the "moccasin incident." Here I was, a privileged white Christian with a sense of entitlement, someone who did not even question that she could fly to the North for the summer to look at and into people's lives and then leave. Here was this Dene woman who had to track us down on her land, on one of the Sahtu Dene sacred sites, to sell her art for reasons that were hers alone. She would leave with the eighty dollars, exchange completed, and I would have these moccasins in my closet for the next twenty-five years, unable to take them out until I had worked out my relationship to them and to Native women.

Two earlier moments in my life marked the beginning of my connection with the harsh realities that faced Native women. One was in the late 1970s when I was coordinator of a one-year federal project on Vancouver Island called the Women's Services Training Program. I was in charge of hiring, coordinating, and training six workers on the North Island. The program was focused on equipping the workers to respond to incidents of spousal abuse. I felt we needed at least one Native trainee and I worked with the Port Alberni Friendship Centre to create a placement. I was fortunate enough to hire Judy Joseph, a Nuu-chah-nulth woman. Leaving aside the details of the short-lived project, one moment was burned into my memory. For the closing of our project we had a family party at my rented cabin in Comox. Judy was a single parent and had taken the bus from Port Alberni. She arrived with her three small sons. All three of them were dressed immaculately with little bow ties and shorts. As I looked as these handsome and shy little boys, I had this sudden flash – at any time she could lose her sons, taken away by social services just because she was Native and a single parent. Hence her vigilance about their appearance among this group of white women, some of whom were connected to social services. My son wasn't even there at the time; he was with his father. Though it was hardly the same situation, I, as a lesbian, had this moment of felt solidarity with Indigenous women who lose (or are in constant fear of losing) their children just because of who they are.

That moment was the closest personal insight I had into one of the many injustices Indigenous women face. Yet the difference in our experience was that I had privilege, both race and class privilege, and I would use both in the court battle that, a few years later, eventually ensued over my son. It was the early 1980s, a time when lesbians still lost their children because they were deemed unfit, especially when the child was a boy. I wanted to take my son with me when I went to Vancouver to attend theology school. My son's father and his wife wanted to keep him here with the new family they had created. I had money from my parents for the court case, and I went into court dressed in a pale blue suit and touting my Oxford education. I won interim custody, but the fight was bitter and ugly, so fortunately his father and I agreed to go to mediation. We ended up with a joint custody arrangement, still rather unprecedented at that time, and my son went back and forth between our homes for over a decade. But I never forgot Judy and that moment of recognition, when the profound wrongness of racist and colonial child apprehension policies, and what they mean for Indigenous women, their families, and communities, became clear to me on a personal level.

During this same period, through an intimate relationship with an Anishinaabe woman, I learned about some of the other injustices and oppression Native women experienced. We lived together for a few years during the late 1970s and early 1980s and, through her, I became involved in education and advocacy around section 12-1(b) of the Indian Act. In 1975, I had read Kathleen Jamieson's book on Native women's loss of status, *Indian Women and the Law in Canada: Citizens Minus.*[1] Yet reading a book is nothing like seeing first-hand the impacts of the Indian Act, which has systematically discriminated against and disenfranchised Native women who married non-Native men. My girlfriend's mother had married a Métis man and so had lost her status. This meant that neither mother nor daughter could vote in band elections, live on reserve, or have the rights to programs, education, and health services for either themselves or their children. They were treated as outsiders by their own community. Worse, in the non-Native community they were challenged as not being "real Indians."

I remember one moment when we were at the passport office in Campbell River where the agent questioned my partner's identity. He wanted to know where she "came from" as she wasn't white. She told him that she was Anishinaabe and that, because of the Jay Treaty, a 1794 agreement between Britain and the United States that recognized and affirmed unimpeded travel rights to First Nations travelling across the border,[2] she wouldn't need a passport to go the United States. The agent knew nothing of the Jay Treaty and basically treated her like dirt because she didn't have a status card. She was in tears after the encounter, feeling both humiliated and angry, and I saw how much power these functionaries had to maintain and/or to deny identity. This was the first time I had encountered overt racism and I was shocked, feeling both powerless and ashamed.

Because of my partner, I was at the periphery of the campaign for status, so I discovered how Native women had been struggling for many years to end this sexist and discriminatory clause of the Indian Act. A determined group of women, including Jeanette Corbiere

Lavell, Yvonne Bedard, Mary Two Axe Early, Sandra Lovelace, and the Tobique women from New Brunswick, was a leading force in bringing the issue of disenfranchisement to the Supreme Court in Canada and, eventually, to the United Nations Human Rights Commission.[3] In 1985, Bill C-31 was finally passed, granting status to thousands of women. But this law changed only some, not all, aspects of this section of the Indian Act. Sub-clauses of the act continued to restrict women from passing on their status: only males could pass on their status to their grand-children. Intrepid lawyer Sharon McIvor won one challenge to this in the BC Supreme Court, and the federal government was supposed to enact legislation to amend the Indian Act. The result was Bill C-3, the Gender Equity in Indian Registration Act, which gave status to more women. McIvor continued to fight the provision that has allowed her brother's grandchildren to have status but not hers, which clearly shows that the law still considers the female line to be lesser than the male. In November 2017, Bill S-3 was finally passed thanks to the work of two Indigenous senators, Lillian Dyck and Sandra Lovelace Nicholas. This bill theoretically ended sex discrimination in the Indian Act, yet it is still to be applied to the thousands of women and their families who were excluded. Considering that many Indigenous nations are matrilineal and that women play a leading role in passing on language, culture, and traditions, the underlying intent of this history of legal gender discrimination has been and continues to be to eliminate or "terminate" the Indigenous population and its legal Rights.[4]

Throughout this history of sex discrimination under the Indian Act, one message has continuously been reinforced: Indigenous women are secondary and inferior. Because women reproduce, the most effective way to erase the Indian population is to disenfranchise them so that they can be more easily assimilated. The legal provisions of the act, which for many years also included the denial of Native women's right to vote, to sit on band councils, and to own property on reserves, have played a significant role in the history of violence against Indigenous women. This devaluing of Indigenous women was internalized not only by settler men but also by many Indigenous men.

In hindsight, I know now that the woman on the Ramparts came from a collective history shaped by the Indian Act, by its sexism and its deliberate abuse of women's rights. Our exchange transpired within the broader context of a history of displacement, residential schools, racism, impoverishment, loss of language, and erosion of culture, not to mention physical and sexual violence against Indigenous women. However, as well, Mary came from a history of survival, resilience, and a rich culture that had not been extinguished, as evidenced by the moccasins she had made with her own hands. I knew little of this history of resilience at the time. Like many Canadians, I was only aware of the "problems" of Native women.

I learned more about Mary's Dene culture and about moccasins many years later through the work of Stephanie Irlbacher-Fox, a non-Indigenous woman who grew up in the Northwest Territories and lives in Yellowknife. In her book *Finding Dahshaa*, she comments: "According to Dene knowledge newly created earth was made beautiful by a moosehide."[5] The Dene make many things out of moosehide – jackets, moccasins, wall hangings, gloves, to name a few – all of which are sewn and beaded. Irlbacher-Fox notes that "moosehide clothing is a signifier of Dene cultural knowledge, artistic ability and artisanal skill."[6] These items are both given in ceremony and used in everyday life. Irlbacher-Fox's purpose in describing the lengthy collective process of tanning moosehide, which is women's work, is to show how it illustrates Dene values, knowledges, and cultural norms, which, in turn, inform Dene approaches to self-determination and governance.

So my moccasins, or, more accurately, Mary's moccasins, were the final product of a similar cultural collective process. The group work of tanning moosehide can take anywhere from ten days to as long as three weeks, followed by the cutting of the hide into different sized pieces. The women use the smaller pieces for moccasins or mittens, the larger for jackets and vests. For moccasins, the delicate sewing of the beads into a unique design is done on the melton vamp, followed by sewing the hide for heels and soles. Moccasins are both works of art and functional items of clothing. Meaning and purpose, art and crafts, are not separate in Indigenous cultures. As with Mary's moccasins, each design is unique; while many beadwork patterns are common to a particular cultural group, each has some individual artistic deviation. Throughout the process of making moccasins, specific cultural values and teachings are transmitted from older women to younger ones.

I was first introduced to beading by Alice Olsen Williams, an Anishinaabe quilt and bead artist from Curve Lake First Nation. My Anishinaabe girlfriend and I were visiting Alice at Curve Lake and, seeing my fascination with beading, she helped me make a bead loom. Alas, this rustic tool still lies unused in a closet. I loved the beautiful hair ties and hair clips made of bead work that I had been given, but I had no patience or time for the delicate and concentrated work of beading.

Like the tanning of moosehide, beadwork is often done in groups of women. My first successful attempt at beading only occurred a few years ago when I was part of a work party that was making a children's drum, an initiative of the Sisters Drum Circle of which I was then a part. Several women were scraping a hide outside, and I confess I did not last long at that endeavour, realizing my ability to stay present while scraping fat and hair off a wet skin was not great. So I went inside and joined the beading group, which was making the bag for the drum. Cree Elder Lillian Daniels patiently showed me how to create a border around the beadwork on an old moccasin vamp I had brought. Having no confidence in my own abilities I had cut this piece from a pair of falling-apart moccasins (not my Dene moccasins!) that I had bought years earlier at Curve Lake and had used as slippers for several years. I was thrilled that I could further adorn the beadwork and I was able to stay focused, while at the same time enjoying the conversation, the back-and-forth tales and stories of beading that the women in this circle were sharing. Perhaps because I had started my piece with a group of women it was the only piece of beading I ever finished.

Native American beader and academic Jenell Navarro describes this collective beading process as a ceremony, as medicine, as a time during which kinship relationships are strengthened, stories are shared, culture is transmitted, and the principle of reciprocity, of gifting, is reinforced.[7] Navarro speaks about an ontology of the beads, of how the beads are sentient beings with a life of their own. Cree beader Tara Kappo describes beads as "other than human kin" that transmit the energy of connection between beader and the person who is receiving the bead work.[8] Prior to Europeans introducing glass beads, Indigenous women used, and continue to use, shells, porcupine quills, turquoise, bone, nuts and seeds, and many other natural materials. Noting the difficult lives of many Métis women who beaded, Métis visual artist and beader Christi Belcourt observes that "part of the process of creating beauty is healing yourself and it's therapeutic. I think it is a form of prayer."[9]

One year I invited Alice Olsen Williams to be a speaker for one of my courses at Concordia. She shared with us how the concept of the

"artist" is a Western construct and how, in her culture, imagination
and being inspired to make beautiful things are part of everyday life.[10]
She spoke about why the Anishinaabe people wore moccasins, how the
subtle hide allowed the feet to feel the connection with the land and do
the least amount of damage when walking on the earth. "The teachings,"
Alice shared, "tell us we are to walk gently and softly on this Land – of
which we are a part."[11]

Over the years I realized that selling moccasins and other beautiful
things was one of the few ways that Indigenous women, especially
those living in isolated communities like Fort Good Hope, could
get money. Mavis Erickson, Carrier lawyer and former chief of the
Carrier Sekani Tribal Council, speaking at a 2011 UBC gathering titled
"Colonialism and Violence against Indigenous Women," described the
profitable sewing work of her mother. In the 1950s, there had been
an international market for Indigenous women's handicrafts, especially for moccasins, from her territory. Many women could become
self-sufficient, sharing their money and watching over their children,
as they created and sold their work. Her words gave a context to the
old pictures of women selling their baskets on the side of the road in
Gespe'gewa'gi. From the turn of the nineteenth century on, women sold
their baskets on the roadways because this was one of the few ways
they could acquire the cash to feed families that were often starving.
However, by the late 1980s and 1990s, both the moccasin and basket
markets were undermined by cheap factory-made replicas, first from
the southern United States and later from Asia.

When I was teaching at university I discovered critiques of tourist consumption of Indigenous crafts that made me question my own
motives for buying Indigenous art.[12] Now, in the twenty-first century,
wealthy consumers from the West can travel anywhere on the globe and
bring back, often at ridiculously low prices, Indigenous arts and crafts
to place in their homes as collector's items. This is not much different
than what occurred in the eighteenth, nineteenth, and twentieth centuries, when imperial powers stole cultural objects from Asia, Africa, and
the Americas for personal and museum display and for profit. Laura
Donaldson, a Cherokee literary critic, writes about the fetishization of
Indigenous art forms. She points out how specifically white feminist
women in North America collect sacred objects from other cultures,
often Indigenous, to fill a spiritual hole in their own lives.[13] One danger

of this culture of tourism and the commoditization of sacred objects is that it reinforces the stereotyping of the Indigenous "Other," fixing them in the past. Another is that these art forms are taken out of context and the historical and cultural meaning of their design is lost. Worse, non-Indigenous artists copy Indigenous designs without knowing their history or role in the culture, a form of cultural appropriation that Coast Salish artist Shain Jackson says "has a serious economic, as well as cultural cost."[14]

I am now aware that I am contributing to Indigenous women's economic development when I buy moccasins, jewelry, baskets, and blankets. Every year when I go back to the Gaspé I buy baskets from the Mi'gmaq Coop in Gesgapegiag, near Maria. The baskets are made by the local women, and there is a flyer and DVD available for customers explaining the history and process of making the baskets from the sacred black ash tree. Each basket has the name of its maker on the bottom. It is still possible to buy moccasins that are not made in a factory. Recently, I discovered an ad in the Globe and Mail showing a pair of moccasins similar to my Dene ones. I Googled the website to find that they cost three hundred dollars and were made by Rosa Wedzin from Behchokö in the Northwest Territories; they were for sale on the Tłįchǫ Online Store operated by the Tłįchǫ Ndek'àowo Government (formerly known as the Dogrib Nation). Not only is the community in control of the marketing, but these moccasins are valued for what they are worth and are described on the Tłįchǫ Ndek'àowo Government website as part of transmitting "knowledge to future generations."[15] I was reminded of Chelsea Vowel's challenge: "You can't afford $200 for beaded and fur-trimmed moose-hide moccasins? Perhaps you should consider going without until you can."[16]

In 2008, the Interfaith Summer Institute for Justice, Peace and Social Movements, where I worked, hosted a gathering called "Indigenous Worldviews on Truth and Reconciliation." Bernadette Spence, a Cree committee member who was one of our cultural advisors, suggested we give tiny moccasins as a gift to participants as a sign of the baby steps we would be taking as we begin the reconciliation journey. We didn't have the money to commission a local Cree woman to make a hundred pairs of tiny moccasins (another interesting funding non-priority), so we decided to replicate an idea that was used at Bernadette's work-place, the Vancouver Aboriginal Child and Family Services Society, to acknowledge the Truth and Reconciliation Commission. This was a picture of baby moccasins on a postcard. At the end of the event we gave each participant the postcard as a gift and as a sign of the relationship that we were committing to enter into as the truth and reconciliation process began.

My relationship with my Dene moccasins continued to be fraught with tensions. It would be a few more years before I felt comfortable wearing them. For me, the question of belonging is underlain by my own quest for authenticity, to feel okay about who I am. Authenticity has come to mean accepting who I am, a white lesbian and settler who has had the opportunities to interact with Indigenous women for most of my life. It has meant acknowledging all the complexities of my history and story and having the courage to be honest about them. Finally, I have come to a point at which I occasionally wear my Dene moccasins, mostly in ceremonial contexts. It has been the work, the showing up, and the acknowledgment and affirmation from some of my Indigenous friends that has given me the permission to feel okay about wearing them. My Dene moccasins have become a talisman for me, a sacred object that has been with me over the years as I unlearned and relearned some of the harsh and the beautiful realities of the lives of Native women.

Walking with Our Sisters

I remove my shoes and enter through a doorway that has cedar boughs hanging from the door frame. I turn under the boughs counterclockwise, the direction of the circle in both Kwakwaka'wakw and Coast Salish traditions. After being cleansed by the cedar I enter the room. A hushed silence, broken occasionally by a few gentle murmurings, fills the large band hall. This hall of the K'ómoks Nation has been totally transformed into the ceremonial space, the lodge, of the Walking with Our Sisters (WWOS) memorial installation. In the background, playing softly, are recorded traditional songs sung by women.

There are over eighteen hundred beaded moccasin vamps displayed in this room, all laid out in a design created by the local organizing team. There are also 117 pairs of children's vamps, made for children who never returned from residential school, placed on a raised platform near the centre of the room. Ahead of me are several people moving slowly, pausing, then continuing to walk forward on a winding path of red cloth. The path has been laid between rows of moccasin vamps carefully placed on the floor in pairs. The vamps have been beaded and stitched to honour and remember the murdered and missing Indigenous women and girls. Some of the vamps are placed so that it appears that the women and girls are standing in their moccasins shoulder to shoulder around the periphery of the room, toes facing the visitors. Some are faced forward so that it feels like we, the visitors, are walking with the women and girls.

I stop beside the first row and am immediately overwhelmed. The beauty and intricacy of the beadwork on these vamps is breathtaking. Each pair has been made with love and care either to honour a woman who was personally connected to the beader or to honour all those who have been lost. What is so astounding is that each pair of vamps is different from all the others. Then there are the sheer numbers.

To actually see that many pairs is to get an idea of what devastation this violence against Indigenous women has meant for communities and families, the immensity of this collective loss of women. This is much more than an art exhibit: it is a ceremony that honours and remembers the lives of the murdered and missing women and girls and supports the grieving process of the families and relatives of those who have been lost so unjustly.

As I walk I recognize a beaded eight-point star of the Mi'kmaq; a bit further, on another pair of vamps, is the purple and white Haudenosaunee flag. There is a circle of beadwork around an image of the three Mi'gmaq women from Listuguj who biked across Canada to raise public awareness about the murdered and missing women and girls. Then I see a pair with the wild rose on them, similar to that on my moccasins from Fort Good Hope, and I presume that they have been beaded in Dene country. Another pair from Nunavut: they are made of seal skin and have a tiny ulu sewn on them. So many women from so many First Nations have been lost! There are vamps made with porcupine quills, some of embroidery, and even some of "fusion" art – shells, beads, and felt. I am feeling proud that I am able to recognize the locations and sources of so many of the vamps, when I come across one that stops me. On it is the transposed picture, surrounded by beads, of a transgender woman I had known in the Downtown Eastside. Suddenly my heart swells with sadness. The memorial has become personal. I have to face the pain of this collective loss – a pain that I have managed to cover up by assessing the beadwork. I have to engage emotionally with the deep significance of the hundreds and hundreds of pairs of moccasin vamps in this room.

Walking with Our Sisters is described as a commemorative art instal-lation that honours the lives of the missing and murdered Indigenous women of Canada and the United States.[1] The I-Hos Gallery, owned by the K'ómoks Nation, had offered to hold the memorial in K'ómoks on Vancouver Island in the summer of 2015. The vision for this "memor-ial," a term that the wwos collective eventually came to prefer over "installation," came from Christi Belcourt, a Métis visual artist based in Espanola, Ontario. She had a dream and chose the idea of the unfinished moccasins to represent the unfinished lives of the missing and murdered women: "Moccasins are symbolic of the path a person walks in life and, within some traditions, moccasins are placed on the feet of the person in death to help them on their journey into the next life."[2] Belcourt put a call-out on social media for the beadwork and was soon overwhelmed by the response, receiving six hundred pairs in a few weeks. A WWOS collective formed and the larger vision of a travelling ceremonial memorial emerged. In the meantime, more moccasins arrived. The memorial was designed to offer flexibility so that each host nation or community created the display of the moccasin tops in a layout that was appropriate for their culture.

What made the memorial powerful was that it was framed in ceremony – indeed, that it *was* ceremony. The fact that neither the faces nor the bodies of the missing or murdered women were on display, a symbolic refusal to engage in further exploitation, was an integral part of its creation as an honouring of the women and their families. Each beautiful pair of vamps was made by the hands of women who transmitted their love through the beading, affirming these women's lives. Daughters, sisters, mothers, friends, and even some who did not know any of the missing or murdered women personally had beaded these vamps. Tara Kappo, who is on the national WWOS collective, describes beading as ceremony. She explains how the beading process enacts a relationship and expresses the love and care of the beader.[3] As soon as you walked into the lodge, you could sense the energy of the relationships and the love transmitted through the beading on the vamps.

This relational aspect was reinforced with the presence of the bundle, which was placed in the centre of the lodge. Christi Belcourt explains that a bundle is "a traditional ceremonial term to describe a collection of sacred items."[4] Shalene Jobin and Tara Kappo, who have written about Walking with Our Sisters, describe a bundle as "a collection of items – the physical and non-physical – that are integral to many Indigenous ceremonies ... In Indigenous worldviews, a bundle is actionable; it has its own agency."[5] Situated in the centre of the lodge the bundle reinforced the sense that the spirit world was very much present in this space.

Besides the actual memorial, what has been important for me about Walking with Our Sisters is the vision that guides it. Maria Campbell, a Métis Elder living in Gabriel's Crossing in Saskatchewan, became the Advising Elder on the National Collective for WWOS, and she informed much of the vision. The National Collective developed an impressive information guide for host venues and communities. The guide states that the purpose of the installation is to honour the women, support the grieving families, and raise public awareness around the issue of the murdered and missing Indigenous women, girls, and Two-Spirit people. It provides directions not only regarding how to install and de-install the memorial but also how to support the host communities in following the ceremonial principles that informed this vision from the beginning. It was the WWOS guide that inspired me to throw myself heart and soul into the process of organizing Walking with Our Sisters. The WWOS guide, sent to all of us on the local committee, was way more than a list of pointers on how a gallery should mount an "art exhibit." It offered a way of working together, a model of Indigenous governance, laws, and Protocols.[6] The guide invited the organizers to spiritually ground their work in four basic principles: humility (all who attend are equal and welcome); protocol (traditional Protocols must be followed throughout the project from beginning to end); love (practising kindness, gentleness, patience, and love); and volunteerism (no one is paid for any of the work). As Maria Campbell states in her introduction to the guide, "it is these *Notokew Ahtyokan* traditions and principles that guide this Exhibit."

What inspired me was the fact that this was a different way of educating and organizing around the "issue" of violence against Indigenous women. I had worked in the area of prevention, healing, and education relating to violence against women, including Indigenous women, since the late 1970s. The Women's Services Training Program on Vancouver Island, my work with the Native Family Violence Program at the Native Education Centre in Vancouver, and my work with Alannah Young at the Downtown Eastside Women's Centre in Vancouver had all involved education, engaging with and learning from Indigenous women who had survived various forms of violence, be it racial, sexual, or gendered. In 2004–05, I co-facilitated with Nisha Sajnani a popular theatre violence prevention program for the South Asian Women's Centre in Montreal. In Vancouver for several years I had participated in the 14 February Women's Memorial March, which has many ceremonial aspects. However, WWOS offered an approach that was unlike anything I had experienced previously. Its purpose was to honour the lives of missing and murdered women, girls, and Two-Spirit loved ones and to support their families. WWOS, in moving from community to community across the country, provided a safe and ceremonial venue for people who might never attend a memorial march or even know much about the murdered and missing Indigenous women. It went beyond advocacy and education to incorporate and embody Indigenous ways of knowing and being in its very structure. In this way, it modelled the strengths of Indigenous cultures and what Jobin and Kappo describe as "an alternative way of connecting to human relations, passed on relations, and with non-human beings."[7]

While I had no family member who had been murdered or was missing, I was connected with some of the families of women who had disappeared. One of my students whom I had taught in high school in the mid-1970s worked the streets in Vancouver. One day, when I was attending a memorial for the women in the Downtown Eastside at First United Church, I heard her name read from a list of missing women. I was stunned and asked myself what I could have done differently as her teacher so many years earlier. A few years later a close friend adopted two girls who were her cousin's son's daughters: the girls' mother had been murdered in Vancouver. When the girls were teenagers they had lost their sixteen-year-old cousin, who was murdered by another predator in Vancouver. Then there were other Indigenous friends and colleagues, and several of the Indigenous students I taught at university, whose family members or neighbours had been murdered. There were the missing relatives of the women I had worked with at the Downtown Eastside Women's Centre in Vancouver. I have come to the conclusion that most of us, Indigenous or not, who live in this country called Canada are within the infamous seven degrees of separation from murdered and missing Indigenous women. Despite those who protest they know no Indigenous people, I am sure these people would be surprised at the connections.

So I came to Walking with Our Sisters with a passion to support its vision. Here was a project framed in ceremony, designed by Indigenous women, that brought the strengths and gifts of Indigenous cultures to the process and that did not present the women as victims but as family members who were present by their absence. Many non-Indigenous people would get educated by attending the memorial, and family and friends of lost ones could grieve in a good way. In K'ómoks, we were fortunate to have workers from Tsow-Tun Le Lum, a residential treatment centre on Vancouver Island near Nanoose Bay, offer culturally appropriate support for all those who were emotionally affected by the memorial.

I had two roles with wwos. I became part of an outreach team, tasked with e-mails, workshops, and community conversations, the objective being to engage as many people as possible with the memorial, educate them about the murdered and missing Indigenous women, and encourage them to attend it when it came to K'ómoks in the first two weeks of August. I also volunteered to be one of the attendants during the memorial, a role that involved explaining some aspects of the installation to the visitors.

I learned a lot during the eight months I was involved with the Walking with Our Sisters project, both about violence against Indigenous women and about working across differences in small communities. This was the first time the memorial had been located within a specific First Nations community, and this generated some insider-outsider dynamics not only between Indigenous and non-Indigenous people but also among Indigenous volunteers inside and outside the community. The volunteers ranged from local K'ómoks Nation community members to Métis and Indigenous women from other communities in the Comox Valley to local settlers. We often ended up working in silos, with no communication between teams. We had different approaches to outreach. Some decided to build a float that they put into both the local Canada Day Parade and the Empire Day Parade. Our outreach group, composed of a Kwakwa̱ka'wakw woman from outside the K'omoks community, a Maliseet woman, and myself, decided to use Métis director Christine Welsh's film *Finding Dawn* as a tool to facilitate community conversations.[8] We offered this film in six different communities – two in churches, two at friendship centres, one at the University of Victoria, and one on Denman Island, where a group of Metis and non-Indigenous women had already beaded moccasin vamps for the memorial. We applied the ceremonial principles that informed the wwos guide, a local Elder opened and closed each gathering, and the Tsow-Tun Le Lum cultural support workers attended each gathering. I was fortunate to work with an outreach team of like-minded women (including a visual artist of Jewish heritage who later joined us) who were committed both to raising public awareness through community discussions and to applying the ceremonial principles whenever possible. These women are now friends.

As with most significant human endeavours, there is the ideal and then there is the reality. We are human beings who, with all our failings, are struggling to survive and co-exist within the dynamics of colonialism. Within the larger organizing committee, we were challenged by disagreements about fundraising, T-shirt designs, different outreach approaches, publicity, and extended programming. I often found it very painful to engage with viewpoints that were so different from mine and that of our team. I would often phone my Métis friend Marjorie, a Two-Spirit Elder who lives in Duck Lake, to ask for guidance in navigating these challenges. Marjorie encouraged me to hang in and trust the principles and process of wwos. The difficulties inherent in our process forced me to keep revisiting the wwos guide and to struggle with how to apply its principles of gentleness, patience, kindness, and love, especially when I was often triggered into feelings of anger and exclusion.

Through Walking with Our Sisters, my understanding of violence against Indigenous women was broadened. Part of the outreach job of our team involved contacting family members to invite them to parts of the ceremonies that were only for the families. I was fortunate to be able to contact Melina Laboucan Massimo, whom I had met previously. Melina's sister Bella had been murdered in Toronto in 2013, and her family had contributed a pair of vamps to the memorial in Bella's honour. Melina has been an outspoken advocate for a family- and community-controlled inquiry into the murdered and missing women. A member of the Lubicon Cree First Nation, she is a fierce defender of the land against resource extraction. She has been involved, as a Greenpeace staff person, in the fight against the tar sands and is one of the founders of the Tar Sands Healing Walk.[9] Melina wrote about her sister's "mysterious" death (Bella had "fallen" from the thirty-first floor of a high-rise) and made the broader connections that provide the context for these attacks on Indigenous women. "The industrial system of resource extraction in Canada is predicated on systems of power and domination. This system is based on the raping and pillaging of Mother Earth as well as violence against women. The two are inextricably linked."[10]

It is not a coincidence that violence against Indigenous women occurs at the same time as companies rapaciously extract resources from the earth and waters. A denial of the sacredness of the earth is linked to a denial of the sacredness of women's bodies, in particular,

Indigenous women's bodies. Melina and Erin Konsmo, a member of the Walking with Our Sisters National Collective, have been part of an education project and toolkit that has brought together the issues of violence against women and violence against the land.[11] Young women activists like Melina and Erin, who are making the links, point the way forward for settlers who are trying to figure out what "to do." As with Walking with Our Sisters, they operate within a holistic framework that includes ceremony, the spirit world, and the links between the different devastations on our planet.

During the time of the memorial, we organized a workshop for youth called "Our Vision for Justice: A Workshop for Indigenous Girls, Young Women and Two-Spirit Youth," facilitated by Chaw-win-nis (Tla-o-qui-aht and Cheklesaht Nuu-chah-nulth, then prevention manager at the Victoria Sexual Assault Centre) and Sarah Hunt (Kwakwaka'wakw, assistant professor at UBC). While we initially asked them to do a workshop, I had been thinking of doing one for the larger community. But Chaw-win-is and Sarah were clear: they wanted it to be only for Indigenous youth. The work they did that day, some of which was shared in an open invitation to the public for the last hour, pointed a way forward. Using art and teachings from their two cultures, they demonstrated honouring Indigenous girls, young women, and Two-Spirit youth, providing a basis for equipping these youth to speak back against sexualized violence out of a place of dignity and sense of kinship.[12] Chaw-win-is and Sarah Hunt continue to be articulate speakers and writers on the need to link body sovereignty and land sovereignty and on how Indigenous traditions and laws can be mobilized to protect Indigenous women's bodies, not just the waters and the land.[13]

I was passionate about and moved by Walking with Our Sisters. Over the years of teaching about colonialism and its impacts on Indigenous women I had learned, through listening to the voices and writings of Indigenous women, that the context of the seemingly unending violence against them is linked to the long history of settler colonial undermining of their power. Early settlers were uncomfortable with the prominent roles – political, social, economic, and spiritual – that Indigenous women had in their communities. The European model of womanhood had women isolated in single-family households, doing domestic duties, and being faithful and subservient to their husbands. In many Indigenous nations, it was the women who carried the clan

knowledge and held the land for the next generation. The many provisions of the Indian Act, the reserve system, residential schools, and
the Sixties Scoop (in which Indigenous children were taken from their
homes to be adopted and fostered by non-Indigenous people) all led to
a systematic erosion of Indigenous family lives and Indigenous women's
connection to the land. What the wwos memorial has done, besides
providing a ceremonial way of addressing the grief of family members
and honouring the women, girls, and Two-Spirit loved ones who are
missing and murdered, is to invite those whose hearts have been closed
to feel the immensity of this loss and to witness the reaffirmation of the
sacredness of Indigenous women. This is decolonization.

For eight months, I lived and breathed Walking with Our Sisters. I
met wonderful Elders, the amazing women who spoke at our workshops along with the film *Finding Dawn*, the women and men from
Tsow-Tun Le Lum, and the family members who showed up at our
presentations. The outreach work was exacting: making posters along
with endless e-mails and calls, promoting the memorial, working with
host communities, and debriefing our team and supporting those who
felt excluded. Yet the challenges we all faced in the organizing leading up
to the actual installation were transformed by the memorial itself, where
we all worked together. Everyone chose to move beyond the conflicts
to support each other and those who attended the memorial – more
than four thousand people, the majority non-Indigenous. Through vis-
ually and ceremonially representing these women as sacred daughters,
mothers, aunties, sisters, and friends, wwos reframed the dominant
media script, which presents Indigenous women as victims. It left many
profoundly shaken, and it educated them not only about the extent
of the violence but also about the richness of the Indigenous cultures
that each of the moccasin vamps' creators drew upon in honouring the
women. Walking with Our Sisters spoke to the heart, not the head. In
its honouring of relationships – those who had gone before us, those yet
to come, and those here now – it made the entire organizing committee
recognize that each of us, in our own way, is doing her best to make this
world a safe place for Indigenous women.

A Water Journey:
Indigenous Water Laws

In the spring of 2004, my friend and colleague Alannah Young invited me to attend the Three Fires Midewiwin initiation ceremonies in Bad River, Wisconsin. At that time we were facilitating and writing together, so she wanted me to better understand Anishnabe tradition and how embodied it was. I felt honoured, but a bit uncertain whether I should go. I knew little of the Midewiwin society. I discovered that it was known as a secret society partly because of how it, like many other Indigenous ceremonies, had been outlawed by the Indian Act between 1886 and 1951. I would learn later that the Midewiwin was known as the "Grand Medicine Society" of the Anishnabe, although a common translation of Midewiwin is "Way of the Heart."[1] I wavered for a few weeks, worrying that it was going to cost me a considerable amount to go and that it would interrupt my work. However, in the end I decided to go, justifying my decision by considering that I would be supporting Alannah in her initiation and that I would certainly be learning more about Anishnabe culture. So in early June, I joined Alannah and her friend Alex in Winnipeg, where we rented a car to drive to Wisconsin.

There are many moments that are seared in my memory of that trip, not the least being the fact that we were stopped at the border. Our car was pulled over and then taken apart, and we were separated from Alex. I was terrified as Alannah and I were taken into a windowless room where a tough young white woman, stocky with mousy brown short hair and a gun on her uniformed hip, went though our bags, which she had placed on a cold steel counter. She said she needed to look at both Alannah's large gift bundle, which she was bringing for the ceremony, and her personal medicine bundle. Alannah was acting calm, which I then couldn't understand but now see as strategic. I was very upset as I felt that the woman had basically violated the sacredness of the bundles. In a rare moment of bravery, I took a chance that the woman was probably Christian, and told her the medicine bundle was just like a special bag holding a Bible and prayer beads – it was something that you were respectful of. She looked at me, paused, and then continued. I think she had never seen a medicine bundle before, and she glanced in it and then closed it without emptying it. Eventually they let us go.

During the long drive to Bad River there were several times when Alannah would reach into a small pouch of tobacco beside the driver's seat and put a pinch out the window. At first I was afraid to ask as I hated showing my ignorance, but I eventually queried her. She replied that each time we had passed an animal that had been killed on the road she offered tobacco with a prayer so that the animal's spirit could pass easily to the other side. Well, that shook me. What I had understood previously as just "road kill," animals unlucky enough to cross the road and be hit by a car, were in fact relatives, beings whose spirit and death needed to be acknowledged and prayed for. Because the tobacco offering embodied a prayer I could not easily forget it, and it eventually became a ritual I continue to perform whenever I am driving.

I was entering into a world that was governed by a totally different set of laws from the one that governed the dominant society with which I was so familiar. I have learned that it is not appropriate to talk about what happens in ceremony, so I don't feel comfortable talking about the details of the Midewiwin Lodge, beyond the fact that there was no cost to attend, that meals were provided daily to over five hundred people, and that we all contributed to the work of preparing the Lodge, the food, and the many tasks required to keep a camp comprised of so many people running smoothly.

It was here, at Bad River, that I began to experience a shift in my relationship to water. On the first morning we went to the sunrise ceremony, and it was there that I observed the women's water ceremony. This involved specific water songs, body movements, and gestures; the blessing of the water; and then the sharing of the blessed water with all present. I was struck by the length of time given to this ceremony, by the fact that the water was contained in copper vessels, and by the haunting water songs. It was a ceremony that occurred daily during the five-day lodge, after the men's pipe ceremony, and it seemed to represent a gender balance in roles and responsibilities. I had never seen water revered in such a way and it stopped me in my tracks. I was learning that water is sacred and that, in the Anishnabe tradition, the protection of water is the specific responsibility of women, who are called the life givers.

But there was more. It seemed that many of these women had an activist relationship with water. Alannah pointed out to me women whom she called "Water Walkers." I discovered these comprised a small group of Midewiwin women who had committed to walk in ceremony around the Great Lakes in order to educate people about the sacredness of water and the need to protect it. A few of the women at Bad River had just returned from the second annual walk, this time around Lake Michigan. One of them was the late Josephine Mandamin, the grandmother who had initiated the walks. I could barely walk ten kilometres on a hike without being exhausted, and here were these women walking hundreds of kilometres! Yet I still had no idea of the extent of their commitment.

The territories of the Anishinaabe people are around all the Great Lakes, and the first ceremonial walk was held in 2003 around Lake Superior. In the years that have followed the Water Walkers have routinely covered distances of anywhere from five hundred to more than a thousand kilometres in a walk. Drawing on Anishinaabe teachings on water and women's responsibilities for water, these women have covered great distances with the goal of changing public perception of water from that of a resource to that of a sacred being, a spirit that must be treated as such. Their purpose has also been to honour the water, to restore a relationship with the spirit of the lakes through ceremony. The walkers' intent has also been to strengthen actions for the protection of clean water for future generations. The Water Walkers begin and end each day with a water ceremony. The walk is always led by a woman carrying a copper vessel of water, and there is always a man or a woman carrying an eagle staff beside her. Others follow in solidarity and, in relay style, shift roles. As they pass through the different communities on their way they are joined by some who walk with them for shorter periods of time. The water walkers have a website, the Mother Earth Water Walkers, which includes information about many water-organizing and water-violation events.[2]

I attended the spring ceremonies in Bad River two more times, and each time I had the privilege of meeting different Water Walkers. I was struggling to connect what they were doing with my growing awareness that there was significant need to bring the element of the sacred into water activism at home. Then, in 2007, Dorothy Christian, from the Secwepemc and Syilx Nations, and I organized a symposium called "Protecting Our Sacred Waters" for the Interfaith Institute for Justice, Peace and Social Movements at Simon Fraser University, of which I was then the director. We were facing several critical issues: the privatization of BC rivers for small hydroelectric dams, threats of bitumen-filled pipelines to the coast, lack of clean drinking water in many First Nations communities, and the ongoing pollution of our rivers, lakes, and oceans. Our focus was to bring forward the resources of religious and spiritual teachings in the fight to protect water. We had speakers from Hindu, Christian, Sylix, and Nlaka'pamux traditions. We also invited the late Violet Caibaiosai, one of the Mother Earth Water Walkers who lived in Roseau River, Manitoba, to speak of her experience and teachings.

I offered to host Violet at my place. As soon as she arrived in Vancouver, before she had unpacked her bag, Violet asked me if we could go down to the ocean so she could acknowledge and honour the waters of the territory of the local nations. Vancouver has always been an intertribal gathering place, and the Tsleil-Waututh (Burrard), xʷməθkʷəẏəm (Musqueam), and Skwxuwu7mesh (Squamish) Nations all have ancestral connections to the waters of the harbour and bays of the city. It was a cool evening, and there were not many people around when we arrived at Spanish Banks, one of Vancouver's beaches. Violet walked right to the tide line, took a pinch of tobacco out of a small deerskin pouch she was carrying, and then said a prayer before offering the tobacco to the water. She then turned to me to see if I wanted to take some tobacco to offer. I was moved and quite humbled to be included and took a pinch from the pouch that she offered to me. Somewhat self-consciously, I said my hurried private prayer and then clumsily threw my tobacco into the water, noticing that I had dropped more on the sand than in the water.

That moment was the small beginning of my relating to water in an embodied way, as something more than an object (i.e., as just a resource for my drinking, bathing, and swimming). In Anishinaabe traditions, tobacco, called *sema* in the Anishinaabemowin language, serves to lift up prayers to the Creator. Offering tobacco to the water is a daily ritual for many Anishinaabe women. It is an act of gratitude and an honouring of the spirit of the water. And it is a ritual that all are encouraged to perform. Since then I have done it consistently over the years, though I confess it is often a struggle for me to maintain an embodied awareness of water as a spirit and relative. Because I have lived by the Salish Sea here in British Columbia, now residing by the Gorge Waterway in Victoria, and am often on the east coast by the Atlantic in the Baie de Chaleurs, I have many opportunities to honour and thank the ocean waters as well as many rivers I have crossed. Over the years I have gradually learned to perform this simple ceremony of offering tobacco to the water in a respectful way, and sometimes I can actually sense the water spirit I am acknowledging. But I admit there are times when I catch myself just throwing the tobacco into the water and turning back almost immediately to move on to my next task. Then I know I still haven't "got it."

What I would call my disassociation from water as a living spirit is a product of my culture, which treats water as an abstraction, as something lacking an ecological relationship to other beings. I learned much from Violet, and also from Ardith Walkem, a Nlaka'pamux lawyer who defends Indigenous water rights and who spoke at our Protecting Our Sacred Waters Symposium. She told us that there were Indigenous laws and Indigenous ecological knowledge that could guide us in reversing the destructive path that we were on in our relationship with water and land. She argued that we needed to do more than learn about Indigenous laws to transform this relationship. She called for a shift in "how we view water and our relationship with the world."[3] After the symposium I searched out Walkem's writings and found an article titled "Water Philosophy" in which she states:

> A Nlaka'pamux elder once told me that the problem with the newcomers was that they were famished. She explained that newcomers never stop eating away at the waters, at the land, at the trees, at the fish. Newcomers would log, mine, build subdivisions and highways, and fish to the point of extinction and still never feel full or satisfied.[4]

This really caused me to pause. Did I have that famished way of being in the world? And what would transform it? How could I change how I experienced water? I was great at grasping intellectual concepts, or so

I thought, but how to get these Indigenous laws to sink in? "Grasping" and "sinking," two different metaphors for how we can relate to the one thing that humans are totally dependent on to live – water.

Walkem's phrasing brought me directly to the somatic work I have done over the years. I am interested in the deeper layers of how we internalize the cosmologies in which we are raised, and how the body and psyche are shaped by the systems in which we live. And, as the Nlaka'pamux Elder said in plain language, there is a somatic component to greed and endless consumption. The economic and social structures that support this greed have great names that scare off or distance many –"capitalism," "heteropatriarchy," and "white supremacy." Yet these systems shape the psyches of those who benefit from them and of those who are oppressed by them, and this is played out in how we live in our bodies. The newcomers' hunger of which the Elder spoke, our emptiness, speaks to a deep spiritual hole.

I connect the Elder's words with the somatic language of body-mind psychotherapy, in which I had trained. My teacher, Susan Apoyshan, talked about being stuck in a grasping action state. She warned: "over-using our ability to grasp and pull limits our ability to receive in a satisfying way."[5] Body-Mind Psychotherapy is informed by Buddhist psychology, which identifies one of the three personality types, before transformation, as the grasping or greed temperament. This temperament is at the basis of always wanting more, of seeking into the future, and of addiction.

There is a body-mind psychotherapy exercise that involves water. I observe how I usually drink a glass of water. Sure enough, I notice I push forward, reach out, and grasp my water glass without even being aware of the gesture of pulling it towards my mouth. I gulp it down and then move on. The next time, I slow down the process. I become conscious that I am about to have a glass of water. I become aware of pulling the glass towards my mouth and then allow my lips, mouth, and throat to feel the water before sensing it move down my esophagus into my stomach. I watch myself yielding, receiving the gift of water to my body as if for the first time. I suddenly feel gratitude for that glass of water. Unfortunately, I do not often practise this conscious awareness of drinking water. My habit is still to grab a glass and gulp it down. I gulp down my food when I eat. This inability to receive and to yield to the gifts of the moment is a somatic component of the grasping of the water and the land of which the Nlaka'pamux Elder was speaking. Taking no time to pause in gratitude and reciprocity, we move on to grab the next thing.

I am primarily an educator, so I began to explore activities that would help people experience this visceral sense of connection with water. I noticed my lack of awareness of where water comes from, to which water bodies my own body is connected, as another example of my disconnection from water. I learned from Chinese Canadian Rita Wong, the tireless water warrior, another experiment with a glass of water. At a reading from her powerful poetic reflection on water, *Undercurrents,* she invited us to take a moment to consider the source of the last glass of water we had drunk.[6] Where was that water yesterday, last week, last month, a year ago? And where will it go after it leaves our bodies? Where will it go in a day, a week, a month? As I conducted this exercise, I realized how I was literally physically connected through the water I drank to the watershed of the Trent River in the Comox Valley where I was living at the time. Rita and Dorothy Christian have written an article in which they challenge readers to reimagine themselves as a living part of a watershed, with which they are interdependent and upon which they are dependent.[7] A watershed is incorporated into our bodies through the air we breathe and the water we drink, and *its* history is part of *our* history. Even if you drink water from a plastic bottle, you can ask, "Where does it come from, and where does it go?" Water always has a context; it is always in place. Water is a process.

This awareness helped me to expand upon the fact that the body is 60 to 70 percent water. All the fluids in our body are replaced seventeen times a year, exchanging with the water systems around us through drinking, breathing, eating, peeing, sweating, or crying. So we are viscerally connected to all other beings through water. I need this concreteness to understand the fact that when we take the time to actually trace our water, we discover that there is only a finite amount of it in the world. This water connects us to places, people, and creatures we have not seen, life that is far away from us, life in the future, and life that came long before us. As Mi'kmaq anti-fracking activist Suzanne Patles, from the Mi'kmaq community of Elsipogtog, has said, water connects us to our ancestors who came before us and to the generations ahead.[8]

Many Indigenous languages, which are centred around verbs rather than nouns, describe water in terms of how it moves, sounds, and looks – for example, rain falling, ice melting. In Ojibwemowin the word for bay is "to be a bay." As Robin Wall Kimmerer states in her book *Braiding Sweetgrass,* "a bay is only a noun if water is dead." She continues: "The verb wiikwegamaa – to be a bay – releases the water from bondage and lets it live. 'To be a bay' holds the wonder that, for this moment, the living water has decided to shelter itself between these shores, conversing with cedar roots and a flock of baby mergansers."[9] The English language falsely holds water temporarily in suspension, even though it continues to move.

Madeleine MacIvor, a Cree-Metis colleague aware of my interest in embodiment, connected me with the work of the Moroccan French anthropologist Frédérique Apffel-Marglin, who studied the ceremonies of Indigenous peoples in the Andes of Peru and in Orissa, India. Apffel-Marglin illustrates that an embodied connection to water undermines many aspects of the Western scientific worldview, including our understanding of the human person.[10] She notes that, in Indigenous worldviews, there is a continuity and flow between bodily fluids and the earth, a moving back and forth. She challenges the notion of the biological body as a Western construct that views the body as a distinct object, separate from nature and the spirit world, with very fixed boundaries.[11] She argues that, if we can experience the body as more fluid, as very much part of the environment surrounding it, then this can shift how we understand human will and autonomy. We are not as autonomous as we like to think, and it is this ability to have fluid boundaries that supports relationship, that deep sense of connection that is possible both with the spirit of water and with the human, non-human, and more-than-human worlds. In line with the notion of the limits to human autonomy, she cites research from the Andean Altiplano that illustrates how agency is held by non-human entities, including the waters.[12]

All this has affected how I relate to water and understand the water bodies around us. Connection to place and watersheds/water bodies is an extension of our bodily awareness. So the notion of water as spirit and relative is quite concrete. We have relationships with water bodies that are living beings that have their own needs for harmony and balance. All the struggles informed and led by Indigenous peoples to stop pipelines, fracking, or dams – whether we're speaking of Standing Rock in North Dakota, the Site C dam in British Columbia, the Unist'ot' en Camp and the many nations and groups resisting pipelines in British Columbia, or the Mi'kmaq stopping fracking at Elsipogtog in New Brunswick – are grounded in listening to water and the belief that "water is life." The practice of listening to water's needs, of having a reciprocal relationship with water, challenges the colonial pattern of assuming humans know best for the natural world.

In my pedagogical practice I wanted to share some of the embodied ways of relating to water that I had learned. In the spring of 2012, Alannah and I contributed a workshop called "Moving with Water" to a symposium on protecting water titled "Downstream: Reimagining Water."[13] This event brought together artists and water protectors from many nations and was held at the Emily Carr College of Art by False Creek in Vancouver. We had developed and offered this workshop over a period of a few years. Its objective was to bring an embodied and spiritual dimension to water protection and activism. We were able to integrate ceremony with Anishinabe and Coast Salish teachings about water, and combine these with movement activities that explored our internal relationship with water. We taught water songs, supported the creation of ritual dances, and encouraged participants to include ceremony in their public water activism.[14] It is important to continue to encourage an embodied awareness of and relationship with water as sacred, especially at a time when water wars, including legal cases over pipelines and dams, are being fought on a solely material level.

Through many events like "Downstream" my understanding of human relationship with water has evolved as more and more people, Indigenous and non-Indigenous, address the need to change the terms of how we protect and relate to water. At the Downstream symposium, Stó:lō Elder and author Lee Maracle stated that she was uncomfortable with the "water-is-a-human right" argument and she talked about humbling oneself to water. She added, unequivocally: "we don't own the water, the water owns itself." And it follows that if we don't own the water, then "we can only engage with it in relationship. We have to seek permission from it and to use it, we must care for it."[15]

The fundamental teaching about water – water is life – that you find in all Indigenous traditions has several dimensions to it. Water is alive; it is sacred; it is part of a holistic system, a greater interconnected whole; and we have obligations, responsibilities, to water as a relative with whom we are in relationship. Kim Anderson, a Cree-Métis educator, interviewed several Métis, First Nations, and Inuit grandmothers in order to capture how they conveyed these spiritual qualities of water and the significance of the spirit of water in creating and sustaining life.[16] The grandmothers told stories that centred on how water is understood and related to in land-based communities, and how the central role of water in maintaining good health is dependent on how well we manage our relationships with it. Women's special bond with water comes from our earliest connection with it, both carrying the waters of gestation and being held in our mother's waters before birth. If we are disrespectful or careless with this life force, we put ourselves at risk. All the grandmothers stressed that ceremony with water is important because it involves the intentional act of connecting, renewing, and maintaining relationship with the spirit of water.

My own involvement with activism to protect water has led me to the discovery of the world of Indigenous water law. Anishinaabe lawyer Lindsay Borrows referred me to the work of Danika Billie Littlechild, a Cree lawyer who is articulating a way to bring Cree water law into dialogue with Canadian water law.[17] Littlechild shows clearly how First Nations experience of water goes way beyond access to safe drinking water. One cannot hunt or fish if water has been polluted, dammed, or drained. But even more is at stake. In Littlechild's words:

Indigenous water use also includes use for ceremonial, spiritual and community purposes. Identity formation and linguistic diversity can be compromised. When First Nations lose access to a sacred or traditional water source, they lose access to the beings and spirits that inhabit that water source. This loss ripples out. Stories, songs, dances and even Indigenous words related to that water source are also lost. The foundational elements of Indigenous legal traditions and knowledge systems are at risk.[18]

Dorothy Christian told me about the work of Sam Marlowe (Syilx), who works on Indigenous water Rights in Dorothy's territories, which are those of the Syilx (Okanagan) and Secwepemc (Shuswap) Nations. Marlowe tells the Secpwecemc Beaver and the Porcupine story, and illustrates how it provides guidelines for ethical relationships with water.[19] "The customary laws that are embedded within the oral trad-ition of the Secwepmec concurrently provide information on needs of the water-dependent species and instructs the Aboriginal people of their responsibilities to the natural world environment."[20] Indigenous stories are not fanciful myths; rather, they provide a balanced perspective on the needs of all water-dependent species. With more research I discovered that some of the Midewiwin Water Walkers had contributed to a report, "Anishinaabe Nibi Inaakonigewin," translated loosely as "Anishinaabe Water Law," which reflects on their traditional teachings and water stories.[21]

These encounters with Indigenous water laws have been my introduction to the world of Indigenous law. The term "Original Instructions" is used by some nations to describe the teachings in Indigenous traditions that form the basis of Indigenous law and that govern human relations with all living beings.[22] Each Indigenous tradition has its Original Instructions, which as humans we ignore at our peril. Indigenous legal orders are informed by these teachings. Indigenous law is different from what is called "Aboriginal law," which is an area of state law that deals with Indigenous Rights. Cases that involve nations asserting their fishing Rights or land Title through the Canadian court system are part of Aboriginal law and, hence, are still involved in the colonial legal system, using the colonial language and framework. Indigenous law existed long before the colonizers arrived. It is found in stories, dances, songs, ceremonies, art work, languages, and traditions. Each Indigenous nation has its own distinct legal traditions. Indigenous law, grounded in the Original Instructions, articulates a cosmology of interrelationship with all beings and addresses the duties and responsibilities that flow from these relationships.[23]

In 2016, West Coast Environmental Law, supported by the Indigenous Law Research Unit of the Faculty of Law at the University of Victoria, established the Revitalizing Indigenous Law for Land, Air and Water (RELAW) project. RELAW's purpose is to train community members to gather stories that can be the basis of creating contemporary legal instruments that can inform "creating water policies, marine use plans, environmental codes of ethics, consent regimes, and environmental assessment practices all rooted in their own laws."[24] This, to me, is one of the most hopeful things that has happened in a long time as it means that individual communities are being trained to develop their own legal principles, which can then inform their decision making around resource development. It also gives settlers principles they can defend as allies and broadens their understanding of their own responsibilities to water. West Coast Environmental Law has also developed a brief to show how Indigenous water law fits within the framework of the UN Declaration on the Rights of Indigenous Peoples.[25] One of the objectives of RELAW is to pressure government and corporations to take Indigenous law more seriously, which is something that settlers can take part in, advocating for Indigenous water law to guide how all water is protected.

I approach water protection from an interfaith perspective. Because I am living in and on Indigenous lands I need to educate myself and learn ways of acting that respect Indigenous worldviews and that enable me to live within Indigenous systems of law. At the same time I need to call to account the Christian tradition. The dominant culture's representation of water as an object and resource to be used by humans is very much a product of a colonial reading of the Bible – that is, a reading that legitimates human domination of the earth. As an alternative to colonial Christianity, which imposed its laws on the original peoples, I teach how the Bible was used to justify imperial domination of lands and all that existed on them – humans, animals, women, and waters. I draw from the work of Botswanan biblical scholar Musa Dube, whose postcolonial feminist reading of the Hebrew and Christian scriptures is grounded in South African Indigenous Traditions and holds up the sacredness of the land and the waters.[26] There is now a school of postcolonial eco-feminist theologians that is rereading biblical texts through the lens of an ethic that challenges the anthropomorphism, the human centredness, of colonial Christianity.[27]

On the Christian activist front there is the Watershed Discipleship movement, which is informed by bioregionalism, Indigenous solidarity, and an anti-colonial reading of the Bible.[28] It shares the value of affirming and living out of a sense of the sacredness of place and has many affinities with Indigenous worldviews. The hub of this movement, which has followers across the continent in both the United States and Canada, is Bartimaeus Cooperative Ministries (BCM), located in the Ventura River watershed in southern California.[29] Ched Myers, who is an activist biblical scholar and co-founder of BCM with his Mennonite partner Elaine Enns, promotes Watershed Discipleship. In 2016 he edited a collection of writing (to which I contributed the foreword) by young Christian activists and scholars on water, local sustainability, and restorative justice for the land.[30] In his introduction, Ched invites

Christians to locate themselves in place. This means, specifically, to become connected to the particular watershed that they inhabit and to integrate a watershed ethos into the way humans live so as to cultivate an ethical and reciprocal relationship with land, waterways, and the peoples who live within them. He proposes that restorative justice should be extended to non-humans and offers a rereading of the parable about judgment day, in which Jesus explains to the disciples that he is the person whom we either responded to or ignored during the course of our lives, the person who was hungry, thirsty, naked, in prison, or ill. Ched posits, "Might not the Jesus of Matthew 25 also ask, 'I was an endangered Steelhead Trout, and you did not restore my habitat?'"[31]

Going back to Indigenous teachings, the questions are: "How can I be responsible to this place, to the waters of this place?" and "How can I locate or relate myself to the existing agendas and laws of the people and this place?" This is not an easy process for newcomers. I give one example of a starting point for myself. In Victoria, British Columbia, there is a walk around the Gorge, an inland waterway connected to the Juan de Fuca Strait. The Gorge was at one time a key source of food – oysters, ducks, herring – for the Songhees and Esquimalt, Straits Salish peoples who form the Lekwungen Nation. Now its waters are surrounded by condominiums and homes with private docks and are populated by paddle boarders, kayakers, canoes, and motor boats. The walk is for pedestrians and cyclists. At one point, beside a tall black orb that digitally records the number of cyclists that pass it per day, stands a totem pole carved by Charles Elliot (Temosen) of the Tsartlip First Nation. At the base of the pole is a plaque identifying this as the Water Keepers' Pole. At the bottom is Frog, atop Frog is a Salish Welcome Warrior figure carrying a paddle and wearing an Osprey headdress. Above Osprey is Killer Whale and, finally, Kingfisher, "who announces the arrival of anyone or any new change in the realm of the water keepers and dwellers as custodians of the great marine paradise." I know now that this pole is not for decoration: it is a statement of connection and an affirmation of Indigenous law.

I had never before considered these various non-human creatures as water guardians. I was expecting water protection knowledge to only come from humans. My friend Joy Illington, a long-time advocate for Indigenous Rights, was with me the first time I saw this pole and she told me that there is a story behind each of its figures. If I am to learn more about how I can be respectful of the waters in this place, I must learn more about these stories and pay attention to what is happening with these beings. Right now the killer whale's existence as a species in the Pacific Northwest is threatened by pipeline tanker traffic and the existence of open-net salmon fish farms. If we destroy the killer whale, we destroy one of the water keepers. Protecting the killer whale is not about protecting tourism (this is a human-centred perspective), it is about maintaining the interconnection between clean water, the whales, the salmon, and the entire ecosystem.

Settlers have much to learn from Indigenous ethics and laws around water and land. There are always ways to contribute to water protection and to support Indigenous water protectors. Water walks are now spreading across the continent. If you are infirm or unable to take several weeks out of your life (that is commitment!), you don't have to be a walker. You can support with a financial contribution or by contacting others who may be able to join. There is so much water that needs protection, from Standing Rock to the Peace River threatened by the Site C dam in British Columbia, the oceans and lakes. There are more than a hundred Indigenous communities in Canada without clean drinking water. The invitation in the phrase "water is life," which has become a rallying cry since Standing Rock, is to protect water in a way that honours its sacredness and recognizes it is a spirit and a relative. It is an invitation to approach water in ceremony and to perform our activism prayerfully and with reverence. To change how we relate to water requires a different way of being. It can begin with being grateful for each glass of water we drink. It can continue as we stand with all Indigenous and non-Indigenous protectors of the water. We can support and promote Indigenous law and live our sacred obligations to the other-than-human world that require us to uphold Indigenous water laws. In this way, we can change how we live on this land and how we relate to the waterways that surround us.

Ceremony

It is 1990 and I am attending my first sweat lodge. It is being held at the Chawathil First Nation reserve. Chawathil is part of the Stó:lō Nation and is on the north side of the Fraser Valley, near Hope, at the foot of a tall mountain. I had been invited to attend by Ida John, who was the field supervisor of Caroline Caldwell, one of the students at the Native Family Violence Program at the Native Education Centre. I had mentioned to her a few weeks earlier that I was heartbroken because my partner of seven years had just left me. Ida suggested I come to the sweat as a way of healing. So that morning I packed up a cotton nightdress, bought a package of tobacco as an offering, and headed out on Highway 1 for the adventure.

I drive into the community feeling quite anxious. I finally find Ida's house. Not far away from it is a low roundish structure covered with a black tarp. I figure this is the sweat lodge. After being warmly greeted by Ida, we change at her house and head out to the lodge. It is a mixed sweat in that men and women are together during the ceremony.

The lodge leader is a male Elder from the Stó:lō Nation who begins his teachings in the sweat with a plea to the Creator to have pity on him as a weak human being, and he prays for more humility. I am used to priests and ministers presenting a certain level of moral superiority, so this is somewhat of a shock. Then he invites us to share first in a round of prayers of gratitude, something that was somehow missing from my experience of Christian liturgies. I am inspired hearing the different things people are thankful for. However, soon it becomes so hot I can barely think. I crawl out with some of the participants after the second round, after the door has been opened to let in some fresh air, and collapse on the damp cool ground. I watch a few of the men jump into a pond beside the sweat. It is early May so I think they are

crazy as the water is freezing. By the third round, I feel I can't handle
any more heat. Ida suggests I just wait out the last round and prepare
for the feast that would follow.

I look at my watch that I left by my towel on the ground. It is already
past one and the sweat is not over yet. I have already been there for
four hours. A feast! I don't have time for that. I have to get back to
Vancouver by mid-afternoon for a 3:00 p.m. appointment. So, feeling
somewhat awkward as I am leaving before the end, I say goodbye to Ida
and thank the leader, change in the house, pack up my gear, and head
back to Vancouver. The sweat has been good as a physical experience
and the teachings and heat have made me forget my problems; yet I am
somewhat annoyed not only that no one had told me how long the
actual sweat would take but also that there was a feast afterwards.

I look back at this experience now with amusement. I was driven by
the clock, already into the future, so barely present when I was there. I
was unprepared for the feast and had brought no food. I expected to be
told what to do rather than just learn by observation. I had not asked
questions regarding the appropriate Protocols to follow before I went.
I had no idea how much I had to learn.

Ten years later, in 2000, I was invited to another sweat ceremony and
eventually joined a sweat lodge community. This was the sweat lodge
hosted by the First Nations Longhouse community at the UBC First
Nations House of Learning. Because UBC and FNHL are on the territory
of the xʷməθkʷəy̓əm (Musqueam) Nation, the founders of the lodge had
asked the Musqueam's permission to have a sweat lodge on their land.
Although many Coast Salish people participate in sweat lodges, these
are not part of the Coast Salish tradition. However, late Musqueam
Elder Vince Tsimlano Stogan said it was important to support the lodge
because students from all First Nations attend UBC. Two lodges, one
for men and one for women, were established at FNHL by Michael and
Pemina Yellowbird from the Three Affiliated Tribes (Mandan, Hidatsa,
and Arikara) when Michael was a faculty member in the early 1990s.
When I began to attend, two of my friends, Madeleine MacIvor (Cree-
Metis) and Alannah Young (Anishnabe Cree), were then leading the
women's lodge. They both incorporated the teachings of Pemina as well
as those of Nlaka'pamux Elder N'kixw'stn James. The FNHL lodge was
a "teaching lodge" and served to educate students and build up their
leadership abilities as well as provide spiritual support for students,

faculty, and staff. Because Madeleine and Alannah ran it as a teaching lodge, I learned a lot by osmosis.

My learning about Indigenous ceremony has been largely through the body. The sweat was an embodied experience at several levels. First, I discovered that the ceremony involved way more than the actual sweat. A feast was always an integral part of the ceremony, not just an add-on. So too was preparation of the wood, the keeping of the fire that heated the rocks, the setting up of the lodge beforehand, the preparation of the food, the eating together, the cleaning up after the feast, the taking down of the lodge afterwards, watching the fire until it burned out on its own, and all the other work that was part of a sweat. It was all ceremony. I had to let go of my obsession with time scheduling and be willing to commit most of the day. And I learned discipline. The sweats were usually one day a month, sometimes two. Sometimes I just didn't feel like going, especially in the winter if it was snowing or cold, or if it was solstice and you had to be there in the dark before sunrise. It involved a lot of preparation – a gift of tobacco or cloth for the leaders, making food for the feast, bringing a sweat dress, and wearing a skirt before and after. I didn't always understand why we followed certain Protocols, like wearing a skirt, but I was taught that if I chose to participate in ceremony, especially as a novice, I was to follow the Protocol established by the sweat lodge leader. As an outsider, it is not my prerogative to get involved in debates about wearing a skirt. I can remember always feeling nervous about doing things "right" and being uncomfortable with how much preparation was involved. However, no one seemed upset when I did something "wrong." Once I arrived on site and participated in the work my discomfort shifted and I was able to move into ceremonial time.

Equally significant was the sense of community. Because it was a university context, many students came and went, yet there was a core group – mostly faculty, some graduate students and staff – who came month after month and were faithful over the years. The lodge was welcoming of all people and, perhaps because of my interfaith working relationship with Alannah and Madeleine, and later my experience as director of an interfaith institute at Simon Fraser University, I felt comfortable there and attended regularly. Eventually, being present at this lodge became part of my own spiritual practice. My commitment included responsibility to the relationships that developed over the years with the regular attendees, with what was loosely called the "UBC sweat community." Even if some of us only saw each other at the sweats, there continued to be this connection.

The heat was not too bad in the women's lodge. As Madeleine once said, women suffer enough so it is fine for the sweat to be gentle. My relationship with rocks, fire, earth, water, and plant medicines has transformed over the years. I now have an embodied sense that rocks have spirits and understand, if only slightly, the teaching that they are our oldest living relatives. I appreciate the fire for how it heats the rocks and the warmth it gives in the winter as we huddle by it waiting to go into the lodge. I now understand a bit more the Dene men whom I had observed many years earlier offering tobacco to the fire before they warmed their drums. I have learned that the fire carries our prayers to the Creator when we offer it tobacco. I so appreciate the smell and firmness of the earth as we enter the lodge, what some describe as the womb of the earth, and I love being able to sit or lie down on the cedar branches that hold her coolness and solidity – what a gift when it is too hot! I am in awe of the transformation of water into steam as it touches the hot rocks. I savour the smell of the cedar boughs on the floor and don't even have a problem with the prickly branches that sometimes stick into my bottom. I have learned respect for the different plant medicines that are brought into the ceremony and have felt their power.

It was through the sweats that I was first taught a different way to relate to plants. Every spring, we tore down the old lodge and built a new one. This involved, among many tasks, going to pick cedar for the floor of the lodge. I first went with Madeleine, who gave me some tobacco and clippers and instructed me to offer some tobacco and say a prayer to the cedar tree before I cut off any of the branches. Without her guidance, I would have just torn off many branches. As I would later learn, as with wild crafting of plants, I was not to take as much as I wanted but only what I needed. So I moved from tree to tree only taking a bit from each. I prayed to the cedar and asked its permission and thanked it for letting us have a few of its branches. I confess that at first my mind was sceptical about saying a prayer to a tree and offering tobacco, and I was often just going through rote gestures. However, over the years, I have learned great respect for the cedar tree, for the work it does for us in cleansing spaces and healing, not to mention its fundamental historical role as the main provider for almost all the living needs of Coastal peoples – for big houses, canoes, bowls, clothing, cooking, poles, the list goes on. From Terri-Lynn Williams Davidson, a Haida singer and lawyer, I learned that cedar is "a cultural keystone species" and how the Haida regard the cedar as their Big Sister.[1] To see cedar as a relative was new for me, and I still strive to remember and enact that relational understanding.

My embodied involvement in ceremony was solidified by the singing that was part of it. I had been told by my mother that I had a terrible voice and I believed her. Yet in a sweat lodge I was able to lose my awkwardness over my gravelly voice. We could not see each other in the darkness and there was no judgment about how each person sang. So I learned to sing with my whole heart and voice. Alannah or Madeleine would pass out rattles (called shakers in some Indigenous Traditions), so my body was engaged in song. Some brought their drums into the sweat, and I eventually had the privilege of making my own drum and bringing it in. Through all this I discovered that I could sing, that songs were medicine, and that singing was an integral part of the healing power of the sweat.

Other ceremonies took place around the lodge and the lodge community. Sometimes there were pipe ceremonies. I remember a Lakota pipe ceremony, an initiation ceremony for a young girl, in which the girl reenacted the movements of the White Buffalo Calf Woman who gave the first pipe to the people. I especially remember a pipe ceremony that I was invited to in North Vancouver. It involved the passing on of a pipe from an older woman to a younger one, both of whom regularly attended the FNHL sweat. The latter was finishing her doctorate in psychology at UBC and was gradually assuming some ceremonial leadership in her work and community. This particular ceremony was integrated into the sweat lodge of Art Leon (from Sts'ailes, or Chehalis), Alannah's partner, and was on the territory of the Squamish Nation in North Vancouver. It was my first time in a mixed sweat after many years, and I was worried about making a faux pas, not doing things "correctly." And I feared the heat of a mixed lodge. However, once inside the lodge, I calmed down and observed with fascination the passing on of the pipe that occurred during the second round, the women's round. The pipe was being given by the elder women as an acknowledgment of the leadership responsibilities that the younger woman was assuming in receiving it. The words spoken were very powerful, and I saw them as a sanctification of her role in her community and as a holding up of her gifts.

This ceremony had an unexpected effect on me. I felt sadness and a pang of loss as I compared it to my Catholic tradition. Here I was, a Catholic woman, by that time with two ministry degrees, who had never had any public or collective ceremonial acknowledgment of her role and responsibilities. While the fact that I couldn't be ordained because I was a woman, not to mention a lesbian, has led me into worlds I may never have entered if I had done something like parish ministry, the lack of ceremonial recognition has been painful. Here I was being exposed to a culture that had a different notion of spiritual leadership. It was based on demonstrated responsibility, hard work, commitment, reliability, and lifeways, and it affirmed the gifts of each person in whatever role she had in her community. As I watched the naming of the responsibilities that came with being a pipe carrier, I felt admiration for this way of honouring a person's spiritual dimension. I also felt sorrow and anger for my own Catholic culture, which has so few ways of sacralizing the responsibilities and roles of laypeople, especially women, within a community. With the lodge leaders that day – a male and a female for balance, and the woman Elder who had passed on her pipe –"leadership" seemed to be horizontal rather than vertical.

Over a period of about twelve years I was invited to other ceremonies at the First Nations House of Learning's Longhouse Community. Some were graduation ceremonies, one was a memorial for one of the members of the sweat community who had passed on, two were engagement ceremonies, and one was a ceremony that acknowledged the appointment of someone at the university. This was a Musqueam witnessing ceremony that affirmed and inaugurated Stephen Toope when he became president of UBC in 2006. Over the years, I have observed this Musqueam witnessing ceremony integrated into the programs of some conferences that were held at the Longhouse. Jo-Ann Archibald Q'um Q'um Xiiem (Stó:lō), at that time dean of Indigenous Education, explained at the annual Indigenous graduate symposiums at FNHL that the Musqueam are a Coast Salish people and that one of their Protocols is this form of witnessing. It involves calling specific people to report back to their communities what they have just seen and heard. It is a ceremonial way of incorporating accountability into an event.

I didn't really understand the importance of witnessing until Alannah and I started to work with the Elders of the LE,NONET Project at the University of Victoria in 2009. The Elders advisory group, composed of Coast and Straits Salish members as well as a Metis Elder, decided to incorporate a witnessing ceremony into the Aboriginal cultural aware-ness training we were developing for the staff and faculty. It involved inviting four people from among the participants who had strategic connections in the university – in other words, who had specific spheres of influence – to assume the responsibility of reporting back to their constituency what they had seen and heard. They also reported back to the group at the end of the training, which, by enabling us to see it through their eyes, was a way of summarizing for the rest of us what we had learned or missed. This responsibility was given to them in a solemn ceremonial context. The ceremony was led by Wayne Charlie, a Quw'utsun Mustimuhw (Cowichan Tribes) Traditional Knowledge Keeper and Speaker.[2] The four witnesses were asked to be represent-atives for the rest of the group, yet all of us were invited to witness as well and to report back to our communities, families, and friends what we had seen and heard. The gravity of the occasion, the fact that the Speaker spoke his language, hul'q'umi'num, which was translated into English by another Elder, affirmed the seriousness with which each of the four was appointed and with which all of us were to understand our responsibilities.

Witnessing is a Coast Salish legal practice with a long history. The ceremony and practice of witnessing has always been very much part of oral societies because there were no signed documents. The witnesses were the official record keepers. They had the responsibility of passing knowledge on to future generations, of carrying history and authen-ticating what really happened. As the ceremony is practised today, it evokes both reciprocity and responsibility. We are invited out of the role of passive observers to be active listeners, so there is a bond between speakers and listeners. Musqueam Elder Larry Grant, who led several of the witnessing ceremonies of which I have been part, has described witnessing as follows:

We call witnesses to be the keepers of our history when an event of historic significance occurs in the Coast Salish world. We do this in part because our traditions are oral, but also in the recognition

of the importance of conducting business and building and
maintaining relationships, in person and face to face ... We call
on all the members of the audience to record this event in their
minds and their hearts and to share the story of what happened
here today.[3]

I have had the privilege of attending other ceremonies over the years.
I have been present at four Midewiwin initiation ceremonies, three
of which were are part of the Three Fires Midewiwin Lodge at Bad
River, Wisconsin, and one at the Minweyweygaan Midewiwin Lodge at
Roseau River, Manitoba. I first attended the lodge in Bad River to support Alannah when she was initiated into this Midewiwin Anishnabe
society in 2004. I attended two more ceremonies there, one at which
I accompanied an Anishnabe friend, Lorraine, who had never been
to a Midewiwin ceremony, and the other as an extended member of
Alannah's large family. In 2014, I went as a support for Alannah when
she was initiated into the second degree at the Minweyweygaan Lodge
at Roseau River. My experience at these Midewiwin ceremonies, which
stretched over four or more days, has been one of the most powerful
in my life.

There is a Protocol of not describing what happens in ceremonies,
especially when you are an outsider. I learned about this at the first
Midewiwin ceremony I attended. I was feeling lonely and awkward
at Bad River, being one of a very small number of non-Indigenous at
a ceremony that involved more than five hundred people. I can speak
to how I was mesmerized by the drumming, dancing, and singing.
We were there for four and a half days, immersed from sunrise to
sunset, with work to do as helpers – preparing and sharing communal
meals, dressing and preparing the lodges, listening to teachings, and
supporting the initiates and their families. At one point, I had asked
Alannah to explain what was going on, and she replied: "I can't. We
are in group mind." I am not sure those were her exact words, but the
message was clear – this was about experiencing, and for her to talk
about it would take her out of the embodied collective experience. I
didn't understand what she meant then, but a few years later, by the time
I got to Roseau River, I was more relaxed. I was able to laugh and joke
with a few people who knew me by then, and, by observing, listening,
and paying attention, I began "to get" what was going on. When the

dancing and singing reached its full intensity I was "in it," I had become part of the collective "group mind."

From my own experience of silent retreats in the Christian tradition, the more you talk about a powerful spiritual experience the more it dissipates. Across traditions, there seems to be an unwritten law pertaining to maintaining silence in order to keep spiritual energy alive. Yet there are other reasons for why it is not appropriate for me to describe in detail what happens in a Midewiwin ceremony or inside a sweat. One of these is historical. In Canada, the Indian Act banned ceremonies for many years; participation in some, like the potlatch on the Northwest Coast or the Sundance on the Plains, could and did lead to imprisonment. From the initial law of 1884 on, a culture of secrecy developed, with some ceremonies continuing underground and some being forgotten. After 1951, the ban on ceremonies was lifted; however, caution is still necessary as another problem has emerged.

While there is more respect for Indigenous traditions now, there are still many people who misinterpret various aspects of Indigenous ceremony or who intentionally misuse them by taking them out of context. This appropriation and misrepresentation of Indigenous knowledge and practices is engaged in by non-Indigenous people, usually white. This sort of thing is found not only in many forms of "New Age" spirituality but also in some mainstream circles, where the desire to know about Indigenous ceremony is founded on a belief that if non-Indigenous know more about Indigenous "spirituality" this will end settler ignorance – which, it is assumed, is the main cause of Indigenous oppression. "Spirituality" is a word that many Indigenous people do not use, rooted as it is in a European Christian assumption of the mind-body split and of spiritual life as somehow separate from daily life. Many settlers prefer to see Native spirituality in isolation from the daily realities of Indigenous life – racism, loss of land, violence against Indigenous women, and Indigenous peoples' struggles for sovereignty. Indigenous studies scholar Andrea Smith vehemently challenges any engagement with Indigenous ceremonial practices that does not include taking responsibility to build relationships with Indigenous peoples and their communities and to change the material conditions of Indigenous communities and end the exploitation of their homelands.[4] One of the most common misuses of Indigenous ceremony that I have observed involves people using or appropriating aspects of it solely for their individual healing journey. From what I have observed, these practices are intended to affirm interdependence and to strengthen one's role in the collective.

There are several forms of cultural appropriation. There are non-Indigenous people who claim to be Indigenous spiritual leaders. These "plastic shamans," as many Native people call them, have no connection with any specific Indigenous community or nation, and they charge considerable amounts of money for leading sweats and other ceremonies. The latter are often a mishmash of many traditions. Then there are those who drop in on seasonal ceremonies in the hope that doing so will enable them to extract the core of what it means to be "Indian." The interfaith curious can also fall into the trap of appropriation. These are people who are open to other traditions while being deeply rooted in their own. Their temptation is to draw simplistic parallels between other traditions and their own traditions and, hence, to misinterpret the former. This is a temptation of which I have had to be wary.

As I have learned over the years, it takes much time and commitment to grasp even a small portion of an Indigenous tradition, and I now see that drawing quick comparisons is a colonial practice. Accordingly, I am uncomfortable with the idea of borrowing elements from a distinct culture and religious practice and inserting it into one's own, something I have seen in some white European Christian churches and in some women's "spiritual-but-not-religious" ceremonies. I am not referring here to Indigenous Christians but, rather, to non-Christians who often incorporate smudging and sweetgrass into a ritual or who use the words taken from what seems to be a boundless supply of supposedly Native American prayers that show up on the internet. These practices are not in themselves inherently wrong. The problem occurs when the borrowing is one-sided or misrepresents the cultural meaning of the practice. As a 2016 guide developed by the Intellectual Property Issues in Cultural Heritage Project at Simon Fraser University states: "'Misappropriation' describes a one-sided process where one entity benefits from another group's culture without permission and without giving something in return."[5] Indigenous ceremonies emerged out of specific contexts and histories, and have cultural and place-based meanings. They have rigorous Protocols and are part of a committed way of life. These points are lost when a white shaman offers a sweat in his or her backyard, or when white people attend a Sundance on a drop-in basis.

Indigenous traditions are not conversion religions – that is, they are not designed to convert people and you cannot become Lakota, or Salish, or Mi'gmaq by attending ceremonies. Each Indigenous tradition is tribally specific; certain ceremonies are part of a much larger tradition that is based in kinship, a common history, and relationship to land, language, and territory. Many ceremonies are not public – that is, they are not for non-Indigenous people. There are also what are called intertribal ceremonies, such as sweat lodges based on the Lakota tradition, and some Sundances, which are open to many nations; however, there are many more ceremonies that stay strictly within communities.

The complexity of the issue of outsider misinterpretation and misappropriation is connected to the ongoing debate about who can attend Indigenous ceremonies. The issue of who is allowed to attend a Sundance and when it is appropriate to do so is one that I have wrestled with, both as an outsider and as someone who has been invited to attend as a participant helper. From what I have learned, the Sundance ceremony requires a lifetime commitment. To dance requires eight years at minimum – four years to dance and four years to help and support the dancers in the lodge. Each year that you dance you attend a "pledge meeting" to stay connected to the intention you bring to the dance and to support the community, and you commit to help and provide resources. A friend told me that a Cree Sundance chief was one of the Sundance leaders who for many years did not allow non-Native people to participate because he was concerned that their active involvement might deter Indigenous people who had for years internalized a sense of distrust of white people. Now he supports the option of non-Indigenous people participating as helpers for four years before they can dance. This helper position is "not to earn their way but to familiarize themselves with the ceremony and its purpose in their own life path, as receivers."[6]

For many reasons, I myself have never attended a Sundance. Even though I have been invited to the Sundance that is led by Alannah's husband, Art Leon, I have not been clear on my motives for attending and therefore have chosen to support it financially instead. Possibly this is because I have been to Midewiwim ceremonies and have been part of a sweat lodge community, and possibly it is because I don't want to be a ceremony tourist or even a voyeur. Possibly it is because I practise Zen meditation and don't want to abandon my Christian spiritual practices, which also take time and commitment. As well, I have observed a dynamic where when too many white people show up at a ceremony then Indigenous people gradually disappear. Sometimes this is not just because of their distrust of white people; often, the outsiders try to take over, and so it no longer feels like a welcoming place.

Perhaps I am too scrupulous. Many Indigenous ceremonial leaders practise the principle of non-interference and say nothing when non-Native people show up at a ceremony. They believe each person will take something of value away, and they assure those who think they are just observing that they are in fact participating and are part of the ceremony. As Madeleine MacIvor once said to me, "My teachings about the sweat are that people come for many different reasons, that it is not up to me to judge the reasons, and that there is a place for each one of us inside the lodge."[7]

I am aware that linked to the quest for a "real" spirituality on the part of many non-Indigenous people is a Christianity that has failed them. This is not only because most Christian churches are allied with the dominant society but also because spirituality often takes a back seat to lengthy sermons and a hierarchy from which diversity and difference are excluded. While ex-Christians or those raised without a religious upbringing may choose Buddhism, Hinduism, Islam, Wicca, or Goddess worship, it is not surprising that many want to engage with Indigenous traditions. These traditions are native to this land and have teachings that match the ecological values of many white people. What is challenging for white Christians is the realization that to really understand Indigenous traditions requires both building long-term relationships based on mutual reciprocity and, at the same time, learning about one's own role in colonization and being okay with being uncomfortable in a lot of situations.[8]

This connects to a debate that has touched me personally as someone who has taught about Indigenous Traditions in a university department of religion. This is the debate over who can teach Indigenous spirituality. When I was hired to teach about Indigenous religions at Concordia it took me some time to figure out how I could do this with integrity and from my location as a settler scholar. I changed the course title to "Indigenous Traditions, Colonialism and Women," avoiding the terms "religion" and "spirituality" altogether. I privileged Indigenous women's voices in readings, invited speakers from the traditions we studied, and experimented with Indigenous pedagogies. I shared my perspective, mistakes, and learnings as a settler and did not attempt to explain or interpret Indigenous traditions.[9] By 2015 I was fortunate to be able to pass on the course to one of my former students and teaching assistant, Kahnawa'kehró:non Orenda Boucher-Curotte.

That same year I was privy to an online list discussion among Indigenous academics after the University of Sudbury posted a job description that called for "an expertise in the areas of health and wellness, community-based research, Indigenous knowledge and Indigenous spirituality." As Indigenous traditions are embodied in practices, the discussion focused on whether Indigenous spirituality can be taught and whether there should be any ceremony or practices conducted in the classroom or at the university. I, like many involved in this discussion, was uncomfortable with the term "spirituality" in the job description as it projected a Euro-Western lens onto traditions within which the spirit world is integrated into daily life rather than seen as a separate realm of experience. For me, if the term is used, it is important to clarify that there is a distinction between Indigenous epistemologies and spirituality. Indigenous ceremony is not necessarily "spirituality," as someone like me, raised a Catholic, is primed to understand the word.

In this particular online debate, most were adamant that their spirituality could not be part of any job description and that the university is such a colonizing institution that any practices shared would only be appropriated, misread, or tokenized. Others were reluctant to rule out all traditional practices from the university. Some instructors, like myself, have invited in Elders and Traditional Knowledge Holders who have the liberty to include whatever ceremonial practices they like. I have always checked in with those who have the cultural authority to decide what is appropriate or not in any teaching situation or workshop. What was clear for all those involved in this discussion was that ceremonies and traditional teachings that are the purview of Traditional Knowledge Holders can never be offered as a credit course in the academy.[10] There are many who, like Muscogee Daniel Wildcat, maintain that respect for Indigenous Traditions may mean accepting that non-Indigenous people may never know or understand First Peoples teachings, and that this includes respecting "the right for First Peoples of the Land to keep something to themselves."[11]

In my discipline, religious studies, there are some who feel strongly that we can only teach *about* religion, not "perform" it. You will often find students of religion are invited to go to synagogues, mosques, or churches to observe a religious practice rather than having that practice-performed in the classroom. However, you don't find students regularly invited to Sundances, Midewiwin ceremonies, or sweat lodges, and many Indigenous people feel that all knowledge of ceremonial practice, all teachings, must be kept in the community and should not be open to university students as a course experience. An interesting exception is a course on the Sundance given at UBC and titled "Indigenous Existential Resistance: The Sundance Practice," the purpose of which is "to prepare you to observe our sacred ceremonies."[12] The original idea for the course came from the Kainai Elders who co-designed it. It combines lectures and seminars at UBC in Vancouver and a ten-day land-based experience in southern Alberta, which includes a four-day observation of a Sundance ceremony in the Kainai community.

I do not think non-Indigenous people should teach about Indigenous "spirituality," but they can team up with Indigenous partners. In terms of my own teaching I have often worked, both inside and outside of the academy, with women who are ceremonial practitioners, like Alannah or Marjorie Beaucage. This teaching has usually been in workshops, where the decision to incorporate some aspect of ceremony is informed by the context and the content of the specific event. At a three-day workshop that Alannah and I co-facilitated for some faculty at Concordia University, Alannah wanted to incorporate a cedar cleansing at the end of the day. The process and the material on Indigenous histories and colonialism that we were covering were difficult and painful for some to hear, and it was a way of closing "in a good way." I was nervous about it, partly because of this emphasis in the field of religious studies on the "objective" presentation of religion and partly because of the issues I have just discussed. In this workshop most of the participants were non-Indigenous and would need to contribute to the ceremony. However, I was reminded of something Alannah had said to me years before: that it is the cedar that does the work, not you. So we proceeded, with criticism from some in the religion department at Concordia and with much appreciation from others.

Later I was reminded by Alannah, as someone who is an Anishnabekwe, a Sundancer, a pipe carrier, a sweat lodge leader, and a

Midewiwin woman, that her spiritual expression is an integral aspect of her self-determination as an Indigenous woman. My role was to make space for this in the university, even if doing so was within the context of ongoing colonialism. As I have heard a few other Indigenous academics say, given the holistic nature of Indigenous worldviews, it does not make sense to leave any worldviews at the door, especially when they form the content and context of the discussion. Ceremony itself is informed by dreams, visions, recent experiences, and the ceremonial leader's decisions. Madeleine MacIvor shared with me her knowledge that ceremonial leaders accommodate based on who is attending, what their needs are, and even the weather, as many ceremonies occur outdoors. She added: "Indigenous ceremony is fluid and responsive. There isn't an overriding body that says you must do this or that. Individual ceremonial leaders have the autonomy to conduct ceremony the way they see fit, with the people they want. It is about spiritual self-determination."[13]

It was through ceremony that the difference between the Euro-Western scientific worldview and Indigenous knowledge systems became apparent to me. As anthropologist Frédérique Apfel-Marglin argues, modernity created the separation of facts and values, "the separation of what is to be known and the life of those who know."[14] In Indigenous worlds this separation does not exist, and ritual performance and ceremony regenerate the world – a world in which humans and other-than humans cohabit.[15] Universities and the mainstream school systems are based on this separation of facts and values, hence the discomfort with embodied and land-based approaches to learning and knowing.

My connections to these tensions and history, and my participation in Indigenous ceremony, have affected how I understand interfaith relations. I am now very wary of blurring the lines between traditions, seeking only commonalities. There are profound differences between Euro-Western Christianity and Indigenous traditions. As Mi'gmaq Elder Pnnal Jerome once said to me, with a twinkle in his eye: "Our ceremonies are so powerful because we invite in the ancestors to participate. My great-grandfather is often present but I don't know what St Paul or St John feel like." I am still moved by the practice of offering a "spirit plate" of food for the ancestors at the beginning of a feast. I am amazed how I have let go of past saints and ancestors so easily, and am jolted by this simple gesture. I cannot say that there is an ongoing respect for ancestors or saints in the Christianity within which I grew up – a Christianity that honours the dead and the saints only once a year.

I am uncomfortable when I see the combining or substituting of various traditions within Christian ritual, even though there are many who are fine with it. As Métis Elder Marjorie Beaucage once said to me, a sweetgrass smudge is not the same as incense. It is all about intention. If incorporating aspects of Indigenous ceremony into a Christian ritual is being done simply to make Indigenous people feel more comfortable in church, there is a problem. If it is done to honour Indigenous ways and knowledge, it carries more weight.

I once remarked to Madeleine MacIvor, who is Catholic as well as a sweat lodge leader, a pipe carrier, and a Sundancer, that I was feeling uncomfortable with the amount of voluntary physical pain that I understood dancers underwent in the Sundance. She replied: "This is similar to the suffering of Jesus on the Cross. We suffer with and for our brothers and sisters." She was helping me to understand through my tradition, while at the same time teaching me that the Sundance had many collective "functions" that Christianity did not. Here one tradition can inform the other, but the context and cultural framework of both are vastly different from each other.

As for me, I find it hard to give up wine for Lent (a forty-day period of returning to the core truths of the Christian tradition by fasting, undergoing penance, and alms giving). I wonder at how the Catholic Euro-Christianity I grew up in became so soft. The discipline and engagement with physical endurance that I observe in Indigenous ceremony, including long periods of fasting, are hard to find in my tradition, and this reminds me of the importance of discipline in spiritual practice. Discipline can make a huge difference. One Indigenous practice with which I struggled but now understand is that of refraining from alcohol or drugs for four days before you participate in a ceremony. Now, as mentioned, wine, not drugs, is my vice of choice. At first I used the excuse that because I was new the rule didn't apply to me and that the four-day requirement was maybe only for those who were heavy drinkers. Somehow I didn't take this requirement seriously, figuring that there was a certain forgiving nature about the ceremonies and that I could break the rules because doing so was only "between me and my Maker." If I was at a Midewiwin ceremony for a week, of course I didn't drink because no one else did. However, a Cree friend once told me alcohol stays in your system for four days. When a friend overdid it at a party and was sick for four days after, I got it. So a few years ago, when I joined a women's drum circle, the same requirement, out of respect for the ancestors, the Creator, and the drum, was made. And for some reason I decided to try it. It was not that hard to skip a glass of wine for four days, and I was amazed at how that changed my experience of the ceremony. It meant that the four days before became part of the ceremony, and I came to the circle with a deeper respect for the drum and songs because I had prepared to be there.

At the same time, as in all religious traditions, a certain type of fundamentalism can creep into Indigenous ceremonies. I remember that, during the preparation for the Walking with Our Sisters Memorial in K'omoks in 2105, the national organizing collective advised the local committee not to implement the no-alcohol-or-drug rule for four days before attending the memorial. Its position was that it was more important that people got to attend and be moved by the ceremony than that they be excluded due to a failure to follow Protocol. One Anishinaabe friend remarked to me that when the rules of a ceremony got too rigid, it reminded him of how the church had operated in his community, and for this reason he avoided some ceremonies. Luckily the ceremonial leaders I know caution against the sort of righteousness that can all too easily lead to dogmatic condemnations and rigid rules. They illustrate the importance of context and intention, and point out that their spiritual traditions do not include making harsh judgments of others.[16] As both the Zen meditation I practise and the teachings of Jesus proscribe judgment and critique dogmatism, this position resonates with me. Ironically, I often still have to catch myself when I make judgments about my fellow settlers – for example, those who do participate in Sundances – even though I don't know their reasons, history, or context.

My awareness of respecting difference in religious traditions was solidified when I was acting director of the Interfaith Institute for Justice, Peace and Social Movements at Simon Fraser University between 2007 and 2012.[17] I worked with an interfaith advisory committee consisting of Indigenous, Muslim, Christian, and Hindu women. We were cautious of some interfaith practices that stress dialogue about commonalities and overlook the serious justice issues involved in many encounters between people of different traditions. When we worked with practitioners of many religions, we chose to foreground

Indigenous Knowledge and Traditions at every public event. This was not only because we were visitors and settlers in the territories of the Skwxwú7mesh (Squamish), xʷməθkʷəy̓əm (Musqueam), and mi ce:p kʷətxʷiləm (Tsleil-Waututh) Nations and followed local Coast Salish Protocols but also because generations of colonial policies, supported by Christian mission, had attempted to obliterate these traditions. We brought Indigenous ceremony into workshops and conferences. By beginning and ending an event with Indigenous ceremony, we provided a container or spirit framework for it, which, in an academic environment, was itself transformative. We hoped to pass on the teaching that, from an Indigenous legal perspective, the host's wealth is measured by her or his ability to accommodate and facilitate good relations.

During this process, I discovered and learned to respect the differences between Indigenous Traditions. This included a time when one of Simon Fraser University's Elders, Eugene Harry, came in and offered, to my surprise, a Shaker ceremony for a welcome.[18] What to me was a curious amalgam of Christian and Coast Salish traditions, I later discovered was a religion practised in several Coast Salish communities, extending from Vancouver Island down the coast to northern Oregon. The institute's commitment to foreground local Indigenous ceremony signified that not only were our events being held on stolen land but also that we acknowledged that Indigenous traditions such as the Shaker one are living and dynamic and are capable of both accommodating and hosting us.

So what is the function of ceremony? Linda Hogan, Chickasaw novelist, essayist, and environmentalist, describes a disembodied American whose romantic images of past Indians in the "wilderness" have served to cloak both the genocide of Indigenous peoples and the destruction of land and animals like the buffalo.[19] She describes her process of attending a sweat lodge ceremony as her way of coming back to her own body and to the memory "that all things are connected":[20]

> The intention of ceremony is to put a person back together by
> restructuring the human mind ... We make whole our broken-
> off pieces of self and world. Within ourselves we bring together
> fragments of our lives in a sacred act of renewal, and we reestablish
> our connections with others. The ceremony is a point of return. It

takes us toward the place of balance, our place in the community of all things. The real ceremony begins where the formal one ends, when we take up a new way, our minds and hearts filled with the vision of earth that holds us within it, in compassionate relationship to and with our world.[21]

My Cree friend Bernadette Spence once said to me that "all life is ceremony." That idea has stayed with me. I do love the Christian monastic tradition of praying the hours seven times in a day or evening, of bringing one back to the remembrance of Spirit. But I need daily reminders that I am connected to, not separate from, all the living beings in my world. I need ceremony to bring me back to a life that is not driven by the values of achievement, success, prestige, or making money. It is Indigenous ceremony that has taught me the most about relationship and about the values of respect, reciprocity, and responsibility. It is because these ceremonies are so embodied that I have a glimmer of these teachings. I can read endless books about Indigenous cultures, but unless I have the privilege of embodied knowledge, what I learn will only stay in my head. As Anishinaabe scholar and activist Lynn Gehl remarks: "This embodied knowledge includes who we are as human beings; who we are within the network of community relationships; the importance of women, men, children and Elders in the community; and the importance of living in harmony and balance with people and the natural world."[22] As a form of embodied knowing, ceremony is a portal into the spirit world. Marjorie Beaucage once said to me: "if you don't sit in our circles, be in our ceremonies, dance in our round dances, you will not know who we are."[23]

14

Reciprocity

I am sitting in an uncomfortable plastic seat in a dark lecture hall at Concordia. At the front of the room, opening the conference, is T'hohahoken Michael Doxtater from Six Nations and a professor in education at McGill. He has been speaking in Kanien'kéha, the Mohawk language, for at least ten minutes. I notice the people around me shifting uneasily in their seats. Because I've been living in British Columbia, where Indigenous presence is much more visible than it is in Quebec, I am quite used to Elders and Traditional Knowledge Holders speaking in their own language. So I am comfortable just listening to the sounds of the language and supporting his intention. I wonder if he will switch to English; eventually he does. The English version seems as long as the Mohawk and, again, I see many of the people around me are looking restless, checking their watches. I, however, am entranced by what he is saying.

Kentióhkwa! Sewatahonhsí:iost ken'nikarihwésha, ne káti
Ohén:ton Karihwatéhkwen enkawennohétston.
  Kentióhkwa! (Group assembled here!) Sewatonhonhsí:iost
(Listen well) ken'nikarihwésha (for a short while), ne káti (as)
Ohén:ton (Before/Ahead of) Karihwatéhkwen (The Business/
Affairs/Issues consolidated) enkawennohétston (the words will
be passed).
  "Group of people here! Listen well for a short while, as we pass
the words that come before all other matters."[1]

After inviting us to listen, in a rhythmic voice T'hohahoken continues with a prayer of thanks, first to the people, then he pauses with a refrain that will be repeated after each such prayer – "now our minds are one." He then goes on to thank Mother Earth, the waters, the fish, the plants and grasses, the medicines, the harvest, the fruits, the animals, the trees, the birds, the insects, the thunder, the four winds, the sun, the moon, the stars, the Creator, and then he closes by saying, "now we open our day." I am stunned. It is like a Catholic litany but with way more substance. Not only has he thanked each of these elements but he has also described the gifts given by each one. I am transported to another level, out of this airless conference hall into the world around that holds us, the world of "nature," which we so easily forget in the concrete jungle of an urban university setting. For a moment, I feel I am a very small part in this interconnected world. The words of this prayer have a humbling effect on me: this is gratitude as an invitation to wholeness.

The year was 2009 and I was attending the ninth annual Critical Race and Anti-Colonial Studies Conference of Researchers and Academics of Colour for Equality (RACE) at Concordia University in Montreal. This was the first time I had heard the Ohén:ton Karihwatéhkwen, known among the Haudenosaunee as "The Words That Come before All Else," often translated on the internet as the Thanksgiving Address. In the next few years I discovered that this address is said at the beginning and ending of class by many Haudenosaunee schoolchildren each day, at the beginning and ending of meetings and conferences, and at gatherings of the Haudenosaunee peoples.[2] I had encountered prayers of gratitude in many of the Indigenous gatherings I had attended, but the thoroughness of this one really affected me. Maybe I was at the stage at which I was ready to actually hear what was being said.

Over the next few years I learned there are slightly different versions of this address. In my last two years of teaching at Concordia University I invited two different Kanien'keha:ka (Mohawk) women, Orenda Boucher-Curotte and Kahsennenhawe Sky-Deer, both from Kahnawà:ke, to open and close the course with it. From them I learned to use the term "Kanien'kéha" to describe the language, not the term "Mohawk," and that it was not appropriate to use an Onondaga version (which I had at first given to my students) of the Ohén:ton Karihwatéhkwen when we were in Kahnawà:ke territory as each community has its own version. I struggled for years with the pronunciation of the title of this address, yet realized how important it was that I use the term that Kanien'kéha people use so as to be able to model for students the importance of learning a few words of the local language. Kahsennenhawe sent me the beginner level translation from the Kanien'kehá:ka Onkwawén:na Raotitióhkwa Language and Cultural Center at Kahnawà:ke, and I gave this to my students. How deeply they absorbed it I do not know. What was important for me as a teacher was to ensure that we began and ended the course in a good way, honouring local Protocols. We were learning to approach Indigenous "religions" as living traditions rooted in living languages. Integral to this was gratitude and an acknowledgment of our reciprocal relationship with all living beings.

When I hear the Ohén:ton Karihwatéhkwen now I am reminded to situate myself in the world in which reciprocity is the natural law. I am not in control: none of us is. I believe that until we are all awake enough to see and live a relationship of reciprocity with the sun, moon, waters, plants, and all our other-than-human relatives, as well as our human ones, we will not be successful in ending colonialism. I did not come to this awareness easily. It is one thing to read about a principle like reciprocity; it is quite another to live by it, or even to get a visceral, embodied understanding of it. Years of attending, being part of, and observing Indigenous ceremony has helped me shift my awareness of reciprocity, though not necessarily always my behaviour.

The offering of tobacco and a prayer of thanks to a plant whose leaves, berries, or roots one is harvesting is but one example of the enactment of the principle of reciprocity. However, it has not been easy for me to internalize the teaching that we have a reciprocal relationship with and responsibility to plants. An illustration: me "stalking the wild asparagus" (the title of a book by the late Euell Gibbons).[3] There are wild asparagus growing near tidal flats by my former house in Courtenay. Asparagus spears, grayish green, are very hard to spot as they blend in with the estuary grasses around them. In that area, there are many people hunting the asparagus, mapping where they found it one year and then aggressively picking it as soon as they can the next, usually taking all they can find. So there is already a competition mentality towards scarcity, not to mention the treat of having this rare plant to eat in the spring. The first few years I picked all I could see. Then, as I slowly became educated about reciprocity, I began to offer tobacco, somewhat cursorily, to a few of the plants. I said a quick prayer but still picked all I could find, somehow rationalizing this by recalling the fact that asparagus grow out of rhizomes under the earth and hence convincing myself I was doing no damage and that more would pop up soon. Finally, last year, I steeled myself and only took half of what I saw. This was the first time I began to feel I was involved in ceremony with the plant. You can't do ceremony half-way; offering tobacco and a quick prayer, for example, is not enough. There was a higher law that I was respecting and, in so doing, I was honouring the plant, even though I bemoaned the fact that one of the asparagus pillagers could take the rest.

There are different teachings on the exact amount to take when harvesting plants. Some say to take only 10 percent, others say half, but the goal when harvesting a plant in the wild is to leave the rest so that it can regenerate. This is a ceremonial act, inherent in a worldview that sees all of creation as living beings. These beings are gifting us, hence we have a responsibility to gift back. This functions as a practice of sustainability not just for humans who use the plant but also for all the living beings who interact with that plant as well as for the plant itself.

It is this gifting as a way of functioning in the world, reciprocity as a moral principle guiding action, that has challenged me the most. Somehow I had grown up with a sense of scarcity, which was surely not rational as my family had way more than enough. A scarcity mentality is very much part of Western consumer culture: one never has enough. It is connected to individualism, to a "survival-of-the-fittest" mentality, and to a lack of trust, be it in a higher power or in a collective. So to interact with a culture that has a different relationship to things, to objects, to living beings was, and is, hard for me.

I had to face my own demons in this area at the first giveaway ceremony of which I was a part. This is a ceremony at which a person gives away many gifts, and it is often part of a larger ceremony, such as a memorial potlatch. The first giveaway I attended occurred when someone from the sweat lodge community at the First Nations House of Learning at UBC was moving on. It was his way of thanking the community. After the sweat and feast, a group of us gathered in the Big Hall in the Longhouse. There was a large pile of items up on the dais – blankets, bowls, pots, and other assorted items I couldn't clearly see. After a short speech, he invited several people to be helpers and to pass out the items. The giver was providing instructions about what to give to whom and it was clear that some things were to be given to specific people, while others were more random. I remember catching myself, wanting certain things and feeling disappointed when I was passed over. I was dismayed when I ended up with a new facecloth and a tea towel while the person beside me got a blanket and a pottery bowl. It took me awhile to realize that I had little history or relationship with the giver and that the structure of the giveaway was linked to relationships, those who were Elders and friends, while at the same time there was an element of randomness.

I have attended many more giveaways over the years. My circle consists mostly of Cree, Métis, and Anishnabe people. The giveaways of which I have been part have varied – a young girl giving gifts after her coming of age ceremony; a woman celebrating with the sweat community a year of being alive without incident after a heart attack; someone giving gifts after receiving a pipe; a memorial service at which the wife gave away her partner's sacred objects and items; another memorial at which we all contributed gifts for the giveaway. I have also witnessed substantial gift bundles offered by initiates in Midewiwin ceremonies. I have been part of giveaways at a Cree Feast of the Dead. Last, but not least, I have been given gifts by some of the women with whom I have worked closely. With all of these experiences I was being invited into a relationship of reciprocity.

The giveaways I have attended are not the same as potlatches, though they share some similar underlying principles. I have learned to honour the differences between Indigenous cultures, and, though I have never attended a potlatch, I have learned a bit from friends who have done so. Potlatches are an integral part of all Northwest Coast cultures. They were directly targeted by colonial legislation and authorities, with participants criminalized and even jailed, until the 1951 repeal of the prohibition of Indigenous ceremonies in the Indian Act.[4] Potlatches are ceremonies that affirm a person's clan, rank, or house legitimacy. These long and elaborate ceremonies often take place over a period of days and are linked to a complex system of responsibilities and reciprocity, of which giving abundant gifts is a part. The host family may own specific dances, songs, and names that are part of the ceremony and may pass one or more of these on. The differences between various ceremonies that involve gifting reflect the complex cultures and lands from which they emerged.

Giving gifts had always been a challenge for me, even when I was young and had to endure Christmas and birthdays, the two times when I needed to give gifts. I wasn't that generous in my heart. I could never figure out what to give people and I watched my money closely, not wanting to spend "too much." Gift-giving was fairly limited in my culture, so I found the gift-giving in Indigenous circles excessive. Yet I felt I was being challenged to examine myself. First, I had to pay attention to how I reacted when I didn't get "stuff." What was that about? Envy? Feeling excluded? Probably more the latter. Then I noticed how impressed I was by the number of gifts someone gave and, as well, how many of the items had been made by the giver. This required a considerable amount of effort and often money. I observed how people would prepare over a significant period of time for their giveaway. At one giveaway I attended, a Métis woman had been preparing for two years; she was giving away handmade gifts, expensive bought things, as well as sacred objects. I received a pair of silver-plated candlestick holders, even though my connection with her was only as part of the larger community invited by the hosts for this specific ceremony. A young girl who had the coming of age ceremony spent an entire year preparing gifts for her giveaway. All this was so different from the culture in which I had grown up, where money could be spent on gifts but little time and effort. It would take a long time for me to understand that gift-giving was part of a culture of reciprocity and that reciprocity was linked to maintaining relationship – one of the highest values.

In 2005, I heard the Anishinaabe lawyer Darlene Johnson talk about gift-giving and reparations at a conference titled "Le Devoir de Memoire" in Montreal.[5] She challenged the audience to learn from Indigenous law how Canadians need to repair the wrongs of colonialism. She was speaking specifically about reparations, and about what it means to materially repair the damage done by righting wrongs. She drew from her research on historical Anishinaabe traditions relating to reparations. These involved the entire community of the offender delivering gifts to the families or communities offended. What was most important was restoring relationship with those offended, not punishing the criminal.[6]

When I was director of the Simon Fraser University Interfaith Institute on Justice, Peace and Social Movements I invited Marjorie Dumont (Wet'suwet'en and Gitksan) and Gloria Coles (Kwakwaka'wakw) to give a workshop on restorative justice. They talked about how feasts and potlatches were integral to restoring peace to individuals, families, and communities in their Northwest Coast Nations. Before the workshop, Marjorie and Gloria, both elementary school teachers, had their classes make gifts. In the workshop, after inviting two members of the group to represent a perpetrator and a victim, respectively, they enacted a shaming ceremony, which involved giving gifts to the perpetrator and then giving gifts to the victims. Then all the witnesses were given gifts. I still have my small wall hanging of black felt with a red what-looks-to-be-an-eagle sewn on it, and a thin cedar bark bracelet made by little hands. Both the children in Marjorie's and Gloria's classes and those of us in the workshop were part of this peace-making ceremony.

I first encountered the work of Rauna Kuokkanen at the First Nations House of Learning sweat. Rauna is Sami from Finland and her early work centres on the gift tradition in Sami and other Indigenous societies. The abundance of gifts from the natural world is responded to with ceremony and reciprocity because the interrelatedness of all beings is a given. Giveaways and gifts to the land – be it tobacco, prayers, or careful attention to how an animal is hunted or how salmon bones are returned to the river – both had the same purpose: "to ensure the balance of the world on which the well-being of the entire social order is contingent."[7] Rauna argues that it is only through adopting "the logic of the gift" as the epistemological basis of Indigenous worldviews that Western universities will be able to truly Indigenize.[8]

These experiences spurred me to see if I could find a comparable gift tradition in Christian teachings. If gift-giving was integral to Indigenous law and could be understood as a basis for reparations, then one way for me to undermine the colonial dynamic was to find something analogous in the Christian tradition. I wasn't looking for simplistic comparisons and it wasn't obvious, but, sure enough, it was there, though somewhat hidden by dominant colonial interpretations of the scriptures. I discovered feminist Christian scholars who have been developing what they call a theology of relations, which centres on an ethic of connection.[9] Postcolonial scripture scholars have uncovered how the initial Christian message has been obscured by the vested interests of European colonizers, who read their values into the texts. Stephen Moore, an American white scholar, articulates a "counter-colonial ethic." He gives the example of the story of the widow's mite, in which the widow gives all she has to the temple (Mark 12:41–4), which churches have often used to get people to give most of their money to the church. Moore sees this as the story of a woman who trusted she would be taken care of in a larger community of sharing within an economy whose logic was not that of endless accumulation.[10] Then there is the story of the woman with the alabaster jar who poured expensive ointment on Jesus's feet (Mark 14:3–4), much to the disgust of his disciples who disliked her recklessness and generous treatment of him.[11] And there is the story of the father who used all his resources to welcome back his prodigal son (Luke 15:11–32), and the miracle of the loaves and fishes, with Jesus supposedly multiplying seven loaves and fishes to feed thousands, though this could have been a feast at which everyone shared what they had (John 6:1–14).

It was exciting for me to go back to my own tradition and see how it has been distorted. I looked up in my Concordance, a reference book that sorts biblical texts by key words, and found more than two hundred references to words like "gifts," "giving," "gave." As I sorted through these, I saw that many passages in both the Christian and Hebrew scriptures affirmed relationship, kinship, and a belief in a different way of being and relating than that which one finds in an exchange economy. I was discovering there was a radical generosity principle in my own tradition, a gift economy tradition, and that it could be drawn on to justify our giving back what we have taken from Indigenous people, which, of course, includes land. I was so inspired by this that I eventually wrote an article on "reparations as gift" for a book on Canadian feminist theology.[12]

While my intellectual grasp of gifting has been important for me it has been my wrestling with gifting that has opened up to me the world of reciprocity. I started collecting items that I could use for gifts and began to give gifts more often and more generously. I still am not up to making my own gifts, be it sewing, beading, or whatever. But I collect possible gifts and store them in a gift basket that I have ready for any occasion. I enjoy doing it, and for my sixtieth birthday I held a small giveaway to thank many of the people who had supported me along the way. A few years later it was easy for me to contribute to a giveaway for the funeral of an Elder whose partner invited several of us to do so. At the same time I noticed that I had begun to feel more comfortable and less greedy at the giveaways I attended, and more curious and accepting of whatever happened.

I admire my Indigenous friends who think nothing of giving many gifts and spending significant amounts of money on them. Some spend a considerable amount of money to attend ceremonies like the

Midewiwin or Sundance far away from home as well as contribute time, resources, and money to preparation and to supplying needs. When I was first invited to Midewiwin ceremonies to support my friend and colleague Alannah Young and her family, I was worried about how much the trip would cost. As I watched others and what motivated them, it was clear that it was the ceremony and the relationships that were important, not the money. By my fourth trip, I had decided to let go of the cost because I was learning that this was not about money but about relationships. Yet I admit I still haven't overcome my scarcity mentality, that I worry about money, and that I have trouble believing the universe will take care of me. I have been deeply marked by an individualist culture that has transmitted the message that you have to look out for yourself first. As I watched family members pitch in to help others go to the ceremonies, I realized my white culture would do better to prioritize building relationships and community so that people can take care of each other rather than to focus on saving for the trials of a solitary old age.

In Indigenous traditions, when humans practise ceremony or perform ritual actions, be it with a water body, a plant, or an animal, they are actually affecting the spirit beings associated with those bodies. In other words, a reciprocal relationship is occurring. The non-human world – the plants, the animals, the land, the water – has its own agency. And this belief in the agency of the non-human world is central to the principle of reciprocity. The function of ritual, as Moroccan French anthropologist Frédérique Apffel-Marglin argues, is to perform actions "by which humans, non-humans and other-than-humans intra-act, and mutually weave each other into an achieved continuity, into an achieved livable and regenerated world."[13]

As for European Christianity, with its colonial baggage and history, there is not much embodiment, even when you have considerable ritual, as does the Catholic Church. I can attend a Catholic or Protestant worship service in Montreal or Victoria and sing the words of a song that include praising earth and sky, yet everyone stands stiffly with their hymn books rather than raising their hands to the sky and bowing down to the earth. Of course, to change a culture of disembodiment requires more than simply adding bodily gestures: it requires a visceral experience of living a reciprocal relationship with the other-than-human world, including the earth and the sky.

In its lack of a reciprocal embodied relationship, for example, with salmon, the dominant culture reinforces its devastation of the other-than-human world. I think of clear-cut logging around salmon spawning streams. If there is no ceremony and no recognition of one's relational responsibilities with the trees, no acknowledgment of the trees' relationship with the waters and the salmon, then the result is flooded streams and no salmon runs. There has been no awareness that we are engaging with the spirit of the water, the spirit of the salmon, and the spirit of the trees.

I remember when I heard and later read the Nishnaabe writer and activist Leanne Betasamosoke Simpson refer to the fish nations, I was shocked.[14] Then I realized I was still operating from an anthropocentric worldview. If I saw the fish world, say the Salmon Nation, as a collectivity with which I had a relationship, rather than only in the form of an individual salmon my son caught for our dinner, then I would feel and act differently in terms of my responsibilities to that nation. To give back to the salmon, who give their lives for us, I need to contribute to taking care of the spawning streams and challenge the open-net fish farming of salmon and overfishing by commercial and sports fishers. I need to be actively involved in the practice of reciprocity with the land and the waterways and to learn how to share the salmon and not waste it. Going even further, we need to be in a treaty relationship with the salmon, who are our kin, those to whom we have responsibilities, something I learned from the Métis/otipemisiw academic, writer, activist, and "fish philosopher" Zoe Todd and Nēhiyaw (Cree) activist Erica Violet Lee.[15]

Reciprocity means much more than giving gifts; it is a different way of living out our obligations. We are all part of a complex interconnected network of living beings, the entire world is alive and related, and there are responsibilities and obligations that come with an awareness of this. Ceremony is one vehicle that enables us to come back to this awareness. It is a way of communicating with the spirits of all beings. I feel more in balance after ceremony, as if my rather heightened sense of my human level has come down to meet these relatives who are my equals – the rocks, the plants, the animals – so I am more equipped in my heart to live out the principle of reciprocity.

If all life is ceremony, as Bernadette Spence has reminded me, then, as part of this interconnected web of reciprocal relations, we need to honour and live daily the giftedness of life, to live out our responsibilities to respect and revere and reciprocate for all these gifts. Whether it is offering tobacco or water to a plant I am harvesting, offering tobacco to the Gorge waterway that I cross every day on a bridge, saying a prayer for and offering tobacco to an animal that has been killed and is lying on the side on the road, or saying a grace before a meal and offering an end-of-the-day thanks for the gifts of the day, all these practices have become for me a discipline that reminds me that I am part of an interconnected web of giving and receiving. Seeing life in this way enables us to affirm that spirit is part of all we do and is there to be drawn upon at all times. When I watch or participate in any Indigenous activism, I am aware of how much reciprocity is part of it. There is drumming, prayer, the holding of eagle feathers, smudging, and a range of gestures that affirm the power of the spirit. Thus ceremony is both a form of resistance and a way of maintaining connection with ancestors, drawing their energy into the present struggle. Once I am in the circle of living out reciprocity in order to protect the wild salmon or the Peace River, or to stop a pipeline, I am reminded that, as a settler, I share in the collective responsibility to remedy the colonial wrongs to which my ancestors contributed.

I close with a story from 2010. It is a reminder for me that everything we receive is a gift and that we live in a world in which reciprocity means giving back at every level.

It's still raining as I start to descend the muddy trail down to the beach. Built in a zig-zag, with hand railings made of willow branches, the path leads from the ceremony grounds down to the beach. It is easy to slip and fall on the slick red clay, and I have only one hand free as I clutch my stone, which is in the pocket of my rain jacket, with my left hand. I have had this perfectly round stone on my house altar for four years. One of the reasons I have come back to Bad River is to return it to this beach on the shores of Lake Superior.

The beach is made of fine reddish sand that has eroded from the cliffs that stretch for many kilometres in either direction. It is deserted except for a few teens and children playing in the sand and clambering on the cliff face. In the distance I can see a woman who is taking a break from the Midewiwin ceremony occurring above. Not accessible to tourists, this beach and these cliffs are part of the territory of the Bad River Chippewa, an Anishnaabe/Ojibwe tribe that occupies more than 50,590 hectares on the southwestern arm of Lake Superior. For those who have the opportunity to come here, they may be lucky enough to discover on the beach one of the many rounded stones that the waves that pound these shores have shaped out of the fine clay sand. These stones are known as Spirit Rocks and are said to carry the spirits of ancestors who have come from this region.

I had been given a Spirit Rock by Alannah the first time I went to Bad River in 2004. So, in 2007, the next time I was there and walking on the beach, I thought nothing of picking up this beautiful large stone that seemed to be calling out to me from a cluster of shining stones at the edge of the lapping waves. It was bigger than a large marble, more the size of a golf ball, perfectly round with what looked like a turtle shape made of the same fine clay sand on one side. Given the turtle shape moulded to it, I felt I had found a "special" Spirit Rock, a creation story rock! I picked it up and carefully put it in a ceremony bag I had brought with me.

A few days later, on the plane leaving Duluth to head back to Vancouver, I picked up a magazine called *Wisconsin Native American Communities*. It contained an article about the Bad River Tribe. And there it was, the admonition to not take any Spirit Rocks from Bad River as they contained the spirits of the ancestors.

I turned to Alannah, who was with me on the plane, and asked her, "Is this true?"

She responded, "Yes; in many Indigenous communities the teachings are that if you take one, you must eventually return it. I have heard some teachings say that if you die far away from here, you need to leave instructions so that it will be returned by somebody else for you."

Now here I am, a few years later, clutching my precious stone at the shores of Lake Superior. I hold it in my hand and start praying, thanking the stone for being with me and teaching me this lesson to give back what I have been given. As I stand holding my Spirit Rock and praying I think of this tradition of returning rocks to the place from which they came. In Indigenous traditions, rocks and stones are our oldest living ancestors. In Anishinaabe traditions, the spirits of ancestors are alive and can be called into the present. Then, raised arm, overhand throw, I return this ancestor rock, a gift on loan, to its watery home. If it was hard to let go, at least now I feel at peace.

Living Treaty

I was on my way to Port Daniel on a hot sunny day in July 2005 when I decided to stop at the Mi'gmawei Mawiomi Secretariat (MMS) in Listuguj. The MMS is housed in an old brick building that used to be a Catholic school and is adjacent to the Church of Saint Anne. I was glad to get out of my rental car for what I was presuming would be a brief moment. I was here to pick up the latest edition of the Secretariat's magazine, *Gespisig*, which covers the news and the work of the MMS in the three communities of Listuguj, Gesgapegiag, and Gespeg. However, the door of the Secretariat was locked. I noticed that the parking lot was full and that a lot of people were milling around. Most seemed to be moving down towards the Restigouche River and to the large field that was to the left and below the two buildings. I was curious and decided to follow the crowd. Then I saw a large banner – it was the Listuguj Pow Wow!

I hesitated. I really wanted to go down to the field below but I felt incredibly awkward. I didn't know a soul and I was afraid I would stick out like a sore thumb. After a few agonizing moments of indecision I decided to at least go down the hill and see what was going on. I had been to a few pow wows out west with friends, so I knew they were not closed events, yet I still felt I was an intruder. Once mingling with the crowd, I soon forgot my anxiety as I began to watch the dancing. There was a men's fancy dance competition happening and I was enthralled by the level of dexterity and speed as well as by the regalia of both young boys and older men dancing in a large circle. Lost in the dance, I was no longer self-conscious, and once it was over and there was a pause I wandered around the various booths of crafts and foods that ringed the circle.

I noticed one booth that seemed a bit different, offering no food or crafts, but with posters on a table. A banner over the booth read: "Atlantic Policy Congress." I went over to discover that the posters were present-day renditions of two peace and friendship treaties signed by several Mi'kmaq, Maliseet, and Penobscot chiefs with the English in the mid-eighteenth century. The woman at the booth was both friendly and informative, and told me that these treaties are key to Mi'kmaw title over their unceded territories. I knew nothing about these treaties so I took the posters and an information kit, both of which were free. I now felt I had a legitimate purpose for being here: to learn more about the history and the political situation of the Mi'kmaq.

However, I did not read the posters, which were transcripts of the treaties. Nor did I read the information kit. I was too busy. The posters lay rolled up on one of my bookshelves for several years, as if waiting for me to realize that they were more than pieces of paper. When I finally did unroll them, I had spent almost a decade coming to terms with both my family's and my own relationship to the land that the treaties addressed. I was finally ready to grasp their meaning for a settler like myself.

For many years I lived on unceded Coast Salish territories in Vancouver and later in the Comox Valley, in K'ómoks territory. As is most of British Columbia, these are regions in which there are no historic treaties – that is, treaties that were signed either before or soon after the province joined Confederation. The only historical treaties that exist in British Columbia are the Douglas Treaties, now called the Vancouver Island Treaties, which cover the territories of several nations in southern Vancouver Island, Nanaimo, and Fort Rupert.[1] There are no historical treaties throughout the rest of the province, with the exception of Treaty 8, which includes its northeastern corner.

In 1992, the BC Treaty Commission was established to facilitate the negotiation of treaties in the province. The first "modern" treaty was the Nisga'a Agreement, which came into effect in 2000 and was negotiated separately from the BC Treaty Process, the negotiations having begun in 1976.[2] At the time of this writing, "Final Agreements" had been reached with seven First Nations, including the K'ómoks Nation, and roughly sixty-five of the 198 First Nations in British Columbia are in treaty negotiations.[3] The goal of the treaty process, as stated on the website of Indigenous and Northern Affairs Canada, is "to achieve certainty over ownership, use and management of land and resources, and to enhance economic opportunities for First Nations, British Columbians and all Canadians."[4]

My experience in the Northwest Territories, where I first learned about land claims and the comprehensive claims process, made me very leery of the treaty process.[5] Through working in the late 1980s with René Fumoleau, the Oblate priest who had written about Treaties 8 and 11, I had learned to be suspicious of government agendas. Modern-day treaties are intended to extinguish Aboriginal Title to the land so that corporations and governments can have "certainty" over ownership, management, and use – in other words, so they can proceed with "business as usual" without legal or political challenges from Indigenous peoples. In 2009 I was lucky to meet Art Manuel, the late Neskonlith activist, and learned more from him about how these modern-day treaties functioned to extinguish Aboriginal Title and Rights.[6] The treaty process set up communities with huge debts as the bands had to repay the money the government loaned them to pay for their lawyers and negotiators.

Given this, I took the position that treaties were all corrupt and therefore irrelevant to me. I remember flying into Saskatoon and seeing in the airport a huge sign announcing, "We are all treaty people." I thought that this was a nice sentiment and that it meant something for those living in the Prairies, where there had been historic treaties.[7] But what could it possibly mean beyond being a nice feel-good gesture towards reconciliation? Then, in the fall of 2012, Idle No More, a movement initiated by four women from the Prairies (three Indigenous [Jessica Gordon, Sylvia McAdam, and Nina Wilson] and one non-Indigenous [Sheelah McLean]), burst onto the national scene. Committed to water protection, I was galvanized by its call to repeal Bill C-45, which the Harper government had just passed and which ended the environmental protection of most rivers in Canada. Like many across the country, I participated in Idle No More Days of Action in the area in which I was then. In mid-March of 2013, Idle No More joined with the group Defenders of the Land to make a series of demands.[8] The fifth of these, which called for the abolition of the Doctrine of Discovery, included a call "to honour the spirit and intent of the historic treaties." This surprised me. Weren't all treaties basically bad? But the words "spirit" and "intent" caught my intention.

I was not living in treaty territory at this time, so if I wanted to find out more about treaties, I felt that now was the time to revisit my Mi'kmaw treaty posters and the two small booklets on treaties I had

picked up at the Mi'gmawei Mawiomi Secretariat in the summer of
2010. I found the posters at the back of my cupboard in the basement.
I unrolled the two of them to discover I had a copy of the Treaty of
1725 and the Treaty of 1752. The first one even had the pictograph
signatures of the chiefs, or ge'ptings, a word which means "they were
responsible for matters of the district as a whole."[9] As I read the treaties,
it became clear that the intention of the British was to make sure the
Mi'kmaq were allies in any upcoming wars. I learned from the booklets
that these were the first of several peace and friendship treaties the
Mi'kmaq had with the British Crown and that, like these ones, none
of them involved or even mentioned ceding land. The Mi'gmaq had a
long history of diplomacy and treaty-making with other Indigenous
nations. These treaties were part of *The Covenant Chain of Peace and
Friendship Treaties*, which were signed in 1725, 1752, 1760–61, 1778,
and 1779 with the British. The Mi'gmaq saw these treaties as a way
"to extend family relations."[10]

It would take me a few more years, and more research and engagement with Indigenous people in the field of Indigenous law, to begin
to grasp what treaty meant. I, of course, first read the treaties with
Euro-Western eyes. The British had wanted these peace and friendship treaties because they did not want to go to war with the Mi'gmaq,
who were allies of the French. Before the colonists arrived, Indigenous
nations on Turtle Island lived by Protocols, diplomacy, and laws that
were specific to each nation and that were linked to the land on which
they lived. These legal traditions informed governance, family life, and
relationships with the land and its creatures as well as trade and relationships with other nations. It was these Indigenous legal traditions
that guided the Indigenous leaders who signed treaties with the French
and the English. Treaty-making with allies had existed long before the
Europeans came. As stated in *Nta'tugwaqanminen*, the book published
by the Gespe'gewa'gi Mi'gmawei Mawiomi that examines the history of
the occupation of Mi'gmaq territory in Gespe'gewa'gi, "central to our
kinship system is the belief that treaties are entered into in order to
extend, strengthen, and incorporate new members into the existing
family systems."[11]

For the British, by contrast, a treaty was just a contract. As Aaron
Mills, an Anishinaabe lawyer, illustrates, the principles of a contract
are fundamentally different from those that underlay Indigenous

understandings of treaty-making. Mills explains that, for the Euro-Western mind, a contract is "the solution to what is imagined as the problem of radical disconnection." In a world of self-interest, "instead of cultivating the kind of genuine non-violent relationships that sustain our connections through periods of conflict ... the contract replaces the need for actual relationships."[12] Mills says that the starting point for treaty within Anishinaabe law is the belief that we are both interdependent and unique. He adds, "Hence Treaties are not legal instruments; they're frameworks for right relationships."[13]

Mills's work has helped me understand better how the intentions of the Mi'kmaq, when signing these treaties, differed radically from those of the British. I learned from the treaty booklets I had picked up at the MMS that treaties are regarded as "sacred covenants" and that the Mi'gmaq signed treaties from within a worldview in which reciprocity and mutuality in relationships are an expression of the spiritual realm, the sacredness of which is confirmed by ceremony.[14] For many years the Mi'kmaq Grand Council met and conducted treaty re-enactment ceremonies at St Anne's Mission at Potlotek (Chapel Island) on 26 July, the feast of Saint Anne – an event that reflected the complex relationship the Mi'kmaq have had with Saint Anne and with Catholicism.[15] For the Mi'kmaq, the treaties were angugamgew'l, meaning they "*added to our relations*" and were crucial to "the extending of our interconnectedness."[16]

Treaty-making was thus a way of extending relationships and had nothing to do with giving away land. Mi'gmaq scholar and activist Fred Metallic places treaty-making within the context of the Mi'gmaq Creation story and speaks to the first treaty being with the animals, the second with the water beings. Both treaties support sustainability, with humans taking only what they need. As Metallic explains, "The first treaty orders land tenure, while the second treaty establishes a water tenure system."[17] The Mi'gmaq ordered their relationship with the land through a system of governance in which extended families had responsibility for select parts of a subdistrict within the territory. This responsibility included patterns of sustainable management and usage.[18] Underlying all of this is a worldview in which all living beings are linked in a kinship system. This kinship system is at the core of Mi'gmag governance, law, and political structures and, hence, is the basis of the Mi'gmaq treaty-making tradition.

The principle of kinship is operative in all Indigenous worldviews in that human beings are part of an interdependent network of kin that includes responsibilities not only to fellow humans but also to non-human beings. All these beings would be considered relatives and would be protected by treaties of peace and friendship, especially as these treaties had nothing to do with giving away land. Anishinaabe lawyer Aimeé Craft writes about what Treaty 1, which covers much of southern Manitoba, including Winnipeg, means from an Anishinaabe perspective: "The core purpose of treaty was to create relationship, not to cede land."[19] For the Anishinaabe who signed Treaty 1 with the Crown, the Queen was a relative, a mother, who had responsibilities and obligations, like any mother.[20] Craft elaborates: "In Anishinabe *inaakonigewin* [law] relationships never end; they are constantly fostered, re-defined, re-examined, and re-negotiated."[21] Craft emphasizes the fact that these treaties are not isolated documents, frozen in time, locked in the past, but are alive and meaningful to this day.

Indigenous worldviews contain a notion of responsibility to the past as well as to the future. Indigenous knowledge systems do not function within a strict linear notion of time (i.e., past, present, and future). Speaking about Blackfoot time, for example, scholar Leroy Little Bear describes how "right now" includes tomorrow and yesterday and that – beyond a two-day limit of yesterday and the day before yesterday, or tomorrow and the day after tomorrow – past, present, and future amalgamate into "is."[22] From this perspective, ancestors, including mine, are never more than two days away, and the same holds true for treaties. Accordingly, the claim of past violations remains in the present. The claim often made by settler governments, that treaties are a thing of the past, is simply not valid.

All this revisiting of treaty-making from Indigenous constitutional perspectives has greatly affected me. I find the emerging framework or language of Indigenous "constitutions" useful, the word "constitution" being sometimes used interchangeably with the word "law" in some Indigenous circles. It encompasses everything from governance to economics to spirituality to relations with all kin.[23] It is this broader framework of Indigenous constitutionalism that provides a challenge to a settler society like Canada.

However, it is clear that, from the government of Canada's perspective, its legal framework must be premised on the need to give corporations and settlers "certainty" about the ownership of land and resources. Eva Mackey, a settler scholar, argues that one of the main problems in moving forward in revisioning treaties is that settlers see the world through a lens that views the concept of private property as a guarantor of certainty. Boundaries and fences protect against uncertainty and against "the chaos and unsettled mobility of a 'state of nature' that is believed to exist outside those boundaries."[24] To own private property provides the illusion of safety and security. Mackey illustrates how this belief in certainty is premised on "fantasies of mastery over nature," on "the fantasy of ownership and control over the past, present and future of one's own body and property" – fantasies that are held by populations who feel they that this certainly is something to which they are entitled.[25] Needless to say, it is not easy to convince settlers, not to mention governments and corporations, to face uncertainty and its concomitant anxiety without also convincing them to accept a shift in worldview.

If settlers assume responsibility for their role in treaties this does not mean that they have to adopt an Indigenous framework; rather, the hope is that they see, hear, and welcome other ways of being in the world and let go of the expectation of certainty and security. In any relationship, if it is to be equal, there must be a recognition and acceptance of the other's position and perspective. Eva Mackey invites us to see treaty as a verb, not a noun, and to see that treaty relationships are an "ongoing exploratory and often uncertain process of building relationship" over time.[26] She adds that relationships are uncertain and so require nurturing, listening, and respecting the other, while each fulfills her or his respective responsibilities.

This understanding of treaty, framed in the context of Indigenous law and ongoing responsibilities between parties, has shifted how I understand my responsibilities in any Indigenous homeland in which I live. At the opening of the 2017 Native American and Indigenous Studies Association Conference in Vancouver, Musqueam Elder Jim Kew said that reconciliation will only be real for his people when "our law is for all."[27] His comment struck me to the core. I live on Indigenous land: Why should not Indigenous law apply to me? That would mean that I would really be living as a treaty person. But, unlike some in Quebec who insist that all newcomers must adopt Canadian and Quebec values and give up their cultures and religions, this doesn't mean I have to give up being who I am. Indigenous law supports difference and uniqueness. As Aaron Mills says, "If you accept the responsibility I am urging you to pick up, you have to be yourself":

> What I am hoping for you is that you'll learn how to create and
> to sustain healthy relationships in the territory of your home,
> and to understand that you are connected to and thus always in
> relationship with everybody there, including all those non-humans
> who fly, walk, crawl, swim, reach, and rumble. This asks you to do
> much more than make space for our voices.[28]

In 2013, Gary Metallic Sr, hereditary chief of the Seventh District of Mi'kmaki, gave notice to the New Brunswick Hydrofracturing Commission that Mi'kmaw land is unceded and protected by the peace and friendship treaties of the 1700s. Fracking of this land without Mi'kmaw consent is a clear violation of their sovereignty. The settlers who supported and allied with the Mi'kmaw resistance to fracking at Elsipogtog in 2013 were living up to their treaty responsibilities. If I support the Mi'gmaq in their resistance, even from a distance, or the Prophet River and West Moberly First Nations asserting their treaty Rights against the provincial government imposition of the Site C dam on the Peace River, it is not just because I want clean water for my children and grandchildren. It is because I have a responsibility, as a settler and as a party to a treaty in which my ancestors were implicated, to support rightful Indigenous claims to sovereignty over the land and waters of their territories.

I have recently moved to Victoria to be closer to family. Now I live in treaty territory that is part of the Vancouver Island Treaties. These involve fourteen Island Nations, the majority in the Victoria area, and were entered into between 1850 and 1854 under the initiative of James Douglas, who was then chief factor of the Hudson's Bay Company. If Douglas's intent was to get these nations to surrender their land, this was not the intent of those with whom he negotiated, who believed they were sharing rather than giving away the land. A recent conference on these treaties, hosted by the Songhees Nation and the University of Victoria, marks the beginning of a process of education for both Indigenous and settler communities: these treaties are living and need to be honoured, and the intent and laws of the initial signatories continue to be valid

today.[29] As Nick Claxton, from the WSÁNEĆ Nation and a professor
of education at the University of Victoria, stated at the gathering, the
question is the same now as it was 160 years ago: "It is about the land
and how we can move forward in a good way."[30]

How can I be here "in a good way?" And how do I move beyond
making space for Indigenous voices, as Aaron Mills so succinctly asks?
I keep learning from Indigenous peoples. Waaseyaa'sin Christine Sy
recently moved to Victoria from Anishinaabe Territory and spoke of
"a long history of taking seriously the act of entering into another person's lands."[31] This involves acknowledging where exactly your residence
is, the place and its history, and learning about the "existing agendas,
visions, wishes of the people of this place." It involves not only learning
as much as you can about the land and the Protocols of the peoples
there but also reflecting on why you are there and where you came from.

I am slowly discovering the colonial history of Victoria and supporting the challenging of this colonial history. My friend Joy Illington
and I recently did a walking tour to discover the First Nations monu-
ments of Oak Bay. These are small cairns with stone carvings by the
WSÁNEĆ artist Charles Elliot (Temoseng) embedded in them. They
provide the traditional place names and stories of each particular location as well as the relationship of the L'kwungen women and men with
the sea and the land.

Indigenous women are inviting us to look at the land in a new way.
Seneca scholar Mishuana Goeman uses the term "(re)map" to describe
how Indigenous peoples are reconstructing spatial geographies "to
generate new possibilities."[32] The connection of Indigenous peoples
to the land is not just in the past. Goeman uses parentheses in the
word "(re)map" because she is reflecting on the work of Indigenous
women who are using both traditional and new stories to see the land
in a creative way. Goeman highlights the work of Mvskoke (Muscogee)
poet Joy Harjo, who combines Creek and Diné stories in her poetry
and somehow poses a way out of the violence of colonial power grids
as she writes lyrically from dreams and landscapes.[33] In Harjo's poem
"A Map to the Next World" Harjo invites her granddaughter to create
her own map through the stories and teachings, and to observe the
price that forgetting has had for her people.[34] I need to move out of my
linear mindset in order to understand how Indigenous relationships to

land are multidimensional, so unlike the blank slate of lines and grids of European mapping.

Isabel Altamirano-Jiménez, a Zapotec scholar at the University of Alberta, and Leanna Parker, a resource sociologist in the field of Native Studies, have argued that it is important to include on Indigenous maps how both women and men related and relate to the land in Indigenous lifeways. They point out that Western mapping is based on seeing land as a resource and hence cannot capture the many layers of "legal, social, and cultural features ... kinship ties and other interpersonal relationships to land, exchange networks, principles of reciprocity and linkages between landscape and the spirit world" that are central to Indigenous worlds.[35] They stress how Indigenous mapping, produced in the context of proving prior occupancy, cannot solely focus on hunting, trapping, and fishing – economic activities usually attributed to men – but needs to include how women have walked and continue to walk the land. It needs to include gathering medicines and berries, making home gardens and places of ceremony.

So my journey continues, now in these territories of the Lekwungen peoples – the Songhees and the Esquimalt, and the WSÁNEĆ peoples. My responsibility is to find out more about the Vancouver Island Treaties, local Indigenous law, and the relationships of these nations to the land. In Indigenous territories there are Protocols for visitors. I hear Joy Harjo's poetic voice in naming one of these in such a beautiful way.

When entering another country do not claim ownership.
It is important to address the souls there kindly, with respect.
And ask permission.[36]

I have been privileged to observe some of the landings of the canoes in the Tribal Canoe Journeys here on the west coast.[37] As each canoe arrives a lead person greets the local nation and requests permission to land in their territory. The canoes are greeted by the chiefs and Elders of that territory and the permission is granted. A significant expression of this protocol occurred here on Vancouver Island when the Anglican bishop of this region, Logan McMenamie, walked 470 kilometres from Alert Bay to Victoria, both as an act of repentance for the role of the church in colonization and to ask permission to "reenter the land" of each First Nation along the way.[38] The Protocol of asking permission creates a framework of respect and reverence for the land and spirits.

However, it is not always easy to follow this protocol when you move to a new place and when you may need some time before you even meet Indigenous people in that area. It was certainly difficult for me when I moved to Victoria. One way I have addressed this dilemma is to always introduce myself as an uninvited guest in a territory. In an indirect way I am saying I have not been given permission to be here. Another Protocol, which I follow, is to briefly name my ancestry, through both my mother's and my father's line. For Indigenous peoples this Protocol is a way of affirming their nations, their kinship relationships, their connection to the land, and their sovereignty over that land. Many Indigenous people want to know the same about their visitors.

As a settler from families with a long history of colonial presence on the land, identifying my genealogy has helped me make sense of my presence on this land. It is not something of which I am ashamed as I did not choose the family into which I was born. Rather, it has helped me to see what responsibilities I have in relation to that genealogy. All those generations behind me meet here in my body and spirit. Who I am is rooted in the colonial past, and to say that those ancestors had nothing to do with me would be disingenuous. For me, the geographical contours of my genealogy inform my responsibility to make space for a different understanding of this land. Living treaty is to live with respect and reverence and a sense of responsibility to the land and the peoples whose original territory one inhabits. It is an invitation into relationship and into another way of living here on this planet. For this I thank all my relations.

PART FIVE

Unsettling Spirit

Lejac Residential School and Rose Prince

We have just passed Vanderhoof and are on the last leg of our drive to Fraser Lake where we will be visiting my godson Charlie, his wife Sheryl, and their little boy Cy. I can see from the map that we are nearly at Lejac. My partner Elisa and I keep our eyes peeled but can see little in the rainy dusk light. There is a dark pine and fir forest on both sides of the highway. In the gloom a small road sign appears, black lettering on white: Lejac. The road opens up to a few fields and a few storefronts on the left, and then the forest returns. I am disappointed. I had wanted to stop and see what remained of the residential school, run by the Oblates of Mary Immaculate for more than five decades. But we are late, and Lejac is soon forgotten as we head into Fraser Lake looking for Charlie and Sheryl's place.

Charlie's dad grew up in Vanderhoof and once told me how in the 1960s groups of young men from the town would go out looking for Native women to pick up and "have sex with" – in my mind, rape. With a wave of nausea I remember how few degrees of separation there are between those of us who consider ourselves "innocent" and those who are directly implicated in violence against Indigenous women. This road we have been driving on is the "Highway of Tears," Highway 16, the road where nineteen murdered and five missing women were last seen. Most of them disappeared in the last two decades.[1] I am glad to finally pull off this road and settle in to the comfort of family visiting.

That night, as we are sitting around the table after supper, Sheryl, a staunch Catholic, offers to take us to Lejac the next day. She says preparations are underway in Lejac for the annual gathering in honour of Rose Prince, a Dakelh woman who died at the school. Sheryl is from Newfoundland, as is her mother, who has dropped by. Both are friends of the local priest, an Oblate from Cape Breton in his late sixties. He has been in charge of the Fraser Lake parishes (two of which are Native, one of which is non-Native) for the past twenty years. Sheryl tells me that the Father is probably at the Lejac site preparing for the big event, which was to happen the next weekend, 6 to 8 July, and she wants me to meet him.

My heart leaps. I'd forgotten about the connection of Rose Prince to Lejac! Rose Prince is considered a saint by many Native Catholics in British Columbia. A young Dakelh (Carrier) woman from Nak'azdli (Nescosli), she attended Lejac as a student and later worked there. Lejac was one of eighteen residential schools in British Columbia. Besides the Oblates, the Sisters of the Child Jesus had been the main staff at Lejac. Rose Prince had been sent to the school when she was seven years old. By the time she was sixteen, her mother and sisters had died from influenza so she decided to stay at the school, doing chores such as mending, sewing, cleaning, and embroidery. She contacted tuberculosis at the school and died in 1949 at the age of thirty-four.[2]

My curiosity about Rose Prince is connected to both my work as a scholar of religious encounters between Indigenous and settler traditions and my own religious questioning. In many ways, she represents the seemingly contradictory convergence of the Catholic and Dakelh traditions in the most contested forum of today, the residential schools. I have trouble understanding how, for some Dakelh people, the site of a residential school is now a site for healing.

The next morning we head out to Lejac with Charlie, Sheryl, her mother, and little Cy. The land where the Lejac residential school stood belongs to the Nadleh Whut'en First Nation. The school opened in 1922 and housed children from Prince George north to Dease Lake, and everywhere in between, until it closed in 1976. Justified as a haven for orphans of various epidemics, the Spanish flu of 1918 being one, it was part of a systematic federal policy of eliminating local Indigenous languages, breaking up family ties, and transforming these children into "civilized" Christians. In particular, Lejac is known (or not known) for the tragic deaths in January 1937 of four students – Maurice Justice, Allen Willie, Johnny Michael, and Andrew Paul – ages eight and nine, who were found frozen in the snow in minus-thirty-degree weather. They had run away from the school and were trying to get home to Nautley, their reserve community, only ten kilometres away.[3]

I feel a mixture of apprehension, curiosity, and dread as we enter Lejac. We take a left turn towards the lake at a sign on the road that we missed last night. Set within a wooden arch, with the name of the Nadleh Whut'en Nation carved on the top, is a large signboard announcing the Rose Prince Annual Pilgrimage from 6 to 8 July 2012, and the name "Rose of the Carrier" at the bottom. In the centre is an image of Rose and the words "everyone welcome."

This piece of land is a small section of the four reserves around the lake allocated to the Nadleh Whut'en. Roughly thirty band members live here. As we drive onto the gravel road we pass a few small wooden houses and trailers on the right. Over to the far left a cook shack is being built by what looks to be two paunchy older white guys. Closer to the road, there is a large fenced-in area that looks desolate, with several concrete blocks and empty trailer pads surrounded by weeds and a few tufts of tall grass. Charlie tells me that in 2011 the Endako mine had housed some three hundred workers in Atco trailers on this site. They had been hired to build a new processing plant for the mine. The Nadleh had to lease their land for one more colonial project, with the only jobs being that of managing the site, and now there is only the ugly remains of this transgression of their space.

On the right is a rolling grassy plain that leads down to the lake. It is a sunny day and Fraser Lake is a deep blue, with a light breeze blowing off it. There is no trace of the school, which was torn down by the Nadleh in the 1980s. What remains is a white fenced graveyard off to the right and, at the lake end of the field, a small shrine constructed like at teepee. Since 1991, there have been annual pilgrimages to the gravesite, organized by the Oblates. To the left, sloping down to where the gravel road veers towards the lake, is a hillside with the letters "R" "O" "S" "E" on it, each about a metre long, made of large white-painted stones. Climbing this hillside to the plain above are wooden stairs with what appears to be a small platform at the top.

The field is hauntingly empty now, yet there is something about this site that gives the appearance of ceremonial grounds. In my mind's eye I can see teepees, people camping in trailers, and possibly a riser for the Elders who need to sit. Near the graveyard are stations of the cross, wooden cross posts with small plaster stations at the top, obviously recently dug into the wet earth. I go over and read the lettering on one station, La Condemnation. I ask myself, "Why aren't the signs written in English or Dakelh rather than French?" Then I recall that the Oblates were initially a French order. I also remember that, regardless of whatever colonial language in which the words are written, it doesn't matter to the people who come here, especially the Elders who may still speak Dakelh, the language of the Yinka Dene. They will infuse each station with their own meaning.

We walk over to the chapel where Sheryl introduces me to the priest, a fairly rotund man with white hair. He is being helped by a young white woman with long brown hair in a braid. She is sweeping out the shrine. I flash back to myself in the late 1980s, with my long hair in a braid, when I earnestly went up North to do my field placement with the Oblates who were "working with the Indians."

I attempt to initiate a conversation with the priest and name my Oblate connections, but he is not interested. I want to find out more about the pilgrimage and Rose Prince's status in the church's line-up for prospective saints, but he answers evasively as he clearly does not want to talk to me and turns back to his task. I am irritated, but the feeling of being patronized or ignored by priests is so old and familiar that I let it go. Long ago, I learned that the Catholic ordered priesthood is an elite fraternity and that it has little interest in female interlopers.

I spend a few minutes watching as they haul out from the back of the shrine black plastic bags full of Styrofoam cups, little flags, votive candles, and various Catholic bric-à-brac. The priest complains about how the mice have gotten into everything, and there is the sour smell of mouse droppings and camphor, with chewed cloth and dust balls all over the floor. A large framed picture of what looks like Saint Anne and baby Jesus with mandarin characters on the bottom leans against a plaster statue of a blond Virgin Mary. A wooden cross is on the wall at the back of the little room.

I ask if there is a picture or statue of Rose Prince. The priest moves over to the pile and hauls from the back a painted portrait of the famed Carrier woman. It feels strange that this picture is brought out only once a year. Possibly more ironic is that there seems to be only white people here preparing for an event at which the majority of the participants will be Native. The priest comments with evident frustration, "Nobody has come to help and there is so much work to do." "Nobody" meaning the Native community. Someone behind me remarks under his breath, "Typical, letting others do the work for them," and I bristle.

This scenario could easily be that which occurred twenty-five years earlier when I was working with the Oblate Camille Piché in the Northwest Territories. Camille would work tirelessly, with little help, preparing for funerals, weddings, and baptisms, and every year bringing Elders to the Lac Saint Anne pilgrimage in Alberta, yet the people would show up only for the event. I think to myself: "Why would people want to show up to do the work when the white church is still running the show? Who has the power and is in control of this event?" From what I can see here, much of this pilgrimage still reflects the colonial pattern of the relationship between the Native locals and the church.

I decide to leave the busyness of the chapel preparations and go to the graveyard. Rose Prince's grave is off to the right of it, encircled by a low white wooden fence. As I approach it, I can sense an energy that is very different from that of the chapel I have just left. In 1951, part of the cemetery in which Rose Prince was buried was relocated for the railway line. When Rose's casket was being disinterred, the cover fell off and her body was discovered to be just as it had been when it was buried, with no signs of decomposition.[4] This "incorruptibility" of her unembalmed body was considered a sign of the supernatural and was the beginning of the rumours that spread of her legendary power.

Today there are tobacco and stone offerings and some wilted flowers covering the grave. Several rosaries hang from the gravestone. I can see where people have taken some of the precious dirt from the grave (the dirt is supposed to have miraculous healing powers). Devotees take away small handfuls of the dirt or rub it on their hands and feet. Many miraculous healings have been credited to "Rose of the Carrier." Devotion to Rose Prince extends beyond Lejac. My friend Madeleine, who attends the Catholic Kateri mission church in Vancouver with her aged Cree mother, told me that several of the old women there are fervent devotees of Rose Prince. One has a picture of Rose that she places on her body whenever she feels pain.

Yet this graveyard is deeply disturbing for me as it represents the contradictions I hold within myself regarding Christianity, the Catholic Church, and being a settler on territories that have been stolen from Indigenous peoples. It has been a long struggle for me to figure out where to position myself in the discussions and debates about residential schools and the Truth and Reconciliation Commission. It has always been easy for me to place the schools in the context of a colonial policy of genocide and assimilation. My structural analysis is clear, but my conflict appears when I write about it or spend time with the players. I know too many personally, on both sides of the fence – and some who straddle it. It is when we get into the reality of daily life that things get messy and unclear – like the fact that sometimes a thousand Indigenous Catholics and even some non-Indigenous people come to pray to Rose Prince at the site of a residential school notorious for abuse and neglect.

I offer some tobacco and pick up a small pinch of the dirt. There are gravestones for a few Oblate brothers, two Sisters of the Child Jesus, and a few women who seem, from my limited knowledge of local names, to be Dakelh. On the other side of the cemetery are two rows of plain white crosses. I walk over and see that these crosses are for children who attended the school, all of whom seem to have died in the 1930s and 1940s. While I have taught in my university courses about residential schools, listened to stories of survivors' experiences at Truth and Reconciliation hearings, and seen films, videos, and pictures, this is the first residential school graveyard I have been in. The residential school graveyards and the missing children have been one of the biggest areas of contention in the Truth and Reconciliation Commission's work. Some claim that there are as many as fifty thousand missing children, lost from their families, who died at residential schools – from abuse, TB, other illnesses, neglect, or even murder – and whose remains are still to be found. The TRC, in response to these undocumented claims, took a systematic approach to the question of missing children and had archeologists examine the gravesites and burial grounds around each school. The "count," at the close of the commission, was thirty-two hundred, and the work to record the deaths of children is ongoing through the TRC's National Residential School Student Death Register.[5]

But those are just numbers, and here I am at the actual graves of some children who have died in the context of a colonial project designed "to kill the Indian in the child."[6] These are Native children who were killed. I stand for a long time in silence, my heart heavy with sorrow and a desire to honour these little bodies. Then I slowly move from cross to cross, reading aloud to myself the names on each cross. I come to an empty space between two crosses and I wonder if it is an unmarked grave. Where are the other graves? There must be more than these two rows, I think to myself. Whatever the conclusion of the numbers debate will be, it is here, in the graveyard, that I sense both grief and an unfinished history. For cultures that believe ancestral remains must be returned to their home territory, to have children missing, to not know where they have died or been buried, is both a tragedy and a betrayal. For a short time as I stand here I can be a witness to these spirits still hovering between worlds.

It is time to go. There is not much else for me to see. As we drive out of the grounds I look back to see Fraser Lake sparkling in the sun. I need to understand more about this pilgrimage and how some Dakelh can see this as a holy place. I feel very confused and disturbed.

That was in 2012, and I was learning about how much the residential schools are part of my history as a settler. I see now how I directly benefit from the Indian Act, the dislocation of communities, and these residential schools – policies and institutions that intended genocide and the assimilation of Indigenous people so that we could occupy their land. And my personal history is a bit closer to this Catholic pilgrimage than is that of most settlers. As a Catholic woman training for ministry in the late 1980s, my field placement was with some of the Oblates in the Northwest Territories. Since the early 1990s, I have been close to some of the Sisters of Saint Anne, another religious order that worked in some of the residential schools in British Columbia. I have had spiritual directors who were Sisters of Saint Ann and one who had worked in residential schools when she was younger. I am friends with a Sister who has been involved for years in the residential schools settlement process. At the same time, I have worked alongside and with Indigenous women who attended residential schools and/or whose parents did. I am connected to a family with a devastating history relating to residential schools, a family that has played a prominent role in the Truth and Reconciliation Commission. I have heard about and witnessed the negative and devastating impacts of residential schools on families and personal lives. I have been involved in facilitating healing workshops at which residential school survivors told their painful stories. I have attended TRC hearings at which these stories have been told in public.

As a result, I have heard many sides of the story. Friends and colleagues who are children of residential school survivors tell of being brought up in dysfunctional and broken homes. Some of the residential school survivors are extremely bitter and angry; others, who have transcended their rage, still call for justice and the recovery of land, language, and traditions as the only feasible steps on the road to reconciliation. Some will have nothing to do with Christianity; others are still Christian. I know some Indigenous people who are deeply critical of the Truth and Reconciliation process, and others who are deeply involved. I know many who reject the word "reconciliation" altogether as just a rhetorical tool to protect "settler innocence." I have known Elders who have difficult, if not horrific, stories to tell of residential school but who can still talk from a place of kindness. And there are the few residential school attendees I have met who were not abused and who felt they benefitted from the education, even as they acknowledge the colonial policies that meant the loss of language and culture.

Then there are my friends from religious orders, particularly women, who now know they contributed to a process of cultural genocide. Many of them have died; some of those remaining have a strong sense of guilt; others emerged from paralysis to do the best they can within the institutional framework of which they are a part. It is challenging to discover that your vocation as a religious woman is now being exposed as integral to the white helper colonial project. I do not judge the individuals who struggle to make some restitution, especially as I see how the women's religious orders are and were overpowered by the male ones, and how the patriarchal structures of the Catholic Church have contributed to preventing the church from taking full responsibility for its role in our colonial history.

When I got home, I Googled Lejac on the internet. I found a blog by a man named Verne Solanas, from Babine Lake.[7] The blog was mostly a site providing pictures of student life for former students of Lejac. I noticed on it a dialogue he had had with an angry survivor who named some of the abuses that occurred at Lejac. Solanas had responded that it was better and safer for him to be at residential school in the 1960s than on the reserve. I realized that, although I wanted him to be angrier, what he said could well have been an accurate reflection of the state of his community in the North, devastated by residential school legacies, alcohol, and welfare dependency. Unfortunately, this is the only story many settlers want to hear. For them, it justifies residential schools and enables them to conveniently overlook the larger purpose of the schools and the violence that occurred within the larger dynamic of colonialism, which amounted to a systemic genocidal effort to eradicate culture, language, and family ties by breaking down community and destroying Indigenous peoples' connection to their lands.

I discovered online a 2008 CBC radio documentary on Rose Prince that had been made during that year's pilgrimage. The main storyline is the tale of a Dakelh woman who, with her mother, is attending the pilgrimage for the first time and is very conflicted. Her mother had been at Lejac and had endured both physical abuse and language suppression. In the documentary a few women Elders from Stony Creek share their memories of Rose Prince, affirming that, in her gentle and kind ways, she truly was a saint who helped others cope with the difficulties of residential school. The documentary then moves back to the daughter. For her, the place carries the memories of so many generations of pain. Yet she does see Rose Prince as what she calls a "prayer warrior," like her own mother. At the end of the piece she comments that when she sees "the seagulls, the gentle breeze and the beauty of the site now," she feels that "perhaps some of the best healing can come at the point where the abuse started."[8]

The term "prayer warrior" jolts me. As a person of faith I know there are unseen realms around us, realms of spirit, of spirits. When these old women come to pray to Rose Prince, it does not mean that they are unaware of the injustices and abuses of the residential schools. They are able to gain access to a realm of mystery and spirit that contains these contradictions. Like Rose Prince they aspire to live as holy women in a distorted unbalanced world and to call on the spirit realms for help. I am drawn to the pilgrimage for this very reason – that there is room for prayer at the site of oppression. I do not believe we can resolve this history with hate and rage for that will only produce more violence.

Rose is an ancestor, someone from the spirit world to whom you pray. The English language cannot capture how the Dakelh see her, so the church blunders on, missing the point. I worry that the Catholic Church is using Rose Prince, like Kateri Tekakwitha, as a sanitized Native holy woman who can keep the local Aboriginals on board. Yet it is clear that the Carrier version of Rose Prince is theirs alone. Settler scholar Jo-Anne Fiske has written how "by the Catholic faith she [Rose Prince] transcends colonial evil to impart hope and redemption in terms of the

Carrier cosmos."[9] The Carrier pray to her and find healing in the dirt from her grave; and, for some, her gravesite is a place of reunion for residential school survivors seeking some peace.

Lejac holds many contradictions, and its history, as a landscape of religion and spirit, continues to evolve. Jo-Anne Fiske told me that, because the band allowed the Endako mine to use part of the land for trailers, "some in the community now feel that the spiritual power of the site has been violated, and ceremonies have been done in late 2011 and in 2012 to purge the site, [including] both Catholic and traditional rites."[10] The Nadleh Whut'en Nation is also pursuing a number of claims for the loss of the lands and other losses as a consequence of the school's being there.

A geography of spirit can be traced here at Lejac – of oppression, resistance, resilience, resurgence, and moments of grace. I am now more comfortable with my ambiguous feelings. As a settler I believe that we too, in our bodies, hearts, and minds, must be liberated from our participation in a colonial structure. If, as many believe, Rose Prince was able, within an oppressive system, to maintain her integrity as a Dakelh woman, then perhaps that is the starting point for those of us whose integrity is challenged by the fact that we are also part of ongoing colonial structures.

Can You Hear the Drum?
Indigenous Christianities

We had parked the car at one of the UBC parkades and were hurrying along the sidewalk because we thought we were late. I was with my Cree friend Bernadette Spence and her cousin Myrna. It was late fall 2009 and the event that night, being held at the UBC Museum of Anthropology, was the official announcement in British Columbia of the Truth and Reconciliation Commission. Several leaders from the mainstream denominations would be present to say they were "in" and committed to the process. Bernadette and Myrna had been students at schools in Manitoba and they were looking forward to finally seeing some commitment from both churches and government to expose and address the legacy of residential schools.

The sidewalk was fairly crowded with people going to the event, and I noticed what looked like a procession coming towards us from the opposite direction, from the direction of the Vancouver School of Theology. I suddenly remembered that the churches had decided to process to the event from VST as a show of collective witness. Some of the residential school survivors were at the head of this fairly large group. Our little trio arrived at the crosswalk the same time as did the procession. And I was torn by what was a huge dilemma for me: Do I stay with my friends or join the church procession? I had a few seconds to decide. I felt no connection to any of the churches that were there. I was critical of the apologies, which, though well meaning, had not included a commitment to decolonize the churches or to give back church land and properties. The Roman Catholic Church was the worst as it had avoided direct accountability in its representation of itself as separate entities (religious orders, dioceses, national office – a convenient legal reality). I had no relationship with the two people at the head of the VST procession, one of whom (the principal at the time) had not supported the Interfaith Institute, of which I was the coordinator, for the short time that it was at VST before it moved to Simon Fraser University. All this played through my mind in nano-seconds. Then I decided to go with Bernadette and Myrna, and I followed them as they joined the end of the residential school survivors' procession.

That moment has stayed with me because it represented so clearly my ambivalent relationship with mainstream Christianity. I have often looked back and wondered if I was just being cowardly, not wanting to stand with the churches in front of my friends. Yet my choice represented with whom I wanted to stand, and with whom I had a relationship. Possibly my own marginalization from the churches, my fear of betraying my friends, and an unwillingness to stand with the churches at this historic moment, were all factors. Yet I still called myself a Christian, felt that I bore responsibility for the injustices that the churches had imposed on Indigenous peoples and that I needed to account for my faith and its role in the violence. But I was not bound by the institutional structures of the churches. I was angry with the churches and, in particular, with the Catholic Church for side-stepping the larger issues of land occupation and the genocide of Indigenous people, not to mention the exclusion of women and LBGTQ people from the circle of sacred beings. A few years earlier I had spoken about and written a theological article on the need for reparations, but I saw no interest among the churches in addressing something so controversial, especially the question of the return of land.[1]

For more than a decade previously I had managed to find spiritual sustenance with what can be called alternative Christian communities. During the 1990s I had the gift of silent retreats at Glenairlie, a property of the Sisters of Saint Anne, which I attended along with Catholic Workers, people who worked at L'Arche, and other Christian social justice activists. In 2000, I began a relationship with a queer-positive community in Toronto that had grown out of the Toronto Catholic Worker. In Quebec, I found a community of French-speaking feminist Catholics in Montreal called L'Autre Parole, which met in house church groups throughout Quebec as an alternative to going to church.[2] So I was able to maintain connection with the rich resources of my tradition through people who were not afraid to address its legacy of violence and conflict. In later years, I attended United Church services and felt somewhat at home there, partly because the United Church has been struggling to transform its residential school legacy and has addressed issues of sexuality and gender oppression.

In 2011, somewhat to my surprise because of my "alternative" church practices, I was invited to present a paper at the Ecumenical Canadian Theological Students' Association Conference in Winnipeg. The title of the conference was "Can You Hear the Drum? Aboriginal Spiritualities in Theological Education," and my presentation was to be on how I taught about Indigenous traditions and colonialism at Concordia – that is, it was to be on my teaching methodology. I had not expected the invitation because I was so critical of the churches, and, for many reasons, I was torn as to whether to attend.

I did not like the term "Aboriginal spiritualities," a phrase that is often used to describe Indigenous traditional practices. The term is usually used to focus on ceremonies as separate and distinct from relationship to the land, from Indigenous governance, and from language. The word "spirituality" carries the freight of the Western mind-body split reinforced by Christianity, conveniently separating the material and spiritual world for the benefit of those who want to exploit the former. As well, the word "Aboriginal" is a term that has been used by the federal government to limit Indigenous sovereignties and the concept of Indigenous nationhood. It has been used as a blanket term to erase the differences between the many nations in Canada. So, for me, a conference using this term in its title reflected how churches are so easily made complicit in government agendas. Last, I was leery of Indigenous Christians. I knew there were a lot of them, but I still couldn't understand how they could be Christian given the terrible history of Indigenous peoples and the churches. Yet the other part of the title intrigued me. "Can you hear the sound of the drum?" This was an invitation to listen, and these words held emotional resonance for me as the drum – drumming – had become important in my life.

The first Indigenous drumming I heard was in Denendeh in 1986. At what I then called Fort Rae, now Behchokǫ̀, I had watched a group of about eight Dene men first offering tobacco to a large fire and then warming these large circular hand drums. Then, forming a half circle, they began to drum and sing. It was the most haunting sound I had ever heard. Over the next four summers, when I was in the Northwest Territories facilitating the Denendeh Seminar, I was able to hear the

Dene drumming several times. Twice we were invited to what are called tea dances, at which there are what are called drum dances. In a drum dance everyone, as many as a hundred people or more, dance clockwise in a slow circle, passing and sometimes turning to face the drummers.

The last year I was in Snowdrift, now called Łutsel K'e, I saw a hand drum in the community craft store and, while hesitant and not knowing if I was doing the right thing, I bought it. My Dene drum sat in my basement, unused for more than a decade. Then I started working with Alannah Young, who was a singer and drummer. I had the Dene drum so I brought it along and Alannah taught me to sing and to drum as we incorporated song into the many workshops and trainings we did. I learned about Protocols about songs and about drums. The ideal was to be given a drum or to make your own. I began to appreciate the saying that the drum connects us to the heartbeat of the earth. I learned that the drum itself is a relative, a sacred being, a gift from the Creator, which you treat with respect, a being that you don't leave lying on the floor or throw into the back of a car. Over the years, drumming and singing has become a way of erasing all thought and worry from my mind; I feel a sense of oneness with the song, the other drummers, and the earth.

Some say you need to give your first drum away. I sure didn't like that teaching as I was quite attached to my Dene drum by then. My drum, which was large, and made of caribou hide, had to be warmed up to sound good. Obviously there were no fires to warm drums where Alannah and I worked, so sometimes I would stand holding my drum by a heater and pray that the skin would tighten up. Then, in 2003, when I was moving to Montreal, out of the blue I was given a drum by a group of women with whom I had worked at the Hospital Employees Union. They had bought the drum at the Vancouver Friendship Centre and one of them, Ana Rahmat, had made the drumstick with a tip of soft purple leather. I was thrilled. But then I realized that, if I was to follow the teachings and Protocols around drums, I would have to give away my Dene drum. This was hard for me as my Dene drum contained part of my history as well as having a unique sound. However, eventually I decided I would give it away, and before I left for Montreal I gave it to Carol Muree Martin, who is from the Nisga`a/Gitanyow Nation and was a tireless advocate for women, and worked at the Downtown Eastside Women's Centre. I knew she would use it or pass it on in a good way.

One of the most powerful drumming experiences I have had was at a women's drum circle I attended at the First Nations House of Learning at UBC. This particular drum circle was a one-time event that had occurred because a powwow drum had been left there for a few days and Alannah had managed to get permission for a group of women, mostly Indigenous students, to use it. A powwow drum is a large drum, and anywhere from four to ten people sit around it in a circle. Often it is only men who sing using a drum like this, though this is changing. Alannah had been teaching me some public songs. These are different from private songs, which belong to an individual or family and can only be sung by a family member. I was thoroughly enjoying pounding the drum and singing my heart out in harmony with the other women. I could feel the power of the collective resonance of voices and vibrations. Then Alannah introduced an intertribal Lakota Sundance song. The Sundance is an exacting physical ceremony during which participants dance for four days without food and water, and offer their suffering for an intention. Whether specific or communal, the intention is to alleviate the suffering of others in their community, be that suffering in the form of illnesses, addiction, suicide, the impacts of residential schools, a housing crisis, or whatever. The song honours the suffering of the people. I had heard this song several times before, but this time, as we began to sing and drum, I suddenly felt a rush of tears, a deep sadness. In that moment, I felt connected to the collective pain of the women in this circle and to the larger community of pain behind them. Somehow my personal pain had transformed into this sense of collective suffering. A window had opened onto an aspect of Indigenous ceremony and community of which I had had no previous experience.

In 2103, I had the opportunity to make my own drum. I was at an expressive arts therapy conference at the Quw'utsun' Cultural and Conference Centre in Duncan on Vancouver Island, and one of the workshops was drum making, led by Tousilum, Ron George, a Quw'utsun' Elder with whom I had worked several years earlier at the LE,NONET Project at the University of Victoria.[3] I was so pleased to be able to make my own drum and to actually know the teacher. I have carried this drum with me ever since. There is something special about singing and drumming with a drum you have made yourself. You have a visceral connection to the deerskin, the sinew that binds it to the frame, and to the ceremony and teachings that were given during the drum making.

In the summer of 2016 I joined an all Nations women's drum circle
in Courtenay. In the fall of the next year, at a feast hosted by this drum
circle to honour the bringing forth of a children's drum that had been
in the making for at least a year, several Elders were asked to speak. A
Cree Elder, Phil Umpherville, told the story of how he had been raised
in an isolated Cree village in northern Alberta. The first drumming he
ever heard was that of Dene drummers who had come to visit. There
were no drums in his community as Christianity had destroyed any
connection to their traditions. He remarked not only on how the power
of the drumming haunted him but also on how it struck him that the
Dene, even when Christianized, had managed to keep their drumming.
I thought then of a comment by the Anglican Indigenous bishop Mark
MacDonald, who said that, in some of the more Northern and remote
communities, the people's worldview was completely Indigenous, even
if many of the people themselves were Christian.[4]

So, looking back at the Canadian Theological Students Association
conference, "Can You Hear the Drum?," I wonder if that experience at
the powwow drum or the memory of those Dene drummers I had heard
at Behchokǫ̀, or even some angel or spirit guide nudged me to go. I was
glad I did as, at that conference, I discovered an Indigenous Christianity
that was both thriving and critical of colonialism. I now see a profound
meaning in that conference title, "Can You Hear the Drum?" It was an
invitation to listen, not judge, and to pay attention. Several moments
from that conference still stay with me.

The sun is high in the sky and I am standing far from the shade in
this circle, feeling my sunscreen-free face burning. Each person, one
at a time, in this circle of about a hundred people, is stepping forward
and walking up to the old rusty oil drum in the centre. Each pauses,
says a prayer, and then offers his or her pinch of tobacco to the sacred
fire in the drum. They then walk around the medicines that have been
placed in wooden bowls on a red cloth beside the drum and proceed to
walk clockwise, in the Cree way, back around the circle to their place.
I can tell this ceremony will take a long time. I am near the end of the
circle far from where the tobacco offering has started. Getting hotter
by the minute, I take off my sweater and try to shield my eyes. Except
for my checkout time at my hotel and missing lunch, which seems to
loom larger than my physical discomfort in the heat, I am okay with
the long time it will take for this closing ceremony to be finished. I have

learned that ceremonies take time, that you cannot rush them, and that part of the experience is getting comfortable with dis-ease. If I think this noonday sun is pitiless, I can't imagine being in a Sundance, where people dance four days in the hot sun.

The oil drum, cut in half, with holes in the bottom to give the fire more air, has sat on the concrete pavement for the last three days. It holds the sacred fire that has been present day and night throughout the conference. Three helpers, Native men ranging in age from twenty-five to forty, are the fire keepers, rotating the duty of watching and feeding the fire so that it never goes out. They have sat on lawn chairs to the side and have chatted with whomever has come to watch the fire with them. Some come to pray and offer tobacco to feed the fire. The practice of having a sacred fire burning throughout the life of a ceremony is common to many Indigenous cultures on Turtle Island. To be able to have it here, on this urban campus in the concrete wilderness of downtown Winnipeg, is a gift, and it has provided me with a container for my own ambivalent feelings as I navigate this conference.

Carmen Lansdowne, who is a Heiltsuk United Church minister and one of the keynote speakers, has already challenged the title of the conference and the notion of "Aboriginal spirituality." In my small discussion group an Anishinaabe woman has patiently explained to the mostly white participants that this is not about sweats and pipe ceremonies but rather, for her, about living on the land and having a relationship with it. In our final small group this same woman shares with us that, for her, the highlight of the conference was going out to the fire and offering her tobacco with her prayers. She knows this is what centres her, and she is now more ambivalent about the church work she has been doing. As for me, for several years I have been suspicious of Native people who identify as Christians, thinking that they are still colonized and have not yet seen the strength of their own traditions. Now, after this conference, I realize it is not that simple.

I suspect there are other shifts like this happening at the conference. I look around at the circle. The majority are white theological students, ministers, and seminary staff, with a smattering of students of colour, all of whom have come to learn more about Indigenous traditions. There are several Elders who are Indigenous clergy and a few middle-aged Indigenous women who work for various churches. There are the firekeepers and the resource people like myself, half of whom are non-Indigenous. In this final circle, we pray that we can move forward from this conference in a good way. Mushkegowuk Cree knowledge keeper Andrew Wesley, who is an Anglican priest, has given us our ceremonial instructions. Eva Solomon, an Objibwe Catholic and a Sister of St Joseph of Sault Ste Marie, and who is also a pipe carrier and sweat lodge leader, has sung and drummed a beautiful Anishinaabe woman's morning song, followed by a song in English.[5] This song seems strangely dissonant to my ears after hearing only drum songs sung in local languages on the Northwest Coast. Eva has finished and now we stand holding our tobacco to our heart with our left hand and watching the slow but steady movement of offerings to the fire.

The silence is broken by the sound of jingling bells. Four young Blackfoot women from Alberta, wearing jingle dresses, have suddenly left their place in the circle and are beginning to move into the centre, dancing. Cheryl Bear, a Carrier woman and Four-Square Church minister, begins to drum and sing for them, in English, a Christian hymn. The young women are dancing around the fire, getting in the way of those who are moving forward to offer their tobacco. I look at the Elders who are leading the ceremony, but their faces are impassive. The young dancers have come with Terry LeBlanc, who is a slim middle-aged guy with white hair in a ponytail and a vest with a Navajo design on it. LeBlanc is Mi'kmaq and is the manager of this little dance troop, called "Dancing the Way." He is also from NAIITS, the North American Institute for Indigenous Theological Studies, an evangelical Christian organization that promotes Indigenizing Christianity.[6] While NAIITS represents a progressive shift among evangelicals, I am uncomfortable with this dancing intervention. My understanding is that the Jingle Dance is either a ceremonial medicine dance used in a healing ceremony or else is part of a powwow competition. Yet these dancers have moved into the circle and are bringing what to me feels like spectacle into a solemn ceremony led by Cree Elders in their own territory. I wonder if attention to ceremonial Protocol is something that can disappear when the universalizing, and, in my mind, still colonialist aspects of Christianity get in the way, as seems to be happening with these "Dancing the Way" dancers, who "dance for Jesus."

But who am I to be a stickler for Protocol? This closing represents the tension that runs through the conference and through me. How do you lightly hold together Christianity and Indigenous traditions? Within

Indigenous Christianity in North America there is a strong evangelical movement, here represented by NAIITS, and then a more "mainstream" type that identifies with a specific denomination, whether Anglicanism, Catholicism, or the United Church. Many of these groups seem to hold the Indigenous and the Christian traditions together. What I have seen here is that many Indigenous people are followers of the Jesus of the Bible, not of the church.

Andrew Wesley is Mushkegouk Cree from James Bay and an Anglican priest. He was raised speaking his own language, and at the conference he shared his Mushkegowuk creation story. I could see that he had melded the two traditions together so as to provide an Indigenous reading of a biblical text. One morning he got up to speak, and he turned and asked all of us if we knew our creation story. Wesley, with short white hair and shoulders slightly hunched from age, startled me as I have had trouble relating to the creation stories in the Bible. He then went on to remind us of the story of the disciples who are confused when Jesus asks, "Who do you say I am?" (Mark 8:29). Wesley remarked that the disciples could only answer if they knew who they were and from where they came. And then he looked at the group and said, "We all have to know who we are if we are going to have an authentic relationship."

In Indigenous ways of knowing it is presumed that the Creator made each of us complete and that we can find answers within ourselves. And knowing who you are and where you come from is central to everyone's recovery from colonialism. I was reminded that settlers like me need to look at how we have constructed our identities in relationship to whiteness and dominance as well as in relation to our ancestors. We need to reconstruct our identities and find our own creation stories. As with all settlers, until I have done my own work, reconciliation between Indigenous and non-Indigenous peoples will be an unrealizable dream.

The evangelicals at the conference were working hard at decolonizing their Christianity. I would have liked to hear a bit more about land and sovereignty from them, but I was still challenged. The late Richard Twiss was one of the keynote speakers. He was a Lakota who lived in Oregon, with butt-length black hair, jeans, checked shirt, and cowboy boots, and he worked as a travelling evangelical whose talking style combined stand-up comedy and Indian humour with old-time preaching. He challenged the white folks in the audience to question how whiteness could be reconciled with a genuine Christianity and alerted us to the fact that Indigenous theology was replacing frontier theology. He left us with his closing question – "What is postcolonial Christianity going to look like?"

My attention comes back to this closing circle around the rusty drum. My turn is coming soon. A Mohawk-Ojibwe woman has walked around the circle and authoritatively told us "as one returns, one goes forward," so no one can rush this or cheat and go in twos or threes. I remember Carmen Lansdowne's talk in the Convocation Hall the day before. Her energetic one-year-old son Gabriel was crawling in the centre of the circle when he noticed two sunbeams that had each created a patch of sun on the maroon carpeted floor. He crawled towards them. First he entered one patch of sun and explored it and then, noticing the other, he moved over into it. He kept going back and forth until he was tired and crawled away, crying for his grandmother who was watching him. For many of us, his movements were a metaphor for what the conference was about. Two patches of light, separated, not melded, from each of which we could feel something.

It is finally my turn. My hand is now all moist from the heat, and, after forty minutes in the sun, the soggy tobacco is sticking to my palm. I walk forward, pause to ask the tobacco and the fire to carry my prayers to the Creator for this journey we are all on, and I ask for humility so that I will not be so judgmental of those who have chosen different paths. Then I brush the sticky strands into the fire. I am grateful for this experience. I have heard many drums at this conference but the one that holds my heart today is this old rusty oil drum in the centre of the circle.

Returning to the Heart

The church hall is filling up quickly, despite the howling wind and pelting rain outside on this March evening. We are showing *Finding Dawn*, a film directed by Métis filmmaker Christine Welsh. It gives a human face to some of the women across Canada who have disappeared and been murdered; it also gives a human face to their families and describes the impact this has had on them. It shows how Indigenous women are working to change the racism and colonial conditions that are at the root of the violence. I am co-facilitating this event at Comox United Church with Maxine Matilpi, a Kwakwaka'wakw educator and lawyer. This is the first of a series of community conversations we have initiated as part of the Walking with Our Sisters Memorial, which is coming to K'omoks in July of 2015. Our purpose is to educate the wider community around the broader issues connected to the violence against Indigenous women and girls, and to promote the memorial as part of a longer process of supporting the families of the women and finding justice for them.

Evelyn Voyageur, a Kwakwaka'wakw Elder, opens the evening. She explains how prayer is different from Christian prayer in her culture, and she offers, in her language, an acknowledgment of the gifts of the land and an affirmation of our intentions this evening in honouring the murdered and missing women. This is followed by the introductory remarks of the Tsow-Tun Le Lum healing team, two men and two women, Elders and counsellors from this residential treatment program on Vancouver Island on the territory of the Snaw-Naw-As (Nanoose) Nation. They introduce themselves by their lineage and nation, and explain their role in offering cultural support to anyone who may be triggered or disturbed by the content of the film. Then, after Maxine and I acknowledge that the spirits of the missing women are here with us in this room, we watch the film.

After the film ends several people are crying, including a few men. We invite the participants to hold a few minutes of silence to allow themselves to process whatever they are feeling. Then we ask everyone to break into small circles to share how the stories in the films connect to their lives. While there are a few Indigenous women in the room, the majority are white. As a facilitator, I remind the crowd that we are not here to jump to problem-solving, a reaction so common among white people; rather, we are here to witness the pain and suffering of the families and to connect it with our own lives.

One of the Tsow-Tun Le Lum Elders, Dean Mason from Snuneymuxw First Nation, is sitting on a side bench, watching as the participants engage in intense conversations in the small groups. I am not in a group, and this enables me to observe the overall dynamics in the room. I sit with Dean, who is not a big chatterer, for a few minutes. He looks at the people talking and says only this: "Until we can feel we cannot become human."

I once heard Cree lawyer and writer Tracy Lindberg speaking at UBC. I remember her saying: "Think of these words and teachings I share as snowflakes; some will fall on you and some won't. Don't try to recall those that don't stick. You may not be ready to hear them." I was ready that day in Comox. I had spent the last twenty years of my life thawing my own heart. Even a few years ago I would have been in one of those small groups immediately recommending political and economic solutions to the outrageous injustices that Indigenous women have faced rather than sharing my feelings or personal connection to their reality. Not that there aren't solutions out there, but if my heart is not open I can neither embrace our common humanity nor get to the deeper level of seeing how I have been part of the problem. And I cannot build genuine relationships with the Indigenous people around me, a necessary step in any process of real change.

Flash forward, three years later. I am sitting in the Ceremonial Hall of First Peoples House at the University of Victoria. It is the fall of 2018 and I am attending as a witness the Sunday "open program" of the Sisters Rising Intergenerational Forum to Honour Indigenous Gender Well-Being. I watch in awe as groups of young Indigenous women speak to their work using art to reclaim their traditional gender teachings and "restory and rebody" the colonial gender violence to which Indigenous women and Two-Spirit people have been subjected. Four adolescent girls, wearing red ribbon skirts, from the Indigenous Young Women's Utopia group from Saskatoon and Treaty 6 territory, shyly read their collective poem of resistance to colonial violence. A young woman from the SENĆOŦEN-speaking peoples on the Saanich peninsula shares, with confidence and skill as a speaker, information about Project Reclaim, which is using plant-based medicines to help people heal from violence. A group of young Indigenous women and women of colour speak to the two public murals they have created as a local branch of the Fearless Collective, a group that originated in India to challenge rape culture and gender violence with "participatory storytelling and art that replaces fear with trust, creativity and collective imagination in public space."[1] I am excited and moved by all these young women and the vision that propels this larger Sisters Rising project and its commitment to dignity, respect, kinship, and consent. In the final session we are asked to make our own art piece and to state our commitment, what we will do as witnesses to what we have seen today. I commit, at a minimum, to write about the project and to find other ways that I can show up and challenge the racism and colonialism that have made young Indigenous women so vulnerable to colonial gender violence. Because I realize writing is not very embodied, I commit, in my future workshops, to teach and encourage embodied exploration of dignity, respect, and consent.

I link these two experiences of wwos and the Sisters Rising project because the latter, also initiated by Indigenous women, points out how someone like me can act to prevent violence against Indigenous women, girls, and Two-Spirit Queer (2SQ) persons. So often settlers of all types will say, "But what can I do?" Each of us can do something in our own sphere of influence. Sisters Rising is "a community-based research project for Indigenous girls, youth of all genders, and communities speaking back against sexualized violence."[2] It is a program that offers arts-based workshops with young Indigenous women from the ages of thirteen to thirty to support the recovery and honouring of traditional gender teachings, using land-based materials and medicines to make art and to embody the connection between the land and the body. At the heart of Sisters Rising is the impetus to move "our stories away from risk and damage and to focus on resurgence and sovereignty, sovereignty over our lands and bodies."[3] The motto is "Body Sovereignty is Land Sovereignty." In teaching the values of dignity, respect, and consent the project underscores not only how Indigenous people never consented to violations of their lands, bodies, cultures, and languages but also that, even now, Indigenous nations don't have the right under Canadian law to veto the extraction of resources on their land. Much of my work seems to be about embodiment and the decolonization of the body, and this is now informed by Sisters Rising's vision.

This insistence on honouring the bodies of women, children, and Two-Spirit Queer peoples is at the heart of the work of Indigenous feminists who have so clearly and eloquently made the connections between body sovereignty and land sovereignty. The bodies of Indigenous women and Two-Spirit Queer people are the markers of the violence of settler colonialism. Two Indigenous feminist theorists, Michi Saagig Nishnaabeg Leanne Betasamosoke Simpson and Kwagiulth (Kwakwaka'wakw) Sarah Hunt, centre gender and embodiment in their analysis of both settler colonialism and decolonization. Simpson asks, "What does it mean to use the bodies, minds and experiences of Indigenous children, women and 2SQ people as the measure of success of our movements?"[4] Sarah Hunt, like Simpson, urges the exploration of decolonization in daily life and, with non-Indigenous scholar Cindy Holmes, explores how one can live daily "a decolonizing queer practice."[5] Simpson quotes Sarah Hunt in calling for an end to "privileging so-called men's work over women's" and insists that "we must treat body sovereignty with the same urgency and importance as political sovereignty."[6] So the work around child protection, prevention of violence against Indigenous women, and strengthening families is as important as is the work of "manning" blockades and supporting political title work.

It has been Indigenous writers and activists like Simpson and Hunt, and groups like Walking with Our Sisters and Sisters Rising, who have most unsettled me. In the chapters in this book I explore my experiences of both colonization (i.e., of being implicated in colonization) and decolonization. I use the title *Unsettling Spirit* because my journey has very much shaken up how I understand my relationship to land, to the body, to religion, and to my connection to the spirit world. I have been exposed to ways of thinking and being in the world that challenge the ways and being that are dominant in the culture in which I live. By an "unsettled spirit" I mean one that has to constantly re-examine its understanding and to revisit, reinterpret, and renew its relationship

with the spirit world. For me this has been about cosmology and worldview – about how I understand, think, and live in the world and with
the earth.

To get at "the heart of the matter," I want to return to the heart feeling
that was identified by Elder Dean Mason during the wwos event. He
actually didn't use the word "heart," but that was how I interpreted it. I
want to share how my Western understanding of heart has been cracked
open through my brief encounters with Indigenous languages. Over
the years I have had the privilege of listening to Coast Salish speakers
who always introduce themselves and their teachings in their language.
hən̓q̓əmin̓əm is the language of the xʷməθkʷəy̓əm Musqueam. I have
heard one phrase, written as "nə́c̓aʔmat tə šxʷq̓ʷeləwən ct" in one version, repeated often. After a long time of listening to Salish speakers, it
is the one phrase I recognize, and every so often I hear just the word
"šxʷq̓ʷeləwən." The phrase is transcribed into English as "Natasamaht
Shqwaluwun" from Hul̓q̓umín̓um̓, the dialect of central and south
Vancouver Island Coast Salish peoples. I have seen it loosely translated
as "one heart one mind, "and this meaning resonated with me. I was
thinking that this phrase captured my concept of the integrated body-
spirit and that "Shqwaluwun" must mean "the heart." I have learned
enough to know that Indigenous languages are quite complex, so I
decided, before writing about it, to ask Larry Grant, a Musqueam Elder
whom I have known over the years, how he would translate it.

Larry, whose Musqueam name issʔəyəɬəq, is in his early eighties
and was, at that point, still teaching one of the Musqueam language
courses at UBC. Was I in for a surprise and a much needed lesson! It
turns out that most words in hən̓q̓əmin̓əm are composites of different "morphemes" – that is, the smallest unit of a language that has
its own meaning. Larry showed me how nə́c̓aʔmat tə šxʷq̓ʷeləwən ct
broke down into eight different units, and he explained that how the
speaker interprets the meaning varies. In other words, there is no fixed
meaning. The last part of the word šxʷq̓ʷeləwən, əwən means "inside
body." So even though this phrase often gets translated as "we are of
one heart and mind," there is literally no mention of a physical or even
a mental heart in the phrase. In the Musqueam tradition, the heart and
mind function as one, so sometimes the phrase could refer to a heartfelt
thought. "We are one together in the heart inside your body" is one
possible translation. Larry added that, more often, the phrase "is used

to indicate thought and mental strength or resolve that has been said by the old people and carries on in today's contemporary life."[7] Larry once warned me that English is a conceptual language and that the colonial mind wants definitive answers.[8] Needless to say, I left that exchange with Larry realizing how little I know.

Now I was curious: Did this hold true for other Indigenous languages? I asked Pnnal Jerome in Gesgapegiag what the translation of heart would be in Mi'gmaq. He wrote down the word *Nweta 'git*. Then he said it meant the whole person, not just the heart. He told me that the Mi'gmaq don't separate the heart from the mind or the spirit from the person. He said there was no comparable translation in English but that the closest he could come was "being whole and connected with everything." He then reminded me that in the Mi'gmaq language "so much is coming from the inner spirit."[9]

Then I spoke to the lawyer Lindsay Borrows, an Anishinaabemowin speaker. She told me that the morpheme *De* means both "heartbeat" and "centre," and she referred me to her book on the relationship between her language and Indigenous law. I discovered that the morpheme *De* is found in the word *Madewe*, translated as "sound"; *Dewe'igan*, drum; *Ishkode*, fire; and *Midewewin*, sometimes translated as "Way of the Heart." And *De* is found in many more Anishinaabemowin words as well.[10]

I share my little journey into a few Indigenous languages to remind myself just how much non-Indigenous people can project onto Indigenous traditions. One of the greatest errors of the colonizer has been to assume that Indigenous traditions are "simple" or that we can eventually fully understand them. I learned long ago how mistaken I was to think the Midewiwin initiation ceremony was "like baptism." Once again I need to remember to respect the differences between traditions and to catch my colonial mind when it wants to universalize.

I am still a reluctant Christian, as the flaws, sins, and errors in institutional Christianity are so apparent and glaring. But I love the Bible and believe in its original teachings and continue to learn much from Indigenous and non-Indigenous peoples who are decolonizing reading the Bible and Christian theology.[11] My search for the heart has brought me back to my own Christian tradition and the heart teachings that are central to both Judaism and Christianity. In the Hebrew and even early Christian understanding, the heart did not refer specifically to the blood-pumping organ that we think of nowadays. The heart was viewed as the centre of a person, the place where one's deepest desires and convictions lay. In Hebrew the word for heart, "Lev" or "Levav," meant the centre of thought and spiritual life, so the heart-mind. When referring to the actual characters in the Hebrew language, the meaning is "the authority within."[12]

In the Hebrew Bible those who inflicted evil were described as having hearts that were hardened (Exodus 4:21, 7:3; Isaiah 63:17; Psalms 95:8). But transformation was possible. The prophet Ezekiel called for hearts of stone to be turned to "hearts of flesh" (Ezekiel 36:26). Jeremiah invited people to return to God with their whole hearts (Jeremiah 24:7). There are constant admonitions in the Psalms to not harden your hearts. In a Concordance, which is an alphabetical index of the principal words in the Bible, there are literally hundreds of passages that contain the word "heart" or its variations. Throughout these ancient texts there seems to be a visceral awareness of how abuse of power comes with disassociation from the body and heart. The counter to this is a heart of flesh within which the Spirit lives. It is easier to follow God's laws when the heart is open and can sense that Spirit, which to me means being embodied, connected to all living beings. The logical corollary is that God's laws, similar to Indigenous laws, are based on justice and respect for all Creation, and one may gain access to these laws through the awakened heart. Through the heart we move beyond judgment and division to see our essential oneness with all living beings.

From Indigenous traditions I have learned that humans are not separate, and the various heart teachings have taught me to see the heart-mind beyond the individual to the collective, to the community, to all living beings and the nation, to all relatives. It is an invitation to oneness, a state I profoundly believe is affirmed in the mystical traditions of Christianity. If my heart is open then I am part of all of it – the land, the animals, the birds, the snakes, the weeds, the lizards, the grasses. I am part of the sorrow and joy of others. My relationship with my heart is also embodied. My somatic training has helped me to process feelings through my body, and it has been mindfulness, specifically in Zen Buddhist practice, that has given me the skills to put my awareness in my heart area when I am stuck in my head area. In Buddhism there is the concept of the non-separate heart-mind, hence the heart is the centre of wisdom.[13]

258   Unsettling Spirit

I have always liked the passage from the prophet Jeremiah in which he talks about the laws of God being written on our hearts. "I will put my Teachings into their innermost being and inscribe it upon their hearts" (Jeremiah 31:33, Jewish Study Bible). This is part of a longer passage in which God promises a new covenant with the Israelites after many years of their refusal to follow the laws given to them at Sinai. The teachings, the laws, will not be new, but how they are learned will be. Many settler Christians and some Indigenous Christians are bringing this idea of a new covenant to their understanding of treaty.[14] Settler theologian Jennifer Henry sees this promise of God to transform the human heart as an invitation for settlers to come to our treaty relationships with a renewed heart and a commitment to embrace the intentions that they held for the original signers.[15] It is this biblical lens of the laws of God written on our hearts that has helped me grasp, however superficially, another level of Indigenous teachings. Indigenous laws are also heart connected and expressed through Indigenous languages. As Lindsay Borrows writes: "Indigenous languages need bodies to live in ... When laws are 'written' on people's hearts, just as languages go to the core of their being, then revitalization occurs."[16]

I cannot forget that European Christianity became far removed from its origins in tribal Palestine occupied by the Romans. Over several centuries it became the vehicle of colonialism, capitalism, patriarchy, and white supremacy. The binary thinking, the dualism of the Western worldview that it has carried, has been counter to any deep spiritual and religious practice rooted in the heart-mind body. The binaries of body/spirit, black/white, mind/body, heart/head, humans/nature, right/wrong, good/evil, and so on that underlie these systems and structures make it hard for settlers to see connections and relations, and to allow for difference. Tom McCallum, a Métis Elder, once cautioned me about using the title "Towards Right Relationship," a phrase often used in Christian contexts, when I was organizing an interfaith event on reconciliation in 2008. He said the language of right and wrong was far removed from the principle of seeking balance in relationship, which is itself grounded in the interconnectedness and interrelatedness of people and non-human beings.

So what can a balanced relationship look like? I remember the words of a young woman whom I once observed leading a youth workshop:

she spoke of two canoes travelling together, parallel with one another, on a river. She warned that if you try to get into someone else's canoe you will tip it over. She spoke of how the settlers had climbed into the canoe of her people but that now Indigenous peoples were righting their canoes and continuing on their journey, maintaining their independence and autonomy but still sharing the same river with the settler canoe. This image of the two canoes travelling in the same direction, separate but related, has its origins in the Covenant Chain, which was made between the Haudenosaunee and the Dutch in 1613 and which still guides Haudenosaunee foreign policy.[17] It was recorded in the Two Row Wampum, or Kaswentha, a white shell belt with two purple rows. Wampum belts were used to transcribe treaties, and this particular one was recorded and explained through oral tradition as a relationship between two vessels travelling side by side but "never crossing paths, never interfering in the other's internal matters."[18] While the Two Row Wampum expresses the principles of autonomy and non-interference, there are three rows of white beads between the purple rows that bridge the parallel rows. Dale Turner (Anishinaabe) explains that these reflect the principles of respect, reciprocity, and renewal that must guide the relationship between the two parties in the agreement. Turner stresses that, within this relationship of respect, the respective partners always retain their "distinct political entities."[19]

I believe in the possibility of non-Indigenous people partnering with Indigenous nations over shared land. The original treaties and the Two Row Wampum belts were and are about sovereign nations respectfully engaging with each other without interference. They are more about co-existence than about reconciliation, which, for me, is a very fuzzy concept and one that often serves to maintain the status quo. My journey has been about identity and a changing worldview: how to acknowledge and accept my responsibilities as a settler who has benefitted from stolen land; how to learn from another way of relating to and living with land; how to live responsibly and respectfully as someone who is part of a treaty relationship; and how to live out of an ethic of reciprocity. It has also been a voyage of self-discovery in learning that it is not all about me. I have learned that personal journeys need to engage with the collective heart, the collective body that includes the land. I am reminded of the simple question asked by some of my Indigenous friends: How can I be a good relative wherever I am on this land?

Lee Maracle (Stó:lō) is a writer and speaker who doesn't hold back from speaking harsh truths to settlers.[20] I once heard her say she does not agree with those Indigenous people who speak of sending all those born of European ancestry back to Europe. Settlers and Indigenous people are here to stay and there is still the possibility of transforming our relations between one another. I share an example from Eva Mackey's work, which focuses on how settler attachment to the concept of private property is a critical deterrent to decolonization. Mackey examines the relationship between a group of settler Americans and the Onondaga Nation in New York State.[21] The Onondaga Nation was asserting its right to exercise its responsibility to the well-being of the land and was supported by a settler group, NOON, Neighbours of the Onondaga Nation. The Potawatomi ethnobotanist and writer Robin Wall Kimmerer, in an article on the Onondaga land title action initiated in 2005, invited settlers to engage in becoming Indigenous to place. Kimmerer clarifies that her invitation is not asking settlers to appropriate Indigenous culture, or to become Indigenous, but, rather:

> to throw off the mindset of the frontier, the mindset that allows people to bury sacred sites under industrial waste, to fill a lake with mercury. Being Indigenous to place means to live as if we'll be here for the long haul, to take care of the land as if our lives, both spiritual and material, depended on it. Because they do.[22]

It is this frontier mindset with which settlers must wrestle and let go. This involves accepting a different way of thinking and being – one that does not see land and water as resources but as living relatives, as kin, which have their own rights and to which we have responsibilities and obligations. The pioneering, trailblazing, conqueror-of-nature persona, which sees land as private property and the earth as a set of resources to be exploited, must be transcended if we are to become equal partners on shared land.

Anishinaabe legal scholar Aaron Mills says, "Our foundational commitment is to reconcile our life way (and the constitutional order it gives rise to) with the earth way."[23] Mills proposes "rooted constitutionalism" as a viable third option between resurgence and reconciliation, two approaches to decolonization that he analyzes as flawed and counter to the deep teachings from the earth: "From within a rooted constitutional framework, reconciliation between peoples is a coherent project only if each is first reconciled with the earth way."[24]

My journey into decolonization has never been linear. It is more like a spiral, and each time the spiral circles round I understand a bit more. I still have to wrestle with the cowgirl within. I have had to learn to be in my body in a different way and to come home to my heart and to my ancestry. That has meant having some compassion for myself and for all of us who are on this journey together. Vine Deloria Jr, the great Lakota Sioux theologian and writer, once said that we live in a moral universe, that there is "a direction to the universe," and that "nothing has incidental meaning and [that] there are no coincidences."[25] When I look back at that Saint Anne car ornament that I bought so many years ago, I see that there was nothing random about that act. Not long ago, I decided to hang it on my car mirror. I don't care what people think as she means a lot to me. I like to see Saint Anne dangling peripherally in my vision. She is a non-dual figure for me and she is a reminder of my treaty responsibilities. In a way, she represents the contradictions and confluences of my life. There is no easy solution to more than 525 years of colonialism in this land called the Americas. But at least I have found fellow travellers in many traditions who see that the way through is on the path that embraces the spirit dimensions of life.

Afterword

I have written this book both for the general reader and for those who want a scholarly reflection on decolonization. Here I offer suggestions and resources for those who are interested in further reading or who teach in this area. My approach is interdisciplinary, partly because I have taught in the intersectional field of religion within women's studies and First Peoples studies. As someone engaged in practice I have needed insights from many fields to enrich my work as a facilitator, educator, and sometimes as an activist. So I offer here some of the varied work that has influenced me and that complements my own.

The work I have done as an educator and the stories I share about my personal journey are informed by several schools of study that address the complexity of decolonization. All recognize the structural dimension of colonization and all include a holistic understanding of the human person's interconnection with all beings. At the same time, I explore a transsystemic approach – that is, I incorporate insights from Indigenous Knowledge Systems while continuing to operate through a Western lens.[1] Accordingly, I have chosen to centre Indigenous writers in the chapters in this book and I continue to do so in now offering some reflections on related academic frameworks to which this work contributes.

The process of decolonization is multifaceted and requires more than a critical consciousness that recognizes intellectually what needs to be done to move us out of colonial structures. The process differs for Indigenous and non-Indigenous peoples. I agree with those who maintain that decolonization is ultimately about returning land to Indigenous peoples. Eve Tuck (Unangax Aleut) and Wayne Yang warn that it is easy to "facilitate settler innocence" by falling into the trap of what they call "decolonization as a metaphor."[2] Their article, widely quoted, appeared in the first issue of the online journal *Decolonization:*

Indigeneity, Education, and Society in 2012, and it has set the tone for many of the issues that have followed, mostly from Indigenous perspectives.[3] However, from my experience working with settlers, I know that it is not going to be easy to move most to accept that material reparations and Indigenous title to land, as well as the prioritization of the needs of animal, plant, and fish nations, are necessary for genuine decolonization and reconciliation. However, there are many scholarly fields that address the mechanisms that contribute to resistance to decolonization.

One such field is "affect studies," which looks at how feelings, which include sensations in the body and emotions, are structured by experiences of dominance and oppression. I was first introduced to this field by settler scholars Randelle Nixon and Katie MacDonald's article on the Kony 12 video.[4] Feelings that we think are ours alone, especially our emotional responses to others, are in fact always to some extent shaped by socio-historical factors.[5] So, because they have internalized stereotypes, prejudices, and racist attitudes that affect their emotional responses, it is difficult for some settlers to feel a connection to the families of the missing and murdered Indigenous women, or to impoverishment and lack of housing for many families on reserve land, or to black people who have been carded or killed by police. In my chapters on the Great White Helper I reflect on the connection between emotions, the body, and the structures of authority and power.

If decolonization of the body is one of the central themes in my life, it is partly because, as an educator, I have struggled with how to approach decolonization in learning and teaching. I began my journey in the 1980s as a popular educator and gradually realized that "conscientization" – increasing the critical consciousness of people – was not enough. In training in somatic psychotherapy and in engaging with the field of ministry and later religious studies and interfaith relations, I was able to bring to my work a holistic approach that included body, spirit, mind, and emotions, all of which are necessary to engage in any process of decolonization. I have been greatly influenced by theories and methods of Indigenous pedagogies, in particular the work of Wanosts'a7 Lorna Williams (Lil'wat) and Q'um Q'um Xiiem Jo-Ann Archibald (Stó:lō).[6] The ongoing work of Mi'kmaq educator and scholar Marie Battiste has shaped how I understand the mechanisms of "cognitive imperialism" that have structured Western education at all levels.[7] Alannah Young Leon and I are part of a growing cohort of educators from many nations who teach and theorize embodied learning and its relationship to decolonization, many of us having been inspired by the work of the late Roxanna Ng.[8] Alongside all these educators I see decolonization as a holistic process that involves an intimate connection between bodies and land. While I have written elsewhere about my pedagogy, in chapters 12, 13, and 14 of this book I reflect on how I gradually experienced this embodied connection between body and land.

While since the 1990s biblical studies, in both Africa and Latin America, have contributed much to illustrating how the Bible was interpreted to justify colonialism, theology in North America has been slow to catch up.[9] Indigenous theological reflection is a growing field, its way led by Vine Deloria Jr with his *God Is Red*, published in 1973.[10] In Canada, Heiltsuk scholar and minister Carmen Landsdowne has written about an Indigenous and postcolonial missiology.[11] The first work I encountered by a settler theologian was *Following Jesus in Invaded Space* by Australian Chris Budden.[12] Canadian settler theologian and activist Jennifer Henry has offered biblical and theological reflections on Indigenous solidarity, and settler theologian Jöelle Morgan has articulated a settler theology of liberation.[13] In Quebec, two scholars in religious studies at the University of Montreal, Jean-François Roussel and Denise Couture, have engaged in dialogue around decolonization with theologians from the Global South. Roussel has edited a collection on decoloniality, derived from the World Forum on Theology and Liberation held in Montreal in 2016.[14]

While my work is framed within an interfaith perspective rather than within theology, my focus on decolonizing the body and a holistic methodology of decolonization may contribute to the field of theology. The final chapters of this book, "Lejac," "Can You Hear the Drum," and "Returning to the Heart," illustrate the challenges to settler theology brought about through contact with the complex reality of the traditional practices of Indigenous people. Any dualistic thinking (e.g., "Indigenous Traditions = good/Christianity = bad") or the drawing of simplistic parallels between traditions is undercut by learning that Indigenous epistemologies and ontologies reject dualism and and honour complexity and difference.

Throughout this work, I engage with and explore differences between Western and Indigenous epistemes. I believe I have a responsibility to do this. Settler researcher Chris Hiller draws from the ethical reflections of Sami scholar Rauna Kuokkanen to stress "the importance of coming to a place of humility as well as *responsibility* in relation to Indigenous worldviews, where we listen not only to the insights Indigenous epistemes might offer us, but also listen to hear what such epistemes might *demand* of us."[15] This, I suggest, is the core task facing settler theological reflection on decolonization.

This book is in conversation with the significant field of "settler colonial studies." The late Australian ethnographer Patrick Wolfe was one of the first to define settler colonialism as a structure and not as a single event: "Settler colonies were (are) premised on the elimination of native societies ... in order to make way for 'a new colonial society on the expropriated land base.'"[16] What is particular to settler colonial states like Australia, New Zealand, Canada, and the United States is the ongoing effort to eradicate Indigenous peoples through the imposition of settler values and laws. Within the growing field of settler colonial studies scholars are analyzing the various mechanisms – legal, economic, social, epistemological, educational – that settler colonialism uses to weaken and undermine Indigenous presence on the land.[17] I refer to some of these mechanisms – residential schools, the creation of reserves, the outlawing of ceremonies, and, in particular, the attempt to erase Indigenous women and their power through the Indian Act. To this list I add the construction of the role of the Great White Helper.

I am grateful for the early work of historian Victoria Freeman, a precursor of settler colonial studies, who documented her family's settler history back several generations and who inspired my reflection on my own family history of colonial dispossession.[18] Paulette Reagan's book, *Unsettling the Settler Within*, identifies how the collective Canadian identity is grounded in settler consciousness and a distorted history of Canada.[19] Another groundbreaking work for me is Eva Mackey's analysis of how the Western institution of private property and its function of giving settlers "certainty" is used to justify not only land takeovers but also settler resistance to Indigenous assertion of sovereignty.[20] Besides these brilliant analyses of settler colonialism, exciting and innovative research is now being done on the different ways in which settler consciousness and identity is transformed. This includes examining pedagogical strategies as well as the impact of Indigenous solidarity and ally politics on settlers who are conscious of the need to address Indigenous sovereignty and land title.[21] In reflecting on my own experience, using autoethnography, and in particular by focusing on decolonization of the body, this book contributes to the study of changing settler consciousness through affirming relationship and engagement with embodied Indigenous Traditions.

While all these writers and schools of thought have played a part in my own learning, I chose to centre Indigenous teachings and Indigenous writers because it has been my engagement with Indigenous epistemologies and ontologies that has most affected me. It is important for readers to know just how much work, both popular and scholarly, is being produced in Indigenous circles. I agree with those who caution against focusing too much on settler colonial studies as it is only through engaging with "Indigenous peoples' articulations" that we can affectively grasp "a relational approach to settler colonial power."[22] In other words, the relational centre of Indigenous worldviews is what fundamentally contests the settler worldview while, at the same time, offering an alternative vision. In my chapters titled "Ceremony," "Reciprocity," and "Living Treaty," I discuss how this relational approach, and the Indigenous legal orders and principles that inform the ceremonies and the teachings, has played the main role in transforming my settler consciousness.

In terms of the broader political framework within which I position this work, I have some allegiance to resurgence asa political project that prioritizes Indigenous legal systems and Indigenous nationhood. For some Indigenous scholars it includes "the politics of refusal," emphasizing the revitalizing of cultures, languages, laws, and Indigenous governance while refusing to put energy into seeking recognition by the Canadian state or any settler colonial institution.[23] "Radical resurgence" is the term preferred by Leanne Betasamosoke Simpson (who distinguishes it from the term "cultural resurgence")because it is political and anti-capitalist, offering an alternative to the present global economic regime of extractivism, which threatens the survival of humans and many species on the planet.[24]

While I support this vision of resurgence, I am interested in how Indigenous and non-Indigenous people can work together. Scott Lyons (Ojibwe/Dakota) uses the term "Indigenism," defined as a global political project that focuses on "promoting Indigenous culture in opposition to neoliberalism and 'settler culture'" and "on ecological sustainability, collective land rights, the primacy of Indigenous ways of knowing and Indigenous values, and the political virtue of respectful co-existence."[25] For me reconciliation must fall within this framework. As with the Two Row Wampum, Indigenous principles, values, and laws can point towards what coexistence can look like. One of the more positive reflections on the possibilities of interdependence between settler and Indigenous peoples is the recent collection *Resurgence and Reconciliation: Indigenous-Setter Relations and Earth Teachings*, edited by senior scholars John Borrows, Michael Asch, and James Tully.[26] Authors in this collection address how reconciliation with the earth, grounded in Indigenous lifeways and sustainable reciprocal relationships, can generate "transformative resurgence and reconciliation."[27]

My work has been deeply informed by and points towards Indigenous law. As a scholar of religion I view Indigenous legal traditions as similar to all wisdom traditions that provide guidelines on how to live respectfully with each other and with the earth. I have only begun to explore the depth and complexity of the many Indigenous legal orders, each of which is grounded in specific languages and lands, and transmitted through stories, dances, ceremonies, songs, and much more. Throughout this work I refer to different Indigenous legal scholars. Anishnaabe lawyer John Borrows's *Canada's Indigenous Constitution* is an introduction to the legal constitutions of several Indigenous nations.[28] The work of Val Napoleon, Cree, and Hadley Friedland, who have developed a methodology for articulating the law embedded in Indigenous stories and traditions, is groundbreaking.[29] Napoleon has led the way at the University of Victoria Faculty of Law's Indigenous Law Research Unit, which is supporting communities to recover and revitalize their laws related to land, waters, governance, justice, and citizenship.[30] The work of the Indigenous Law Research Unit, and of Napoleon and Friedland, in promoting gender justice inside Indigenous law and in offering Indigenous legal principles to address domestic violence, victimization, and child welfare, is cutting-edge and can inform not only state legal systems but also community practice.[31]

For those interested in the area of solidarity with Indigenous assertions of sovereignty, there is a growing body of work by both activists and scholars. The collection *Alliances: Re/Envisioning Indigenous-Non-Indigenous Relationships*, edited by settler educator Lynne Davis, brings together reflections and examples from both Indigenous and non-Indigenous writers regarding how settlers and Indigenous people can work together.[32] In the past few years there have been discussions regarding the meaning of solidarity, the terminology of allyship, and decolonizing solidarity.[33] As American activist and scholar of whiteness David Leonard says, the label "ally" doesn't cancel out whiteness and privilege. Rather than labelling, Leonard stresses the need for committing to racial justice, for action not just talk, and for accountability.[34] Gord Hill, a Kwakwaka'wakw grassroots activist, prefers the term "supporter" as traditionally Indigenous nations made alliances with other nations, and alliances are based on *shared interests and mutual benefits* (his emphasis).[35] Harsha Walia's article "Moving beyond a Politics of Solidarity towards a Practice of Decolonization" is an excellent analysis of how Indigenous self-determination is intertwined with all struggles for justice, and of how decolonization within a relationship framework is essential.[36] Emma Battell Lowman and Adam Barker, in their book *Settler*, in reflecting on Indigenous solidarity argue that the term "ally" should be used only as a verb.[37] They suggest it is necessary to acknowledge and name one's settler identity as a first step towards any change. They say that "the key guiding principle for settler Canadians is that decolonization is and must be 'Always in Relationship.'"[38] What settlers are invited to do is to enter the frame of accountability to kinship, to act as if all beings – human and non-human – are our relatives.

For me, always uncomfortable with labels, what I have learned over the years is that it is only in building relationships with Indigenous people that accountability can begin. You need to show up, again and again. You cannot think your way into relationship, you have to live it, and that takes years. It has been my relationships, over time, with Indigenous women and men that have played the largest role in decolonizing my settler consciousness and, I hope, some of my behaviour. In learning from relationships and in exploring how embodied relationship with all living beings is critical to the decolonization process, I hope I have contributed to broadening the concept of what solidarity with Indigenous peoples can look like.

Notes

Foreword

1 See Freeman, *Distant Relations*; Lowman and Barker, *Settler*; DiAngelo, *White Fragility*.

2 For the claim that the genre of autobiography is "Eurocentric," see Portillo, *Sovereign Stories*, 103. Also discussed in 1985 was the idea that the Indian autobiography "has no prior model in the collective practice of tribal cultures." See Krupat, *For Those Who Come After*, 31.

3 See Reder, "Âcimisowin as Theoretical Practice"; "Writing Autobiographically"; "Native American Autobiography"; "Indigenous Autobiography in Canada."

4 Rachel Taylor, writing on Indigenous publishing protocols, notes that "Indigenous storytellers often start with who they are and where they are from, where they got the story, and why they have the right to tell it." See Taylor, "Gathering Knowledges," 1.

5 Like territorial welcomes or acknowledgments.

6 For example, Copway, *Life, History, and Travels*.

7 See Sarris, *Keeping Slug Woman Alive*; Archibald, *Indigenous Storywork*; Wesley, "Twin-Spirited Woman"; Knight, *Dispossessed Indigeneity*; Abel, "NISHGA"; Taylor, "Gathering Knowledges."

8 See also Episkenew, *Taking Back Our Spirits*.

Introduction

1 There are many terms used to describe Indigenous peoples of this land: "Indigenous," "Aboriginal," "Native," "Indian," "Métis," "Inuit," "First Nations." The term "Aboriginal" is found in section 35 of Canada's Constitution Act, 1982, and refers to Indian, Métis, and Inuit peoples. The term "First Nations" refers to specific bands on reserve lands and not to

the larger historical territories of nations. The term "Indigenous" is used internationally, as in the United Nations Declaration of Indigenous Peoples. I occasionally use the term "Native" as a more informal term. I more often use "Indigenous" as it also describes ways of knowing, epistemologies, and knowledge systems of the many Indigenous nations. "Indian Country" is more an insider term, and I use it sparingly and within quotes to indicate as much. A helpful guide to clarifying terminology questions is Métis writer and educator Chelsea Vowel's *Indigenous Writes: A Guide to First Nations, Métis and Inuit Issues in Canada*. See Vowel, *Indigenous Writes*, 5–12.

2   Truth and Reconciliation Commission, *Canada's Residential Schools: Reconciliation*, 3.

3   Simpson, *As We Have Always Done*, 45 (emphasis in original).

4   Lowman and Barker, *Settler*, 15.

5   Jafri, "Privilege vs. Complicity."

6   For more on definition of settlers see Vowel, *Indigenous Writes*, 13–22. Vowel's website and blog, https://apihtawikosisan.com/, provides an introduction to a range of Indigenous issues.

7   The spelling of "Mi'gmaq" varies across Mi'gma'gi (or Mi'kma'ki), which is the word for the territory of all seven districts of the Mi'kmaw Nation, which includes what is now known as Newfoundland, Nova Scotia, New Brunswick, northern Maine, Prince Edward Island, Isles de la Madeleine, and the Gaspé Peninsula. The term "Mi'kmaw"(or "Mi'gmaw") is used as an adjective. Following an Indigenous principle of honouring linguistic diversity rather than standardizing language and orthographies, I use the different spellings when referring to the different regions of Mi'gma'gi. The same applies for my use of the terms for the Anishinabe peoples, who are also called "Anishinaabe," "Anishnabe," "Anishinabek," and "Nishinaabe" in different regions of the Great Lakes, Ontario, and Quebec. Likewise in my use of the terms "Métis," "Metis," and "Metisse," which reflect regional variations.

8   A few years after I graduated, Margaret Power would leave the position of principal of the Sacred Heart Convent to move to Little Burgundy in Montreal where she became an advocate for people on welfare and founded l'Organisation d'aide aux assistés sociaux. Margaret Power received an honorary doctorate from Concordia University in 1994. See Habib, "Honorary Degree Citation."

9   Richard Twiss, Keynote Address.

10 Palmater, *Beyond Blood*.

11   Throughout this book I capitalize all terms that refer to Indigenous identities, including Indigenous institutions and collective rights. I follow here the Indigenous style guide authored by Gregory Younging. See Younging, *Elements of Indigenous Style*.

12   Nadeau, "Decolonizing Religious Encounter," 168.

13   For a contemporary discussion of the debates and tensions around the use of the term "religion," see Juergensmeyer, "2009 Presidential Address."

14   Hilland et al., "An Indigenous Law Response."

Chapter One

1   Choquette, *Oblate Assault*; Mishler, "Missionaries in Collision."

2   Cooke and Piché, *Liidli Koe*, 11.

3   Ibid., 24–5.

4   The pope did return to Fort Simpson for a few hours in 1987 on his way to the United States. The crowd this time was much smaller. Many had read his aborted visit in 1984 as a sign that the Catholic Church had "had its day" in the North. See CBC Digital Archives, "Fog Prevents Fort Simpson Stop."

5   For a similar image of the Catholic Ladder, see Royal BC Museum, "The Catholic Ladder."

6   Huel, *Proclaiming the Gospel*, xix.

7   In 1974, Prime Minister Pierre Trudeau appointed Justice Thomas Berger to head the Mackenzie Valley Pipeline Inquiry to assess the social, environmental, and economic impacts of building a natural gas pipeline down the Mackenzie Valley to the South. Berger's report, published in 1977, was clearly pro-Indigenous and pro-protecting the environment and resulted in a moratorium for the pipeline project. See Berger, *Northern Frontier, Northern Homeland*.

8   L'Arche is an international organization dedicated to providing support and homes for people with intellectual disabilities. It was founded by Jean Vanier. See L'Arche Internationale, https://www.larche.org/.

9   The Oblates had many missions in the eastern Northwest Territories, northern Alberta, Saskatchewan, and Manitoba, and they used the Cree hymnal throughout. However, there are nine Indigenous languages spoken in the Northwest Territories, of which Cree is only one: Dogrib, Dënesųłiné (formerly called Chipewyan), Gwich'in, Inuktitut, Inuinnaqtun, Inuvialuktun, North Slavey, and South Slavey. See "Chipewyan Language."

10 Michael McNally, in a book on Ojibwe singers and hymns in Minnesota, illustrates how the Ojibwe made room for their cultural identity in the hymns, despite the efforts of the missionaries who had translated them to assimilate the people into their version of Christianity. See McNally, *Ojibwe Singers.*

11 Grey Nuns of Montreal, http://www.sgm.qc.ca/en/main-nav/who-we-are/grey-nuns-of-montreal/.

12 The Fort Providence community has erected a monument that commemorates the names of the three hundred children who died in the school. They are buried in a common grave, eighteen metres by twelve metres. See CBC News, "Documented N.W.T. Residential School."

13 Cooke and Piché, *Liidli Koe,* 20.

14 For an introduction to popular education, see the classic text by Paulo Freire, *Pedagogy of the Oppressed.*

15 For a Potawatomi understanding of strawberries, see Kimmerer, *Braiding Sweetgrass,* 22–5. For a Nishnaabe understanding, see Simpson, *Dancing on Our Turtle's Back,* 94–5. For a Dene understanding, see Boivin, "Sharing Bioethics." In the languages of all three women the word for "strawberry" refers to the heart.

Chapter Two

1 Fumoleau, *As Long.*

2 Taken from my personal journal from the summer of 1988.

3 Dene Nation, "Dene Declaration," in Watkins, *Dene Nation,* 3.

4 Coulthard, *Red Skin, White Masks,* 66.

5 Ibid., 75.

6 For the early history of Project North, which had worked since 1975 to support Aboriginal rights, see Cynthia Llewellyn, "Project North."

7 The Chipewyan (also known as the Denesuline) in the Snowdrift/Lutsel k'e region are part of the Dene Nation, as are the Tłįchǫ (formerly known as the Dogrib), Slavey, Gwich'in, and Yellowknives.

8 Coulthard, *Red Skin, White Masks,* 76.

9 Ibid., 76.

10 This collection is located at the Northwest Territories Archives in Yellowknife. See Rene Fumoleau Fonds, NWT Archives, https://www.nwtarchives.ca/fonds_display.asp?Fonds_Number=12.

11 Fumoleau, *Here I Sit; The Secret; Way Down North.*

Chapter Three

1   "Mission," Online Etymology Dictionary.
2   Mesters, *Defenseless Flower.*
3   Peelman, *L'Inculturation.*
4   Arrupe, *Jesuit Apostolates,* 173.
5   Greer, *Mohawk Saint.*
6   Ibid., 199–200.
7   Tekakwitha Conference, "Conference History"; Greer, *Mohawk Saint,* 203.
8   I capitalize Elder when referring to someone who has a role as a Traditional Knowledge Holder in a community and is recognized as such by the community. I use a lower case "e" for elders who are of a certain age but do not necessarily have this role of knowledge and tradition sharer.
9   The Tekakwitha Conference continues to exist today, bringing together Catholic Indigenous people from all over the United States and Canada. Tekakwitha Conference, "Conference History."
10 Andraos, "The Church," 134–5.
11 Ibid., 138; Andraos, "Indigenous Leadership."
12 Andraos, "Indigenous Leadership," 62.
13 Ibid., "The Church," 133.
14 Smith, "The Church," 517.
15 For an overview of the complex nature of Native Christian missionary encounters, see Martin and Nicholas, *Native Americans.*
16 George Blondin, cited in Cooke and Piché, *Liidle Koe,* 19.
17 Pesantubbe, "Foreword," xii.
18 Lansdowne, "Bearing Witness"; "About Me."
19 Warrior, "Native American Perspective," 264.
20 Tinker, *Missionary Conquest.*
21 Dube, *Postcolonial Feminist,* 117.
22 Ibid., 128.
23 Ibid., 193.
24 Hanley, *History,* 117–24. See also Thiel, "Catholic Ladders."
25 For other images of the Catholic Ladder and its history as a pictorial catechism, see "'Catholic Ladder' Pictorial Catechisms," Special Collections and University Archives, Marquette University, June 2009. http://www.marquette.edu/library/archives/News/spotlight/01-2009.shtml.
26 Friesen, "Great Commission," 37.

Chapter Four

1 Exposing that settlers choose to see themselves as innocent and not complicit in the structures that create the marginalization of Indigenous, black, migrant, and impoverished people has been part of the work of Sherene Razack, whose writings have influenced my thinking for many years. See Razack, *Looking White People in the Eye*; and "Gendered Racial Violence."

2 For an analysis of this sense of entitlement to space, see Razack "When Place Becomes Race."

3 Peggy Macintosh's well-known article, "White Privilege: Unpacking the Invisible Knapsack," first appeared in *Peace and Freedom Magazine* in 1989.

4 Roediger, *Towards the Abolition*, 13.

5 Baldwin, "On Being White," 2.

6 Du Bois, *Black Reconstruction*, 700.

7 Roediger, *Colored White*, 64.

8 Baldwin, "On Being White," 1.

9 For an excellent historical overview of the many ways white women were complicit in the regulation and attempted domestication of Indigenous women in Canada, see Pickles and Rutherdale, *Contact Zones*.

10 Roger, "Making White Women," 127.

11 On offering appropriate gifts of respect to Elders, see Younging, *Elements*, 36–7.

Chapter Five

1 I wrote my doctorate of ministry dissertation, "Restoring Sacred Vitality," on this program. See Nadeau and Young, "Educating Bodies"; "Decolonizing Bodies"; and "Restoring Sacred Connection."

2 See Crawford O'Brien, *Religion and Healing*, for examples of a range of Indigenous healing approaches.

3 Nadeau and Young, "Restoring Sacred Connection."

4 Nadeau and Young, "Decolonizing."

5 In 2019 the Downtown Eastside Women's Centre released a comprehensive report with thirty-five recommendations that "shift the lens from pathologizing poverty towards amplifying resistance to and healing from all forms of gendered colonial violence." See Martin and Walia, *Red Women Rising*.

6   See Brantbjerg, "Hyporesponse."

7   Apoyshan, *Natural Intelligence*; *Body-Mind Psychotherapy.*

8   Brantbjerg, "Moaiku."

9   Kleinman and Desjarlais, "Violence, Culture."

10 Ibid., 177.

11 Martin-Baro, *Writings.*

12 Anderson, *Recognition of Being*, 57.

13 Million, *Therapeutic Nations.*

14 Ibid., 6.

15 Ibid., 5, 101.

16 Ibid., 6.

17 Ibid., 161.

18 Fassin and Rechtman, *Empire*, 279.

19 Ibid.

20 Million, *Therapeutic Nations*, 150.

21 See Ontario Federation of Indigenous Friendship Centres, "Trauma Informed Schools."

22 Gross, *Anishinaabe Ways*, 33–51.

23 Ibid., 46.

24 McCormick, "Healing."

25 Ubelacker, "Health Solutions."

26 Kassam, "Ratio of Indigenous Children."

27 "Spiderweb of relations" is Leroy Little Bear's term, cited in Carrière and Richardson, "From Longing," 55.

28 Carrière and Richardson, "From Longing," 55.

29 Spence, "Indigenization of Child Welfare." The Vancouver Aboriginal Child and Family Services Society's website is http://www.vacfss.com/.

30 Linklater, *Decolonizing Trauma Work.*

31 Focusing Initiatives International, "Indigenous (formerly Aboriginal) Focusing-Oriented Therapy Initiative," https://focusinginternational.org/aboriginal-focusing-oriented-therapy-initiative/.

32 Charleson-Touchie and Parsanishi, "Trauma and Culture."

33 Million, *Therapeutic Nations*, 162.

34 Kiera Ladner, cited in Million, *Therapeutic Nations*, 179.

Chapter Six

1   For a brief bibliography on the Christian roots of social work, see Kelly, "Christianity and Social Work."

2   Kipling wrote "The White Man's Burden: The United States and the Philippine Islands" to encourage the United States to take up the burden of empire as had Britain. See Kipling, "White Man's Burden."

3   See Apoyshan, *Natural Intelligence*; *Body-Mind Psychotherapy*.

4   Apoyshan, *Body-Mind Psychotherapy*, 52.

5   Brantbjerg, "From Autonomic Reactivity." Brantbjerg has published most of her papers in Danish but several are available in English on her website, http://www.moaiku.com/.

6   Brantbjerg has integrated the systems-oriented language and methods of systems-centred training into her approach to trauma therapy. See "Systems-Centered Training," https://www.systemscentered.com/.

7   Brantbjerg, "Exploring One-Up."

8   E-mail communication with Susan Cook, 21 July 2018.

9   Okun, "White Supremacy Culture."

10   Ibid., 4.

11   Nadeau and Sajnani, "Creating Safer Spaces."

12   I Love First Peoples, https://www.ilovefirstpeoples.ca/.

13   Anne McClintock's book *Imperial Leather* is a classic, examining the white woman's role in British imperialism. For a nuanced study of the relationship and roles of settler women interacting with Indigenous women in Canada's colonial past, see Pickles and Rutherford, *Contact Zones*. For a critique of Western white feminist response to the War on Terror, see Thobani, "White Innocence." For a critical examination of peace and development projects and socially responsible tourism, see Mahrouse, "Questioning Efforts That Seek to Do Good."

14   Invisible Children, *Kony 2012*.

15   Nixon and MacDonald, "Being Moved," 113–14.

16   Cole, "White Savior."

17   Truth and Reconciliation Commission, *Canada's Residential Schools: Reconciliation*, 102.

18   Ibid., 110.

19   Ibid., 43.

20   The Indian Residential Schools Settlement Agreement was the result of a class action suit. It established a multibillion-dollar fund to help residential school Survivors in their recovery. The Truth and Reconciliation

Commission was funded through the Settlement Agreement. Call to Action No. 61 calls for permanent funding for healing and recovery projects, and for churches to support regional dialogues with Indigenous leaders. Truth and Reconciliation Commission, *Canada's Residential Schools, Final Report*, 112.

21 Medina, *On the Doctrine of Discovery*; Canadian Ecumenical Anti-Racism Network, *Truth and Reconciliation*.

22 Canadian Ecumenical Anti-Racism Network, Noteboom, and Metcalfe, *Truth and Reconciliation*.

23 Heinrichs, *Wrongs to Rights*; Woelk and Heinrichs, *Yours, Mine, Ours*; Friesen and Heinrichs, *Quest for Respect*.

24 Ibid., *Unsettling the Word*.

25 KAIROS Canada, "What We Do"; "Indigenous Rights"; "Missing and Murdered Indigenous Women and Girls"; "Blanket Exercise."

26 "World's First Indigenous Law Degree," *UVic News*, 21 February 2018; See "Indigenous Law," in Truth and Reconciliation Commission, *Canada's Residential Schools: Reconciliation*, 79.

27 United Church of Canada, "Anti-Black Racism."

28 Dismantling Racism Works, "Web Workbook."

29 Canadian Ecumenical Anti-Racism Network, *Cracking Open*.

30 Personal conversation with Dr Jane Dawson, 13 September 2018.

31 Todd, "Indigenizing Canadian Academia."

32 Ibid.

33 Ibid.

34 A church exception comes from the London Conference of the United Church, which, in April 2016, transferred land from the United Church of Canada back to the Delaware Nation. See United Church of Canada, "A Historic Land Transfer." A university exception is the University of British Columbia, which is in the process of forging an ongoing relationship with the Musqueam people on whose land the university sits, and with the Okanagan peoples on whose land UBC Okanagan sits. This relationship goes beyond acknowledgment of territory to, for example, co-hosting conferences in the Musqueam community, co-signing memoranda of affiliation, and developing principles for collaboration. See University of British Columbia, "Musqueam and UBC." http://aboriginal.ubc.ca/community-youth/musqueam-and-ubc/.

35 McCardle, "Board Appoints."

36 McCardle, "Change Must Come."

37 Unitarian Universalists White Supremacy Teach-In, "Essential Elements."

38   Lane-Gatez and Connor, "Institutional Assessment."
39   Tuck and Yang, "Decolonization Is Not a Metaphor," 12.
40   See Alfred, "Reconciliation as Recolonization"; and Coulthard, "Recognition."
41   Simpson, *As We Have*, 49.
42   Ibid.
43   Manuel and Derrickson, *Reconciliation Manifesto*, 302.
44   St Denis, "Roundtable."
45   In most cases I have chosen not to italicize words from Indigenous languages in this text. I take the lead from Tasha Beeds, nêhiyaw and Métis, who maintains that nêhiyawêwin (Cree) "must be placed beside English in an equal textual position" rather than be italicized as a foreign language. She refers to nêhiyaw words as carrying "spiritual power" and giving them "living space." Beeds, "Rethinking," 138.

Chapter Seven

1   A reminder here that there are regional variations in the spelling of Mi'gmaq. In the Gespe'gewa'gi region, Listuguj and Gesgapegiag use Mi'gmag. In Gespeg, Micmac is more common. This reflects something common to many Indigenous languages – diverse orthographies. Mi'kmaq is used in most of the eastern districts, based on the Smith-Francis orthography; in New Brunswick one can find both that system and the Pacifique-Millea system; while in Quebec the standard usage is Mi'gmaq, which is from the Listuguj or Metallic system. See Battiste, "Narrating Mi'kmaw Treaties," 10.
2   Gesgapegiag is the Migmaw name for the land designated to the Mi'gmaq as the Maria reserve in 1853. While there have been some additions to this land base in the last 150 years, it remains around 538 acres in size. See Beaulieu, *Localisation des nations*, 108–9.
3   For an Indigenous analysis of the history of the pass system, see the 2015 documentary *The Pass System*.
4   Inez Talamentez has been an associate professor for several decades at the University of California Santa Barbara, where she has taught and mentored numerous scholars in the area of Native American religious traditions. Inez insists that the only way to understand and study an Indigenous religious tradition is by learning the language.
5   Michael McNally is an Anishinaabemowin speaker and author of several books on Ojibwe religion and Christianity, including *Honoring Elders: Aging, Authority, and Ojibwe Religion*.

6   Tinker, *Spirit and Resistance*, 37–54.
7   Cherry and Mukunda, "Case Study."
8   Nadeau, "Relation et responsabilité."
9   Younging, Dewar, and DeGagné, *Response*.
10 CBC Radio, "This Is Our Birthright."
11 Curtis, "Kahnawake Evictions."
12 Hamilton, "Mikinaks Call Themselves."
13 Vowel, *Indigenous Writes*, 43; Saul, *Fair Country*.
14 Tuck and Yang, discussed in Vowel, *Indigenous Writes*, 43.
15 Poliquin and Dubuc, *L'Empreinte*; Vowel, *Indigenous Writes*, 44–5.
16 Palmater, *Beyond Blood*.
17 Ibid., 202.
18 Ibid., 216.
19 Hill, *Blood*.
20 McIvor, "What Does the Daniels Decision Mean?"
21 Palmater, *Beyond Blood*, 218.
22 Tallbear, *Native American DNA*.

Chapter Eight

1   Mi'gmawei Mawiomi Secretariat, *Nm'tginen*.
2   For a history of Mi'kma'ki, see Paul, *We Were Not Savages*.
3   The Mi'gmawei Mawiomi Secretariat is the administrative body of the Mi'gmawei Mawiomi and follows the directions of the leadership of three Mi'gmaq communities – Gesgapegiag, Gespeg, and Listuguj – which are located in Gespe'gewa'gi, the seventh district of Mi'gma'gi. All three are on the north shore of the Baie de Chaleurs, on the Gaspé Peninsula. The Secretariat is based in Listuguj and its role is to represent the political, cultural, and economic interests of Gespe'gewa'gi. See the organization's website at https://www.migmawei.ca/.
4   Dumais was a pioneering feminist theologian in Quebec. She was the inspiration for and co-founder of Autre Parole, an ongoing organization of feminist Christians across Quebec founded in 1976. I participated in the group when I lived in Montreal. Dumais published two books, *Femmes et mondialisation* and *Femmes et pauvreté*. She co-edited *Souffles de femmes* with Marie-Andrée Roy. Monique Dumais died in September 2017.
5   Ursulines, "Discover."
6   For an introduction to counter-mapping, see "Counter-Mapping Colonization," in Eades, *Maps and Memes*, 96–121. For an overview

of the field, see University of Victoria Ethnographic Mapping Lab, "Indigenous Mapping."

7   See Compton, "Seven Routes," as an example.

8   Cartier, *Relations*, 109–12. For a detailed description of his eight-day interaction with the Mi'gmaq, see Gespe'gewa'gi Mi'gmawei Mawiomi, *Nta'tugwaqanminen*, 168–9.

9   Gespe'gewa'gi Mi'gmawei Mawiomi, *Nta'tugwaqanminen*, 168–9.

10   *Histoires.*

11   Ibid., 15.

12   Ibid.

13   Ibid.

14   French speakers, especially settlers, in the Gaspé, use the term "Micmac," not "Mi'gmaq."

15   Gespe'gewa'gi Mi'gmawei Mawiomi, *Nta'tugwaqanminen*, 170.

16   Ibid.

17   Mi'gmawei Mawiomi Secretariat, *Nm'tginen*, 5–7; Gespe'gewa'gi Mi'gmawei Mawiomi, *Nta'tugwaqanminen*, 71–90, 169–71.

18   Reid, "Doctrine," 335–59.

19   Ibid., 338.

20   Fitzmaurice, "On Nobody's Land," 35–7. An accessible resource on the Doctrine of Discovery is Woelk and Heinrichs, *Yours, Mine, Ours.*

21   Mackey, *Unsettled*, 45.

22   Ibid.

23   Denis Wood, cited in Roberts, *Contested*, 128 (emphasis in original).

24   McMartin, "Surveys," 181.

25   Ibid., 182.

26   Annett, "Gaspee Expedition."

27   Gespe'gewa'gi Mi'gmawei Mawiomi, *Nta'tugwaqanminen*, 98–9; Metallic and Chamberlin, "Encountering," 391.

28   Annett, "Gaspee Expedition."

29   Cole Harris, cited in Eades, *Maps and Memes*, 81.

30   Cartier used the term "sauvage," literally translated as "savage" in 1534. The word is still in use in some communities in Quebec today.

31   Eades, *Maps and Memes*, 81.

32   For a detailed history of forestry on the Gaspé coast, see Pinna et al., *Portrait forestier.*

33   Harris, *Making Native Space.*

34   A copy of both letters in author's possession.

35 Henderson, *Míkmaw Concordat*; Battiste, *Living Treaties.*
36 Chiac is a variety of Acadian French heavily mixed and structured with
    English. It has various Aboriginal language influences as well, especially
    Mi'kmaq. It is mostly spoken in southeastern New Brunswick, but versions
    of it can be found in the Gaspé.
37 Dell and Schlie, *Way We Were*, 22–5.
38 Pinna et al., *Portrait forestier*, 25–7.
39 Raibmon, "Unmaking," 57.
40 Ibid., 59.
41 Razack, "When Place Becomes Race," 5.

Chapter Nine

1   Daniel Heath Justice uses the term "other-than-human" rather than "non-
    human" because of its relational possibilities. Heath Justice, *Why Indigenous*,
    253. I use "non-human" when referring to the work of an author who uses
    the term.
2   Gespe'gewa'gi Mi'gmawei Mawiomi, *Nta'tugwaganminen*, 137.
3   Ibid., 139.
4   Ibid., 140.
5   Metallic, "Strengthening Our Relations," 64.
6   Ibid., 67.
7   Ibid., 68–9.
8   Colonial nostalgia is a term used by Derek Gregory, discussed in Erickson,
    "Embodied Heritage," 324.
9   Erickson, "Embodied Heritage," 324.
10 Cascapedia River Museum, "Welcome."
11 In 2018, the museum made a request of the Mi'gmawei Mawiomi
    Secretariat for the map of the Mi'gmaq place names on the river. Telephone
    conversation with museum staff member Julie Schlie, 7 May 2019.
12 Unama'ki Institute of Natural Resources, "Netukulimk."

Chapter Ten

1   Jamieson, *Indian Women.*
2   Aboriginal Rights and Research Office, Mohawk Council of Akwesasne,
    "Aboriginal Border Crossing."
3   For the story of the Tobique women, see Silman, *Enough Is Enough.*

4 For an overview of this history and the complexities of status under the Indian Act, see Vowel, *Indigenous Writes*, 25–35.

5 Irlbacher-Fox, *Finding Dahshaa*, 37.

6 Ibid.

7 Navarro, "Beading a Path."

8 Kappo, Todd, and Lee, "Beyond Ontology."

9 Belcourt, *Beadwork*, 18.

10 For Alice's quilt work, see http://www.pimaatisiwin-quilts.com/.

11 Alice Olsen Williams, e-mail communication, 6 March 2016.

12 Ryan and Aicken, *Indigenous Tourism*; Johnson, *Is the Sacred for Sale?*

13 Donaldson, "Medicine Women."

14 CBC Radio, "Indigenous Culture."

15 Tłı̨chǫ Ndek'àowo Government, "Fine and Decorative Arts."

16 Vowel, *Indigenous Writes*, 89.

Chapter Eleven

1 Walking with Our Sisters, "About."

2 Walking with Our Sisters, "Information Guide," 7.

3 Kappo, Todd, and Lee, "Beyond Ontology."

4 Belcourt, *Beadwork*, xiii.

5 Jobin and Kappo, "To Honour," 13.

6 The Walking with Our Sisters *Information Guide for Host Communities and Venues*, which was periodically updated, was only available for the host communities.

7 Jobin and Kappo, "To Honour," 147.

8 Welsh, *Finding Dawn*.

9 Wong, "Healing Walk."

10 Laboucan-Massimo, "It Felt Like."

11 Women's Earth Alliance and Native Youth Sexual Health Network, "Violence."

12 For another example of this ongoing transformative work with Indigenous youth. see Sisters Rising, a community-based research project for Indigenous girls, youth of all genders, and communities speaking back against sexualized violence. https://onlineacademiccommunity.uvic.ca/sistersrising/.

13 Chaw-win-is (Ruth Ogilvie), "Remaking Balance"; Hunt, "Justice at the Shoreline," "Representing Colonial Violence."

Chapter Twelve

1   See http://www.anishinaabe.ca/index.php/tag/ojibwa/.
2   Mother Earth Water Walk.
3   Walkem, Presentation at "Protecting Our Sacred Waters."
4   Walkem, "Water Philosophy."
5   Apoyshan, *Natural Intelligence*, 72.
6   Wong, Reading from *Undercurrent*; Wong, *Undercurrent*.
7   Christian and Wong, "Untapping."
8   Patles, Presentation given at strategy session.
9   Kimmerer, *Braiding Sweetgrass*, 55.
10 Apffel-Marglin, *Subversive Spiritualities*.
11 Ibid., 141.
12 Ibid., 134.
13 Downstream: Reimagining Water, "Downstream."
14 For a description of this workshop, see Nadeau and Leon, "Moving."
15 Maracle, "Water," 38.
16 Anderson, "Aboriginal Women."
17 Littlechild, "Transformation."
18 Ibid., 6.
19 Marlowe, "Oral Narratives," 177.
20 Ibid., 178.
21 Craft, "Anishinaabe Nibi Inaakonigewin Report."
22 Nelson, *Original Instructions*.
23 For an introduction to Indigenous law, see Borrows, *Canada's Indigenous Constitution*. For examples of Anishinabe law, see Borrows, *Drawing Out Law*; and Craft, *Breathing Life*. For a Cree example, see McAdam, *Nationhood Interrupted*.
24 West Coast Environmental Law, "RELAW Project"; "RELAW: Revitalizing."
25 West Coast Environmental Law, "Between Law and Action."
26 Dube, *Postcolonial Feminist*.
27 Two examples are Wainwright, "Healing Ointment"; and Yee, "Reflections on Creation."
28 Watershed Discipleship.
29 Bartimaeus Cooperative Ministries.
30 Myers, *Watershed Discipleship*.
31 Ibid., "Critical Contextual," 27.

Chapter Thirteen

1   Gid7ahl-Gudsllaay Terri-Lynn Williams-Davidson, *Out of Concealment*, 47.

2   In the Coast Salish tradition speakers have a very specific role. Musqueam Elder Larry Grant told me that "a speaker, if designated by the host, is the 'voice' of the host as a diplomatic loudspeaker and will have to convey the words of the host and, through time, sometimes acquires the knowledge of many families. If a speaker is on his/her own, he or she is someone who carries or imparts teachings/laws or historical knowledge as they know it to inform others." E-mail communication, 25 January 2018.

3   Larry Grant, cited in Gaertner, "Aboriginal Principles," 141.

4   Smith, *Conquest*, 119–35.

5   Intellectual Property Issues in Cultural Heritage Project, "Think before You Appropriate," 3.

6   Bernadette Spence, personal conversation with author, 29 June 2018.

7   Madeleine MacIvor, e-mail communication with author, 7 January 2018.

8   For an excellent "how-not-to" guide for Christian outsiders who attend Indigenous ceremonies, see Dykstra, "Watch and Pray."

9   For a description of my teaching process see Nadeau, "Decolonizing Religious Encounter?"

10 For a nuanced discussion about bringing Indigenous spirituality into the university, specifically social work, see Lavallée, "Blurring the Boundaries."

11 Wildcat, "Respecting," 23.

12 See University of British Columbia, Department of Education Studies, "Summer Institute 2018."

13 Madeleine MacIvor, e-mail communication with author, 7 January 2018.

14 Apffel-Marglin, *Subversive Spiritualities*, 156.

15 Ibid., 156–7.

16 See Williamson, "Of Dogma and Ceremony," for an Anishinaabekwe/Nehayowak perspective.

17 The website for the Interfaith Institute for Justice, Peace and Social Movements ceased to operate when there was no longer institutional funding for the project. A collective continued with the same name, organizing events on a smaller scale. The group has a Facebook page and a website: https://interfaithinstitute.ca/.

18 For an introduction to the Indian Shaker Church and its founder, Jonathan Slocum, a Squaxin with relations to the Skokomish and other Coast Salish

peoples in the Puget Sound area, see Irwin, *Coming Down*, 266–7.

19 Hogan, "Department of the Interior," 159–74.

20 Ibid., 172.

21 Ibid., 173.

22 Gehl, *Claiming Anishinaabe*, 112–13.

23 Marjorie Beaucage, phone communication with author, 26 November 2017.

Chapter Fourteen

1 These opening words of the Ohén:ton Karihwatéhkwen are from a version produced by the Kanien'kehá:ka Onkwawén:na Raotitióhkwa Language and Cultural Center and have been adapted for use in the Kahnawà:ke Tsi Ietsenhaientáhkhwa Tsi Nitewawennò:ten Tánon Tsi Niionkwarihò:ten Tsi Ionteweiehstáhkhwa (MCK Language and Culture Training Center at Kahnawà:ke) for instructional purposes only.

2 For more on the Ohenton Kariwahtékwen and its importance in the education of Mohawk children, see White, *Free to Be Mohawk*, 87–90.

3 Gibbons, *Stalking the Wild Asparagus*.

4 Many books have been written on the potlatch tradition. On criminalization, see Cole and Chiakin, *An Iron Hand upon the People*. For an example of how potlatches functioned in the kinship economy of the Gitksan and Wetsuwit'en, see Daly, *Our Box Was Full*.

5 Johnston, "Aboriginal Traditions."

6 Ibid., 158.

7 Kuokkanen, *Reshaping the University*, 33.

8 Ibid.

9 See Rubenstein, "Relationality"; and Tanner, *Economy of Grace*.

10 Moore, "Mark and Empire," 147.

11 Kunder, "Beautiful Recklessness."

12 Nadeau, "Restoring Relationship."

13 Apfel-Marglin, *Subversive Spiritualities*, 163.

14 Simpson, *Dancing on Our Turtle's Back*, 109–10, 116n153.

15 Kappo, Todd, and Lee, "Beyond Ontology." Todd and Lee represent a new generation of Indigenous activists and writers. Todd's blog is *Urbane Adventurer*, https://zoestodd.com/, and Lee's is *Moontime Warrior*, https://moontimewarrior.com/.

Chapter Fifteen

1   See Vancouver Island Treaties, http://hcmc.uvic.ca/songheesconference/.

2   Nisgaʼa Lisims Government, "Understanding the Treaty."

3   These are the numbers claimed by the BC Treaty Commission, "Frequently Asked Questions."

4   Indigenous and Northern Affairs Canada, British Columbia Treaty Negotiations Process.

5   For the federal government's definition of comprehensive claims, see Indigenous and Northern Affairs Canada, Comprehensive Claims.

6   See chapter 15, "No Half Measures," in Manuel and Derrickson, *Unsettling Canada*, for a detailed analysis of the BC Treaty Process.

7   These treaties àre known as the Numbered, or Post-Confederation, Treaties and were signed between 1871 and 1921 between the British Crown and various leaders from the many First Nations that occupied what is now most of Ontario, the three Prairie provinces, a large proportion of the Northwest Territories, and the northeast corner of British Columbia. For an informative and useful explanation of the Numbered Treaties and both settler and Indigenous perspectives on treaty-making, see the video series "Trick or Treaty," part of the University of Alberta's free online course, Indigenous Canada, https://www.coursera.org/learn/indigenous-canada/lecture/HEe1s/numbered-treaties-part-1.

8   Idle No More, "Idle No More and Defenders of the Land"; Manuel and Derrickson, *Unsettling Canada*, 217.

9   Gespeʼgewaʼgi Miʼgmawei Mawiomi, *Ntaʼtugwaganminen*, 102.

10   Miʼgmawei Mawiomi Secretariat, *Treaty Relationship*, 15.

11   Gespeʼgewaʼgi Miʼgmawei Mawiomi, *Ntaʼtugwaganminen*, 97.

12   Mills, "What Is a Treaty?," 213.

13   Ibid., 225.

14   Miʼgmawei Mawiomi Secretariat, *Miʼgmewey Politics*, 14–15; Metallic, "Treaty," 47.

15   Augustine, "Negotiating," 22; Joe B. Marshall in Conversation with Jaime Battiste, in Battiste, "Treaty Advocacy," 153. On the origins of the uniqueness of Miʼgmaq Catholicism, in which traditionalism and a blend of appropriated Catholicism stand side by side, see Henderson, *Miʼkmaw Concordat*, which explains the constitutional agreement that incorporates Miʼkmaq legal traditions and that was negotiated between the Miʼkmaq governing body and the Vatican between 1610 and 1630.

16 Mi'gmawei Mawiomi Secretariat, *Treaty Relationship*, 3 (emphasis in
    original); Metallic, "Treaty and Mi'gmewey," 46.
17 Metallic, "Treaty and Mi'gmewey," 46.
18 Gespe'gewa'gi Mi'gmawei Mawiomi, *Nta'tugwaganminen*, 169–70.
19 Craft, *Breathing Life*, 114.
20 Ibid., 89.
21 Ibid., 113.
22 Little Bear, "Native Science."
23 See Borrows, *Canada's Indigenous Constitution*, for an overview of the
    constitutional orders of the Mi'kmaq, Haudenosaunee, Anishinabek, Cree,
    Métis, Carrier, Nisga'a, and Inuit.
24 Mackey, *Unsettled Expectations*, 33.
25 Ibid., 34, 35.
26 Ibid., 141.
27 Kew, Opening Ceremony.
28 Mills, "Nokomis," 24.
29 Vancouver Island Treaties, Presentations.
30 Claxton, *Vancouver Island Treaties Presentation*.
31 Waaseyaa'sin Christine Sy, "From Territorial Acknowledgements."
32 Goeman, *Mark My Words*, 3.
33 *A Map to the Next World, Conflict Resolution for Holy Beings,* and *She Had
    Some Horses* are just a few of the many poetry books Joy Harjo has written.
34 Goeman, *Mark My Words*, 19–21.
35 Altamirano-Jimenez and Parker, "Mapping," 95.
36 Harjo, *Map to the Next World*, 77.
37 "Tribal Canoe Journeys."
38 Forget, "BC Bishop's 470-km Walk."

Chapter Sixteen

1 Many in the North believe the numbers may exceed thirty. Carrier Sekani
   Family Services has produced a website that not only honours the memory
   of the victims but also documents a prevention strategy based on the
   fulfillment of the thirty-three recommendations of the Highway of Tears
   Symposium. See Carrier Sekani Family Services, "Highway of Tears."
2 Hume, "Canada 150."
3 Kujarta, "Four Deaths, No Action."
4 Fiske, "Pocahontas's Granddaughters," 670–1.

5 Truth and Reconciliation Commission of Canada, *Canada's Residential Schools: Missing Children.*

6 The phrase "kill the Indian in the child," wrongly attributed to Duncan Campbell Scott, who was deputy superintendent of Indian Affairs from 1913 to 1932, has been frequently used to describe the assimilationist aim of the residential school system, an aim that had genocidal results. It was used by Prime Minister Stephen Harper during his 2008 apology to former residential school students. Truth and Reconciliation Commission, *Honouring the Truth,* 369.

7 I accessed this blog in August 2012. It is no longer online.

8 Trumpener, "Miracles."

9 Fiske, "Pocahontas's Granddaughters," 676.

10 E-mail communication with Jo-Anne Fiske, 8 September 2015. In 2019 the Nadleh t'en First Nation approved having this same site, adjacent to the pilgrimage site of the former school and the extant graveyard, used for construction workers working on the LNG pipeline, starting in the fall of 2019. This would provide the Nadleh'ten, as hosts, with employment opportunities. E-mail communication with Jo-Anne Fiske, 23 April 2019.

Chapter Seventeen

1 Nadeau, "Restoring."

2 L'autre Parole is a collective of feminist and Christian women active in Quebec since 1976. For its publications over the years, see L'autre Parole, "Revues."

3 See https://www.uvic.ca/services/indigenous/students/lenonet/index.php for a description of the initial LE,NONET Project.

4 MacDonald, "Word Is Becoming Flesh," 92.

5 Eva Solomon has been on the board of the Tekakwitha Conference, started a new order called the "Companions of Kateri," and is co-producer of Kateritv.com, whose purpose is "to delve more deeply into the Aboriginal part of the Catholic Church." See Kateri Television, "About Us."

6 NAIITS: An Indigenous Learning Community, http://www.naiits.com/.

Chapter Eighteen

1 Fearless Collective, https://fearlesscollective.org/.
2 Sisters Rising, https://onlineacademiccommunity.uvic.ca/sistersrising/.
3 Sabrina de Finney, Engaging Youth and Community Responses to Sexualized Violence Forum, University of Victoria, 27 October 2018.
4 Simpson, *As We Have Always Done*, 51.
5 Hunt and Homes, "Everyday Decolonization," 154–72.
6 Simpson, *As We Have Always Done*, 53.
7 Larry Grant, e-mail communication with author, 25 January 2018.
8 Ibid., 18 November 2017.
9 Pnnal Jerome, personal conversation, 28 August 2018.
10 Borrows, *Otter's Journey*, 4–5.
11 See Afterword.
12 See Ancient Hebrew Research Center, Hebrew Word Definitions, "Heart," http://www.ancient-hebrew.org/vocabulary_definitions_heart.html.
13 Y. Wong, "Please Call Me." 254.
14 For an Indigenous example see Stan McKay, "Understanding the Treaty."
15 Henry, "Decolonizing," 12.
16 Borrows, *Otter's Journey*, xii.
17 Hill, "Travelling," 30.
18 Ibid.
19 Dale Turner, quoted in Mackey, *Unsettled Expectations*, 136. For original, see Turner, *This Is Not a Peace Pipe*, 54.
20 Maracle, *My Conversations*.
21 Mackey, *Unsettled Expectations*, 145–64.
22 Kimmerer, "Rights" (emphasis added).
23 Mills, "Rooted Constitutionalism," 156.
24 Ibid., 159.
25 Deloria, "If You Think," 46.

Afterword

1 For an analysis of transsystemic knowledges, see Battiste, *Decolonizing Education*.
2 Tuck and Yang, "Decolonization," 9.
3 See https://jps.library.utoronto.ca/index.php/des.

4   I refer to the *Kony 2012* video in my essay "Decolonizing the White Helper and Reconciliation."

5   Nixon and MacDonald, "Being Moved." See also Ahmed, *Cultural Politics of Emotion*; Massumi, *Parables for the Virtual*; and Clough, "Afterword."

6   Lorna Williams teaches about the connection between the land and our bodies. See Snively and Wanosts'a7 Lorna Williams, *Knowing Home*, an excellent resource and introduction to Indigenous Knowledge Systems for teachers of all ages. Jo-Ann Archibald's *Indigenous Storywork* models both Indigenous pedagogy and a methodology for working with Indigenous Knowledge Holders.

7   Battiste, *Decolonizing the Learning Spirit*.

8   Nadeau and Leon, "Embodying"; See Batacharya and Wong, *Sharing Breath*.

9   See Piu-Lan et al., *Empire*.

10   Deloria Jr, *God Is Red*; See also Tinker, *American Indian Liberation*; and Charleston, *Four Vision Quests*, as examples of Indigenous theology.

11   See Lansdowne's work at www.carmenlansdowne.com.

12   Budden, *Following Jesus*.

13   Henry, "Decolonizing Our Hearts"; Morgan, "Restorying toward a Theology of Decolonial Healing."

14   Roussel, ed., *Decoloniality and Justice*.

15   Hiller, "Tracing the Spirals," 426 (emphasis in original).

16   Wolfe, "Settler Colonialism," 388.

17   Veracini, *Settler Colonialism*.

18   Freeman, *Distant Relations*.

19   Reagan, *Unsettling*.

20   Mackey, *Unsettling Expectations*.

21   See the issue of *Settler Colonial Studies* 7, no. 4 (November 2017), "Pathways," edited by Davis et al.

22   Snelgrove, Dhamoon, and Corntassel ("Unsettling Settler Colonialism," 4) quoted in Davis et al., "Editorial."

23   The more well-known theorists of resurgence and refusal are Taiaiake Alfred, Jeff Corntassel, Leanne Betasamosoke Simpson, Audra Simpson, and Glen Coulthard.

24   Simpson, *As We Have*, 49.

25   Lyons, *X-Marks*, 64.

26   Asch, Borrows, and Tully, eds., *Resurgence*.

27   Borrows and Tully, "Introduction," in *Resurgence*, 7.

28   Borrows, *Canada's Indigenous*.

29 Friedland and Napoleon, "Gathering."

30 Indigenous Law Research Unit, https://www.uvic.ca/law/about/indigenous/indigenouslawresearchunit/index.php.

31 Indigenous Law Research Unit, Gender Inside Indigenous Law Toolkit and Casebook; Friedland, *The Wetiko*.

32 Davis, *Alliances*.

33 Morris, "Decolonizing Solidarity."

34 Park, "Challenging Racism."

35 Hill, "On the Question."

36 Walia, "Moving Beyond."

37 Lowman and Barker, *Settler*, 116.

38 Ibid., 117.

Bibliography

Abel, Jordan. "NISHGA." PhD diss., Simon Fraser University, 2019.

Aboriginal Focusing-Oriented Therapy and Complex Trauma Certificate. Justice Institute of British Columbia. www.jibc.ca/node/14350.

Aboriginal Rights and Research Office, Mohawk Council of Akwesasne. "Aboriginal Border Crossing Rights and the Jay Treaty of 1794." Kentenhko:wa. 19 November 1999. http://www.akwesasne.ca/node/119.

Act to Amend the Indian Act in Response to the Superior Court of Quebec Decision in Descheneaux c. Canada (Procureur général), S.C. 2017, c. 25. http://www.parl.ca/DocumentViewer/en/42-1/bill/S-3/royal-assent.

Ahmed, Sara. The Cultural Politics of Emotion. New York: Routledge, 2004.

Alfred, Taiaiake. "Reconciliation as Recolonization – Highlights." Tehaiá:iake Indigenist. September 2016. https://taiaiake.net/2016/10/03/reconciliation-as-recolonization-highlights/.

Almond, Paul. The Deserter. Montreal: Paul Almond, 2012.

Altamirano-Jiménez, Isabel, and Leanna Parker. "Mapping, Knowledge, and Gender in the Atlantic Coast of Nicaragua." In Living on the Land: Indigenous Women's Understanding of Place, ed. Nathalie Kermoal and Isabel Altamirano-Jiménez, 85–106. Edmonton: Athabaska University Press, 2016.

Anderson, Kim. "Aboriginal Women, Water and Health: Reflections from Eleven First Nations, Inuit, and Métis Grandmothers." Prairie Women's Health Centre of Excellence (2011): 1–32. http://www.pwhce.ca/pdf/womenAndWater.pdf.

– A Recognition of Being: Reconstructing Native Womanhood. Toronto: Second Story Press, 2000.

Anderson, Kim, Maria Campbell, and Christi Belcourt, eds. Keetsahnak: Our Missing and Murdered Indigenous Sisters. Edmonton: University of Alberta Press, 2018.

Andraos, Michel. "The Church and Indigenous Cultures: Beyond the Violent Encounter with 'Modernity.'" In *Theology and the Crisis of Engagement: Essays on the Relationship between Theology and the Social Sciences*, ed. Jeff Nowers and Néstor Medina, 128–40. Eugene, OR: Pickwick, 2013.

– "Indigenous Leadership in the Church: The Experience of the Diocese of San Cristóbal de las Casas, Chiapas, Mexico." *Toronto Journal of Theology* 21, 1 (2005): 57–65.

Anglican Church of Canada. "A Charter for Racial Justice in the Anglican Church of Canada: A Working Document of General Synod." https://www.anglican.ca/about/ccc/cogs/arwg/charter/.

Annett, Kenn (with excerpts from the SPEC). "The Gaspee Expedition and Other Matters (1758)." Gaspesian Heritage Web Magazine. http://gaspesie.quebecheritageweb.com/article/gaspee-expedition-and-other-matters-1758.

Apffel-Marglin, Frédérique. *Subversive Spiritualities: How Rituals Enact the World*. New York: Oxford, 2011.

Apoyshan, Susan. *Body-Mind Psychotherapy*. New York: W.W. Norton and Co., 2004.

– *Natural Intelligence*. Baltimore, MD: Lippincott, Williams and Wilkins, 1998.

Archibald, Jo-Ann. *Indigenous Storywork: Educating the Heart, Mind, Body, and Spirit*. Vancouver: UBC Press, 2008.

Arrupe S.J., Pedro. *Jesuit Apostolates Today: An Anthology of Letters and Addresses*, ed. Jerome Aixala, S.J. St Louis: Institute of Jesuit Sources, 1981.

Asch, Michael, John Borrows, and James Tully, eds. *Resurgence and Reconciliation: Indigenous-Settler Relations and Earth Teachings*. Toronto: University of Toronto Press, 2018.

Augustine, Stephen J. "Negotiating for Life and Survival." In *Living Treaties: Narrating Mi'kmaw Treaty Relations*, ed. Marie Battiste, 16–23. Sydney, NS: Cape Breton University Press, 2016.

Baldwin, James. *I Am Not Your Negro: A Major Motion Picture Directed by Raoul Peck from Texts by James Baldwin*. New York: Vintage International, 2017.

– "On Being White ... And Other Lies." Reproduced from *Essence* (April 1984). http://www.cwsworkshop.org/pdfs/CARC/Family_Herstories/2_On_Being_White.PDF.

Bartimaeus Cooperative Ministries. www.bcm-net.org.

Batacharya, Sheila, and Yuk-Lin Renita Wong. *Sharing Breath: Embodied Learning and Decolonization*. Edmonton: Athabaska University Press, 2018.

Battiste, Jaime. "Treaty Advocacy and Treaty Imperative through Mi'kmaw Leadership: Remembering with Joe Marshall." In *Living Treaties: Narrating Mi'kmaw Treaty Relations*, ed. Marie Battiste, 138–65. Sydney, NS: Cape Breton University Press, 2016.

Battiste, Marie. *Decolonizing Education: Nurturing the Learning Spirit*. Saskatoon: Purich Publishing. 2013.

– "Narrating Mi'kmaw Treaties: Linking the Past to the Future." In *Living Treaties: Narrating Mi'kmaw Treaty Relations*, ed. Marie Battiste, 1–15. Sydney, NS: Cape Breton University Press, 2016.

– ed. *Living Treaties: Narrating Mi'kmaw Treaty Relations*. Sydney, NS: Cape Breton University Press, 2016.

Baum, Gregory. *The Church in Quebec*. Montreal: Novalis Press, 1992.

Beaulieu, Jacqueline. *Localisation des nations autochtones au Québec: Historique foncier*. Québec: Gouvernement du Québec, Ministère du Conseil exécutif, Ministère de l'énergie and des ressources, 1986.

Beeds, Tasha. "Rethinking Edward Ahenakew's Intellectual Legacy." In *Mixed Blessings: Indigenous Encounters with Christianity in Canada*, ed. Tolly Bradford and Chelsea Horton, 119–41. Vancouver: UBC Press, 2016.

Belcourt, Christi. *Beadwork: First Peoples' Beading History and Techniques*. Owen Sound, ON: Ningwakwe Learning Press, 2010.

Berger, Thomas. *Northern Frontier, Northern Homeland: The Report of the Mackenzie Valley Pipeline Inquiry, 1974–1977*. Vancouver: Douglas and McIntyre, 2010.

Bluubox, "Essential Elements: What to Address in Your UU White Supremacy Teach-in." http://www.blacklivesuu.com/teach-in-resources/.

Boivin, Lisa. "Sharing Bioethics." *Indigenous Bioethicist*, 5 October 2015, https://indigenousbioethicist.wordpress.com/.

Borrows, John. *Canada's Indigenous Constitution*. Toronto: University of Toronto Press, 2010.

– *Drawing Out Law: A Spirit's Guide*. Toronto: University of Toronto Press, 2010.

Borrows, John, and James Tully. "Introduction." In *Resurgence and Reconciliation: Indigenous-Settler Relations and Earth Teachings*, ed. Michael Asch, John Borrows, and James Tully, 3–25. Toronto: University of Toronto Press, 2018.

Borrows, Lindsay. *Otter's Journey through Indigenous Language and Law.* Vancouver: UBC Press, 2018.

Brantbjerg, Merete Holm. "Exploring One-Up and One-Down Roles through Body Awareness." *System-Centered News* 23, 1 (2015). http://www.moaiku.com/.

– "From Autonomic Reactivity to Empathic Resonance in Psychotherapy." *Body, Dance and Movement in Psychotherapy* 13 (2018). https://www.tandfonline.com/eprint/GVkNqhCUYVKtTRQWarvw/full

– "Hyporesponse: The Hidden Challenge in Coping with Stress" (2009). http://moaiku.dk/moaikuenglish/englishlitterature/articles_pdf/us_letter/hyporesponse_21_usl.pdf.

– "Moaiku: Relational Trauma Therapy – A Psycho-Motor and Systems-Oriented Approach." http://www.moaiku.com/.

British Columbia Treaty Commission. "Frequently Asked Questions: Treaties and Negotiations." http://www.bctreaty.ca/faq.

Budden, Chris. *Following Jesus in Invaded Space: Doing Theology on Aboriginal Land.* Eugene, OR: Pickwick, 2009.

Canadian Ecumenical Anti-Racism Network. *Cracking Open White Identity towards Transformation.* Toronto: The Canadian Council of Churches, 2012.

Canadian Ecumenical Anti-Racism Network, Peter Noteboom, and Jeffrey Metcalfe. *Truth and Reconciliation and the Doctrine of Discovery: Select Responses of Member Denominations of the Canadian Council of Churches to TRC Call to Action No. 49.* Toronto: Canadian Council of Churches, March 2017.

Carrière, Jeannine, and Cathy Richardson. "From Longing to Belonging: Attachment Theory, Connectedness, and Indigenous Children in Canada." In *Passion for Action in Child and Family Services: Voices from the Prairies*, ed. Sharon McKay, Don Fuchs, and Ivan Brown, 49–67. Regina: Canadian Plains Research Center, 2009.

Carrier Sekani Family Services. "Highway of Tears: Preventing Violence against Women." http://www.highwayoftears.ca/.

Cartier, Jacques. *Relation.* Critical edition by Michel Bideau. Montreal: Presses de l'université de Montréal, 1986.

Cascapedia River Museum. "Welcome." http://www.cascapedia.org/home/.

CBC Digital Archives. "Fog Prevents Fort Simpson Stop on 1984 Papal Visit." http://www.cbc.ca/archives/entry/1984-papal-visit-fog-prevents-fort-simpson-stop.

CBC News. "Documented N.W.T. Residential School Deaths Too Low." CBC.ca, 28 February 2013. http://www.cbc.ca/news/canada/north/documented-n-w-t-residential-school-deaths-too-low-1.1346213.

CBC Radio. "Indigenous Culture Needs to Be Appreciated, Not Stolen, Says Artist." Tapestry, 5 October 2018. https://www.cbc.ca/radio/tapestry/cultural-appreciation-vs-cultural-appropriation-1.4386343/indigenous-culture-needs-to-be-appreciated-not-stolen-says-artist-1.4386363.

– "'This Is Our Birthright': Indigenous Senators Call on PM to End Discrimination against Women in Indian Act." The Current. 2 November 2017. http://www.cbc.ca/radio/thecurrent/the-current-for-november-2-2017-1.4382427/this-is-our-birthright-indigenous-senators-call-on-pm-to-end-discrimination-against-women-in-indian-act-1.4382545.

Charleston, Steven. The Four Vision Quests of Jesus. New York: Morehouse, 2015.

Charleson-Touchie, Anita, and Dea Parsanishi. "Trauma and Culture." Faculty of Medicine, UBC Learning Circle, Centre for Excellence in Indigenous Health. 23 October 2014.

Chaw-win-nis (Ruth Ogilvie). "Remaking Balance: Decolonizing Gender Relations in Indigenous Communities." In For Indigenous Minds Only: A Decolonization Handbook, ed. Waziyatawin and Michael Yellow Bird, 245–63. Sante Fe: School for Advanced Research Press, 2012.

Cherry, Alissa, and Keshav Mukunda. "A Case Study in Indigenous Classification: Revisiting and Reviving the Brian Deer Scheme." Cataloging and Classification Quarterly 53, 5–6 (2015): 548–67.

"Chipewyan Language." Wikipedia. https://en.wikipedia.org/wiki/Chipewyan_language.

Chiron de La Casinière, Annik. Voyage au pays des Mi'gmaq: Canada, debut du XXIe siècle. Paris: Cartouche, 2010.

Choquette, Robert. The Oblate Assault on Canada's Northwest. Ottawa: University of Ottawa Press, 1995.

Christian, Dorothy, and Rita Wong. "Untapping Watershed Mind." In Thinking with Water, ed. Astrida G. Neimanis, Cecilia Chen, and Janine MacLeod, 232–53. Montreal and Kingston: McGill-Queen's University Press, 2013.

Claxton, Nick. Vancouver Island Treaties Presentation. https://vimeo.com/227565288.

Clough, Patricia. "Afterword: The Future of Affect Studies." *Body and Society* 16, 1 (2010): 222–30.

Cole, Douglas, and Ira Chaikin. *An Iron Hand upon the People: The Law against the Potlatch on the Northwest Coast.* Vancouver: Douglas and McIntyre, 1990.

Cole, Teju. "The White-Savior Industrial Complex." *Atlantic,* 21 March 2012. https://www.theatlantic.com/international/archive/2012/03/the-white-savior-industrial-complex/254843/.

Compton, Wayde. "Seven Routes to Hogan's Alley and Vancouver's Black Community." In *After Canaan: Essays on Race, Writing, and Region,* 112–17. Vancouver: Arsenal Pulp, 2010.

Cooke, Lanny, and Camille Piché. *Liidli Koe: Two Rivers of Faith.* Yellowknife: Native Communications Society, 1984.

Copway, George. *The life, history, and travels, of Kah-ge-ga-gah-bowh (George Copway): A Young Indian Chief of the Ojebwa Nation, a Convert to the Christian Faith, and a Missionary to his People for Twelve Years, in Regard to Christianity and their Future Prospects.* Philadelphia: J. Harmstead, 1847.

Coulthard, Glen. "Recognition, Reconciliation and Resentment in Indigenous Politics." Simon Fraser University Office of Community Engagement. 16 May 2016. https://www.youtube.com/watch?v=usrJlFVpKaM.

– *Red Skin, White Masks: Rejecting the Colonial Politics of Recognition.* Minneapolis: University of Minnesota Press, 2014.

Craft, Aimée. *Breathing Life into the Stone Fort Treaty: An Anishinabe Understanding of Treaty One.* Saskatoon: Purich Publishing, 2013.

Craft, Aimée, with the assistance of a group of gifted law students. "Anishinaabe Nibi Inaakonigewin Report: Reflecting the Water Laws Research Gathering Conducted with Anishinaabe Elders, 20–23 June 2013, at Roseau River, Manitoba." Revised Spring 2014. http://create-h2o.ca/pages/annual_conference/presentations/2014/ANI_Gathering_Report_-_June24.pdf.

Crawford O'Brien, Suzanne J., ed. *Religion and Healing in Native America: Pathways for Renewal.* Westport, CT: Praeger, 2008.

Curtis, Christopher. "Kahnawake Evictions: Mohawks, Feds on Legal Collision Course." *Montreal Gazette,* 12 April 2016.

Daly, Richard. *Our Box Was Full: An Ethnography for the Delgamuukw Plaintiffs.* Vancouver: UBC Press, 2005.

Davis, Lynne. *Alliances: Revisioning Indigenous and Non-Indigenous Relationships*. Toronto: University of Toronto Press, 2010.

Davis, Lynne, Jeff Denis, and Raven Sinclair, eds. "Editorial: Pathways to Settler Decolonization." *Settler Colonial Studies* 7, 4 (2017): 393–7.

Dell, Rachel Campbell, and Julie Schlie. *The Way We Were: Vignettes of Grand Cascapedia and Saint Jules: A Cascapedia River Museum Exhibit*. Cascapedia-St Jules: Cascapedia Museum, 2014.

Deloria, Vine Jr. *God Is Red: A Native View of Religion*. New York: Putman, 1973. (30th anniversary edition, Golden Colorado: Fulcrum Publishing, 2003.)

– "If You Think about It You Will See That It Is True." In *Spirit and Reason: The Vine Deloria, Jr. Reader*, ed. Barbara Deloria, Kristen Foehner, and Sam Scinta; foreword by Wilma P. Mankiller, 40–60. Golden, CO: Fulcrum Publishing, 1999.

DiAngelo, Robin. *White Fragility: Why It's So Hard for White People to Talk about Racism*. Boston: Beacon Press, 2018.

Dismantling Racism Works. "Web Workbook." http://www. dismantlingracism.org/.

Donaldson, Laura. "On Medicine Women and White Shame-ans: New Age Native Americanism and Commodity Fetishism as Pop Culture Feminism." In *Gender and Religion: An Anthology*, ed. Elizabeth Castelli, 237–53. London: Palgrave/St Martin's Press, 2001.

Downstream: Reimagining Water. "Downstream: A Poetics of Water, a Research-Creation Project." 2011. http://downstream.ecuad.ca/.

Driver, Tom F. *The Magic of Ritual: Our Need for Liberating Rites That Transform Our Lives and Our Communities*. San Francisco: HarperSanFrancisco, 1991.

Dube, Musa W. *Postcolonial Feminist Interpretation of the Bible*. St Louis, MO: Chalice Press, 2000.

Du Bois, W.E.B. *Black Reconstruction in America: An Essay toward a History of the Part Which Black Folk Played in the Attempt to Reconstruct Democracy in America, 1860–1880*. New York: The Free Press, 1965.

Dumais, Monique. *Femmes et mondialisation*. Montreal: Médiaspaul, 2009.

– *Femmes et pauvreté*. Montreal: Médiaspaul, 1998.

Dumais, Monique, and Marie-Andrée Roy, eds. *Souffles de femmes: Lectures féministes de la religion*. Paris: Éditions Paulines, 1988.

Dykstra, Laurel. "Watch and Pray: A 'How-Not-To' Guide for Christians." In *Quest for Respect: The Church and Indigenous Spirituality*, ed. Jeff Friesen and Steve Heinrichs, 167–8. *Intotemak Trilogy*. Winnipeg: Mennonite Church of Canada, 2017.

Eades, Gwilyma Lucas. *Maps and Memes: Redrawing Culture, Place, and Identity in Indigenous Communities*. Montreal and Kingston: McGill-Queens University Press, 2015.

Episkenew, Jo-Ann. *Taking Back Our Spirits: Indigenous Literature, Public Policy, and Healing*. Winnipeg: University of Manitoba Press, 2009.

Erickson, Bruce. "Embodied Heritage on the French River: Canoe Routes and Colonial History." *Canadian Geographer/Le géographe canadien* 59, 3 (2015): 317–27.

Fassin, Didier, and Richard Rechtman. *The Empire of Trauma: An Inquiry into the Condition of Victimhood*, trans. Rachel Gomme. Princeton: Princeton University Press, 2009.

Fearless Collective. https://fearlesscollective.org/.

Fellows, Mary Louise, and Sherene Razack. "The Race to Innocence: Confronting Hierarchical Relations among Women." *Journal of Gender, Race and Justice* 1 (1998): 335–52.

Finney, Sabrina de. Paper presented at Engaging Youth and Community Responses to Sexualized Violence Forum, University of Victoria, Victoria, British Columbia, 27 October 2018.

Fiske, Jo-Anne. "Pocahontas's Granddaughters: Spiritual Transition and Tradition of Carrier Women in British Columbia." Special Issue: Native American Women's Responses to Christianity. *Ethnohistory* 43, 4 (1996): 663–81.

Fitzmaurice, Andrew. "On Nobody's Land: Understanding Terra Nullius." In *Yours, Mine, Ours: Unravelling the Doctrine of Discovery*, ed. Cheryl Woelk and Steve Heinrichs, 35–7. Winnipeg: Mennonite Church of Canada, 2016.

Forget, André. "BC Bishop's 470-km Walk a 'Small Step on a Journey toward Reconciliation.'" *Anglican Journal*, 1 April 2016. https://www.anglicanjournal.com/b-c-bishop-s-470-km-walk-a-small-step-on-a-journey-toward-reconciliation/.

Freeman, Victoria. *Distant Relations: How My Ancestors Colonized North America*. Toronto: McClelland and Stewart, 2000.

Freire, Paulo. *Pedagogy of the Oppressed*, 30th Anniversary Edition. New York: Bloomsbury Academic, 2000.

Friedland, Hadley. *The Wetiko Legal Principles: Cree and Anishinabek Responses to Violence and Victimization*. Toronto: University of Toronto Press, 2018.

Friedland, Hadley, and Val Napoleon. "Gathering the Threads: Developing a Methodology for Researching and Rebuilding Indigenous Legal Traditions." *Lakehead Law Journal* 1, 1 (2015–16): 17–44.

Friesen, Jeff, and Steve Heinrichs, eds. *Quest for Respect: The Church and Indigenous Spirituality*, ed. Jeff Friesen and Steve Heinrichs, *Intotemak Trilogy*. Winnipeg: Mennonite Church of Canada, 2017.

Friesen, Katerina. "The Great Commission: Watershed Conquest or Watershed Discipleship?" In *Watershed Discipleship: Reinhabiting Bioregional Faith and Practice*, ed. Ched Myers, 26–43. Eugene: Wipf and Stock, 2016.

Fumoleau, René. *As Long as This Land Shall Last: A History of Treaty 8 and Treaty 11, 1870–1939*. Calgary: University of Calgary Press, 2004.

– *Here I Sit*. Montreal: Montreal: Novalis, 2004.

– *The Secret*. Ottawa: Montreal: Novalis, 1997.

– *Way Down North: Dene Life, Dene Land*. Montreal: Novalis, 2010.

Gaertner, Dave. "'Aboriginal Principles of Witnessing' and the Truth and Reconciliation Commission of Canada." In *Arts of Engagement: Taking Aesthetic Action in and beyond the Truth and Reconciliation Commission of Canada*, ed. Dylan Robinson and Keavy Martin, 135–55. Waterloo: Wilfrid Laurier Press, 2016.

Gehl, Lynn. *Claiming Anishinaabe: Decolonizing the Human Spirit*. Regina: University of Regina Press, 2017.

Gendlin, Eugene T. *Focusing*. New York: Bantam Dell, 2007.

Generative Somatics: Somatic Transformation and Social Justice. www.generativesomatics.org.

Gespe'gewa'gi Mi'gmawei Mawiomi. *Nta'tugwaganminen Our Story: Evolution of the Gespe'gewa'gi Mi'gmaq*. Halifax: Fernwood, 2016.

Gibbons, Euell. *Stalking the Wild Asparagus*. New York: McKay Co., 1962.

Gid7ahl-Gudsllaay Lalaxaaygans/Williams-Davidson, Terri-Lynn. *Out of Concealment: Female Supernatural Beings of Haida Gwaii*. Vancouver: Heritage House, 2017.

Goeman, Mishuaua. *Mark My Words: Native Women (Re)mapping Our Nations*. Minneapolis: University of Minnesota Press, 2013.

Greer, Allan. *Mohawk Saint: Catherine Tekakwitha and the Jesuits*. New York: Oxford University Press, 2005.

Grey Nuns of Montreal. http://www.sgm.qc.ca/en/main-nav/who-we-are/grey-nuns-ofmontreal/.

Gross, Lawrence W. *Anishinaabe Ways of Knowing and Being*. London: Routledge, 2014.

Habib, Henry. "Honorary Degree Citation – Margaret Power." Records Management and Archives, Concordia University, June 1994. http://archives.concordia.ca/power.

Hamilton, Graeme. "Mikinaks Call Themselves Quebec's Newest Aboriginal Community, Others Are Calling Them a Fraud." *National Post*, 7 July 2016. http://nationalpost.com/news/canada/the-mikinaks-call-themselves-quebecs-newest-aboriginal-community-others-are-calling-them-a-fraud.

Hanley, Philip M. *History of the Catholic Ladder*. Fairfield, WA: Ye Galleon Press: 1993.

Harjo, Joy. *Conflict Resolution for Holy Beings*. New York: W.W. Norton and Company, 2015.

– *A Map to the Next World: Poetry and Tales*. New York: W.W. Norton and Company, 2000.

– *She Had Some Horses*. New York: W.W. Norton and Company, 1983.

Harris, Cole. *Making Native Space: Colonialism, Resistance, and Reserves in British Columbia*. Vancouver: UBC Press, 2002.

Heath Justice, Daniel. *Why Indigenous Literatures Matter*. Waterloo, ON: Wilfrid Laurier Press, 2018.

Heinrichs, Steve, ed. *Unsettling the Word: Biblical Experiments in Decolonization*. Winnipeg: Mennonite Church of Canada, 2018.

– *Wrongs to Rights: How Churches Can Engage the United Nations Declaration on the Rights of Indigenous Peoples, Intotemak Trilogy*. Winnipeg: Mennonite Church of Canada, 2016.

Henderson, James (Sákéj) Youngblood. *The Míkmaw Concordat*. Halifax: Fernwood, 1997.

Henry, Jennifer. "Decolonizing Our Hearts: Biblical and Theological Animation of Indigenous Rights Solidarity in Canada." Unpublished paper available at jenniferjubilee@gmail.com.

Hiller, Chris. "Tracing the Spirals of Unsettlement: Euro-Canadian Narratives of Coming to Grips with Indigenous Sovereignty, Title, and Rights." *Settler Colonial Studies* 7, 4 (2017): 415–40.

Hill, Lawrence. *Blood: The Stuff of Life*. Toronto: House of Anansi, 2013.

Hill, Gord. "On the Question of Allies." 22 December 2016. https://warriorpublications.wordpress.com/2016/12/22/on-the-question-of-allies/.

Hill, Susan. "Travelling Down the River of Life Together in Peace and Friendship, Forever: Haudenosaunee Land Ethics and Treaty Agreements as the Basis for Restructuring the Relationships with the

British Crown." In *Lighting the Eighth Fire: The Liberation, Resurgence, and Protection of Indigenous Nations*, ed. Leanne Betasamosoke Simpson, 59–72. Winnipeg: Arbeiter Ring, 2008.

Hilland, Andrea, Ardith Walkem, Gwaai Edenshaw, Robyn Gervais. "An Indigenous Laws Response to the Boushie/Fontaine Verdicts." University of Victoria Legacy Gallery, 27 October 2018.

Histoires et souvenirs, 150e Port-Daniel, 1855–2005. Port-Daniel, QC: Corporation de la relance économique, 2005.

Hogan, Linda. "Department of the Interior." In *Minding the Body: Women Writers on Body and Soul*, ed. Patricia Foster, 159–74. New York: Anchor Doubleday, 1994.

Huel, Raymond. *Proclaiming the Gospel to the Indians and the Metis*. Edmonton: University of Alberta Press, 1996.

Hume, Stephen. "Canada 150: Rose Prince a Saint to Many." *Vancouver Sun*, 25 February 2017. http://vancouversun.com/news/local-news/canada-150-rose-prince-a-saint-to-many.

Hunt, Sarah. "Justice at the Shoreline: Redefining Spaces of Sovereignty through Coastal Wisdom." Presentation at First Peoples House, University of Victoria, Victoria, British Columbia, 8 March 2018.

– "Representing Colonial Violence: Trafficking, Sex Work, and the Violence of Law." *Atlantis* 37, 2 (2015): 25–39.

Hunt, Sarah, and Cindy Homes. "Everyday Decolonization: Living a Decolonizing Queer Politics." *Journal of Lesbian Studies* 19, 2 (2015): 154–72.

Idle No More. "Idle No More and Defenders of the Land Join to Call for Sustained Campaign of Action." 18 March 2013. http://www.idlenomore.ca/about-us/alliances/item/215-defenders-of-the-land.

I Love First Peoples. https://www.ilovefirstpeoples.ca/.

Indigenous and Northern Affairs Canada. Comprehensive Claims. https://www.aadnc-aandc.gc.ca/eng/1100100030577/1100100030578.

– The British Columbia Treaty Negotiations Process. https://www.aadnc-aandc.gc.ca/eng/1348230937078/1348231345065.

Indigenous Law Research Unit. University of Victoria Law Faculty. https://www.uvic.ca/law/about/indigenous/indigenouslawresearchunit/index.php.

Indigenous Law Research Unit. *Gender Inside Indigenous Law Toolkit*, University of Victoria, 2016. https://www.uvic.ca/law/assets/docs/ilru/Gender%20Inside%20Indigenous%20Law%20Toolkit%2001.01.16.pdf.

– *Gender Inside Indigenous Law Casebook.* University of Victoria, 2016.
    https://www.uvic.ca/law/assets/docs/ilru/Gender%20Inside%20
    Indigenous%20Law%20Casebook%2001.01.16.pdf

Intellectual Property Issues in Cultural Heritage Project. "Think before
    You Appropriate: Things to Know and Questions to Ask in Order to
    Avoid Appropriating Indigenous Cultural Heritage." Vancouver: Simon
    Fraser University, 2015. https://www.sfu.ca/ipinch/sites/default/
    files/resources/teaching_resources/think_before_you_appropriate_
    jan_2016.pdf.

Interfaith Institute for Justice, Peace and Social Movements. "Vision and
    Mission." https://interfaithinstitute.ca/.

Invisible Children. *Kony 2012.* 5 March 2012. https://www.youtube.com/
    watch?v=Y4MnpzG5Sqc.

Irlbacher-Fox, Stephanie. *Finding Dahshaa: Self-Government, Social
    Suffering, and Aboriginal Policy in Canada.* Vancouver: UBC Press, 2009.

Irwin, Lee. *Coming Down from Above: Prophecy, Resistance, and Renewal
    in Native American Religions,* foreword by Philip J. Deloria. Norman:
    University of Oklahoma Press, 2008.

Jafri, Beenash. "Privilege vs. Complicity: People of Colour and Settler
    Colonialism." *Federation for the Humanities and Social Sciences, Equity
    Matters.* 21 March 2012. http://www.ideas-idees.ca/blog/privilege-vs-
    complicity-people-colour-and-settler-colonialism.

Jamieson, Kathleen. *Indian Women and the Law in Canada: Citizens Minus.*
    Ottawa: Canadian Advisory Council on the Status of Women, 1978.

Jobin, Shalene, and Tara Kappo. "'To Honour the Lives of Those Taken
    from Us': Restor(y)ing Resurgence and Survivance through Walking with
    Our Sisters." In *Surviving Canada: Indigenous People Celebrate 150 Years
    of Betrayal,* ed. Kiera Ladner and Myra Tait, 131–48. Winnipeg: Arbeiter
    Ring Publishing, 2017.

Johnson, Alison. *Is the Sacred for Sale? Tourism and Indigenous Peoples.*
    London: Earthscan, 2006.

Johnston, Darlene. "Aboriginal Traditions of Tolerance and Reparation:
    Introducing Canadian Colonialism." In *Le Devoir de mémoire et les
    politiques du pardon,* ed. Micheline Labelle, Rachad Antonius, et Georges
    Leroux, 141–59. Quebec: Presses de l'Université du Québec, 2005.

Juergensmeyer, Mark. "2009 Presidential Address: Beyond Words and War –
    The Global Future of Religion." *Journal of the American Academy of
    Religion* 78, 4 (2010): 882–95.

KAIROS Canada. "Blanket Exercise Workshop." https://www.kairoscanada. org/what-we-do/indigenous-rights/blanket-exercise.

– "Indigenous Rights: Campaign on the United Nations Declaration on the Rights of Indigenous Peoples." https://www.kairoscanada.org/what-we-do/indigenous-rights/undrip-campaign.

– "Missing and Murdered Indigenous Women and Girls." https://www. kairoscanada.org/missing-murdered-indigenous-women-girls.

– "What We Do: Indigenous Rights." https://www.kairoscanada.org/what-we-do/indigenous-rights.

Kappo, Tara, Zoe Todd, and Erica Violet Lee. "Beyond Ontology: Indigenous Immateriality and Relatedness." Panel presentation, Native American and Indigenous Studies Association Conference, Vancouver, 24 June 2017.

Kassam, Ashifa. "Ratio of Indigenous Children in Canada Welfare System Is 'Humanitarian Crisis.'" *Guardian*, 4 November 2017. https://www. theguardian.com/world/2017/nov/04/indigenous-children-canada-welfare-system-humanitarian-crisis.

Kateri Television. "About Us." http://www.villagersmedia.com/kateritv/about.html.

Kermoal, Nathalie, and Isabel Altamirano-Jiménez, eds. *Living on the Land: Indigenous Women's Understanding of Place*. Edmonton: Athabaska University Press, 2016.

Kelly, Michael S. "Christianity and Social Work." Oxford Bibliographies. http://www.oxfordbibliographies.com/view/document/obo-9780195389678/obo-9780195389678-0266.xml.

Kew, Jim. Opening Ceremony. Native American and Indigenous Studies Association Conference, University of British Columbia. 22 June 2017.

Kimmerer, Robin Wall. *Braiding Sweetgrass: Indigenous Wisdom, Scientific Knowledge, and The Teachings of Plants*. Minneapolis: Milkweed Editions 2013.

– "The Rights of the Land." *Orion Magazine*, November–December 2008. https://orionmagazine.org/article/the-rights-of-the-land/.

Kipling, Rudyard. "The White Man's Burden: The United States and the Philippine Islands, 1899." In *Rudyard Kipling's Verse: Definitive Edition*. Garden City, NY: Doubleday, 1929. http://historymatters.gmu. edu/d/5478/.

Kleinman, Arthur, and Robert Desjarlais. "Violence, Culture and the Politics of Trauma." In *Writing at the Margin: Discourse between Anthropology and Medicine*, ed. Arthur Kleinman, 173–89. Berkeley: University of California Press: 1995.

Kleinman, Arthur, Veena Das, and Margaret Lock, eds. *Social Suffering*. Berkeley: University of California Press, 1997.

Knight, Natalie. "Dispossessed Indigeneity: Literary Evacuations of Internalized Colonialism." PhD diss., Simon Fraser University, 2018.

Kovach, Margaret. *Indigenous Methodologies: Characteristics, Conversations, and Contexts*. Toronto: University of Toronto Press, 2009.

Krupat, Arnold. *For Those Who Come After: A Study of Native American Autobiography*. Berkeley: University of California Press, 1985.

Kujarta, Andrew. "Four Deaths, No Action: 'Notorious' BC Residential School Explored in New Project." *CBC News*, 4 January 2018. http://www.cbc.ca/news/canada/british-columbia/lejac-residential-school-four-boys-runaways-death-1.4473885.

Kunder, Will, "Beautiful Recklessness: A Theological Reflection Based on Mark 14:1–9." *Mandate*, May 2005.

Kuokkanen, Rauna. *Reshaping the University: Responsibility, Indigenous Epistemes, and the Logic of the Gift*. Vancouver: UBC Press, 2007.

Kwok, Pui-Lan. *Post-Colonial Imagination and Feminist Theology*. Louisville, KY: Westminster John Knox, 2005.

Kwok, Pui-Lan, Don H. Compier, and Jorge Rieger, eds. *Empire: The Christian Tradition – New Readings of Classical Theologians*. Minneapolis: Fortress Press, 2007.

Laboucan-Massimo, Melina. "It Felt Like There Was No End to the Screaming Sadness: One Sister's Take on #mmiw." *APTN National News*, 25 September 2014. http://aptn.ca/news/2014/09/25/felt-like-end-screaming-sadness-one-sisters-take-mmiw/.

Landsdowne, Carmen. "About Me." https://www.carmenlansdowne.com/.

– "Bearing Witness: Wearing a Broken Indigene Heart on the Sleeve of Mission Dei." PhD diss., Graduate Theological Union, 2016.

Lane-Gatez, Sharon, and Justin Connor. "Institutional Assessment on Racism Update, January 2018." FGC Friends General Conference, 9 January 2018. https://www.fgcquaker.org/news/institutional-assessment-racism-update-january-2018.

L'Arche Internationale. https://www.larche.org/.

L'Autre Parole. "Revues." http://www.lautreparole.org/revues.

Lavallée, L. "Blurring the Boundaries: Social Work's Role in Indigenous Spirituality." *Canadian Social Work Review* 27, 1 (2010):143–6.

Lee, Erica Violet. *Moontime Warrior: Fearless Philosophizing, Embodied Resistance.* https://moontimewarrior.com/.

Linklater, Renee. *Decolonizing Trauma Work: Indigenous Stories and Strategies.* Halifax: Fernwood, 2014.

Little Bear, Leroy. "Native Science and Western Science: Possibilities for a Powerful Collaboration." Simon Ortiz and Labriola Center Lecture on Indigenous Land, Culture and Community, University of Arizona, 24 March 2011. http://www.youtube.com/watch?v=ycQtQZ9y3lc.

Littlechild, Danika Billie. "Transformation and Re-formation: First Nations and Water in Canada." LLM thesis, University of Victoria, 2014. http://hdl.handle.net/1828/5826.

Llewellyn, Cynthia. "Project North: Coalition for Self-Determination." *International Review of Mission, World Council of Churches* 71, 283 (1982): 353–4.

Lowman, Emma Battell, and Adam J. Barker. *Settler: Identity and Colonialism in 21st-Century Canada.* Winnipeg: Fernwood, 2015.

Lyons, Scott. *X-Marks: Native Signatures of Assent.* Minneapolis: University of Minnesota Press, 2010.

MacDonald, Mark. "The Word Is Becoming Flesh: A Conversation with Indigenous Bishop Mark MacDonald." In *Quest for Respect: The Church and Indigenous Spirituality, Intotemak Trilogy,* ed. Jeff Friesen and Steve Heinrichs, 91–4. Winnipeg: Mennonite Church of Canada, 2017.

Macintosh, Peggy. "White Privilege: Unpacking the Invisible Knapsack." *Peace and Freedom Magazine,* July–August 1989, 10–12.

Mackey, Eva. *Unsettled Expectations: Uncertainty, Land and Settler Decolonization.* Halifax: Fernwood, 2016.

Mahrouse, Gada. "'Questioning Efforts That Seek to 'Do Good': Insights from Transnational Solidarity Activism and Socially Responsible Tourism." In *States of Race: Critical Race Feminism for the 21st Century,* ed. Sherene Razack, Malinda Smith, and Sunera Thobani, 169–90. Toronto: Between the Lines, 2010.

Manuel, Arthur, and Grand Chief Ronald M. Derrickson. *The Reconciliation Manifesto: Recovering the Land and Rebuilding the Economy.* Preface by Naomi Klein. Toronto: James Lorimer, 2017.

Manuel, Arthur, and Grand Chief Ronald M. Derrickson. *Unsettling Canada: A National Wake-Up Call.* Toronto: Between the Lines, 2015.

Maracle, Lee. *My Conversations with Canadians.* Toronto: Book Thug, 2017.

– "Water." In *Downstream: Reimagining Water*, ed. Dorothy Christian and Rita Wong, 33–8. Waterloo: Wilfrid Laurier University Press, 2017.

Marlowe, Sam Gregory. "Oral Narratives, Customary Laws and Indigenous Water Rights in Canada." PhD diss., University of British Columbia, 2013. http://hdl.handle.net/2429/45247.

Martin-Baro, Ignacio. *Writings for a Liberation Psychology*, ed. Adrianne Aron and Shawn Corne. Cambridge: Harvard University Press, 1994.

Martin, Carol Muree, and Harsha Walia. *Red Women Rising: Indigenous Women Survivors in Vancouver's Downtown Eastside*. Vancouver, Downtown Eastside Women's Centre, 2019. http://dewc.ca/resources/redwomenrising.

Martin, Joel W., and Mark A. Nicholas, eds. *Native American, Christianity, and the Reshaping of the American Religious Landscape*. Chapel Hill: University of North Carolina Press, 2010.

Massumi, Brian. *Parables for the Virtual: Movement, Affect, Sensation*. Durham, NC: Duke University Press, 2002.

Masters, Robert. *Spiritual Bypassing: When Spirituality Disconnects Us from What Really Matters*. Berkeley, CA: North Atlantic Books, 2010.

McAdam, Sylvia. *Nationhood Interrupted: Revitalizing nêhiyaw Legal Systems*. Vancouver: UBC Press/Purich Publishing, 2017.

McCardle, Elaine. "Board Appoints Six to Two-Year Commission on Institutional Change." UU World, 22 June 2017. https://www.uuworld.org/articles/commission-institutional-change.

– "Change Must Come if Unitarian Universalism Is to Thrive, Say Co-Presidents." UU World, 23 June 2017. https://www.uuworld.org/articles/co-presidents-report-2017-ga.

McClintock, Anne. *Imperial Leather: Race, Gender and Sexuality in the Colonial Contest*. New York: Routledge, 1995.

McCormick, Rod. "Healing through Interdependence: The Role of Connection in First Nations Healing Practices." *Canadian Journal of Counselling* 31, 3 (1997): 172–85.

McIvor, Bruce. "What Does the Daniels Decision Mean?" *First Peoples Law*, 20 April 2016. https://www.firstpeopleslaw.com/index/articles/248.php.

McKay, Stan. "Understanding the Treaty as Covenant." In *Mamow Be-Mo-Tay-Tah. Let Us Walk Together*, 30–2. Canadian Ecumenical Anti-Racism Network. Toronto: Canadian Council of Churches, 2009.

McMartin, George E. "Surveys of the Province of Quebec." In *Report of Proceedings of the Association of Dominion Land Surveyors at Its*

Sixth Annual Meeting Held at Ottawa, February 19, 20, and 21, 181–7. Montreal: John Lovell & Son, 1889.

McNally, Michael D. *Honoring Elders: Aging, Authority, and Ojibwe Religion.* New York: Columbia University Press, 2009.

– *Ojibwe Singers: Hymns, Grief, and a Native Culture in Motion.* Oxford: Oxford University Press, 2000.

McNally, Michael D., ed. *The Art of Tradition: Sacred Music, Dance and Myth of Michigan's Anishinaabe, 1946–1955.* East Lansing: Michigan State University Press, 2009.

Medina, Néstor. *On the Doctrine of Discovery.* Toronto: The Canadian Council of Churches, 2017.

Mesters, Carlos. *Defenseless Flower: A New Reading of the Bible.* Maryknoll, NY: Orbis, 1989.

Metallic, Fred (Gopit). "Strengthening Our Relations in Gespe'gewa'gi, the Seventh District of Mi'gmagi." In *Lighting the Eighth Fire: The Liberation, Resurgence, and Protection of Indigenous Nations*, ed. LeanneBetasamosoke Simpson, 59–72. Winnipeg: Arbeiter Ring Publishing, 2008.

– "Treaty and Mi'gmewey." In *Living Treaties: Narrating Mi'kmaw Treaty Relations*, ed. Marie Battiste, 42–51. Sydney, NS: Cape Breton University Press, 2016.

Metallic, Fred, and Amy Chamberlin. "Encountering Memories on the Restigouche River." In *Surviving Canada: Indigenous People Celebrate 150 Years of Betrayal*, ed. Kiera Ladner and Myra Tait, 389–97. Winnipeg: Arbeiter Ring Publishing, 2017.

Mi'gmawei Mawiomi Secretariat. *Mi'gmewey Politics.* Listuguj, QC: Mi'gmawei Mawiomi Secretariat, 2010.

– *Nm'tginen: Me'mnaq Ejiglignmuetueg Gis Na Naqtmueg.* Listuguj, QC: Mi'gmawei Mawiomi Secretariat, 2007. https://migmawei.ca/system/wp-content/uploads/2017/07/Nmtginen-book-English-small-size-file.pdf.

– *The Treaty Relationship between Mi'qmaq of Gespe'gewa'gi and the British Crown and Its Implication for the Province of Quebec.* Listuguj, QC: Mi'gmawei Mawiomi Secretariat, 2010.

Million, Diane. *Therapeutic Nations: Healing in an Age of Indigenous Human Rights.* Tucson: University of Arizona Press, 2014.

Mills, Aaron. "Nokomis and the Law in the Gift: Living Treaty Each Day." In *Surviving Canada: Indigenous People Celebrate 150 Years of Betrayal*, ed. Kiera Ladner and Myra Tait, 17–27. Winnipeg: Arbeiter Ring Publishing, 2017.

– "Rooted Constitionalism: Growing Political Community." In *Resurgence and Reconciliation: Indigenous-Settler Relations and Earth Teachings,* ed. Michael Asch, John Borrows, and James Tully, 133–73. Toronto: University of Toronto Press, 2018.

– "What Is a Treaty? On Contract and Mutual Aid." In *The Right Relationship: Reimagining the Implementation of Historical Treaties,* ed. John Borrows and Michael Coyle, 208–47. Toronto: University of Toronto Press, 2017.

Mishler, Craig. "Missionaries in Collision: Anglicans and Oblates among the Gwich'in, 1861–65." *Arctic* 43, 2 (1990): 121–6. http://dx.doi. org/10.14430/arctic1601.

"Mission." *Online Etymology Dictionary.* https://www.etymonline.com/word/mission.

Moore, Stephen. "Mark and Empire: 'Zealot' and 'Postcolonial' Readings." In *Postcolonial Theologies: Divinity and Empire,* ed. Catherine Keller, Michael Nauser, and Mayra Rivera, 134–48. St Louis, MO: Chalice Press, 2004.

Morgan, Jöelle. "Restorying Indigenous-Settler Relations in Canada: Taking a Decolonial Turn toward a Settler Theology of Liberation." PhD diss., St Paul University, 2018.

– "Restorying toward a Theology of Decolonial Healing." In *Decoloniality and Justice,* ed. Jean-François Roussel. São Leopoldo, Brazil: Editora OIKOS, 2018.

Morris, Katie Boudreau. "Decolonizing Solidarity: Cultivating Relationships of Discomfort." *Settler Colonial Studies* 7, 4 (2017): 456–73.

Mother Earth Water Walk. http://www.motherearthwaterwalk.com/.

Myers, Ched. "A Critical Contextual and Constructive Approach to Ecological Theology and Practice." In *Watershed Discipleship: Reinhabiting Bioregional Faith and Practice,* ed. Ched Myers, 1–25. Eugene, OR: Wipf and Stock, 2016.

– ed. *Watershed Discipleship: Reinhabiting Bioregional Faith and Practice.* Foreword by Denise M. Nadeau. Eugene, OR: Wipf and Stock, 2016.

Nadeau, Denise. "Decolonizing Religious Encounter? Teaching 'Indigenous Traditions, Women, and Colonialism.'" In *Mixed Blessings: Indigenous Encounters with Christianity in Canada,* ed. Tolly Bradford and Chelsea Horton, 164–82. Vancouver: UBC Press, 2016.

– "Feminist Anti-Colonial Practice in a Euro-Canadian Context." In *Women's Voices and Visions of the Church: Reflections from North*

America, ed. Letty M. Russel, Aruna Gnanadason, and J. Shannon Clarkson, 66–79. Geneva: World Council of Churches, 2005.

– "Relation et responsabilité: Vers un processus de réconciliation." *Théologiques* 20, 1–2 (2012): 419–52.

– "Restoring Relationship: Towards a Theology of Reparations as Gift." In *Feminist Theology with a Canadian Accent: Canadian Perspectives on Contextual Feminist Theology*, ed. Mary Ann Beavis, 220–34. Ottawa: Novalis, 2008.

– "Restoring Sacred Vitality: Restoring Community Health with Women Who Suffer Routinized Violence." DMin. diss., San Francisco Theological Seminary, 2003.

Nadeau, Denise Marie, and Alannah Young Leon. "Educating Bodies for Self-Determination – A Decolonizing Strategy." *Canadian Journal of Native Education* 29, 1 (2006): 87–101.

– "Decolonizing Bodies: Restoring Sacred Vitality." *Atlantis Women's Studies Journal: Indigenous Women – The State of Our Nation* 29, 2 (2005): 13–22.

– "Embodying Indigenous Resurgence: All My Relations Pedagogy." In *Sharing Breath: Embodied Learning and Decolonization,* ed. Sheila Batacharya and Yuk-Lin Renita Wong, 55–82. Edmonton: Athabasca University Press, 2018.

– "Moving with Water: Relationship and Responsibilities." In *Downstream: Reimagining Water,* ed. Dorothy Christian and Rita Wong, 117–38. Waterloo: Wilfrid Laurier University Press, 2017.

– "Restoring Sacred Connection with Native Women in the Inner City." In *Religion and Healing in Native America: Pathways for Renewal,* ed. Suzanne J. Crawford O'Brien, 115–34. Westport, CT: Praeger, 2008.

Nadeau, Denise, and Nisha Sajnani. "Creating Safer Spaces for Immigrant Women of Colour: Performing the Politics of Possibility." *Canadian Women's Studies: Ending Woman Abuse* 25, 1–2 (2006): 45–53.

NAIITS: An Indigenous Learning Community. http://www.naiits.com/.

Navarro, Jenelle. "Beading a Path to the Future: Indigenous Anti-Violence Work, Community Activism, and Walking with Our Sisters." Panel presentation, National Women's Studies Association Conference, Montreal, 11 November 2016.

Nelson, Melissa, ed. *Original Instructions: Indigenous Teachings for a Sustainable Future.* Rochester, VT: Bear and Co., 2008.

Nisga'a Lisims Government. "Understanding the Treaty." http://www. nisgaanation.ca/understanding-treaty.

Nixon, Randelle, and Katie MacDonald, "Being Moved to Action: Micropolitics, Affect, and Embodied Understanding." In *Sharing Breath: Embodied Learning and Decolonization*, ed. S. Batacharya and R. Wong, 111–34. Edmonton: Athabaska University Press, 2018.

Okun, Tema. "White Supremacy Culture." *dRworks*. http://www. dismantlingracism.org/uploads/4/3/5/7/43579015/okun_-_white_sup_ culture.pdf.

Ontario Federation of Friendship Centres. "Trauma-Informed Schools: 'Ask Me about Trauma and I Will Show You How We Are Trauma-Informed' – A Study on the Shift toward Trauma Informed Practices in Schools." OFIFC Research Series 4 (Summer 2016).

Palmater, Pamela. *Beyond Blood: Rethinking Indigenous Identity*. Saskatoon: Purich, 2011.

Park, Suey. "Challenging Racism and the Problem with White 'Allies': A Conversation with David Leonard." *{young}ist*, 26 December 2013. https://youngist.tumblr.com/post/71231465066/challenging-racism-and-the-problem-with-white.

Patles, Suzanne. Presentation given at a strategy session co-sponsored by the First Nations Studies and English Departments at Simon Fraser University, Harbour Centre Campus, 24 January 2014. https://www. youtube.com/watch?v=lkN1Yz88VDU.

Paul, Daniel. *We Were Not the Savages: Collision between European and Native American Civilizations*. 3rd ed. Halifax: Fernwood, 2006.

Peelman, Achiel. *L'Inculturation: L'Église et les cultures*. Paris/Montreal: Desclée/Novalis, 1988.

Pesantubbe, Michelene. "Foreword." In *Native American, Christianity, and the Reshaping of the American Religious Landscape*, ed. Joel W. Martin and Mark A. Nicholas, xi–xiii. Chapel Hill: University of North Carolina Press, 2010.

Pickles, Katie, and Myra Rutherford, eds. *Contact Zones: Aboriginal and Settler Women in Canada's Colonial Past*. Vancouver: UBC Press, 2005.

Pinna, S., A. Maelfant, B. Hébert, et M. Coté. *Portrait forestier historique de la gaspésie*. Gaspé: Consortium en foresterie Gaspésie-Les-Iles, 2009.

Poliquin, Carole, and Yvan Dubuc, eds. *L'Empreinte*. Quebec: Isca Productions, 2015.

Portillo, Annette Angela. *Sovereign Stories and Blood Memories: Native American Women's Autobiography*. Albuquerque: University of New Mexico Press, 2017.

Raibmon, Paige. "Unmaking Native Space: A Genealogy of Indian Policy, Settler Practice, and the Microtechniques of Dispossession." In *The Power of Promises: Rethinking Indian Treaties in the Pacific Northwest*, ed. Alexandra Harmon, 56–85. Seattle: University of Washington Press, 2008.

Razack, Sherene H. *Dying from Improvement: Inquests and Inquiries into Indigenous Deaths in Custody*. Toronto: University of Toronto Press, 2015.

– "Gendered Racial Violence and Spatialized Justice: The Murder of Pamela George." In *Race, Space and the Law: Unmapping a White Settler Society*, ed. Sherene H. Razack, 121–56. Toronto: Between the Lines, 2002.

– *Looking White People in the Eye*. Toronto: University of Toronto Press, 1998.

– "When Place Becomes Race." In *Race, Space and the Law: Unmapping a White Settler Society*, ed. Sherene H. Razack, 1–20. Toronto: Between the Lines, 2002.

Reagan, Paulette. *Unsettling the Settler Within: Indian Residential Schools, Truth Telling, and Reconciliation in Canada*. Vancouver: UBC Press, 2010.

Reder, Deanna. "Âcimisowin as Theoretical Practice: Autobiography as Indigenous Intellectual Tradition in Canada." PhD diss., University of British Columbia, 2007.

– "Indigenous Autobiography in Canada: Recovering Intellectual Traditions." In *The Oxford Handbook of Canadian Literature*, ed. Cynthia Sugars, 170–90. Oxford: Oxford University Press, 2016.

– "Native American Autobiography: Connecting Separate Critical Conversations." *Lifewriting Annual* 4 (December 2015): 35–63.

– "Writing Autobiographically: A Neglected Indigenous Intellectual Tradition." In *Across Borders/Across Cultures: Canadian Aboriginal and Native American Cultures*, ed. Emma LaRocque, Paul DePasquale, and Renate Eigenbrod, 153–69. Peterborough, ON: Broadview Press, 2009.

Reid, Jennifer. "The Doctrine of Discovery and Canadian Law." *Canadian Journal of Native Studies* 30, 2 (2010): 335–59.

Roberts, Jo. *Contested Land, Contested Memory: Israel's Jews and Arabs and the Ghosts of Catastrophe*. Toronto: Dundurn, 2013.

Roediger, David R. *Colored White: Transcending the Racial Past*. Berkeley: University of California Press, 2002.

– *Toward the Abolition of Whiteness: Essays on Race, Politics and Working Class History*. New York: Verso, 1994.

Roger, Kerstin. "Making White Women through the Privatization of Health and Well-Being in the Context of Psychotherapy." In *Anti-Racist Feminism*, ed. Agnes Calliste and George Sefa Dei, 123–42. Halifax: Fernwood, 2000.

Ross, Rupert. *Dancing with a Ghost: Exploring Indian Reality.*
    Markham, ON: Octopus Books, 1992.
– *Indigenous Healing: Exploring Traditional Paths.* Toronto: Penguin, 2014.
– *Returning to the Teachings: Exploring Aboriginal Justice.* Toronto: Penguin,
    2006.
Roussel, Jean François, ed. *Decoloniality and Justice: Theological
    Perspectives.* São Leopoldo, BR: Editora OIKOS, 2018.
Royal BC Museum. "The Catholic Ladder." https://royalbcmuseum.bc.ca/
    exhibits/tbird-park/html/present/stann/sb3/claddere.pdf.
Rubenstein, Mary-Jane. "Relationality – The Gift after Ontotheology." *Telos*
    123 (2002): 65–80.
Ryan, Chris, and Michelle Aicken, eds. *Indigenous Tourism: The
    Commodification and Management of Culture.* Boston: Elsevier, 2005.
Sarris, Greg. *Keeping Slug Woman Alive: A Holistic Approach to American
    Indian Texts.* Berkeley: University of California Press, 1993.
Saul, John Ralston. *A Fair Country: Telling Truths about Canada.* Toronto:
    Viking, 2008.
Schirch, Lisa. *Ritual and Symbol in Peacebuilding.* Bloomfield, CT: Kumarian
    Press, 2005.
Silman, Janet. *Enough Is Enough: Aboriginal Women Speak Out – As Told to
    Janet Silman.* Toronto: Women's Press, 1987.
Simpson, Leanne. *As We Have Always Done.* Minneapolis: University of
    Minnesota Press, 2017.
– *Dancing on Our Turtle's Back: Stories of Nishnaabeg Re-Creation,
    Resurgence, and a New Emergence.* Winnipeg: Arbeiter Ring, 2011.
Sister Mary of Jesus. "Ursulines [1948]." *The Quebec History Encyclopedia.*
    http://faculty.marianopolis.edu/c.belanger/quebechistory/encyclopedia/
    Ursulines-QuebecHistory.htm.
Sisters Rising. https://onlineacademiccommunity.uvic.ca/sistersrising/.
Smith, Andrea. *Conquest: Sexual Violence and American Indian Genocide.*
    Cambridge, MA: South End Press, 2005.
Smith, Theresa S. "The Church of the Immaculate Conception: Inculturation
    and Identity among the Abishnaabeg of Manitoulin Island." Special Issue:
    "To Hear the Eagles Cry: Contemporary Themes in Native American
    Spirituality." *American Indian Quarterly* 20, 3–4 (1996): 515–26.
Snively, Gloria, and Wanosts'a7 Lorna Williams, eds. *Knowing Home:
    Braiding Indigenous Science with Western Science,* Book 1. Victoria:
    University of Victoria Press, 2016.

"Somatic Psychotherapy." *GoodTherapy.org*. https://www.goodtherapy.org/learn-about-therapy/types/somatic-psychotherapy.

Spence, Bernadette. "Indigenization of Child Welfare as an Institution within an Urban Context: The VACFSS Experience." Paper presented at the First Roundtable on Indigenization, Vancouver, University of British Columbia, 2013.

St Denis, Verna. "Roundtable. Author Meets Critics: On Jaskiran Dhillon's *Prairie Rising* –Indigenous Youth, Decolonization, and the Politics of Intervention." Native American and Indigenous Studies Association Conference, Vancouver, University of British Columbia, 22 June 2017.

Systems-Centered Training. https://www.systemscentered.com/.

Tallbear, Kim. *Native American DNA: Tribal Belonging and the False Promise of Genetic Science*. Minneapolis: University of Minnesota Press, 2013.

Tanner, Kathryn. *Economy of Grace*. Minneapolis: Fortress Press, 2005.

Taylor, Rachel. "Gathering Knowledges to Inform Best Practices in Indigenous Publishing." MA thesis, Simon Fraser University, 2019.

Tekakwitha Conference. "Conference History." http://tekconf.org/conference-history.

Thiel, Mark G. "Catholic Ladders and Native American Evangelization." *US Catholic Historian* 27, 1 (2009): 49–70.

Tłıchǫ Ndek'àowo Government. "Fine and Decorative Arts." https://tlicho.ca/businesses/fine-and-decorative-arts.

Thobani, Sunera. "White Innocence, Western Supremacy: The Role of Western Feminism in the 'War on Terror.'" In *States of Race: Critical Race Feminism for the 21st Century*, ed. Sherene Razack, Malinda Smith, and Sunera Thobani, 127–46. Toronto: Between the Lines, 2010.

Tinker, George. *American Indian Liberation: A Theology of Sovereignty*. Maryknoll, NY: Orbis, 2008.

– *Missionary Conquest: The Gospel and Native American Genocide*. Minneapolis: Fortress Press, 1993.

– *Spirit and Resistance: Political Theology and American Indian Liberation*. Minneapolis: Fortress Press, 2004.

Todd, Zoe. "Indigenizing Canadian Academia and the Insidious Problem of White Possessiveness." *Urbane Adventurer: Amiskwacî*. https://zoestodd.com/2018/05/04/indigenizing-academia-and-the-insidious-problem-of-white-possessiveness/.

"Tribal Canoe Journeys." Wikipedia. https://en.wikipedia.org/wiki/Tribal_Canoe_Journeys.

Trumpener, Betsy. "The Miracles of Rose Prince." CBC Radio, *The Current*. 16 October 2008.

Truth and Reconciliation Commission of Canada. *Canada's Residential Schools: Missing Children and Unmarked Burials – The Final Report of the Truth and Reconciliation Commission of Canada.* Vol. 4. Montreal and Kingston: McGill-Queen's University Press, 2015.

– *Canada's Residential Schools: Reconciliation – The Final Report of the Truth and Reconciliation Commission of Canada.* Vol. 6. Montreal and Kingston: McGill-Queen's University Press, 2015.

– *Honouring the Truth, Reconciling for the Future: Summary of the Final Report of the Truth and Reconciliation Commission of Canada.* Winnipeg: Truth and Reconciliation Commission of Canada, 2015.

– *Truth and Reconciliation Commission of Canada: Calls to Action.* Winnipeg: Truth and Reconciliation Commission of Canada, 2015.

Tuck, Eve, and K. Wayne Yang. "Decolonization Is Not a Metaphor." *Decolonization: Indigeneity, Education, and Society* 1, 1 (2012): 1–40.

Turner, Dale. *This Is Not a Peace Pipe: Towards a Traditional Indigenous Philosophy.* Toronto: University of Toronto Press, 2006.

Twiss, Richard. Keynote Address. Churches Council for Theological Education Conference: Aboriginal Spiritualities and Theological Education. Winnipeg, Manitoba, 16–18 May 2011.

Ubelacker, Sheryl. "Health Solutions for Attawapiskat Must Be Long-Term: Experts." *Globe And Mail*, 17 April 2016. http://www.theglobeandmail. com/news/national/health-solutions-for-attawapiskat-must-be-long-term-experts/article29657501/?page=all.

Unama'ki Institute of Natural Resources. "Netukulimk." http://www.uinr.ca/ netukulimk/netukulimk/.

Unitarian Universalists White Supremacy Teach-In. "Essential Elements: What to Address in Your White Supremacy Teach-in." https://www. uuteachin.org/teachins.

United Church of Canada. "Anti-Black Racism and Afrophobia in the Canadian Context." 1 October 2018. https://www.united-church.ca/sites/ default/files/resources/afrophobia.pdf.

– "Anti-Racism." https://www.united-church.ca/social-action/justice-initiatives/anti-racism.

– *Ending Racial Harassment.* Ed. Susannah Schmidt. www.united-church.ca/ sites/default/files/resources/handbook_racial-harassment.pdf.

– "A Historic Land Transfer." https://www.united-church.ca/stories/historic-land-transfer.

University of Alberta. "Indigenous Canada." *Coursera.org.* https://www.
coursera.org/learn/indigenous-canada/lecture/HEe1s/numbered-
treaties-part-1.

University of British Columbia. "Musqueam and UBC." http://aboriginal.ubc.
ca/community-youth/musqueam-and-ubc/.

– "Summer Institute 2015, Indigenous Existential Resistance: The Sundance
Practice." http://pdce.educ.ubc.ca/summer-institute-indigenous-
existential-resistance-2/.

University of British Columbia, Department of Education Studies. "Summer
Institute 2018, Indigenous Existential Resistance: The Sundance
Practice." http://indigenous.educ.ubc.ca/indigenous-existential-
resistance-the-sundance-practice/.

University of Victoria. Indigenous Academic and Community Engagement.
"LE,NONET: Indigenous Support Student Success at UVic." https://
www.uvic.ca/services/indigenous/students/lenonet/.

University of Victoria Ethnographic Mapping Lab. "Indigenous Mapping
Bibliography." https://www.uvic.ca/socialsciences/ethnographicmapping/
resources/mapping-bibliography/index.php.

Ursulines. "Discover the Great Periods of the History of the Ursulines."
http://www.ursulinesuc.com/en/remembering/the-origins-of-the-
ursulines/.

Vancouver Aboriginal Child and Family Services Society. www.vacfss.com/.

Vancouver Island Treaties. Presentations. https://hcmc.uvic.ca/songhees
conference/index.php.

Veracini, Lorenzo. *Settler Colonialism: A Theoretical Overview.* New York:
Palgrave Macmillan, 2010.

Vowel, Chelsea. *âpihtawikosisân*: Law, Language, Culture. www.
apihtawikosisan.com.

– *Indigenous Writes: A Guide to First Nations, Métis and Inuit Issues in
Canada.* Winnipeg: Highwater Press, 2016.

Waaseyaa'sin/Sy, Christine. "From Territorial Acknowledgements to
Here-ing: (Indigenous) Methodology for Being in Someone Else's
Home." First People's House, University of Victoria, 20 March 2018.

Wainwright, Elaine. "Healing Ointment/Healing Bodies: Gift and
Identification in an Ecofeminist Reading of Mark 14:3–9." In *Exploring
Ecological Hermeneutics*, ed. Norman Habel and Peter Trudinger, 131–9.
Atlanta, GA: Society of Biblical Literature, 2008.

Walia, Harsha. "Moving beyond a Politics of Solidarity towards a Practice of
Decolonization." In *Organize! Building from the Local for Global Justice,*

ed. Aziz Choudry, Jill Hanley, and Eric Shragge, 240–53. Oakland, CA: PM Press. (Toronto: Between the Lines, 2012.)

Walkem, Ardith. Presentation at "Protecting Our Sacred Waters: Intercultural and Interfaith Teachings about Water and Water Privatization." Interfaith Summer Institute, Vancouver, Simon Fraser University, 5 July 2007.

– "Water Philosophy: Indigenous Laws Treat Water with Awe and Reverence Rather Than as a Resource to Be Managed." *Alternatives: Environmental Ideas and Action.* 27 May 2009.

Walking with Our Sisters. "About." http://walkingwithoursisters.ca/about/.

Warrior, Robert Allen. "A Native American Perspective: Canaanites, Cowboys, and Indians – Deliverance, Conquest and Liberation Theology Today." *Christianity and Crisis* 49, 12 (1989): 261–5.

Watershed Discipleship. https://watersheddiscipleship.org/.

Watkins, Mel. *Dene Nation: The Colony Within.* Toronto: University of Toronto Press, 1977.

Welsh, Christine. *Finding Dawn.* Montreal: National Film Board of Canada, 2006. https://www.nfb.ca/film/finding_dawn/.

Wesley, Saylesh. "Twin-Spirited Woman: Sts'iyóye smestiyexw slhá:li." *Transgender Studies Quarterly* 1, 3 (2014): 338–51.

West Coast Environmental Law. "Between Law and Action: Assessing the State of Knowledge on Indigenous Law, UNDRIP and Free, Prior and Informed Consent with Reference to Fresh Water Resources." https://www.wcel.ngo/sites/default/files/publications/betweenlawandaction-undrip-fpic-freshwater-report-wcel-ubc.pdf.

– "RELAW Project: Summer in Review." 18 September 2016. http://wcel.org/resources/environmental-law-alert/relaw-project-summer-review.

– "RELAW: Revitalizing Indigenous Law for Land; Air and Water." http://wcel.org/our-work/relaw-revitalizing-indigenous-law-land-air-and-water.

White, Louellyn. *Free to Be Mohawk: Indigenous Education at the Akwesasne Freedom School.* Norman: University of Oklahoma Press, 2015.

Wildcat, Daniel. "Respecting What We Do Not Know." In *Quest for Respect: The Church and Indigenous Spirituality*, ed. Jeff Friesen and Steve Heinrichs, 21–4. Winnipeg: Mennonite Church of Canada, 2017.

Williams, Alex. *The Pass System.* Toronto: Tamarack Productions, 2015. http://thepasssystem.ca/.

Williams, Alice Olsen. http://www.pimaatisiwin-quilts.com/.

Williamson, Tara. "Of Dogma and Ceremony." *Decolonization: Indigeneity, Education and Society.* 16 August 2013. https://decolonization.wordpress. com/2013/08/16/of-dogma-and-ceremony/.

Wilson, Shawn. *Research Is Ceremony: Indigenous Research Methods.* Halifax: Fernwood, 2008.

Woelk, Cheryl, and Steve Heinrichs, eds. *Yours, Mine, Ours: Unravelling the Doctrine of Discovery. Intotemak Trilogy.* Winnipeg: Mennonite Church of Canada, 2016.

Wolfe, Patrick. "Settler Colonialism and the Elimination of the Native." *Journal of Genocide Research* 8, 4 (2006): 387–409.

Women's Earth Alliance and Native Youth Sexual Health Network. "Violence against the Land, Violence against Our Bodies: Building an Indigenous Response to Environmental Violence." http://landbodydefense.org/ uploads/files/VLVBReportToolkit2016.pdf.

Wong, Rita. "A Healing Walk around the Tar Sands Dead Zone." *rabble.ca.* 10 August 2010. http://rabble.ca/news/2010/08/healing-walk-around-tar-sands-dead-zone.

– *Undercurrent.* Gibsons, BC: Nightwood Books, 2015.

Wong, Yuk-Lin Renita. "'Please Call Me by My True Names': A Decolonizing Pedagogy of Mindfulness and Interbeing in Critical Social Work Education." In *Sharing Breath: Embodied Learning and Decolonization,* ed. Sheila Batacharya and Yuk-Lin Renita Wong, 253–78. Edmonton: Athabasca University Press, 2018.

"World's First Indigenous Law Degree to Be Offered at UVic." *UVic News.* 21 February 2018. https://www.uvic.ca/news/topics/2018+jid-indigenous-law+media-release.

Yee, Gail. "Reflections on Creation and the Prophet Hosea." In *Liberating Biblical Study,* The Center and Library for the Bible and Social Justice Series, vol. 1, ed. Laurel Dykstra and Ched Myers, 65–79. Eugene, OR: Cascades Books, 2011.

Younging, Gregory. *Elements of Indigenous Style: A Guide for Writing by and about Indigenous Peoples.* Edmonton: Brush Education, 2018.

Younging, Gregory, Jonathan Dewar, and Mike DeGagné, eds. *Response, Responsibility, and Renewal: Canada's Truth and Reconciliation Journey.* Ottawa: Aboriginal Healing Foundation, 2010.

Index

*Page numbers in italics refer
to figures.*

Aboriginal, 5, 36, 41, 44, 239; and
    Aboriginal Healing Foundation,
    80, 111; ancestors in Quebec,
    114; as Métis people, 116; in
    section 35, 271n1; as term to
    erase difference, 243
Aboriginal fishing rights, 183; denial
    and criminalization of, 143, 147;
    Mi'gmaq fight for, 143–4
Aboriginal law: difference from
    Indigenous law, 183
Aboriginal Rights and Title,
    31, 41; 1988 Agreement-in-
    Principle for Dene/Metis, 32, 36;
    extinguishment of, 220; Mi'gmaq
    statement of, 120
Aboriginal Rights Coalition, 38, 41,
    42
"Aboriginal spirituality," 33, 243;
    critique of term, 243, 247; as
    "Indian spirituality," 38
affect studies, 264
*Alliances: Re/Envisioning
    Indigenous-Non-Indigenous
    Relationships* (Davis), 268
allyship, 269
Altamirano-Jiménez, Isabel, 227

ancestors, 6, 10, 101, 105, 111,
    228; in blood memory, 117; in
    ceremony, 201–2, 216; connected
    through water with, 180; respect
    for, 203; in Spirit Rocks, 217; in
    time, 223
Anderson, Kim, 79, 181
Anglican Church: and anti-racism,
    95; competing with Oblates,
    19, 37. *See also* McMenamie,
    Logan
anti-racism education, 50, 62,
    63, 101; church programs, 95;
    limitations of, 96; resistance to, 96
Apffel-Marglin, Frédérique: on body
    as fluid, 180; on ritual, 214
Apoyshan, Susan, 77, 87, 178; and
    embodiment practice, 88
appropriation: of ceremony, 195–6;
    cultural, 162
Archibald, Jo-Ann (Q'um Q'um
    Xiiem), 192, 264
autonomy: and autonomous selves,
    78; of ceremonial leaders, 201;
    limits to human, 180; in Two
    Row Wampum, 259; Zapatista
    vision of, 49

balance, 4, 146; ceremony to ensure,
    205, 215; in gender, 43, 174, 192;

gifting and, 212; living in, 205; principles of, 54, 258; in relations based on, 79, 145; with water bodies, 180

Baldwin, James, 63

Barker, Adam, 23, 269

Barnaby, Joanne, 37–8

Barrios, Carmen Miranda, 61

baskets, 127, 133; and women selling, 161; Mi'gmaq baskets, 162

Battiste, Marie, 264

BC Treaty Process, 219; Art Manual on, 220

beading, 159–60, 213; and Indigenous women, 3, 11; as ceremony, 160, 166; beadwork on Dene moccasins, 154; ontology of, 161; in WWOS, 166

Bear, Cheryl, 248

Beaucage, Marjorie, 23, 41, 200; on ceremony, 202, 205; on Daniels case, 116–17

Belcourt, Christi: on beading, 160; and WWOS, 165, 166

Beyond Blood: Rethinking Aboriginal Identity and Belonging (Palmater), 115

Black Lives Matter, 90

Blaney, Fay, 61–2

Blondin, George, 51

blood, 102, 119; bloodline, 145; and identity, 112, 113; as memory, 117; and Métis identity claims, 114–15; one drop rule, 111; politics of, 112; as quantum, 101, 115–16; test, 10, 113, 118. See also Palmater, Pam

Blood (Hill), 116

body, 5, 8, 11; in dualism and binaries, 87, 258; and ceremony, 189–91, 204, 214; connection with land, 265; split in Christianity, 10, 243; in dominance and submission, 87–8, 89–90; as marker of colonialism, 8, 82; in Musqueam language, 255; in skills, 88; and "spirituality," 195, 243; in somatic greed, 178; in sovereignty, 171, 253–4; and trauma symptoms, 75–6, 78; water in, 178–9; as Western construct, 180; whiteness behaviour in, 61, 98; working through, 70

Body-Mind Psychotherapy, 77, 86, 87; embodiment practice in, 88; grasping in, 178

Borrows, John: Canada's Indigenous Constitution, 268, 289n23

Borrows, Lindsay, 182; on "heart" in Anishinaabemowin, 256; on bodies and language, 258

Boucher-Curotte, Orenda (Kahnawa'kehró:non), 199, 207

Braiding Sweetgrass (Kimmerer), 180

Brantbjerg, Merete: and relational trauma therapy, 77; and systems method, 88, 91

Budden, Chris: Following Jesus in Invaded Space, 265

Buddhism, 10, 87, 198, 257

bundle, 173–4; in Walking with Our Sisters, 166; gift bundles, 210

Caibaiosai, Violet, 176

Canada's Indigenous Constitution (Borrows), 289n23

Canadian Ecumenical Anti-Racism Network, 94; on Doctrine of Discovery, 94; workbook on white identity, 95

Carrière, Jeannine, 84

Cartier, Jacques, 124, 126

Cascapedia, 103, 124; Grand Cascapedia, 117, 137, 138; Cascapedia St Jules, 138, 145

Cascapedia River, 143, 144, 145; fishing clubs on, 144; as life line, 147; Mi'gmaq co-management, 14; Mi'gmaq place names on, 147, *148*; origin of name, 144

Cascapedia River Museum, 145–7; and "colonial nostalgia," 145–6

Catholic Church, 3, 19, 22, 115, 214; colonial structures in, 50, 122; in Gaspé region, 139; and inculturation, 45, 51; and Indigenous women saints, 45, 239; patriarchal structures in, 238; and residential schools, 235; as separate legal entities, 241; sidestepping genocide, 242; women and LGBTQ in, 18, 57

Catholic Ladder: description of, 21–2; history of, 53; values in, 54

cedar, 66, 70, 180, 190, 212; as cultural keystone species, 191; cleansing with, 164, 200; as a relative, 191

ceremony: appropriation of, 195–7; attendance at, 197; as collective experience, 194; discipline in, 202–3; as embodied experience, 189, 191, 194, 204–5; as fluid and responsive, 201; as form

of resistance, 216; function of, 201, 204–5; fundamentalism in, 203; Indian Act banning of, 195; intertribal, 197; misuse of, 195–6, 197; responsibility to relationships in, 189, 195

certainty: and BC Treaty Process, 219–20; and private property, 224, 266

Charlie, Wayne, 193

Christian, Dorothy, 176, 182; and Protect Our Sacred Waters, 179

Christianity: and colonial past and present, 3–4, 9, 12; as decolonized, 11; dominant society, 198; anthropomorphism of, 184; and viewing as pagan, 22, 71; civilizing mission of, 65, 93; competing for Native souls, 36; disembodied, 213; dualism and binaries in, 12, 253; European, 9–10, 93, 258; gift traditions in, 212; heart teachings in, 256–7; and imperial domination, 53; in mainstream, 93; monastic tradition in, 205; mystical traditions of, 257; post-colonial, 251; post-colonial feminist, 184; responsibility for, 38; and suffering, 18; as universalizing, 248. *See also* Indigenous Christianity

Claxton, Nick, 226

co-existence, 12, 268; rather than reconciliation, 259

Cole, Teju, 93

Coles, Gloria, 211

colonial: anti-colonial worldview, 82; and Christianity, 3–4, 10, 40,

53, 111; in child apprehension
policies, 157; and dispossession,
33, 266; dynamic, 155; in gender
violence, 252–3; and genealogy,
140; as history, 114, 119, 226; in
legal system, 183, 210; and mind,
256; in nostalgia, 145; as patterns,
67, 181, 235; and power relations,
35; as project, 83, 233, 238;
reading of Bible, 184; structures,
81, 96, 240, 263; policies, 80, 114,
204, 236, 238; practices, 30, 196;
and violence, 78–9, 226
colonialism, 9, 37; in Asian
Canadian communities, 62; body
as site and marker of, 8; history
of, 95; inferiority of Indigenous
knowledge, 73–4; and
Indigenous women, 62, 79; and
individualism, 118; "figurative
genealogy of," 139; in land and
waters as resources, 10, 141; and
mission, 50; ongoing, 201; and
recovery from, 249; in relational
sphere of, 98; and Great White
Helper, 81
comprehensive land claims, 31, 33
Compton, Wayde, 113; and
"retrospeculate," 123
Contré-Migwans, Dolores, 135
conversion, 22, 51; conversion
religions, 54, 197
Coulombe, Jeannine, 24–5
Coulthard, Glen, 31–2
Couture, Denise, 265
covenant, 258; treaties as
sacred, 222
Covenant Chain, 221, 259. See also
Two Row Wampum

cowboys: and Indians, 6, 102; and
racism, 12; theology of, 9
Cree: Feast of the Dead, 210; in
hymnals, 25; sacred site, 46; in
water law, 182; way in a circle,
246
Culhane, Dara, 77

Dakelh (Carrier): language of Yinka
Dene, 234; and Rose Prince,
231–2, 236, 237, 239, 240
Daniels, Lillian, 160
Davis, Lynne: *Alliances: Re/
Envisioning Indigenous-Non-
Indigenous Relationships*, 268
De (centre or heartbeat):
Anishinaabemowin morpheme,
256
decolonization: of the body, 8, 11,
254, 264, 267; as comprehensive
strategy, 75; as holistic process,
265; as making relations in, 11;
meaning of, 3; mechanisms of
resistance to, 264; as more than
critique, 10; not a metaphor,
97, 263 (*see also* Tuck, Eve;
Yang, Wayne); in prevention
of real, 96; private property as
deterrent to, 260; as process, 5,
12, 263; as queer practice, 254; in
reconciliation steps, 98; within
a relational framework, 269;
and resurgence, 98; returning
land, 263; as spiritual journey,
13; in wwos, 172; unmap as
metaphor for, 123; unsettling
spirit world, 11
Deer, Brian, 110; and library
classification system, 110

Deloria, Vine, Jr, 261, 265

Dene, 20, 23, 25, 32, 35; Dene Declaration, 31; drumming, 33, 190, 243–4, 246; moccasins, 154, 162; moosehide and cultural knowledge, 159; as Nation, 30, 36; Rights and Title of, 19, 30, 32; traditional knowledge of, 28; spiritual practices of, 37, 153

Dene Cultural Institute (DCI), 31, 36, 37

Dene Declaration, 31

Dene National Assembly: 1990 assembly, 36, 38

Denendeh Seminar, 19, 28, 29, 30–1, 37; asymmetrical power relations in, 155; content of, 33, 36, 43; at Dettah, 33, 36; as exposure tour, 32; fast on the land, 33, 153; at Fort Good Hope, 29, 30, 153, 154–5; goals of, 37–8; at Hay River, 36–7; impact of, 36–7; limitations of, 35, 39; participants in, 32; at Snowdrift, 31, 33–4, 35. See also Fumoleau, René

Desjarlais, Robert, 78

Dewar, Jonathan, 111

Dewe'igan (drum): in Anishinaabemowin, 256

Dick, Skip, 66

Diocese of Chiapas, 46–9; and Zapatistas, 49

DNA: as racial science, 117

Doctrine of Discovery, 127, 220; TRC Call to Action on, 94; Canadian Ecumenical Anti-Racism Network documents on, 279n21; Mennonite resource on, 94

Donaldson, Laura, 161

Douglas Treaties. See Vancouver Island Treaties

Downtown Eastside Women's Centre (DEWC), 63, 71, 74–5, 167; and Red Women Rising Report, 276n5

Doxtater, T'hohahoken Michael, 206

drum, 243, 245; Dene drumming, 243–4, 246; Protocols around, 244; and public and private songs, 245; women's drum circle, 245, 246

Dube, Musa: and gender lens, 52–3; and sacredness of land and waters, 184

Dubois, W.E.B., 63–4

Dumais, Monique, 122, 281n4

Dumont, Marjorie, 211

Dyck, Lillian, 158

Elders, 46, 58, 118, 227, 233; gifts for, 276n11; and intellectual property, ix; importance for balance, 205; as Indigenous clergy, 247; and Kainai Sundance, 200; making space for, 65–6; Michael McNally on, 280n5; Mi'gmaq interviews with, 123; and Rose Prince, 239; speaking own language, 206, 234; University of Victoria Advisory Group, 66, 193

Elliot, Charles (Temosen), 185, 226

embodied: awareness of water, 176–7, 181; ceremony as, 189–91; in connection to all, 257; critical to decolonization,

269; and explorations, 253; in knowledge, 205; and land-based learning, 265; in listening, 87; offering tobacco as, 174; in relationship as core, 11; relationship with salmon, 215; and spirit world, 11; and reciprocity, 208

embodiment, 8, 254; centred in decolonization, 244; defined as, 87; lack of in Christianity, 214, as practice, 88

Empire of Trauma, The (Fassin and Rechtman), 80

Epsegeneq (the place where one warms up): Mi'gmaw name for Port Daniel, 124, 126

Fair Country: Telling Truths about Canada, A (Saul), 114

Fassin, Didier: *The Empire of Trauma*, 80

Finding Dawn (film by Welsh), 169, 172, 251

First Nations House of Learning, 70, 111, 188, 192, 209

Fiske, Jo-Anne, 239, 240

Following Jesus in Invaded Space (Budden), 265

forestry, 135; Gaspé history of, 132, 138; jobs in, 144; Nadeau family and, 138; as a resource, 140

Fort Providence, 19, 23, 26, 27–8; and residential school, 26

Fort Simpson, 17–18, 23, 25; as Liidli Koe, 19, 20; visit of Pope John Paul II to, 19, 21, 273n4

Freeman, Victoria, 266

Friedland, Hadley, 268

Friesen, Kate, 54

frontier: mentality, 12; mindset, 260; as theology, 250

Fumoleau, René, 19, 29; archives of, 274n10; *As Long as This Land Shall Last*, 30, 39; biography of, 29–30, 39; and critique of comprehensive land claims, 31; as role model, 37, 39; theology of, 30. *See also* Denendeh Seminar

Gagnon family: Anna Mae, 103; arrival in Gaspé, 103; Augustin, 139; Diana, 103; Francois Xavier, 139; Eduard, 139

Geddes, Harriet, 27–8

Gehl, Lynn: on embodied knowledge, 205

gender, 9, 24, 50; and balance, 43, 174; in Bill C-3, 158; as centre of analysis, 254; in challenging colonial violence, 253; in conquest, 52; discrimination in Indian Act, 158; in justice inside Indigenous law, 268; and oppression, 6, 243; in traditional teachings, 252–3

genocide, 4, 204; Catholic Church sidestepping, 242; as colonial policy, 236–7; cultural, 238

George, Deb, 66

George, Ron, 245

Gesgapegiag, 3, 68, 117, 134; and fishing rights, 14; and Mi'gmaq Coop, 162; as reserve, 132, 138; "where the river widens," 144

Gespeg, 107, 134–5, 144, 218; Centre Socio-Culturel de Gespeg, 142; Gespeg Nation, 142

Gespe'gewa'gi, 68, 117, *121*, 127,
141; history of, 221; and women
selling baskets, 16
gift, 11, 216, 247, 162–3; bundles,
210; in ceremony, 189; drum
as, 244; and reciprocity, 211;
responsibility to plants, 209; and
reparations, 211–12; in Sami
society, 212 (*see also* Kuokkanen,
Rauna); sorrow as, 70; tradition
in Christianity, 212–13; of
water, 178
giveaway, 213; ceremony, 209, 210,
211; and potlatches, 210, 211;
and relationships, 210
Goeman, Mishuana, 226
going home, 9, 106; as a settler, 149
Grant, Larry, 65; on Musqueam
language, 255; on witnessing,
193
Greer, Allan, 45–6
Grey Nuns, 24, 26; Sisters of
Charity, 25; partners with
Oblates, 25
Gross, Larry: on post-apocalypse
stress syndrome, 82

Hanuse, Bonnie, 113
Harjo, Joy, 226, 227
Harris, Cole, 131, 132
Harry, Eugene, 204
Haudenosaunee, 6, 165, 259; and
Thanksgiving address, 207
healing, 40; as capitalist industry,
78, 80, 81; church funding of,
94, 95; and culturally specific
approaches, 83–5; deficit model
of, 59–60, 72; as embedded
in systems, 75; in focus on

individual, 77, 79, 81, 196; and
"healing cultures," 85
heart, 210, 248, 252; in
Anishinaabewomin, 256;
in Buddhism, 257; in Coast
Salish languages, 255–6; and
collective, 259; in Judaism and
Christianity, 256–7; in Mi'gmaq,
256; open, 252, 257; renewed
and treaty, 258; and strawberries,
274n15; Western understanding
of, 255
Henry, Jennifer, 258, 265
Highway of Tears, 231
Hill, Gord, 269
Hill, Lawrence, 116
Hiller, Chris, 265
Histoires et souvenirs, 124–5
Hogan, Linda, 204
Hunt, Sarah: protecting women's
bodies, 171; on embodiment and
gender, 254

Idle No More, 220
inculturation, 44, 51; definition of, 45
Indian, 4, 6, 64, 103, 126, 272–3n1;
in fight for souls, 37; figure in
Port Daniel, *125*, 126; "kill the
Indian in the child," 236, 290n6;
playing Indian, 102; racism
towards in Quebec, 103; and
"real" Indians, 113; "vanishing
Indian," 126
Indian Act, 44; banning of
ceremonies in, 50, 173, 195, 210;
denial of Indigenous women's
rights, 266; devaluing of women
through, 118, 158, 172; and
exclusion of Métis, 116; loss of

fishing rights in, 147; section
12–1 (b) of, 157–8; status,
non-status categories in, 112,
132; and structure of Canadian
state, 80–1. *See also* status
Indigenism: definition of, 267–8
Indigenous approaches to wellness,
9; and cultural specificity, 84;
and decolonizing trauma work,
84; emphasis on strengths,
75, 84; and healing trauma,
85; holistic, 85, 87, 264; and
Indigenous governance, 85;
and resources of Indigenous
medicine, 74; rooted in cultural
knowledge, 74
Indigenous Christianity, 246; as
Anishinabe Christianity, 44–5;
evangelical and mainstream,
248–9; at Lac Saint Anne, 46;
Tekakwitha Conference, 45–6.
See also Diocese of Chiapas;
Prince, Rose; Twiss, Richard
Indigenous church, 46;
"autochthonous church," 47;
Catholic resistance to, 49
Indigenous constitutions, 223, 268;
and "rooted constitutionalism,"
261–2. *See also* Mills, Aaron
Indigenous feminists: and women,
children, and 2SQ as centre, 254
Indigenous governance: and
"healing cultures," 85; and
Indigenous law, 95; in Mi'gmaq
principles of, 145; in "politics of
refusal," 267; and WWOS, 157
Indigenous identity: and Indian
Act, 112–13; and Mi'kmaq
citizenship, 115–16

Indigenous law, 12, 185, 186, 268;
difference from Aboriginal law,
183; as Indigenous legal orders,
11, 183, 267, 268; and language,
256; and Original Instructions,
183; in reparations, 211–12; as
supporting difference, 225; and
treaties, 221, 224; University of
Victoria Indigenous law program,
95. *See also* Indigenous water laws
Indigenous Law Research Unit, 183,
268
Indigenous Rights, 36, 37, 42, 47,
185; and Aboriginal law, 183; and
counter-mapping, 123
Indigenous-settler relations, 10, 11;
Mennonite program, 94
Indigenous solidarity, 32, 38, 184,
265; and decolonizing, 269;
impact on settlers, 266. *See also*
allyship
Indigenous spirituality, 38; Call to
Action 60, 93–4; who can teach
debate, 198–9
Indigenous theology: "teologia
india," 48; replacing frontier
theology, 250; of sovereignty, 52
Indigenous traditions, 4;
Christianity and, 248; differences
from and between, 201, 204;
embedded in language and land,
11; as embodied, 11, 267, 199;
healing based on, 40, 74; and
Indigenous law, 171, 183; and
interconnectedness, 54, 257; and
reciprocal relationship, 214; as
religions, 10, 197; respect for,
199; revitalization of, 82; and
rocks in, 41; South African, 184

Indigenous trauma theory: on attachment, 83, 84; decolonizing trauma work, 84; post-apocalypse stress syndrome, 82

Indigenous water laws: Cree law, 182; Sylix and Secwepemc water rights, 182–3; Anishinaabe law, 183; West Coast Environmental Law and UNDRIP, 183–4. *See also* RELAW

Indigenous ways of knowing, 249, 267; in WWOS, 168

Indigenous women, 3, 11; and child apprehension, 157; differences from women of colour, 62; historical prominent roles of, 171; identity for, 112; impact of Indian Act on, 158, 266; marketing handicrafts, 161; needs of urban, 75; and (re)mapping, 226; sacredness of, 172; and Sisters Rising, 253–4; stereotypes of, 155; and struggle for status, 17, 112; WWOS and reframing of, 172. *See also* murdered and missing Indigenous women; violence against Indigenous women

individualism, 118; capitalism based on, 83; in "survival of the fittest," 209; in white culture, 90, 214

intellectual property, ix, 196

interconnectedness: as given in ceremony, 212; and interrelatedness, 54, 149, 258; of people and non-humans, 258; and treaties as extending, 222

Interfaith Institute for Justice, Peace and Social Movements, 176, 211; and respecting difference, 203

Irlbacher-Fox, Stephanie: *Finding Dahshaa*, 159

Ishkode (fire): in Anishinaabemowin, 256

James, N'kixw'stn, 188

Jamieson, Kathleen: *Indian Women and the Law in Canada: Citizens Minus*, 157

Jeannotte, Manon, 107, 142; family history in Port Daniel, 135

Jeannotte, Oscar, 142–3, 144

Jerome, Pnnal, 68, 117, 134, 137, 144; on ceremony, 201; on Mi'gmaq language, 256

Jesuits, 41, 44, 49, 57; and Anishinabe Spiritual Centre, 43, 50–1; and Native Apostolate, 42, 44

Jobin, Shalene, 166, 168

Johnson, Darlene, 211

Joseph, Judy, 156–7

Joseph, Norma, 109

Kahnawà:ke, 60, 110, 207, 208, 113; and blood quantum, 112

Kanien'keha:ka (Mohawk peoples), 11, 135, 207, 208

Kappo, Tara, 160, 166, 168

Kateri Tekakwitha, 45–6, 239, 290n5

Kimmerer, Robin Wall: *Braiding Sweetgrass*, 180; invitation to settlers, 260

kinship: accountability to, 269; attachment and, 83–4; beading and, 160; and Mi'gmaq treaties, 221–2; excluded from Western mapping, 227; principles of, 79; in naming Protocol, 228; and responsibilities, 223; in Sisters Rising, 253; values inherent in, 72

Kleinman Arthur, 78

K'ómoks First Nation, 164–8, 219, 251

Kony 2012 (video), 92, 264

Kuokkanen, Rauna: and "logic of the gift," 212; and responsibility to Indigenous worldviews, 266

Lac Saint Anne, 3, 45–6; as Cree sacred site, 46; pilgrimage at, 235

Ladner, Kiera, 85

land: authority at stake over, 98; constructed as property and resources, 10; Defenders of, 220; dispossession and occupation of, 81, 94, 114; gifts to, 212; and how women walk, 227; legal traditions and, 221; reciprocal relationship with, 185, 215; reconciliation not addressing, 97; and relationship with spirit world, 145; as sacred and alive, 21, 35, 184; and sacred sites, 155; as shared with all creatures, 131; and sovereignty, 171; traditional use, 120, 123; walking softly on, 161. *See also* terra nullius

Landsdowne, Carmen, 52, 265

language (Indigenous): Anishinaabemowin, 256; Cree, 25; Dakelh and Yinka Dene, 234; Dogrib (Tłı̨chǫ), 25; Kanien'kéha (Mohawk), 206–7; hən̓q̓əmin̓əm̓ (Musqueam dialect), 255; hul'q'umín'um'(dialect of central and south Vancouver Island), 193, 255; Mi'gmaq, 256; and missionaries learning of, 44; morphemes and language construction, 255–6; needing bodies, 258; and North Slavey, 30; Ojibwemowin, 180; principle of honouring linguistic diversity, 272n7; South Slavey, 22; and suppression, 239; traditions rooted in, 208

L'Autre parole, 242, 290n2

Lee, Erica Violet, 215

Lejac residential school: dates of, 232; frozen deaths at, 232; graveyard, 236–7; missing children, 236; on Nadleh Whut'en land, 232–3

Leonard, David, 269

liberation theology, 18, 23, 30, 40, 60; Native American critique of, 52

Lindberg, Tracy, 252

Linklater, Renee: on decolonizing trauma work, 84

Listuguj, 122, 132, 134, 145, 165; location of Mi'gmawei Mawiomi Secretariat, 218

Little Bear, Leroy, 223

Littlechild, Danika Billie, 182

Lowman, Emma Battell, 5, 269

Lyons, Scott, 267

McCallum, Tom, 258

McCormick, Rod, 83

MacDonald, Katie, 92

MacDonald, Mark, 246

MacIvor, Madeleine, 180, 188, 202; on ceremony, 198, 201

McIvor, Sharon, 158

Mackenzie Valley pipeline, 23, 38, 41, 273n7

Mackey, Eva: on private property, 224, 260, 266

McMenamie, Logan, 227–8

McNally, Michael, 108

Madewe (sound), in Anishinaabewomin, 256

making space: for Elders and Knowledge Keepers, 65–6; for Indigenous voices, 63; in moving beyond, 225–6; open to Indigenous Knowledge, 68; and setting aside agendas, 67

Mandamin, Josephine, 175

Manuel, Art, 97, 220

maps: in cartographic erasure, 131; counter-mapping, 123; European use of, 129; Indigenous mapping, 227; of land as resource, 227; legitimating private property, 129, 131; unmapping as decolonization, 123; as weapons against Mi'gmaq, 129. *See also* (re)mapping

Maracle, Lee, 181

Marlowe, Sam, 182

Martin, Carol Muree, 244; *Red Women Rising*, 276n5

Martin-Baro, Ignacio, 79

Mason, Dean, 252, 255

Matilpi, Maxine, 251

medicines, 51, 71, 190, 246; and Indigenous mapping, 227; and plant, 28, 74, 127, 190, 253; songs as, 191

Meister, Carlos: and reading the Bible, 43

Mennonite Church of Canada: Indigenous-Settler Relations Program, 94; *Unsettling the Word*, 94

Metallic, Fred, 122: on salmon and Mi'gmaq governance, 145; on Mi'gmaq treaty making, 222

Metallic, Gary, 225

Métis, 19, 31–2, 113, 133; claims to be Metis, 111, 114; and Daniels case, 116; distinct culture, 116; and Lac Saint Anne, 46; and legacy of Indian Act, 116; and Métis Nation, 111; and section 35, 271n1; variant spelling, 272n7

Midewiwin, 113, 117–18, 174, 202; Minweyweygaan Lodge, 194; not to talk about, 195; as Three Fires, 50, 173; as Way of the Heart, 173, 256

Mi'gma'gi: as land of Mi'qmaq Nation, 6, 120; Mi'maq occupation of, 126; seventh district of, 120, *121*, 225

Mi'gmaq: 1853 reserves, 132; at Battle of Restigouche, 130; and fishing rights, 143; greeting Jacques Cartier, 124; history of treaties, 131, 134, 221–2; occupation of Gespe'gewa'gi, 127, 221; presence in Port Daniel, 126, 133, 135–6; rules of law, 126, 131; and salmon, 145, 147; settler misinterpretation of, 134; system of governance, 127, 222; variant spelling, 272n1, 280n1. *See also* Cascapedia River

Mi'gmawei Mawiomi Secretariat (MMS), 120, 218, 221, 281n3; *Nta'tugwaqanminen*, 221

Mi'kmaq, 34, 107; on citizenship,
116 (*see also* Palmater, Pam);
and eight-point star, 165; and
resource management, 147;
resistance to fracking, 179,
181, 225; treaty re-enactment
ceremonies, 222; variant spelling,
280n1
Mi'kmaw Concordat, 134, 228n15
Million, Dian: on adapting to
capitalism, 81; critique of
"therapeutic nations," 79; on
Indigenous governance and
healing, quoting Kiera Ladner
in *Therapeutic Nations*, 85; on
TRC, 80
Mills, Aaron: beyond making space,
225–6; on contracts, 221–2; and
"rooted constitutionalism," 260–1
mission: alternative vision of in
watershed discipleship, 54;
as "Church of the North,"
23; churches in Maria and
Restigouche, 139; civilizing
mission and social work, 64–5,
86; etymology of, 40; as imperial
project, 50, 86; as inculturation,
45; Indigenous theology of, 52;
in Native mission, 9; in Native
ministry, 41, 44; Native American
critique of, 52; and obliterating
Indigenous traditions, 204;
postcolonial feminist alternative
to, 52–3; "reverse mission," 52;
versus an interfaith approach, 49;
and "White Man's Burden," 86.
See also Sacred Heart Mission
MMIW. *See* murdered and missing
Indigenous women

moccasins: Anishinaabe teachings
on, 211; in collective process,
209; Dene, 203, 214; and factory
replicas, 212; for feeding families,
212; in Interfaith Institute event,
214; in transmission of cultural
values, 210; in Walking with
Our Sisters, 216, 218, 227; and
women's economic development,
212–13
Moore, Stephen: and a "counter-
colonial ethic," 212
Morgan, Joëlle, 265
Morgenson, Scott, 111
murdered and missing Indigenous
women, 11; in *Finding Dawn*,
169, 251; Kairos hub on, 95; in
Walking with Our Sisters, 164,
167–8
Murray, Mike, 42–3, 46, 48
Musqueam. See xʷməθkʷəy̓əm
Myers, Ched, 184–5

Nadeau family, 104–5, 136, 137; as
anglicized, 137; Bernard, 137;
Charles Harrington, 138; Charlie
Nadeau Jr, 106; Charlie Nadeau,
Indian agent, 139–40; family
home, 140; Margaret, 140; Paul,
138; Pierre (Peter), 106, 137
Nadleh Whut'en First Nation:
ceremonies to purge, 240; and
pipeline construction camp,
290n10; site of Lejac, 232, 233
Napolean, Val: and gender justice,
268; and Indigenous Law
Research Unit, 268
Native Family Violence Counselling
and Community Services

Training Program (Native Family Violence Program), 40, 57, 71, 167, 187

Navarro, Jenell, 160

nə́ćaʔmat tə šxʷqʷeləwən ct (we are of one heart and mind): in həńq̓əmińəm, 255

Nétsamaat ("we are all One"): in Lkwungen, 98

Netukulimk: and Mi'kmaq sustainable resource management, 147

Ng, Roxanna, 265

Ng, Wenh-In, 62–3

Nicolas, Sandra Lovelace, 112, 158

Nixon, Randelle, 92, 264

Nm'tginen: Me'mnaq Ejiglignmuetueg Gis Na Naqtmueg, 120, 121, 122, 127

non-human(s), 10, 35, 74, 168, 214, 225; agency held by, 180; interconnectedness with, 54; kinship relations with, 72, 223; as other-than-human, 141, 186, 208, 215, 283n1; as relatives, 269; in restorative justice for, 185; as water guardians, 185

non-intervention, 113; ethic of, 67; as non-interference, 118, 198; in Two Row Wampum, 259

North American Institute for Indigenous Theological Studies (NAIITS), 248–9

Nta'tugwaqanminen (MMS), 221

Nweta 'git (whole person): in Mi'gmaq, 256

Oblates of Mary Immaculate, 19, 25; and Catholic Ladder, 53; competing with Anglicans, 37; and inculturation, 44; as language speakers, 22, 30; at Lejac, 231–4; and Rose Prince pilgrimage, 233

Ohén:ton Karihwatéhkwen: in honouring Protocols, 208; as Thanksgiving address, 207

Okun, Tema, 90, 94

Oleman, Gerry, 66

Onondaga Nation, 260

otipimsewak (the people who own themselves), 117

Palmater, Pam, 9; Beyond Blood: Rethinking Aboriginal Identity and Belonging, 115; on blood memory, 117; on criteria for citizenship, 116

Parker, Leanna, 227

pass system, 102

Patles, Suzanne, 179

Patton, Niioieren, 113

Peace and Friendship Treaties, 134; Covenant Chain of, 221; to extend family relations, 221–2; against fracking, 225; and kinship system, 222; Mi'kmaq with British, 134, 219; and Mi'kmaw Title, 219; re-enactment of, 222; Treaty of 1725 and Treaty of 1752, 221

Peelman, Achiel, 44

Pesantubbe, Michelene, 51

pheneticization, 113–14

Piché, Camille, 19, 22, 26, 29, 235; and pope's visit, 21; and Jean Vanier, 23; and Lac Saint Anne pilgrimage, 46

politics of trauma, 8, 9, 75; in colonized subject as victim, 80;

and politics of reparation, 80;
and social suffering, 78, 80–1;
the trauma economy, 80. See also
Empire of Trauma; *Therapeutic
Nations*
popular education, 26, 27, 32, 47,
109; and Jesuit workshops, 42–4;
limitations of, 264; Paulo Freire
and, 27, 61; teaching, 50, 109
Port Daniel, 102–7, 124, 138;
allocation of woodlots, 132; East
and West, 136; "Epsegeneg,"
Mi'gmaw name for, 124, 126; and
Jacques Cartier, 124–6; map of
1756, *128*, 130–1; map of 1787,
128; map of 1888, *129*, 131; map
of 1912, 138; Micmacs in, 133–5;
plaster Indian in, *125*, 126; settler
allotments of 1787 in, *128*, 131–2
Prince, Rose: annual pilgrimage,
233, 237; in Carrier cosmos,
239–40; devotion to, 235;
gravesite of, 235; as "prayer
warrior, 239; time at Lejac, 232
private property: and belonging,
140; as deterrent to
decolonization, 260; facilitated
by reserve system, 132; frontier
mindset and, 260; guarantor
of certainty, 224, 266; maps as
legitimizing, 120, 131
Project North, 18, 32, 38, 40, 41–2
Prophet River First Nation: Treaty
Rights and Site C dam, 225
Protocols, 66, 68, 188, 221; and
ceremony, 196; Coast Salish, 204;
grounded in child welfare, 84;
honouring in classroom, 208;
about songs and drums, 244; as

visitors, 226–7; in witnessing
ceremonies, 192; in wwos, 167

Quesnel, Madeleine, 129, 135

racism, 6, 12, 71, 81, 157; anti-
racism workshops, 63; against
Asian Canadian communities,
62; and blood quantum, 101,
115, 118; in child apprehension
policies, 157; colonialism
reinforced by, 62; culture not a
remedy for, 98; epistemological,
73; in Quebec, 103, 115, 133; and
white supremacy, 90
Raibmon, Paige, 139
Razack, Sherene, 276n1; on
unmapping and white settler
innocence, 140
Reagan, Paulette: *Unsettling the
Settler Within*, 266
Rechtman, Richard: *The Empire of
Trauma*, 80
reciprocity, 11; in ceremony, 205;
ethic of, 259; in giveaways
and potlatches, 210; and
interrelatedness, 212; as
living out obligations, 215; in
maintaining relationships, 198,
210; in Mi'gmaq culture, 134,
222; as principle, 160, 208, 209,
214, 259; in witnessing, 193
reconciliation: church funding of,
94; dysfunctional roles in, 91;
with the earth, 358; with home
place, 54; and Indigenism, 267–8;
as maintaining status quo, 259;
when "our law is for all," 224; as
recolonization, 97; as rhetorical

tool, 238; third option to, 260–1,
268 (*see also* Mills, Aaron); TRC
statement of, 5; and white
authority, 98; workshop on, 65–6
reconciliation and churches: Calls
to Action, 48, 49, 61, 94; healing
and cultural recovery funds,
95; and Kairos programs, 95;
Mennonite Indigenous-Settler
Relations Program, 94; Quaker
Institutional Assessment Task
Force, 97; Unitarian Universalists
of America, 96–7. *See also*
Canadian Ecumenical Anti-
Racism Network; Doctrine
of Discovery
relational: approach to settler
power, 267; centre of Indigenous
worldviews, 267; as field,
85, 88; humans as beings,
78; Indigenous identity as a
process, 116; recognition of
responsibilities, 215; as skills, 70;
sphere of colonialism, 98; and
trauma, 76
relational trauma therapy, 77, 88,
91, 278n5; dominance and
submission in, 88; and stuck
roles, 91
relationship: with ancestry, 118;
beading process and, 166; and
ceremony, 205; in Christian
and Hebrew scriptures, 213;
decolonization and, 269; as
embodied, 11, 215; in gift-giving,
211; as God in, 30; to kinship
network, 83; to land and water,
11, 37, 123, 126–7, 247; and
reciprocal, 34, 185, 208, 214;

as mutually respectful, 5; and
responsibilities, 215, 222; seeking
balance in, 54, 258; with spirit
world, 145; in treaty, 134, 228,
259; with water, 35, 174–5, 177,
181–2
relationships, building, 11, 66, 94,
89; and accountability, 269; as
foundational practice, 85; as
priority, 215; in treaty, 224
relative(s): accountability to, 269;
all beings as, 79; animals as,
73, 174; cedar as, 191; drum
as, 244; as equals, 215; how to
be, 11, 260; of murdered and
missing women, 165; protected
by treaties, 223; Queen as, 223;
rocks as, 190; salmon as, 149;
water as, 177, 180–1, 186
RELAW (Revitalizing Indigenous Law
for Land, Air and Water), 183
(re)mapping: by and with
Indigenous women, 226–7;
as reconstructing spatial
geographies, 226
reparations: in Anishinaabe
traditions, 211–12; as "gift," 213;
necessary for decolonization,
242, 264
reserve, 37, 102, 147; as "making
Native space," 132; Maria, 102,
132, 144; Restigouche, 132; and
status, 132; women off, 75, 157
residential schools, 35, 232; and
conversion, 51; and family
violence, 27; Fort Providence,
26; "to kill the Indian in the
child," 236, 290n6; missing
children in, 236; and National

Residential School Student Death
Register, 236; and Settlement
Agreement, 94, 237, 278n20;
and settler history, 237; severed
relationships through, 80, 172;
sexual abuse in, 19, 38, 40, 50, 81;
and TRC, 93, 236. *See also* Lejac
residential school

*Response, Responsibility,
and Renewal: Canada's
Truth and Reconciliation
Journey,* Aboriginal Healing
Foundation, 111

responsibilities: complex system
of, 210; gender balance in, 174;
and genealogy, 228; and "going
home," 149; interrelationships
and, 183; and leadership, 193;
to non-human beings, 223; of
setters, 259; treaty and ongoing,
224–5; to water, 181, 183;
women's, 175

responsibility: for ancestry and
progeny, 118; as a Christian, 38;
of churches, 94; as collective,
216; denial of settler, 114; in
leadership, 192; and Mi'kmaq
sustainable management, 147,
222; to past and future, 223;
to plants, 208–9; in relation to
Indigenous worldviews, 266; to
relationships, 189; and rescuer
role, 92; with right to fish, 145;
as settler, 225; to treaties, 224,
227–8; in witnessing, 193

resurgence, 240, 253, 260; as anti-
capitalist, 267 (*see also* Simpson,
Leanne Betasamosake); as
movement and framework, 97;

and "the politics of refusal," 276;
as radical versus cultural, 267

*Resurgence and Reconciliation:
Indigenous-Setter Relations and
Earth Teachings* (Borrows, Asch,
and Tully), 268

Richardson, Cathy, 84

Roediger, David, 63

Roussel, Jean-François, 265

Royal Commission on Aboriginal
People, 80

Ruiz, Samuel, 46–7; interfaith
approach of, 48; and theology,
47–8; and Zapatistas, 49

Sacred Heart Convent, 7, 60;
Margaret Power, 8, 272n8

Sacred Heart Mission, 17, 19, 29; in
Fort Providence, 26

Saint Anne, 3–4, 18, 46, 234, 260;
treaty re-enactment at feast of, 222

St Denis, Verna, 98

Sajnani, Nisha, 167

salmon, 124, 141, 186; bones of,
48; law against spearing of, 143;
leasing of rivers in Quebec,
143; log booming and, 144,
146; as medicine, 147; Mi'gmaq
salmon enhancement, 144; and
Mi'gmaq governance, 145; as
nation, 149, 215; as relative, 149;
and restoration, 148; reciprocal
relationship with, 215

Saul, John Ralston: *A Fair Country:
Telling Truths about Canada,* 114

self-determination: Dene approaches
to, 159; for Indigenous women
off reserve, 75; intertwined with
all struggles, 269; Project North

advocacy for, 18; in spiritual expression, 201

settler, 3, 21–2, 110; as background, 158; comfort with healing, 106; culture, 267; decolonization applicable to, 129; definition of, 272n6; as deterritorialized, 10; families, 141, 164, 180–1; first settlers, 180–1; going home as, 197; Mi'gmaq interactions with, 134; practices reinforcing erasure, 183; and private property, 161; privilege, 4; responsibility to remedy, 286

settler colonialism, 10; churches' role in, 93; decolonization and, 98; dynamic around reconciliation, 91; processes of, 5; as structure, 266; structures of, 6; and undermining of women, 171; in unsettling, 11; women and 2SQ bodies and violence in, 254

settler colonial studies, 266, 267

settler innocence, 140, 238, 263

settler narratives, 106, 175–7; binary thinking in, 258; Canada as Métis nation, 114; Christian civilizing mission, 65, 93; ignorance as cause of oppression, 195; nomadic and vanishing, 126. See also terra nullius

settlers, white, 5, 19; either/or mentality of, 98; as feeling threatened, 12; and privilege and discomfort, 13; and stuck in roles, 91

Shaker church, 204, 286n18

Simpson, Leanne Betasamosake, 5, 97, 215; centring embodiment and gender, 254; on radical resurgence, 267

Sisters of Saint Anne, 3, 4, 53, 69, 237, 242; response to Call to Action, 95

Sisters Rising: vision of, 253–4; and Intergenerational Forum, 252–3

Sixties Scoop, 117, 172

Sky-Deer, Kahsennenhawe, 207

Smith, Andrea, 195

Smith, Theresa, 51

Snaw-Naw-As First Nation, 251

Snuneymuxw First Nation, 252

social suffering, 80; definition of, 78; individualization of, 81

Solomon, Art, 41

Solomon, Eva, 248

sovereignty, 36, 109, 266; and control of land, 97; Dene fight for, 30–1; fracking as violation of, 225; and Indigenous law, 95; for Indigenous women off reserve; linking body and land, 171, 253–4; and restriction of food, 143; struggles for, 195; theology of, 52

Spence, Bernadette, 113, 162, 205, 215, 241; on Indigenization of child welfare, 84

status, 115; bills restoring women's, 112, 158; campaign to end discrimination by, 157–8; Indian Act and, 112, 118, 132; Jamieson on loss of, 157; and "real" Indians, 132; rights of, 114

sundance, 112, 214, 245; Indian Act Banning of, 195; outsider attendance at, 196, 197; suffering in, 202; UBC course on, 200

Sy, Waaseyaa'sin Christine, 226

taking space: as bodily space, 63; in design and planning, 63; multiple dimensions of, 67–8
Talamentez, Inez, 108, 280n4
Tallbear, Kim, 117
Tekakwitha Conference, 45–6
terra nullius, 127, 129, 131
Therapeutic Nations (Million), 85
Tinker, George, 52, 108–9
tobacco, 174, 187, 189, 190, 216; for Elders, 65–6; to fire, 190, 243, 246; at grave, 236; offering to water, 176–7; and reciprocity, 208, 212
Todd, Zoe, 96, 215
tourism: culture of, 162; human-centred, 186; and Indigenous art, 161
Traditional Knowledge Holders, 66, 199, 206
trauma, 71; in attachment, 83; body symptoms of, 75; in decolonizing work, 84; "historical trauma," 80–1; Indigenous understandings of, 82, 87; intergenerational, 59, 76; life and death, 76; narrow emphasis on, 74, 77; political ramifications of, 79, 80; and psychosocial trauma, 79; and PTSD, 78; in relational field, 76, 88, 98; and system work, 88; trauma-informed practice, 82. *See also* politics of trauma; relational trauma therapy
TRC. *See* Truth and Reconciliation Commission

treaties: in seigneurie documents, 130; BC historic, 219; Idle No More on, 220; Indigenous understandings of, 224; and extinguishment of Title, 220; Numbered historic treaties, 220, 288n7; Treaties 8 and 11, 39, 220. *See also* Peace and Friendship Treaties
treaty: in Anishinaabe law, 222; as alive today, 223; BC Treaty Process, 219, 220; as contract, 221–2; core purpose of Treaty 1, 223; Jay Treaty, 157; Treaty 8 rights and Site C, 225; as a verb and process, 224
Truth and Reconciliation Commission (TRC), 163, 236, 237, 241; churches' responses to, 93; dates of and Calls to Action, 5; framed as victim-centred, 80–1; and missing children, 236
Tsow-Tun le Lum, 168–9, 172, 251, 252
Tuck, Eve, 97, 115, 263
Turner, Dale, 259
Twiss, Richard, 9, 249
Two Row Wampum, 259
Two Spirit (2SQ), 171, 172, 253; and Elder Marjorie Beaucage, 170; honouring bodies of, 254; violence against, 252; and WWOS, 167

United Church, 65, 168, 242–3, 247, 249; and anti-racism materials, 95
United Nations Declaration of the Rights of Indigenous Peoples:

and Indigenous water law, 184;
Kairos advocacy for, 95; in TRC
Calls to Action 48 and 49, 94;
Mennonite publication on, 94
unmapping, 141; as counter-
mapping, 123; in land use
surveys, 123; in personal, 137; in
undermining innocence, 144
unsettled spirit, 254–5
Unsettling the Settler Within
(Regan), 266
*Unsettling the Word: Biblical
Experiments in Decolonization*
(Mennonite Church), 94–5
Ursulines, 122

Vallières, Pierre, 64
Vancouver Island Treaties, 225, 227;
previously Douglas Treaties, 219
Vancouver School of Theology, 18,
50, 58, 60, 62, 241
violence against Indigenous women,
159, 165, 169, 170, 195; and
Highway of Tears, 231; and
Indian Act, 158; prevention of,
254; and resource extraction,
170; and settler colonialism, 171;
and wwos, 167, 251
Vowel, Chelsea, 114–15, 162;
Indigenous Writes, 272n1

Walia, Harsha: "Moving beyond a
Politics of Solidarity," 269; *Red
Women Rising*, 276n5 (ch. 5)
Walkem, Ardith, 177
Walking with Our Sisters (wwos):
as ceremony, 166, 168, 171; as
decolonization, 172; National
Collective, 166; principles of,

166–7, 169–70; youth workshop
at, 171
Warrior, Robert, 52
water: agency of, 180; anti-colonial
Biblical readings of, 184–5; in
body, 179; ceremony with, 174,
182, 186; disconnection from,
177, 179; embodied connection
to, 180; grasping of, 178–9; in
Indigenous languages, 179–80;
non-human guardians of, 185–6;
offering tobacco to, 176–7;
as spirit and relative, 180–6;
reciprocal relationship with,
181–2; responsibilities to, 181,
185; "water is life," 181, 186;
women's responsibility for, 175.
See also Indigenous water law;
Watershed Discipleship; Water
Walkers
Watershed Discipleship, 54, 184–5;
and Bartimaeus Cooperative
Ministries, 184; and restorative
justice for non-humans, 185
Water Walkers, 183; Mother Earth
Water Walkers, 175, 176
Welsh, Christine: *Finding Dawn*
(film), 169
Wesley, Andrew, 248
West Coast Environmental Law,
183–4
West Moberly First Nation: Treaty 8
and Site C dam, 225
white helper, 9; body behaviours
of, 61–2; in civilizing mission,
64–65; and deficit model of
healing, 59–60; mentality
and colonialism, 81; and
problem-solving, 90; in

religious vocations, 238; and righteousness, 91; in Western feminists, 92; and white man's burden, 86

whiteness, 9, 35; in "ally" label, 269; body behaviours of, 61, 89; in Catholic benevolence, 60; and genuine Christianity, 9, 249; and false self, 61, 63; history of, 64; identities in relation to, 249; invisibility of, 35, 62, 98; as privilege, 90; right identification with, 90; as structural, 96; as wage, 64; in whiteness studies, 63

White Savior Industrial Complex, 93

white supremacy, 90, 98; and Black Lives Matter, 90; as a culture, 90, 94, 95, 96–7; and decolonization, 98; European Christianity as vehicle of, 258; Quakers Task Force on, 97; structural, 96; Unitarian teach-ins on, 97

Wildcat, Daniel, 199

Williams, Alice Olsen, 159, 160

Williams, Wanosts'a7 Lorna, 264

Williams Davidson, Terri-Lynn, 191

witness, 39, 113, 172, 193, 237, 252; in collective witness, 241

witnessing: in Coast Salish ceremony, 192–3; as legal practice, 193–4

Wolfe, Patrick, 266

Wong, Rita: on water, 179

worldview, Euro-Western, 73; as anthropocentric, 215; author's changing, 259; binaries and dualism of, 258; Christianity as antithetical, 9; of heart, 255; and human person, 180; non-validity of Indigenous medicine in, 74; and separation of facts and values, 201; understanding of treaties, 221–2; unlearning of, 5

worldviews, Indigenous: as anti-colonial, 82; body in Indigenous, 180; all creation as living in, 209; gift as epistemological basis of, 212; grounded in kinship, 79, 83, 222, 223; holistic nature of, 85, 201; Indigenous medicine and, 74; as interconnected, 54; and Mi'gmaq and land, 127; relational centre of, 267; responsibilities in, 223, 266; sustainable governance embedded in, 149; as unsettling, 254–5

wwos. See Walking with Our Sisters

xʷməθkʷəy̓əm (Musqueam), 65, 188, 255

Yang, Wayne, 97, 115, 263

Young, Alannah, 63, 70, 167, 173, 188, 264; on drumming and songs, 244–5; and going home, 106; on self-determination, 200–1

Younging, Gregory, 273n11